SUN & MOON SIGNS

JULIA AND DEREK PARKER

Photography by Monique le Luhandre

Illustrations by Danuta Mayer

DK

DORLING KINDERSLEY

London • New York • Stuttgart • Moscow

A DK PUBLISHING BOOK

Editor **Tom Fraser**
Art Editor **Ursula Dawson**
Managing Editor **Krystyna Mayer**
Managing Art Editor **Derek Coombes**
Production **Antony Heller**
U.S. Editor **Laaren Brown**

First American Edition 1996
2 4 6 8 10 9 7 5 3 1

Published in the United States by
DK Publishing, Inc., 95 Madison Avenue
New York, New York 10016

ISBN 0-7894-0367-6

Reproduced by GRB Editrice, Verona, Italy

CONTENTS

SUN & MOON SIGNS

ARIES

MARCH 21 – APRIL 20

INTRODUCING
ARIES

ARIES, THE SIGN OF THE RAM, IS THE FIRST SIGN OF THE ZODIAC. THE SUN MOVES INTO ARIES ON OR AROUND MARCH 21, MARKING THE START OF THE ASTROLOGICAL NEW YEAR – ASTROLOGY'S NEW YEAR'S DAY.

Ariens have a psychological need to win and to stand out from the crowd, ahead of all other competition. Here is assertiveness, self-assurance, and an uncomplicated approach to life. In order to achieve their goals, Ariens will strip away everything that is unnecessary to them. Here too is lively enthusiasm and an abundance of physical energy.

Traditional groupings

As you read through this book you will come across references to the elements and the qualities, and to positive and negative, or masculine and feminine signs.

The first of these groupings, that of the elements, comprises fire, earth, air, and water signs. The second, that of the qualities, divides the Zodiac into cardinal, fixed, and mutable signs. The final grouping is made up of positive and negative, or masculine and feminine signs. Each Zodiac sign is associated with a combination of components from these groupings, all of which contribute different characteristics to it.

Arien characteristics

The Arien element is fire – a bright, crackling inner fire that is easily ignited. Ariens must do all that they possibly can to keep this fire alive, for if it vanishes, great potential is lost, enthusiasm dies, and inner fulfillment is sure to be lacking. The sign belongs to the cardinal quality, which makes Ariens outgoing in manner. It is a positive, masculine sign, and therefore its subjects are inclined to be extroverts.

The traditional color of Aries is red, although blue is sometimes suggested, and its ruling planet is the red planet, Mars. Ariens are easily roused to anger, but once they have expressed their feelings, they bear neither malice nor resentment.

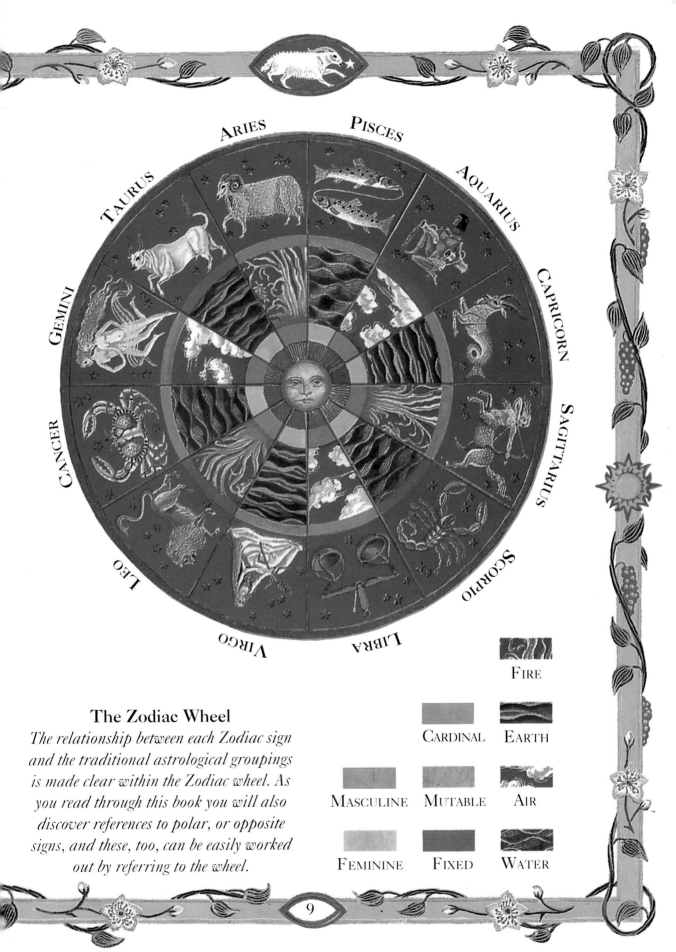

ARIES

PISCES

TAURUS

AQUARIUS

GEMINI

CAPRICORN

CANCER

SAGITTARIUS

LEO

SCORPIO

VIRGO

LIBRA

FIRE

The Zodiac Wheel

The relationship between each Zodiac sign and the traditional astrological groupings is made clear within the Zodiac wheel. As you read through this book you will also discover references to polar, or opposite signs, and these, too, can be easily worked out by referring to the wheel.

CARDINAL   EARTH

MASCULINE   MUTABLE   AIR

FEMININE   FIXED   WATER

MYTHS & LEGENDS

THE ZODIAC, WHICH IS SAID TO HAVE ORIGINATED IN
BABYLON AS LONG AS 2,500 YEARS AGO,
IS A CIRCLE OF CONSTELLATIONS THROUGH WHICH THE
SUN MOVES DURING THE COURSE OF A YEAR.

The Ram is not shown in the earliest Babylonian Zodiacs, and probably first appeared in the charts of Ancient Egyptian astronomers. It can be seen on the walls of the temple of the Egyptian Pharaoh, Ramses the Great, near the Valley of the Kings in Thebes.

The Golden Fleece
In the complicated legend of the golden ram, the Ancient Greeks continued to foster the mythical associations of the creature.

Babylonian votive ram
Since the earliest times, imagery associated with the ram has appeared in the devotional art of many different cultures.

Without elaborating upon the many characters involved, the story is basically as this: Phrixus and his sister, Helle, the children of the Boeotian King Athamas, were quietly walking in a wood one day when they met their mother, Nephele, leading a fine golden ram by the horns. She claimed that Poseidon, the god of the sea, had changed the beautiful Theophane, daughter of Bisaltes, into a ewe and himself into a ram, the better to court her. Nephele's ram was their child. She ordered Phrixus and Helle to ride him to the kingdom of Colchis, by the Black Sea,

Jason steals the Golden Fleece

This painting by Herbert Draper (1864 – 1920) shows Jason escaping from Colchis. To delay their pursuers, Medea, the daughter of the king of Colchis, who had fallen in love with Jason, threw her brother's body into the sea.

and sacrifice him to Ares, the god of war. This they did, and the ram's golden fleece was hung in the temple of Ares at Colchis, where it was guarded by a dragon that never slept.

Many years later, Jason, rightful king of Iolcus in Thessaly, could only claim his throne if he recovered the Golden Fleece. He led the Argonauts, a group of heroes, to Colchis, where, after performing a number of apparently impossible tasks, he took not only the Fleece but also Medea, daughter of the king of Colchis. In fact, if it had not been for Medea's assistance in delaying her father's pursuit, Jason could well have been unable to make his escape. Following his triumphant return, Jason mounted the throne and reigned happily ever after.

Jason's story embodies many of the qualities that are traditionally associated with Ariens: courage, an adventurous spirit, energy, and the need to triumph over adversity.

ARIES
SYMBOLISM

CERTAIN HERBS, SPICES, FLOWERS, TREES, GEMS, METALS, AND
ANIMALS HAVE LONG BEEN ASSOCIATED WITH PARTICULAR
ZODIAC SIGNS. SOME ASSOCIATIONS ARE SIMPLY AMUSING,
WHILE OTHERS CAN BE USEFUL.

Flowers
*The vividly colored geranium and
broom are Arien flowers. It is less
easy, however, to explain the Arien
dominion over honeysuckle.*

HONEYSUCKLE

BROOM

Trees

Because of their prickly nature, all thorn-bearing trees and shrubs are dominated by Aries.

HAWTHORN

MUSTARD POWDER

CAYENNE PEPPER

Spices

Aries is a fire sign, and is therefore said to rule cayenne pepper. The same is true of mustard and tartly flavored capers.

PEPPERMINT

Herbs

Peppermint, which is said to ease digestive complaints when brewed as a tea, has long been associated with Aries.

HOLLY

ARIES
SYMBOLISM

Metal
The Arien metal is iron. In keeping with some of this sign's characteristics, it is strong, direct, and plain.

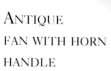

LEAD TOY SHEEP

ANTIQUE
FAN WITH HORN
HANDLE

Animals
Sheep are Arien creatures, due to their association with the ram.

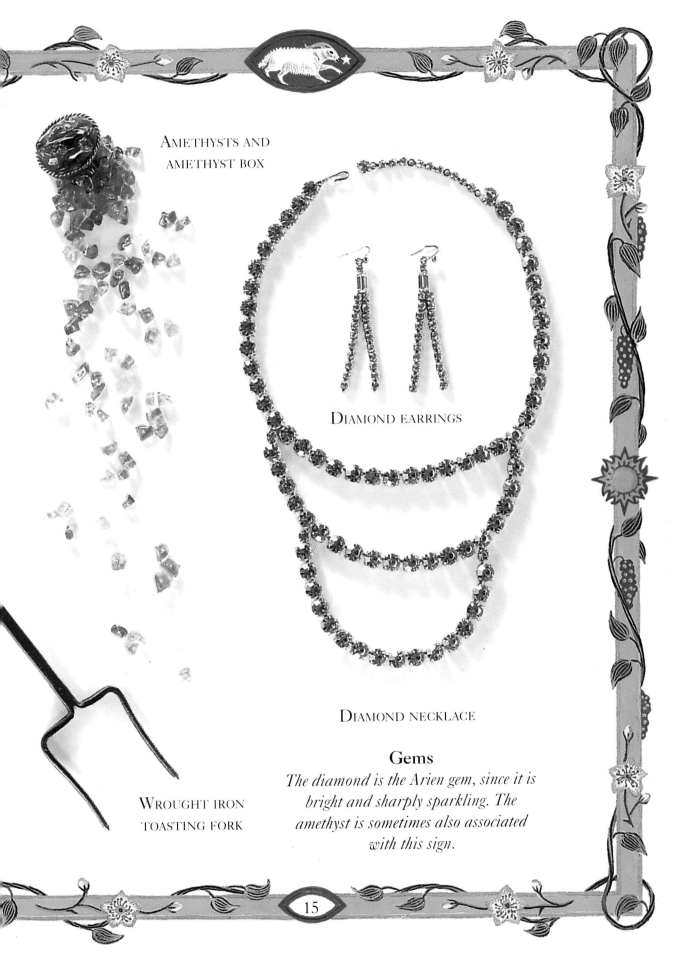

AMETHYSTS AND
AMETHYST BOX

DIAMOND EARRINGS

DIAMOND NECKLACE

WROUGHT IRON
TOASTING FORK

Gems
The diamond is the Arien gem, since it is bright and sharply sparkling. The amethyst is sometimes also associated with this sign.

ARIES
PROFILE

THE OVERALL PHYSICAL APPEARANCE OF THE TYPICAL ARIEN IS
LIKELY TO REFLECT A SENSE OF IMMEDIACY. ARIENS
ARE OFTEN IN A HURRY, AND HAVE NO TIME TO MESS AROUND
WITH UNNECESSARY COMPLICATIONS.

The Arien stance is easily definable: it expresses confidence. You will be likely to stand with your feet placed well apart, distributing your weight evenly. Your gestures will probably be rather uncomplicated – just like the normally straightforward Arien approach to life.

The body
The Arien body is, when in good condition, very wiry, giving the general impression by the very way in which it moves that it is made of elastic. It is important that you keep yourself on the lean side, since if your body becomes sluggish so will your mind, and the whole pace of your life will slow down. It is sometimes the case that an Arien will appear to be leaning

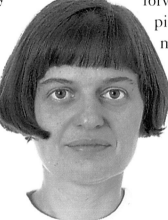

The Arien face
*The Arien glyph is often
visible in the line from the
eyebrows to the nose.*

forward most of the time. This pioneering approach may mean that you are forever searching for your next challenge. It may also mean that you have a tendency to jump forward in emergencies.

The face
Your hair is likely to be rather fine, or even flyaway. Male Ariens sometimes tend to lose their hair as they age – not that this need make them look any less attractive. The Arien forehead is typically broad and open, and the Arien glyph, ♈, can sometimes be seen in the line created by the eyebrows and the often prominent nose. Your eyes will no doubt betray your sense of determination; they will be clear, alert, and often quick-

The Arien stance

The Arien stance, which is very easy to recognize, is a very confident one. Your weight will be distributed very evenly.

moving. Most Ariens possess a strong and distinctive chin that often juts forward. It is unlikely that you find it difficult to break into a smile or grin.

Style

Ariens like casual clothes, uncluttered by fussy detail. At the same time, most people of this Sun sign possess the gift of always being able to look very stylish. Men look good in blazers and sweaters; women in well-matched separates. Clothes that restrict movement may, even on formal occasions, not look appropriate. Ariens can spend quite a lot of money on their wardrobes. It could be that you enjoy wearing the latest, very expensive tracksuits.

Many Ariens own a favorite item of clothing with which they will not, under any circumstances, wish to be parted. This goes against their usual reluctance to be nostalgic.

In general

Ariens are always in a hurry, taking long, determined strides at a quick pace, and often barging through doors without too much concern for others who may be in their wake. As has already been mentioned, you may lean forward when you walk, and this could lead to the development of back problems at some time in your life. You should consciously try to hold yourself more upright, making sure that you keep your head up. In all, your robust approach to life will be reflected in the way you act and dress.

ARIES
PERSONALITY

BECAUSE ARIES IS THE FIRST SIGN OF THE ZODIAC, THOSE BORN
WHILE THE SUN IS TRAVELING THROUGH IT ARE NATURAL
LEADERS. THEY SHOULD BE ASSERTIVE, BUT NEVER RUTHLESS, IN
THEIR DEALINGS WITH OTHER PEOPLE.

Here is a Zodiac group that is positive and enthusiastic in its outlook. Ariens enjoy challenge and should always have some important goals to achieve. You probably have a high physical energy level, and it is important that you express this positively and assertively. You can do this by developing a fast-paced lifestyle that is demanding both at work and in leisure. This will satisfy your Arien psychological motivation, which is to always win and to be way out ahead of all your competitors.

At work
The straightforward Arien outlook on life is admirable: a daunting problem can be solved in a matter of minutes. In fact, those of us who allow side issues to clutter up our attitudes and opinions could take lessons from Ariens. Of course, this can lead to the one real drawback of the Arien personality. In your determination to

deal with problems briskly, you may all too easily oversimplify a situation. When working on complicated projects, Ariens should have opportunities to confer with someone who can cope with the more detailed areas of the plan.

Your attitudes
Your main vice is selfishness, and no matter how well adjusted you are, or what other planets provide counter-influences, this trait can emerge. It can nearly always be traced back to the "me first" syndrome. Self-awareness, and a little forethought when dealing with other people's feelings, will help enormously in overcoming this unpleasant tendency.

Many people of this sign have a propensity to take risks. If this side of their nature is controlled and kept within certain limits, this becomes a positive adventurousness which is, of course, marvelous. If it is not, the

Mars rules Aries

Mars, the Roman god of war, represents the ruling planet of Aries. The influence of Mars, which has a strong sexual emphasis, relates to the masculine side of an Arien's nature.

individual will sometimes act in a rather hot-headed or foolhardy manner – and learn the hard way.

The overall picture

The Arien energy level, both physical and emotional, is very high. Indeed, inner fulfillment will only come when you use your body and your mind like a single well-adjusted and oiled machine. You should aim to do this during for your whole life. This is one of the signs requiring a good measure of independence. Ariens do not suffer fools gladly, and you will make quite sure that you do things in your own way. Freedom of expression is important to you.

ARIES
ASPIRATIONS

WHATEVER THEIR CAREER, ARIENS ASPIRE TO REACH THE TOP
OF THE LADDER. YOU NEED CHALLENGE AND MUST BE
ABLE TO EXPRESS YOURSELF THROUGH YOUR WORK. OF COURSE,
IT ALSO HAS TO INTEREST YOU.

Professional sports
*An above-average number of
professional athletes have a strong
Arien influence. Winning is important
to them, and it calls up all their
inherent energy.*

GUNMETAL
STOPWATCH

Motoring
*Cars can be a passion for Ariens.
However, their natural
exuberant haste
can often make them
impatient drivers.*

BRASS CAR HORN

1920s
MOTORING MAP

Engineering

Ariens of both sexes make good engineers and, in their spare time, are often enthusiastic amateur motor mechanics. They seem to positively enjoy getting their hands dirty.

1927 CIGARETTE CARDS DEPICTING ENGINEERING

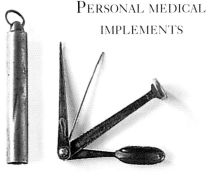

PERSONAL MEDICAL IMPLEMENTS

Medicine

There is a traditional link between the medical profession and this sign. Perhaps because Aries rules the head, Ariens also make good psychiatrists.

DENTAL MIRROR

Dentistry

Although Capricorn rules the teeth, Ariens are often drawn to working in the dental profession.

DENTAL PROBE

BRASS HORSE

Physical work

Arien energy is well suited to many different forms of physical activity, including farming.

ARIES
HEALTH

FOR ARIENS TO KEEP HAPPY AND HEALTHY, THEY HAVE
TO BURN UP ENERGY THROUGH EXERCISE. IF YOUR
WORK AND PLAY ARE PHYSICALLY DEMANDING, THEY WILL
HELP YOU TO STAY IN GOOD SHAPE.

The pioneering spirit of Aries is usually motivation enough to keep you moving, but at times when life lacks challenge, even the most energetic Arien will become lazy.

Your diet
Although you may like spicy foods, these are seldom good for Ariens. You will thrive on traditional, even bland, dishes. Your diet may also benefit from being supplemented with the cell salt potassium phosphate (Kali. Phos.), which is thought to build brain cells, help prevent headaches, and alleviate depression.

Taking care
Ariens are not the most careful of Zodiac types, and you will tend to cut and burn yourself more than is common. Learn to be cautious, especially when cooking or working with sharp tools. The Arien body area is the head, and it is true to say that Ariens either suffer badly from headaches – sometimes due to minor kidney disorders – or never have any. Ariens sometimes find it hard to modify an exercise regimen. As you get older, this could cause you to damage your body, and all of your old injuries may come back to plague you.

Italian red onions
Most strong-tasting foods, such as onions and leeks, are associated with Aries.

Astrology and the body

For many centuries it was impossible to practice medicine without a knowledge of astrology. In European universities, medical training included information on how planetary positions would affect the administration of medicines, the bleeding of patients, and the right time to pick herbs and make potions. Each Zodiac sign rules a particular part of the body, and early medical textbooks always included a drawing that illustrated the point.

ARIES AT
LEISURE

EACH OF THE SUN SIGNS TRADITIONALLY SUGGESTS SPARE-TIME
ACTIVITIES, HOBBIES, AND VACATION SPOTS.
CONSIDER SOME OF THESE SUGGESTIONS – THEY OFTEN SUIT
ARIEN INTERESTS.

Travel
*You will enjoy adventurous holidays,
especially while you are young. Seeing the
world will probably be more of a priority
than comfort. Try England, Poland,
France, Syria, and Israel
for vacations.*

POSTAGE STAMPS

VOLT-
METER

Car maintenance
*Ariens enjoy driving
and maintaining their cars. The
latter can, in fact, prove to be a
lucrative hobby.*

WALKING BOOTS

Horse-riding
*You may enjoy pony trekking
and spending long days in
the fresh air, whatever
the weather.*

HORSE'S BIT

Manual work
Iron is the metal of Mars, the planet that rules Aries. There is a long tradition that links Ariens with metalwork, tools, and machinery.

PAINT-STRIPPING TORCH

Mountaineering
The spirit of adventure possessed by many Ariens often attracts them to climbing and hiking.

1930s SPORTS CIGARETTE CARDS

Sport
Ariens need to exercise for both physical and psychological reasons. Football, hockey, and boxing are all possibilities. You will enjoy team sports, especially if you are the captain.

ARIES IN
LOVE

ONE OF THE MOST PASSIONATE SIGNS OF THE ZODIAC, ARIENS
FALL IN AND OUT OF LOVE VERY QUICKLY. BUT A
TENDENCY TO SWEEP PROSPECTIVE PARTNERS OFF THEIR FEET
CAN END IN DISASTER.

You must learn to listen to your partner's needs and ensure that selfishness does not spoil this wonderful sphere of life for you.

Pleasant romantic dinners and big nights out are sure to be part of the more mature Arien approach. When they are young, however, Ariens may seek affection in the backseat of an old jalopy. All Ariens should ensure that their approach is not too gushing and fast for many people.

As a lover

Those partners on the receiving end of your admiration will no doubt find the experience both lively and enjoyable. In most cases, your enthusiasm is likely to be infectious, and the individual involved will find it both easy and pleasant to be swept up into a fastpaced, sexually rewarding experience.

Types of Arien lover

Many Ariens have a beautifully poetic streak in their expression of love. This is something that one does not automatically expect to find in those who tend to rush things. However, Ariens must be aware of the possibility that once they are in love, an uncharacteristic element of possessiveness may spoil their relationships. This type is, on the other hand, usually prone to be marvelously sensual and warmhearted. Some Ariens are marked by a happy-go-lucky flirtatiousness, which can lead them toward duality and result in a great many awkward complications. Others will probably be so jealous of their independence that they will delay committing themselves to marriage until later than average. When in love, many Ariens enjoy surprising their partners. The small, unexpected gift will be presented quite frequently, and it is in winning ways such as this that they score highly. Many Ariens are considered to make excellent husbands and wives. They will, more often than not, encourage their spouses to express their potential in their own ways and, perhaps because they themselves have an independent spirit, are highly unlikely to create an unpleasant, claustrophobic atmosphere within any partnership. These particular Ariens should make sure that they do not choose partners who will attempt to inhibit their own positive and lively, energetic personalities.

ARIES AT HOME

THE WARM AND WELCOMING ARIEN HOME WILL BE COMFORTABLY, SOLIDLY, AND UNFUSSILY FURNISHED. SHADES OF RED WILL ENHANCE THE FEELING OF WARMTH, AND THE BEDROOM, IN PARTICULAR, WILL HAVE A SENSUAL ATMOSPHERE.

Many Ariens will enjoy spending time on improving their home. They may, for example, replan their kitchen or garden, and then do all of the work themselves. It is in fact the process of doing the work, rather than the end result, which provides real pleasure for an Arien.

You will probably prefer living near a busy street to setting up home in a peaceful rural setting. One important thing to consider is that as an Arien you will not want to be hemmed in or feel restricted.

Candelabra
This wrought iron candelabra has been made from the Arien metal.

furniture. Furthermore, having spent time choosing pieces, you will not want to waste more time, money and energy, starting to look for new items after only a couple of years. You must, however, be rather careful that you initially take your time when deciding to buy new furniture.

Soft furnishings

Ariens like their homes to have a warm, colorful glow. You probably enjoy creating an overall atmosphere that appears pleasing and informal to all who enter it.

Ariens are not usually very adventurous when it comes to choosing wallpaper and drapes. You may well prefer plain, clear colors.

Furniture

Ariens tend to be rather careless, and hate anything insubstantial. You will therefore usually choose durable

Antique swords

Mars, the planet of war, rules Aries. It is therefore hardly surprising that many Ariens decorate their homes with weapons.

Even though very young Ariens will probably choose vivid or even garish designs (for duvet covers, for instance) this tendency usually diminishes as they become older. By the time they eventually feel ready to set up their own homes a certain restraint is likely to emerge, which will make the final effect both interesting and tasteful.

Decorative objects

The decorative objects that Ariens will enjoy owning reflect certain elements of the individual's personality. Your sexual energy may well be considerable, so a reproduction of some famous erotic painting could easily end up hanging on your wall. Alternatively, a reproduction of a painting by the very famous Arien painter, Van Gogh, could find a place in the Arien home. His energetic painting of bright sunflowers sums up so much that is typical of this Sun sign.

Mars, the planet of war, rules Aries, and the Arien metal is iron. You could therefore end up possessing some weapons, such as an antique sword, or a flint-lock pistol.

Armchair and cushions

The principal Arien color is red, so there will be a good deal of it in their homes. They also like solid, functional furniture.

THE
MOON
AND
YOU

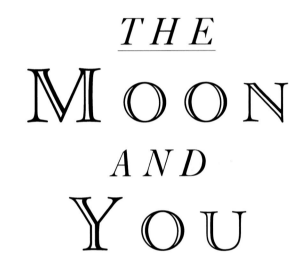

THE SUN DECREES YOUR OUTWARD
EXPRESSION, YOUR IMAGE, AND MANY
IMPORTANT PERSONALITY TRAITS. THE
MOON, ALTHOUGH MERELY THE EARTH'S
SATELLITE, IS ASTRONOMICALLY THE
SECOND MOST IMPORTANT BODY IN THE
SOLAR SYSTEM. FROM THE SIGN THAT IT
WAS IN AT YOUR BIRTH, IT INFLUENCES HOW
YOU REACT TO SITUATIONS, YOUR
EMOTIONAL LEVEL, AND, TO A CERTAIN
EXTENT, WHAT YOU HAVE INHERITED FROM
YOUR PARENTS AND ANCESTORS. HAVING
FOUND YOUR MOON SIGN IN THE SIMPLE
TABLES ON PAGES 606 TO 609, TURN TO THE
RELEVANT PAGES AND TAKE A STEP
FORWARD IN YOUR OWN SELF-KNOWLEDGE.

THE MOON IN
ARIES

WITH THE SUN AND MOON BOTH IN ARIES AT THE TIME OF YOUR BIRTH, YOU WERE BORN UNDER A NEW MOON. ARIES IS A FIRE SIGN, AND THIS ELEMENT POWERFULLY INFLUENCES YOUR PERSONALITY AND REACTIONS.

Should you study a list of your Sun sign characteristics, you will probably recognize that a great many of them apply to you. Out of a list of perhaps 20 traits of a Sun sign listed in books or magazines, most people will strongly identify with 11 or 12. For you, however, the average increases considerably because the Sun and Moon were both in Aries when you were born.

Self-expression
Your Sun sign denotes fiery, positive emotion, and so does your Arien Moon. Obviously, with such a powerful force at your disposal, you will understand that it is essential for you to express your feelings and to use your emotional energy positively. Do not bluster about or flare up unnecessarily: learn to control your emotional energy and use it calmly and constructively. Your Sun sign makes you assertive and your Moon

sign emphasizes this as your main motivation. You should also be aware that you may be terribly prone to hastiness and could act prematurely.

Romance
The most serious Arien fault is selfishness and, more than for other people of your Sun sign, it could very easily mar your personal relationships. You can react to your partners in a self-centered way, putting your own interests first and ignoring their needs and suggestions. But once aware of the pitfalls of selfishness, you make a wonderful, passionate lover.

Your well-being
The effect of your Aries Moon on your health will be to increase your vulnerability to all Arien ailments. Most importantly, your inherent hastiness will incline you to be yet more accident-prone. The emotional intensity of your Moon underscores

The Moon in Aries

the likelihood of headaches. If they persist, it could be as the result of a mild kidney disorder, so arrange to have a medical checkup.

Self-control and the conscious awareness that you can overdo things are essential to your well-being.

Planning ahead

The Arien enterprising spirit will put you in good stead when it comes to finance. Ariens are extremely decisive, but due to your Arien Moon you may well react to situations without due thought. Be careful, for instance, when you invest, since mistakes can easily be made.

Parenthood

You will be a lively, energetic parent, who will encourage your children in every area of their lives. But because you are so enthusiastic about your own interests, it may be all too easy for you to make the mistake of ignoring their individual tastes.

THE MOON IN
TAURUS

TAURUS IS AN EARTH SIGN, AND ITS QUALITIES ARE IN STRIKING
CONTRAST TO THOSE OF YOUR FIERY ARIEN SUN SIGN.
THEY WILL TEND TO MAKE YOU FAR LESS LIKELY TO EMBARK
ON UNWISE PREMATURE ACTIONS.

The qualities attributed to Aries and its neighboring sign, Taurus, are totally opposite – so the fact that the Moon was in Taurus when you were born adds a very different dimension to your personality. If you are aware of these contrasting qualities, you will be able to express them without too much internal conflict.

Self-expression
Your Taurean Moon gives you an extremely useful tendency to react to situations both constructively and thoughtfully. You will not find it difficult to control a sense of urgency or hastiness, and will always want to think things through carefully.

Taurus and Aries are very much emotionally oriented signs, but you find it relatively easy to control your emotional flow and expression. At times, however, you will find it more difficult to throw off your anger than many Ariens do. Be careful that an inherent tendency toward resentment and brooding does not mar your admirably straightforward Arien approach to life.

Romance
Arien selfishness, coupled with a tendency to be possessive of your partner, can be a big stumbling block in an emotional relationship. Make sure that you use the affectionate, positive passion of your Moon to the full when responding to your partner. Allow the zest for love and sex that you obtain from your Aries Sun to color your emotional relationships.

Your well-being
Taurus rules the throat, and at the first sign of a cold, you may well lose your voice and come down with a very sore throat. Many Ariens are wiry, but your Taurean Moon could add a lot of bulk to your frame. You may find it

The Moon in Taurus

extremely difficult to resist rich, sweet food. Weight gain could be a real problem for you.

Planning ahead

The Taurean business sense often beautifully complements the Arien sense of enterprise. In fact, many people of your Sun sign are lucky enough to possess two different sources of income.

You have an extremely powerful intuitive streak when it comes to dealing with money and will take fewer risks than many Ariens. Enterprise and good business sense, along with enthusiasm and a by no means small regard for luxury, all go well together.

Parenthood

Arien enthusiasm will color your attitude to your children, but you may sometimes find yourself being over-possessive. Watch out, too, for problems with the generation gap – you can appear far more conventional to your children than you realize.

THE MOON IN
GEMINI

A COMBINATION OF ARIES (A FIRE SIGN) AND GEMINI (AN AIR
SIGN) WILL, WHILE INCREASING ARIEN IMPATIENCE AND
RESTLESSNESS, GIVE YOU FAST RESPONSES TO SITUATIONS, A NEED
FOR IMMEDIATE ACTION, AND LOTS OF BRIGHT IDEAS.

Fire and air blend well: Aries fire motivates you and colors your self-expression, while the airy Gemini Moon spurs you forward, keeps you alert, and ensures that you never waste a moment.

If your life is unrewarding, you will suffer much more than most Ariens. Avoid false starts and the temptation to give up because you are bored. If you succeed in this, you will control what amounts to your most severe problem: a pathological hatred of boredom.

Self-expression
Although Arien directness is present in your personality, it is very easy for you to get sidetracked by the versatility that derives from your Moon sign. Allow the latter tendency some expression within the confines of a few well-chosen interests, and let it support a wider dimension within your career.

You may, perhaps, not entirely trust your powerful Arien emotions. Be very careful not to suppress the expression of your feelings, nor, as you are more likely to do, simply to rationalize them out of existence.

Romance
You will possess plenty of Arien passion, and it will be clearly expressed through sex and other aspects of your emotional life. You are more than likely to be a good communicator and will respond very fairly to your partner's desires and suggestions. Most fortunately, the inherent Arien selfish streak will be considerably mitigated in you.

Your well-being
The Geminian body areas are the hands and arms, so be extra careful that the Arien tendency to be accident-prone does not lead you to cut or burn them. Your Geminian

The Moon in Gemini

Moon may provoke periods of nervous tension. This, coupled with the Arien tendency to overdo things and the need for a constant use of mental energy, could make relaxation difficult for you.

Planning ahead
In some spheres of your life, a cunning streak could combine with Arien selfishness and the desire to be first in all things. You will plan your every action and will not be averse to scheming that will put you ahead of competitors. You will certainly voice your opinions, and your dynamic force will let you lead others skillfully.

Parenthood
You will make an extremely lively parent and will find it very easy indeed to keep up with what your children are thinking, and with their various interests and crazes. In fact, it could be that you will become the trendsetter, because your Geminian Moon instills a particularly strong interest in what is new and original.

THE MOON IN
CANCER

A COMBINATION OF THE FIRST ZODIAC FIRE SIGN (ARIES) AND THE FIRST WATER SIGN (CANCER) BLENDS ASSERTIVE ENTHUSIASM WITH AN INSTINCTIVE CARING, PROTECTIVE RESPONSE. IT WILL ALSO HEIGHTEN YOUR EMOTIONAL LEVEL.

The tremendously high emotional voltage of your Sun and Moon combination is a vital key to your whole personality. As the Moon traditionally rules Cancer, its effect on you is even more powerful than it is on those who have it in another sign.

Self-expression
While Aries is extroverted, Cancer tends to be introverted, and you have some of the qualities of both. But there are, of course, areas where Aries and Cancer meet. Both signs are, for instance, of the cardinal quality, and share an important and expressive outgoing nature. You are generally forthright – Aries sees to that – but the Moon is also likely to make you tender, caring, and sympathetic.

Your Moon sign will probably make you somewhat apprehensive when challenged; it will make you intuitive, which is good, but it will also make you a worrier. Couple this with a

powerful Cancerian imagination, and when something troubles you, you can easily begin to feel that your world has collapsed around you.

While much about the Cancer personality is gentle and tender, there is, conversely, also a lot of toughness present, and this is very good when blended with more forthright, assertive Arien qualities.

Romance
You have the high, fiery passion of Aries plus the sensual, caring, and tender expression of love typical of Cancer. This is a pretty stunning combination, but you may find that you sometimes smother your partners with affection. Try not to be too sensitive, sentimental, or nostalgic.

Your well-being
You will work extremely hard, and could feel wound up at times; develop relaxation techniques to counter the

The Moon in Cancer

tendency. Most Ariens cope well with stress, but the Cancerian inclination to worry may stop you from taking as philosophical an attitude to problems as you otherwise might. Stress could also affect your digestion, so look carefully at your diet. It may be that you would benefit from eating far less spicy food.

Planning ahead

Your Cancerian Moon will, in general, make you marvelously – and usefully – shrewd. This is especially true when it comes to business and finance. Follow your powerful instincts, but do not let any fiery Arien enthusiasm entirely quench deep-rooted caution.

Parenthood

You will enjoy family life enormously and may be eager to have children. But even though you will be an excellent and energetic parent, when your children want to leave home, you may find it hard to let them go. Right from the start, avoid an instinctive tendency to overprotect them. While you will want to give your children a happy home, beware of trying to make it too comfortable.

THE MOON IN
LEO

YOUR LIFE CAN OFTEN BE HECTIC BUT, BECAUSE YOU HAVE AN INSTINCT FOR GETTING THINGS RIGHT, YOU WILL NOT BE INCLINED TO TAKE SHORTCUTS TO ATTAIN YOUR GOALS. THIS CAUTION WILL TEMPER UNDUE HASTE OR CARELESSNESS.

You possess very powerful feelings, and will enjoy expressing them, and your opinions, forcefully and to great effect.

Self-expression

Your Arien ability and motivation to win and to lead is enhanced by Leo's instinctive organizational ability. You should, can, and must aim to go far, but without hurting others. The chances are that with this combination you are a born leader, and if you achieve inner fulfillment, others will gladly follow your example.

You may tend to react in a somewhat pompous and bossy way at times and, if accused of this, your Arien Sun will encourage you to feel embarrassed. In fact, Aries is one of the least pompous of the 12 Zodiac signs. Therefore take heed: the influence from the Moon sign is powerful, and does influence the way other people react to us.

In anyone who has an influence from Leo, there is usually an urge for some form of creative expression. Ariens often love bright, vivid colors, so you may like to paint – but you will probably not be terribly patient. Do not, therefore, concern yourself with detail. Just slap the paint on liberally and have fun, because the act of doing so can be very creative in itself.

Romance

You will make your partners feel wonderful, and be very generous with romantic and flattering gifts. Your zest for sex will encourage and help relax the shiest of partners.

When angered, you will become a real lion – if in sheep's clothing. But any resentment or brooding after you have had your say would be most uncharacteristic. Magnanimity is always present, even if you are capable of reducing a rival or an enemy to a quivering jelly.

The Moon in Leo

Your well-being

The Leo body area is the spine: look after it and exercise it. If you sit at an office desk all day, get a back-support chair. Because Leo also rules the heart, any Arien sporting activity is important, too. You do not go halfway and, with your Moon in a fire sign, you could succumb to the Arien problem of burning yourself out of both physical and emotional energy.

Planning ahead

The Arien enterprising spirit is a very necessary asset for you, since you really love luxury and expensive quality. You are often attracted to things that are well beyond your price range. If you are enterprising and creative, work hard, and make large amounts of money, you will achieve great inner fulfilment.

Parenthood

You will be a loving, if somewhat domineering, parent. If you curb the latter trait, you will be a great source of inspiration to your children, giving them every encouragement. Even when you have no alternative but to criticize them, you will do so in such a way as to encourage their efforts.

THE MOON IN
VIRGO

THE ARIEN NEED FOR ACTION BLENDS WELL WITH VIRGO'S
QUICK BUT CAREFUL RESPONSES TO SITUATIONS. YOU
WILL BE FAR LESS LIKELY TO MAKE SILLY MISTAKES THAN
OTHER PEOPLE OF YOUR SUN SIGN.

Your Moon in Virgo, which is an earth sign, gives your character a dimension that is very much in contrast to your fire sign Arien Sun.

Self-expression
While having the typical quick Arien grasp of a situation, you respond not only practically but also very analytically, seeing every loophole. Try not to become damningly critical of other people, for a very understandable tendency not to suffer fools gladly can go a bit too far at times, especially when Arien hasty action meets with Virgoan fussiness.

You are among the most practical of Ariens, being capable of either theoretical or active work, but may not be terribly patient. Take a break rather than struggling on to the point where you want to give up.

Although Ariens are certainly not celebrated for their shyness, it is just possible that in some way you have had to come to terms with a degree of reticence. Maybe it has inhibited you in just one area of your life, perhaps as the result of critical put-downs from your parents when you were young. Your Virgoan modesty could have predominated until the positive force of Aries came into its own.

Romance
Your Arien emotion is dampened by the qualities of your Moon sign. It will lead you to think sensibly before overwhelming your partner with passion. When you are annoyed you may tend to carp and nag, but you will rarely be resentful.

Your well-being
The Virgoan body area is the stomach. You need an above-average amount of fiber, and might respond well to a vegetarian diet. The Moon in Virgo can also cause a considerable buildup of tension: Many Sun sign Virgoans

The Moon in Virgo

suffer from migraines, and because Aries rules the head and makes its subjects prone to bad headaches, you could sometimes succumb to them. Find a way to counter stress; note its early symptoms, and try to distance yourself from any problem. This is vital if you are to remain productive.

Planning ahead

Ariens are generous; Virgoans, on the whole, are not. There is clearly a potential conflict between the two. If it is troublesome, then make every effort to keep the Virgoan level of your personality under control.

Parenthood

All Ariens have the capacity to enjoy parenthood, but be careful that you are not more critical toward your children than you realize. They could easily take you more seriously than you might imagine. When they do, make it up to them with some special treats to show how sorry you are.

THE MOON IN
LIBRA

ARIES AND LIBRA ARE POLAR OR OPPOSITE SIGNS, WHICH MEANS
THAT YOU WERE BORN AT THE TIME OF THE FULL MOON.
ALWAYS GUARD AGAINST RESTLESSNESS, AND DO NOT ALLOW
INDECISION TO MAR YOUR ARIEN ENTHUSIASM.

All of us, in one way or another, tend to express certain attributes of our polar, or opposite, Zodiac sign. In your case, this is Libra, which is straight across the Zodiac circle from Aries. Because the Moon happened to be in that sign when you were born, this polarity is expressed in a very interesting way: you will react to people with much greater consideration for their feelings than most people of your Sun sign.

Self-expression
You can be diplomatic and tactful, and when the going gets tough, you will recognize any negative symptoms of stress and really kick back and relax.

Having said that, most people born like you, at the time of the Full Moon, are prone to restlessness, and all too often harbor some kind of inner feeling of discontent. You must be on your guard against this. Perhaps you tend to change occupations rather too

often, and therefore never manage to completely satisfy your sense of inner fulfillment. Examine your attitudes and opinions occasionally, as they may tend to be overvolatile or, conversely, stuck in a rut.

Romance
Your Libran Moon sign makes you diplomatic, far more tactful, and less hasty than most Ariens. Libra is, emotionally, not a very powerfully charged sign. It is enhanced by fiery Arien warmth, while Arien sexual passion is softened by warm affection and a beautiful expression of romance. Any selfishness is considerably mitigated in you, although you may suffer twinges of resentment from time to time.

Your well-being
The Libran body area is the kidneys, and as a result of the polar lunar influence, you may have slight kidney

The Moon in Libra

upsets. You could also suffer from many Arien headaches. No doubt you find rich, expensive, and delicious food hard to resist. If you tend to put on weight easily, keep up the exercise and sporting activities – otherwise your gourmet interests may damage your physique.

Planning ahead

Your Libran Moon sign inclines you to luxury – something many Ariens are not too obsessed about. But if you really do enjoy luxurious living, it is clear that you should exploit your enterprising qualities as much as you can. You will do well to be one of those Ariens who has two sources of income (apart from anything else, the variety will satisfy you).

Parenthood

You are an excellent parent and will be sympathetic to your children's opinions; you will not want them to be clones of yourself. A hint of Libran indecisiveness could, however, be irritating for them at times.

THE MOON IN
SCORPIO

THE FIERY EMOTION OF ARIES AND THE INTENSE EMOTION OF
SCORPIO BUILD POWERFUL RESOURCES ON WHICH TO DRAW
DURING HARD TIMES. BE CAREFUL THAT JEALOUSY DOES NOT
DESTROY YOUR ARIEN STRAIGHTFORWARDNESS.

There is a long-standing tradition that links Aries with Scorpio: both were ruled by Mars until the discovery of Pluto. After considerable discussion, Pluto was designated as the ruler of Scorpio.

Self-expression

Your resources of emotional, as well as physical, energy are considerable. You have what it takes to achieve a great deal. If you really concentrate on your objectives, you will express your potential to the full. But if you fail to do this, you are likely to suffer from an unpleasant sense of discontent.

A full, busy, rewarding life and a deep involvement in both work and spare-time activities is what you need. Stagnation is your great enemy. You have a liking for mystery, ranging from detective fiction to the occult. If you feel attracted to the latter, or think you have a psychic side to your nature, do not play around with

seances or Ouija boards. Seek sound professional advice from someone who is regarded as trustworthy.

Romance

Your need for sexual fulfillment is above average. Make sure that you find a partner who is sympathetic to your demanding needs and who is as lively as you are.

Your deep and passionate emotions mean that you can respond to certain situations with a show of jealousy and, perhaps, possessiveness. Your suspicions may well be unfounded, so be careful how you express them.

Your well-being

The traditional Scorpio body area is the genitals. "Safe sex" may therefore prove to be absolutely essential for you to keep your health.

With this Sun and Moon combination, your physical energy level is very high, so exercise is

46

The Moon in Scorpio

terribly important to you. One of your important activities should be athletic – all kinds of swimming are excellent for you. Do not ignore your Arien competitive spirit, spiked with Scorpio emotions.

Planning ahead

As long as you control your Arien enthusiasm when faced with get-rich-quick schemes, you are usually very shrewd when dealing with money. Use your intuition to discover weaknesses and foresee problems. In general, you should invest in big companies with steady growth.

Parenthood

You will be an excellent parent, but try not to force your own interests on your children, since you may tend to dominate them. Your psychological and emotional energy is infectious. By all means let it affect your children, and be proud of their progress, but allow them to be themselves.

THE MOON IN
SAGITTARIUS

YOU RESPOND TO SUGGESTIONS AND CHALLENGES IMMEDIATELY
AND WITH A NATURAL ENTHUSIASM. SINCE ARIES AND
SAGITTARIUS ARE FIRE SIGNS, YOU MAY HAVE TO DEVELOP YOUR
STAMINA, OR YOUR PROJECTS COULD EASILY FIZZLE OUT.

You are truly blessed; an Arien Sun and a Sagittarian Moon is an extremely positive combination. With your straightforward attitude to life, you are well able to assess problems and to put them into a coherent perspective.

Self-expression
Your powerful fire element prompts you to live a full life, but it does not encourage you to cope with detail. Your boredom level is very low, and can lead you to cast aside a project or ambition just because something else seems more attractive.

You are somewhat overly optimistic, and disappointments can spread a layer of gloom over your life. Still, this should not last – soon you will be off on another venture. You do need variety in your activities, perhaps involving moving from a physically demanding project to one that exercises your brain.

Try, however, to develop consistency of effort and a little more patience. You are more versatile than most Ariens, but to avoid exhaustion, make sure that you set aside time each day for relaxation and contemplation. Some of your deepest instincts incline you to a philosophic approach to life, and to an interest in esoteric subjects such as religion.

Romance
You are a lively, passionate lover whose many delightful ways will endear you to a partner. There will, however, be an element of duality in your nature that could create some sticky situations. You should also guard against a tendency to be offhand with people.

Your well-being
The Arien body area covers the hips and thighs. Arien women with a Sagittarian Moon will tend to put on

The Moon in Sagittarius

weight in these areas quite as readily as their Sagittarian Sun sign sisters. The Sagittarian body organ is the liver. If you like rich dishes, heavy food, and red wine, you would therefore be wise to keep a hangover cure at the ready.

Take care that undue haste does not lead to you incurring long-lasting sports injuries.

Planning ahead
You are very prone to risk-taking. When you are confronted by a challenge, you will respond almost instantaneously. Be careful, since this could be foolhardy. Get-rich-quick schemes could have an almost irresistible attraction, and you may have a strong gambling streak.

Parenthood
You could scarcely be a more lively and enthusiastic parent, but because you will be so anxious for your children to progress in life, you might find it difficult to adjust to a child with a slower rate of progress than you would like. Try to be patient, and make sure that you take enough time to listen to your children attentively and sympathetically.

THE MOON IN
CAPRICORN

YOUR PRACTICAL CAPRICORNIAN MOON WILL ENCOURAGE YOU TO
ACHIEVE ARIEN OBJECTIVES. TO BE FIRST IS IN YOUR NATURE.
CONFRONTED WITH CHALLENGES, YOUR REACTION IS AMBITIOUS:
YOU ASPIRE TO REACH THE TOP.

You may take life more seriously than any other Moon sign Capricornians. This does not, however, mean that your outlook will be negative. The Moon in Capricorn gives you a marvelous, offbeat sense of humor.

Self-expression

Your Arien desire to be first will be encouraged by the Capricornian ambition to "climb every mountain." You will not only reach the top, but you could also be the first of your peer group to do so.

Oddly enough, given your Arien assertiveness and Capricornian instinct for progress, doubts will creep in from time to time when you are confronted with challenges. This is most likely if your parents were at all domineering or unsympathetic. Counter such uncertainties by recalling that you are a free agent and have what it takes to win.

Romance

Emotionally, Capricorn is a cool sign, so your Arien passion will be kept under control and carefully directed. You may find it easier to be faithful to a lover than many people of your Sun sign. You may also tend to respond well to partners who are either wealthier than you or seem to be of a superior social class. This may not always be a good thing.

Because Capricorn is an earth sign, you possess plenty of practical caution. Do not allow this to dampen your pleasure when it comes to love.

Your well-being

The Capricornian body area is the knees and shins. Capricornians are prone to stiffness in the joints, so rheumatic pains and arthritic conditions are not unknown to them. These ailments are less likely to afflict you if you exercise. If, however, you should sustain an injury while

The Moon in Capricorn

exercising, especially to your knees, go to a physical therapist at once. Otherwise long-term damage or cartilage problems may occur. Most Ariens find it easy to keep up sports and exercise regimens, and exercise is just as important for you as it is for those with different Moon signs.

Planning ahead

Caution and a practical instinct will act in your favor where financial and career matters are concerned. While, as an Arien, you will like striding forward, and perhaps taking risks, with the Moon in Capricorn you will prefer a carefully regulated pace, both in climbing the career ladder and in increasing your bank balance.

Parenthood

You will want only the best for your children. Be careful, however, about working extra hours or bringing work home in order to provide materially for your children. Make sure that you take time to enjoy their company and to have fun with them.

THE MOON IN
AQUARIUS

THE MOON IN AQUARIUS IS INVENTIVE, ORIGINAL, GLAMOROUS,
AND COOL, WHILE ARIES IS WARM AND PASSIONATE. BE AN
INDIVIDUALIST, BUT TRY NOT TO LET YOUR AQUARIAN MOON
DISTANCE YOU FROM YOUR ARIEN QUALITIES.

You are among the most inventive of Ariens and are capable of having truly original ideas. What is more, you have the enthusiasm to bring these ideas to fruition. Your potential is great and should not be ignored or suppressed.

Self-expression

Aries is a sign needing considerable independence, and Aquarius is the most independent sign in the Zodiac. It is therefore hardly surprising that you like to do things your own way and will respond very negatively to anyone who tries to boss you around or cramp your style. It is necessary for you to learn from your own mistakes, even if this means doing things the hard way.

Because Aquarius is of the fixed quality, you could well surprise others by reacting very stubbornly at times. You will also have a tendency to be unpredictable, which can often be appealing. Be careful, however, that this trait does not go hand in hand with Aquarian selfishness.

Romance

Because of your Aquarian Moon, you may tend to rationalize your emotions, or even to detach yourself from them, especially during the early stages of an emotional relationship. But there is also a very romantic side to your Aquarian Moon and an instinctive liking for glamour. These traits will inevitably color your attitudes.

An overall need for independence may mean that you put off forming a permanent relationship or marriage until quite late in life. Your sex life will, however, have the usual exuberance of Aries.

Your well-being

Aquarius rules the ankles and the circulation. You could feel the cold more than most Sun sign Ariens, and

The Moon in Aquarius

it is important that you keep your circulation in good order. If you can keep active, you should also avoid developing stiffness in the joints, to which Aquarians are prone.

Planning ahead

The Aquarian attraction to the glamorous and romantic often creates a desire for expensive, glitzy things, unusual objects for the home, and costly original clothes and perfumes. It is in these areas that Arien enthusiasm could grab you and encourage you to spend an excessive amount of money.

Parenthood

You should not find it difficult to keep up with your children's interests. At times, you may even overtake them in following fads, so you should have no problem with the generation gap. Do, however, control any tendency to be unpredictable, since children like to know where they stand.

THE MOON IN
PISCES

BY COMBINING YOUR FIERY ARIEN QUALITIES WITH THE PISCEAN SENSITIVITY OF YOUR EMOTIONAL REACTIONS, YOU WILL MAKE THE MOST OF THESE VIVIDLY CONTRASTING CHARACTERISTICS.

Aries is often said to be the pioneer of the Zodiac, and Pisces the poet, so it is not surprising that you are an individual with contrasting sides to your personality.

Self-expression

Your Arien Sun gives you all the positive, forthright qualities that are associated with the sign. In fact, it could eclipse the influence of your sensitive, intuitive Moon. You may sometimes lack Arien self-confidence when confronted with a challenge. Have you a deep-rooted tendency to shy away from some situations?

Looking at this combination in another way, it is likely that you are far more caring and sympathetic than many Ariens. You will certainly spend time, energy, and money helping other people, and this could occasionally leave you feeling drained. You could well be creative, in a variety of ways. Your Piscean instinct will incline you to work behind the scenes, while your Arien Sun will want you to be in the spotlight.

Romance

Your fiery Arien emotion is combined with the emotion of Pisces, which is a water sign. This makes you a caring lover, sensitive to your partner's needs. But beware of a negative Piscean trait: deceptiveness. This is often brought on by a tendency to take the easy way out of situations.

Your well-being

The Piscean body area is the feet. You may hate the restriction of wearing shoes, especially high-heeled shoes, and going barefoot will therefore have its attractions. But remember the Arien tendency to be accident-prone, which could mean that you are easily susceptible to cut and scraped feet, bunions, or corns. You may not enjoy the rough and

The Moon in Pisces

tumble of the sports that Ariens usually like. Bearing in mind your Arien strength and vitality, however, you could well be attracted to gymnastics when you are young, and to any kind of dancing. This, and perhaps ice skating, should be particularly good for you.

Planning ahead
Enthusiasm, the inability to adopt a firm position, and a tendency to be impractical could make you fall for risky financial schemes. If, like many Ariens, you have an enterprising streak, you may need a good business partner to steady you and to keep the books. Beware of overextending yourself financially.

Parenthood
You will be sensitive to your children's needs, but may tend to worry about them too much – more, in fact, than most other Ariens. Instead of allowing your admirable Piscean imagination to invent all sorts of catastrophes that may have happened to your children, put this imagination to use in devising your own bedtime stories to enthrall them. You will not find this difficult.

SUN & MOON SIGNS

TAURUS

APRIL 21 – MAY 21

INTRODUCING
TAURUS

TAURUS, THE SIGN OF THE BULL, IS THE SECOND SIGN OF THE
ZODIAC. IT REPRESENTS A DESIRE FOR STABILITY IN
ALL THINGS, AND AN OVERALL NEED FOR BOTH EMOTIONAL
AND MATERIAL SECURITY.

Taureans like creature comforts, enjoy sweet, rich food, and are very sensual. They make marvelous lovers, but are often too possessive, and can go so far as to treat their partners as if they owned them.

Here, too, is excellent business sense. While not quick to learn, once Taureans absorb a concept, they will seldom forget it.

Traditional groupings

As you read through this book you will come across references to the elements and the qualities, and to positive and negative, or masculine and feminine signs.

The first of these groupings, that of the elements, comprises fire, earth, air, and water signs. The second, that of the qualities, divides the Zodiac into cardinal, fixed, and mutable signs. The final grouping is made up of positive and negative, or masculine and feminine signs. Each Zodiac sign is associated with a combination of components from these groupings, all of which contribute different characteristics to it.

Taurean characteristics

As the first sign of the earth element, Taurus is characteristically plodding, reliable, and predictable. Being ruled by Venus, however, it also bestows on its subjects great natural charm, and gives them the reputation of being the best-looking Zodiac group.

Taurus is a sign of the fixed quality, so stubbornness can often be present in its subjects. It is therefore very important for Taureans to learn to keep an open mind. Taurus is also, in spite of the symbolic Bull, a feminine or negative sign, which has the effect of inclining its subjects to be introverted.

The Taurean colors are those governed by the planet Venus: pastel blues, pinks, and greens.

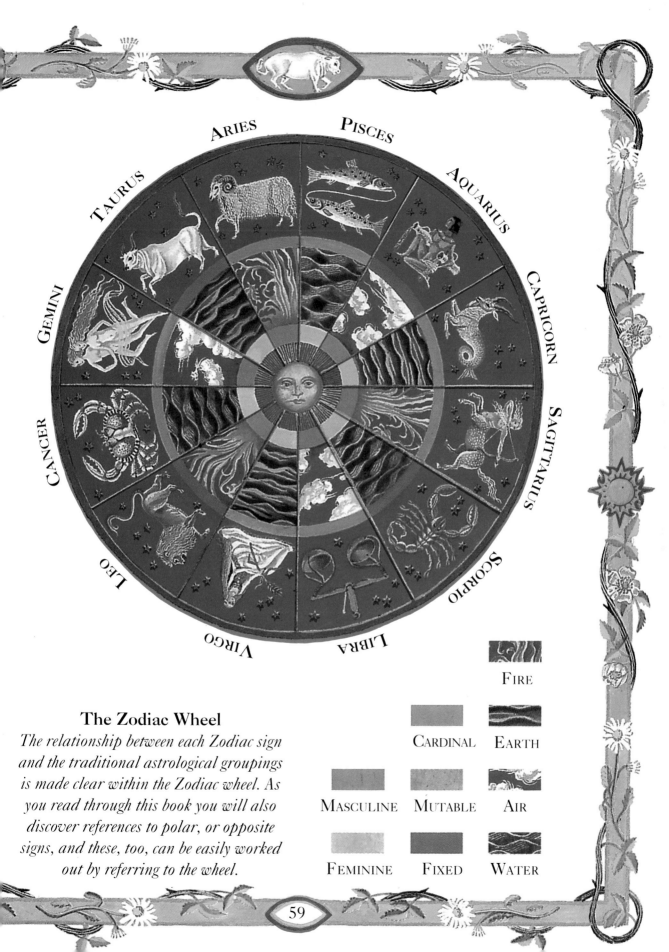

ARIES

PISCES

TAURUS

AQUARIUS

GEMINI

CAPRICORN

CANCER

SAGITTARIUS

LEO

SCORPIO

VIRGO

LIBRA

The Zodiac Wheel

*The relationship between each Zodiac sign
and the traditional astrological groupings
is made clear within the Zodiac wheel. As
you read through this book you will also
discover references to polar, or opposite
signs, and these, too, can be easily worked
out by referring to the wheel.*

FIRE

CARDINAL   EARTH

MASCULINE   MUTABLE   AIR

FEMININE   FIXED   WATER

TAURUS
MYTHS & LEGENDS

THE ZODIAC, WHICH IS SAID TO HAVE ORIGINATED IN BABYLON
AS LONG AS 2,500 YEARS AGO, IS A CIRCLE
OF CONSTELLATIONS THROUGH WHICH THE SUN MOVES
DURING THE COURSE OF A YEAR.

The first myth associated with this constellation concerned the Babylonian "Bull of Heaven," Ishtar and Anu, and Gilgamesh, the great epic hero of Babylon.

Ishtar, the goddess of lechery, fell violently in love with the hero Gilgamesh. He knew, however, that she had disposed of her previous lovers in various unpleasant ways, and that she was both faithless and unreliable. Finding herself rejected, Ishtar appealed to her father, Anu, king of the gods, to create a giant Bull of Heaven that would kill Gilgamesh. This bull was Taurus.

A variety of myths

Various other bulls have been associated with the constellation. There was the white bull mentioned by the Roman poet Virgil, which was said to open "the gate of the year with his golden horns." White bulls were also sacrificed at sunset on the fifth day of the Babylonian new year festival, when the equinoctial New Moon appeared in the sign of Taurus.

Europa and the bull

Much better known than this or the Babylonian Bull of Heaven is the bull in the Greek legend of Europa.

Zeus, king of the gods, fell in love with the king of Phoenicia's extraordinarily beautiful daughter, Europa. In order to deceive her into submitting to his dubious intentions, Zeus turned himself into an incredibly handsome bull and set himself to graze among her father's herd. When Europa, who was playing by the seashore with her friends, saw Zeus as the bull, she was overcome by how majestic, yet gentle, he seemed.

The abduction

Europa approached him, and he knelt in front of her. At this, she climbed onto his back, and put a wreath of

Jupiter carries off Europa

*In this painting by Pierre Gobert (1662 – 1744), Europa is
shown being carried off by the god Zeus, who has disguised
himself as a bull.*

flowers around his horns. Zeus then
sprang immediately to his feet and
swam across the sea to Crete. There
he had his wicked way with Europa
under a plane tree. (This particular
tree was then granted the divine
privilege of keeping its foliage
through all the seasons.) Europa bore
Zeus three children. Among them was
Minos, who later ruled over the island
after the king of Crete, Asterius,
adopted all three children and invited
Europa to become his wife.

Some traditions of Taurus – the
sign of good looks and charm but also
of possessiveness – do seem linked to
that handsome bull who was really a
god in disguise.

TAURUS
SYMBOLISM

CERTAIN HERBS, SPICES, FLOWERS, TREES, GEMS, METALS, AND
ANIMALS HAVE LONG BEEN ASSOCIATED WITH PARTICULAR
ZODIAC SIGNS. SOME ASSOCIATIONS ARE SIMPLY AMUSING,
WHILE OTHERS CAN BE USEFUL.

PRIMROSES

Flowers
*Taurus rules the rose,
primrose, columbine, daisy,
foxglove, poppy, and violet.
The reasons for these
attributions are lost
in the mists of time.*

PINK ROSES

CYPRESS

Spices

Taurus was said by ancient astrologers to rule all spices. Cloves, in particular, fall under the influence of this sign.

Trees

Taurean trees include the ash, cypress, vine, almond, fig, apple, and pear.

CINNAMON STICKS

Herbs

Spearmint is only one of the herbs traditionally linked to Taurus. Among the others, arrack was used to cure throat infections and elder root for snake bites.

SPEARMINT

CLOVES

TAURUS
SYMBOLISM

UNREFINED COPPER

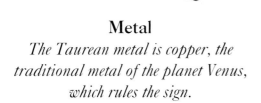

Metal
The Taurean metal is copper, the traditional metal of the planet Venus, which rules the sign.

COPPER BROOCH

TOY BULL
MADE OF LEAD

Gems

The magnificent emerald and the moss agate are Taurean gems. Their only obvious association with the sign is through their color, green, which is a Taurean color.

Moss AGATE

EMERALD BROOCH

NINETEENTH-CENTURY BULL CAN-OPENER

SPANISH CERAMIC TILE

Animals

All types of cattle fall under the domination of Taurus.

TAURUS
PROFILE

Taureans have the reputation of being the best-looking of all 12 Zodiac types. If this is true, you should try hard to maintain your appearance. Unfortunately, this is often a difficult task.

Taureans like to be sure that they are on firm ground, both psychologically and physically. A conventional approach appeals because they prefer established things that are secure and dependable. You are therefore likely to stand with your feet apart, your hands either in your pockets or grasping some all-important possession, for example, a handbag. You will, on the whole, be inclined to present a conventional image of yourself to those around you.

The Taurean face
Your hair is likely to be soft and curly, and may fall well onto your forehead.

women tend to be broad-shouldered and to have thick necks, echoing the powerful build of the animal of their sign. They are capable of having slim waists, and must constantly strive to keep themselves in good shape. Flab can, all too easily, mar their natural good looks.

The body
Taureans often have a firm, and somewhat stocky, but undeniably handsome, frame. Both men and

The face
Taureans often have hair that falls well over their foreheads. Soft curls are quite common, and baldness is rarely seen. The forehead itself is likely to be rather low, and as you get older, you may find pronounced horizontal lines appearing there. Your eyes are probably deep-set, dark, and penetrating, but a softness is possibly

The Taurean stance
You will generally adopt a firm stance, with your feet apart, and clasping a favorite possession.

also visible. The Taurean nose is likely to be broad and rather flat, and the chin is is rarely pronounced. Any increase in your weight, and this is something that you should be wary of, may therefore lead to you developing a double chin. Your mouth is likely to reflect your purposefulness, but it can also reveal your sensitivity.

Style
Taureans will dress in a style conventional for their generation. You may therefore have to be careful that your image does not start to look dated. For women, the look tends to prettiness: pastel colors and the occasional frill or bow at the neck. The men will sometimes sport an attractively floral or pastel-colored tie, for example to relieve a formal city suit. The naturally broad shoulders of Taureans usually require a minimum of padding.

In general
The attractive, warm, and sensual speaking voice that is possessed by many Taureans often enhances their natural good looks. You may have a tendency to move rather slowly and deliberately since, although you are well aware of where you are going, and the way in which you are going to get there, you usually prefer to feel unhurried as you go about your business. Perhaps you should sometimes try speeding up a little, as this might well benefit you both mentally and physically.

TAURUS
PERSONALITY

TAURUS, THE SECOND SIGN OF THE ZODIAC, IS STEADFAST, STABLE, AND CONVENTIONAL IN OUTLOOK. IT IS IMPORTANT THAT TAUREANS DO NOT BECOME SLAVES TO A ROUTINE, OR TOO SET IN THEIR WAYS AND IMMOVABLY STUBBORN.

You are one of the most reliable of all Zodiac types and are also likely to be the most charming. People will soon come to realize that from you they will always be able to expect a warm and affectionate greeting. You have the ability to inspire confidence and will impress everyone with your genuine sincerity.

For you to be completely fulfilled, you must have both emotional and financial security. Indeed, the achievement of this often forms the basic motivation of your life.

At work
You will flourish in a steady, well-paid job, complete with the knowledge that a regular paycheck will be yours. This will enable you to plan your finances with great confidence and let you look toward the future in terms of possessions and purchases. In your case, these will no doubt include a bigger and better house, labor-saving devices to make life easy for you, handsome furniture, and a generally comfortable lifestyle.

Your attitudes
Your need for emotional security is just as strong as your delight in material possessions. There is a danger here, however, since you can unconsciously come to regard your partner as being just another possession. When this happens, the words "my wife" and "my husband" take on quite new – and not altogether pleasant – connotations. More is said on this subject elsewhere (*see pages 76 – 77*), but the tendency must be underscored. Possessiveness is by far the worst Taurean fault, and this is the most dangerous area in which it can be expressed.

Material things, for example your home and its furniture – in fact most objects a Taurean can own – may also become too important to you, just like

Venus rules Taurus
*Venus, the Roman goddess of love, represents the ruling planet
of Taurus and Libra. The influence of Venus extends to art and
fashion, and relates to the feminine side of a Taurean's nature.*

the figures in your bank balance. The trait relates, of course, to your need for security.

The overall picture
Taureans are very often passionate people with strong feelings and opinions. Luckily, you usually express your powerful emotional level in a positive way. Like the Taurean bull, however, while you may be slow to anger, once roused your rage is often considerable. Be magnanimous, and learn to reject resentfulness.

With your liking for the good life, there is a chance that you may feel a conflict between the necessity to work hard, in order to attain that prosperous, luxurious lifestyle, and a certain indulgent laziness.

TAURUS
ASPIRATIONS

FOLLOWING A REGULAR ROUTINE WILL NOT WORRY YOU. YOUR
ORGANIZATIONAL AND MONEY-MAKING SKILLS MAY
HELP YOU TO START YOUR OWN BUSINESS. DO NOT BE AFRAID
OF TAKING OCCASIONAL RISKS.

COIN BALANCE

Finance
*A career in finance may suit
money-loving Taureans.
They will usually take great
care when investing.*

COINS

Arts and crafts
*As an earth sign, Taurus has a strong feeling
for natural materials. Taureans enjoy using
wood or clay, and a variety of fabrics.*

DIVIDERS AND
ARCHITECTURAL PLAN

POLISH BEADWORK

Architecture
*Taureans have a strong sense of
balance and form. They often
design buildings that have an
affinity with the landscape.*

The wine trade

Most Taureans love wine and are discriminating connoisseurs. Some will enjoy making it, either from grapes or from other natural ingredients that come to mind. Restaurant management may appeal.

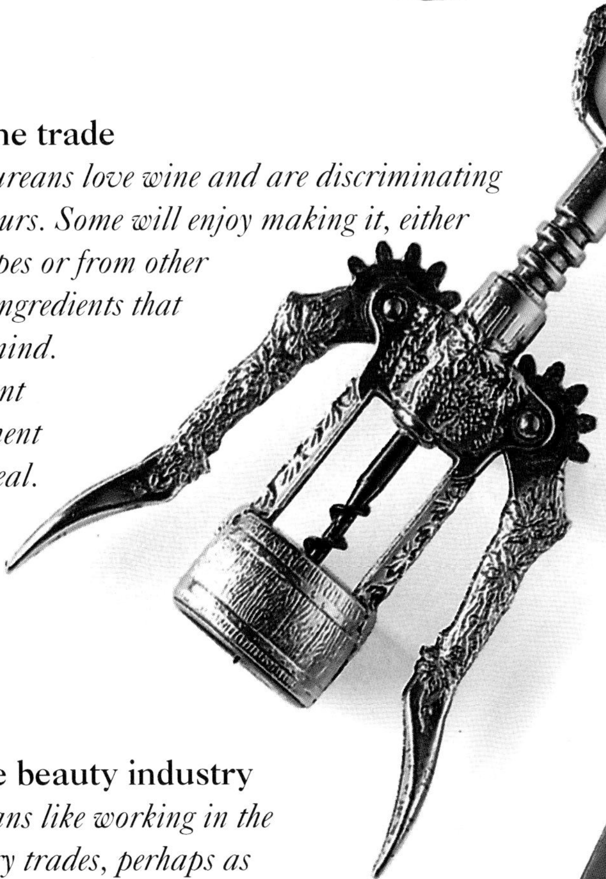

ITALIAN
BOTTLE
OPENER

The theater

Theater work may not provide the security that many Taureans need, but they can be great musicians.

The beauty industry

Taureans like working in the luxury trades, perhaps as beauticians. Their love of nature demands that they use goods produced without harming animals.

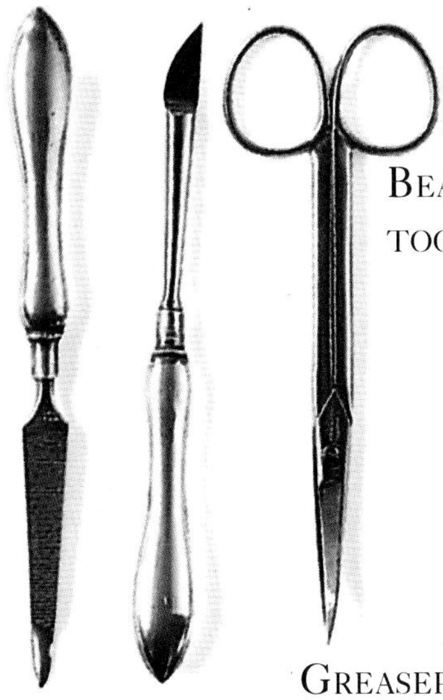

BEAUTICIAN'S
TOOLS

GREASEPAINTS

71

TAURUS

HEALTH

BECAUSE OF THEIR LIKING FOR RICH FOOD, OFTEN COMBINED WITH A SLOW METABOLISM, MANY TAUREANS HAVE A TENDENCY TO PUT ON WEIGHT EASILY. THEIR NECKS AND THROATS ARE VULNERABLE TO INJURY OR INFECTION.

Although Taureans are generally disciplined people, they sometimes find the routine of exercise difficult to maintain.

Your diet

As a Taurean, you no doubt love your food. If you have a slow metabolism, you should therefore do what you can to speed it up, perhaps through exercise, to help you fight weight gain. You may need to supplement your diet with sodium sulfate (nat. sulph.), which helps to eliminate excess water from the body.

Taking care

It should be kept in mind that the planet Venus rules not only the sign Taurus, but also the thyroid gland. If, therefore, you are considerably overweight for no apparent reason, you should think about being tested for possible thyroid inactivity.

The Taurean body area is the throat and neck, so you should take care to sleep with a suitable pillow. You may otherwise find yourself waking up with a stiff neck.

Grapes

Among the foods traditionally associated with Taurus are grapes, cereals, berries, and beans.

Astrology and the body

For many centuries it was not possible to practice medicine without a knowledge of astrology. In European universities, medical training included information on how planetary positions would affect the administration of medicines, the bleeding of patients, and the right time to pick herbs and make potions.

Each Zodiac sign rules a particular part of the body, and early medical textbooks always included a drawing that illustrated the point.

TAURUS AT
LEISURE

EACH OF THE SUN SIGNS TRADITIONALLY SUGGESTS SPARE-TIME
ACTIVITIES. ALTHOUGH THESE HOBBIES AND VACATION
SPOTS ARE ONLY SUGGESTIONS, THEY OFTEN SUIT TAUREAN
INTERESTS AND TASTES.

Gardening
*Taurus is an earth sign and
has always been associated
with gardening, especially
the creation of beautiful
flower gardens.*

GARDENING EQUIPMENT

Comfortable hotel stays
*Taureans need and enjoy
their creature
comforts. When you
are on vacation,
you no doubt like
to relax in the
luxury of an
expensive hotel.*

BRASS HOTEL KEYS

EMBROIDERED HANDKERCHIEF

Embroidery
*Taureans are often patient, with a
fondness for detail. Meticulous work such
as model-making, craftwork, or
embroidery will no doubt fascinate you.*

PASTRY CUTTER

ROLLING PIN

Cookery
*Although this hobby is normally
associated with Cancerians, many
Taureans enjoy baking cakes and
making desserts.*

POSTAGE
STAMPS

Travel
*You hate uncertainty and, having found
your ideal vacation destination, you are
likely to return there regularly. It could be
Ireland, Cyprus, the Greek islands,
Iran, or Switzerland.*

Sport
*Team sports might be fun
when you are young, but
these are likely to be
replaced by games of skill,
like bowling.*

BOWLING BALLS

TAURUS IN
LOVE

WHEN A TAUREAN IS IN LOVE, THE INFLUENCE OF VENUS
RULES THE DAY. UNDER THESE CIRCUMSTANCES, YOU
WILL EXPRESS YOUR VERY BEST CHARACTERISTICS IN A WAY
THAT CANNOT FAIL TO IMPRESS A LOVED ONE.

You may, with your overwhelming need for emotional security, find it hard to step into the vast unknown of a new relationship. Taureans need to be very sure of their partners before making any commitment to them. The worst Taurean fault is possessiveness and, when you are in love, this tendency can be quite vehemently expressed. You may find yourself thinking: "You're mine – all mine!" Together with a tendency to cling, this may create a claustrophobic atmosphere that will put many other Sun signs off. Allowing a partner a little more freedom will be much more productive.

Taureans are very generous lovers, and your gifts may have a good investment value. Naturally, this means that you are investing in your lover's emotions, in anticipation of a long-lasting relationship; but you are also looking to the future in a more material way. If, by some misfortune, the pair of you should fall upon hard times, the gift could be sold.

As a lover
Sexually, you are likely to be an admirable lover. Every move that you make will be unhurried, and every act of love will be

beautifully paced, with consideration for your partner's needs. Joy and passion will combine to the satisfaction of you both. Without a doubt, all Taureans are capable of being exciting lovers. The best kind of Taurean lover is, of course, one who can be both protective and caring.

Types of Taurean lover

Some Taureans can be surprisingly oversensitive. Many of you are nostalgic and may tend to look to the past in a rather sentimental way. This could be a little difficult for a lively, forward-looking partner to cope with. Others of your Sun sign are prone to be more assertive; their passion is intense and fiery. They must take care not to expose a selfish streak that could mar a relationship. There are also those people who express their love in a purel Taurean way, by recognizing every one of the traits that are set out here and by learning to counter any negative possessiveness. Some of you tend to have a flirtatious side to your nature, which lightens Taurean passion. This group tends to be talkative and requires partners with active minds as well as lively bodies.

TAURUS AT HOME

COMFORT IS THE KEYNOTE OF A TAUREAN HOME, WITH TRADITION BEING THE BACKBONE OF THE FURNISHING AND DECOR. WARM PINK OR PALE BLUE COLORS MAY PREDOMINATE. ABOVE ALL, THE ATMOSPHERE WILL BE CALM AND CUSHIONED.

Taureans usually have an overall need to feel secure. A typical Taurean home will be beautiful, large and, above all, very comfortable. This may even be motivated by a conscious effort to show how comfortably placed its inhabitants are. The perfect Taurean house will have a yard, and will preferably be located in the country. If this is not possible, then a quiet suburb should suffice just as easily. When you take time to sit down and relax in your living room, you will want to feel the warmth and the security of a solid, but luxurious and very comfortable armchair.

Your choice of furniture is likely to tend toward the conventional and, if this is the case, you will probably

Elegant flower display
The Taurean home is very likely to boast at least one beautiful display of flowers.

prefer to choose styles that will not date too easily. Wildly fashionable articles are unlikely to hold much appeal for you; you will, in general, want your furniture to be easy on the eye, and very welcoming. It is likely that your furniture will be extremely pretty, perhaps containing soft, delicate shades of pink, blue, and perhaps some very pale green, which are the colors of Venus, the Taurean ruling planet.

Decorative objects
Since most Taureans love flowers, there is a fair chance that you will own plenty of beautiful vases in which to put them. Taureans sometimes have a

Music stand and flute
If, like many Taureans, you play an instrument, you may give it pride of place.

perhaps in a glazed cotton or shiny satin. Frills often abound in the Taurean home, and there will be a proliferation of sheers to enhance windows, or to block out any uninteresting view outside. These will, however, be kept pulled right back if you have a beautiful flower garden of which you are justifiably proud. You probably prefer thick carpets, and will use beautiful rugs not only to preserve your carpets, but decoratively, in their own right, to enhance the look of your home.

collection of books on gardens or gardening. Alternatively, you might accumulate business magazines (some Taureans enjoy thinking about finance as much as gardening).

Soft furnishings
Taureans often obtain terrific pleasure from choosing new drapes and cushions. You will, more than likely, decide upon floral patterns,

Comfortable armchair
The floral pattern on this comfortable armchair is typically Taurean.

THE
MOON
AND
YOU

THE SUN DECREES YOUR OUTWARD
EXPRESSION, YOUR IMAGE, AND MANY
IMPORTANT PERSONALITY TRAITS. THE
MOON, ALTHOUGH MERELY THE EARTH'S
SATELLITE, IS ASTRONOMICALLY THE
SECOND MOST IMPORTANT BODY IN THE
SOLAR SYSTEM. FROM THE SIGN THAT IT
WAS IN AT YOUR BIRTH, IT INFLUENCES HOW
YOU REACT TO SITUATIONS, YOUR
EMOTIONAL LEVEL, AND, TO A CERTAIN
EXTENT, WHAT YOU HAVE INHERITED FROM
YOUR PARENTS AND ANCESTORS. HAVING
FOUND YOUR MOON SIGN IN THE SIMPLE
TABLES ON PAGES 606 TO 609, TURN TO THE
RELEVANT PAGES AND TAKE A STEP
FORWARD IN YOUR OWN SELF-KNOWLEDGE.

THE MOON IN
ARIES

ARIES IS A FIRE SIGN, SO YOUR REACTIONS TO SITUATIONS ARE EN-
THUSIASTIC AND OFTEN EMOTIONAL: UNDER PRESSURE
YOU COULD TAKE HASTY OR PREMATURE ACTION. MAKE AN EFFORT
NOT TO SUPPRESS YOUR TAUREAN CAUTION.

Your Arien Moon enables you to respond to situations with enthusiasm and speeds up your reactions. You could occasionally act hastily, and your Moon could even allow you to take some risks.

Self-expression
Taureans are generally warm people, and because your Arien Moon also provides a highly charged emotional influence, you will have a particularly high emotional level. You will be quick to anger, and may find it a little difficult to get along with some people. But because of the speed with which the Moon works when in Aries, you can throw off anger, and dismiss any outpouring of emotion, more easily than many Taureans.

Romance
You will be a very passionate lover, and because of an element of Moon sign impatience – something that is

virtually unknown to Taureans – you may tend to sweep partners off their feet. You are also less likely to succumb to Taurean possessiveness.

If you have a greater need for independence and freedom than most Taureans, do not ignore this. You most certainly have a very lively zest for love and sex which, coupled with warm Taurean sentiment and affection, plus your delightful sensuous qualities, makes you a wonderful lover.

Your well-being
The effect of an Arien Moon on your health could be to render you prone to headaches. If you suffer from them frequently, do not ignore the possibility that you may be suffering from a minor kidney problem.

You should also remember that Aries is an accident-prone sign and that, through carelessness, you may sometimes cut or burn yourself. If

The Moon in Aries

your responses to situations tend to be hurried, or you are prone to flurries of hastiness, there is a distinct possibility that you could be very vulnerable in this respect.

Planning ahead
Your Taurean business sense may be impeded by your Arien Moon. While it will encourage you to invest your money, you may do so a fraction less wisely than your Taurean Sun sign would have it. You may have a

sneaking regard for quick, risky growth, and could end up learning the hard way – by losing money.

Parenthood
You will be a less conventional, and perhaps less strict, parent than with many Taureans. You will understand when your children wish to express their independence. You will also manage to sidestep the Taurean tendency to spoil them. Encourage family members to exercise plenty.

THE MOON IN
TAURUS

WITH BOTH THE SUN AND THE MOON IN TAURUS AT THE TIME OF YOUR BIRTH, YOU WERE BORN AT THE TIME OF THE NEW MOON. AS AN EARTH SIGN, TAURUS POWERFULLY INFLUENCES YOUR PERSONALITY AND REACTIONS.

Should you study a list of your Sun sign characteristics, you will probably recognize that a great many of them apply to you. On average, out of a list of perhaps 20 traits of a Sun sign listed in books or magazines, most people will strongly identify with 11 or 12. In your case, however, the average increases considerably because the Sun and Moon were both in Taurus when you were born.

Self-expression
Your Sun sign makes you cautious, methodical, and not given to rushing around; your Moon sign encourages you to respond to situations in the same careful manner.

Your Taurean need for security is extremely strong, and your need for emotional security is perhaps second to none. You need a steady routine, like most people of your Sun sign, but with you it goes deeper than that. If, for instance, your schedule is unexpectedly disrupted, you will not find it easy to adjust, and your whole system could suffer.

You may fly into a rage more frequently than other Taureans, and this does not always have positive results: Try to emerge from this type of mood as quickly as you can.

Romance
You can be a wonderfully responsive Taurean lover, as long as you consciously check what may amount to a fatal flaw of being possessive. You could, without thinking, make life claustrophobic for your lover; if accused of this, you should take the rebuke seriously.

Your well-being
Healthwise, you must watch a tendency to put on weight; losing it may not be easy for you. One solution is to try to increase your metabolic rate, which may be naturally slow. For

The Moon in Taurus

instance, try walking a little more quickly and climbing stairs instead of relying on elevators.

Planning ahead

You may be something of a wizard at making money and at stretching your income much further than might seem possible. You have an excellent instinct for investment: Your cautiousness and tendency to go for steady growth ensure that you get the best possible results from your portfolio. Financial risk-taking is not something to which you are normally prone. You do, however, love luxury and creature comforts and will therefore be wise to earn as much money as you possibly can.

Parenthood

While making sure that your children have the best of everything, you may veer between being too strict and spoiling them. They may have more independent spirits than you; do not try to quell this. A show of affection will endear you to them.

THE MOON IN
GEMINI

YOUR GEMINIAN MOON PROVIDES YOU WITH UNUSUALLY RAPID
RESPONSES TO SITUATIONS. SHOULD YOU SUFFER FROM
RESTLESSNESS, ALLOW YOUR TAUREAN STABILITY TO CALM IT.
ANY SUDDEN IDEAS COULD BE VERY ORIGINAL.

Your lighthearted Geminian Moon makes you both original and capable of conveying your ideas to other people easily. You are, no doubt, an excellent communicator, and in all kinds of situations will respond to others in an open, friendly way. You are probably more talkative than many Sun sign Taureans.

Neighboring Zodiac signs are always very different, and from Gemini the Moon gives your stable, down-to-earth Taurean character some delightfully contrasting Geminian facets.

Self-expression
Gemini is not a highly emotional sign, and your reaction to most situations may be remarkably cool and detached. It could also be well spiced with a questioning logic.

But it is likely that, having first been affected by your Geminian Moon, your Taurean qualities soon take over. When your Sun sign dominates, you do anything to get what you want, just the way you want it. In your case stubbornness, supported by verbosity, will definitely come into its own from time to time.

Romance
Your Moon sign will make you express your natural charm and affection in a delightfully flirtatious way. You will enchant and attract lovers, who will not have to wait long to know how you feel about them.

You need a certain freedom of expression in this sphere of your life. Although your Taurean possessiveness may make it difficult, you must also recognize that your partners may need some freedom, too.

Your well-being
The Geminian body area covers the arms, hands, and lungs. In your case, a sore throat could well be followed by

The Moon in Gemini

a chest cough. If the cough persists, do not ignore it, since it could develop into something more serious. Your metabolism is probably considerably faster than that of most Taureans, so a susceptibility to putting on weight could be less of a problem for you. You should enjoy exercise.

Planning ahead

You may not be quite as cautious or as interested in steady financial growth as many Taureans. From time to time you could fall for some enticing get-rich-quick scheme, with awful results. Do not always follow your first reactions to such schemes.

Parenthood

You will have fewer problems with the generation gap than is usual with Taureans, because any Geminian influence encourages one to be future-oriented. In your case it will add a certain youthfulness of outlook that will help you to respond well to the concerns, opinions, and needs of the younger generation.

THE MOON IN
CANCER

WITH THE MOON IN CANCER, YOUR AFFECTIONATE QUALITIES
ARE COMBINED WITH TENDER, CARING EMOTION. YOU
WILL EXPRESS THIS POSITIVELY TO YOUR LOVERS AND FAMILY. BE
SENSIBLE IF YOU ARE SEIZED BY AN IRRATIONAL WORRY.

Earth and water are complementary elements, and the power of your Cancerian Moon (it is strong because the Moon rules Cancer) will vie for expression with your Taurean Sun. Therefore your Taurean qualities will be very powerfully affected by protective instincts. Your need for emotional security, which is so much a part of your Taurean motivation, will also be strongly enhanced and extended toward your loved ones.

Self-expression
All Taureans are practical and have plenty of common sense. Those with the Moon in Cancer have great intuitive foresight and will instinctively know when the time is right to be determined and brave.

You will achieve much, but may be a little undisciplined in your approach to life, sometimes allowing yourself to do what your prevailing mood seems to dictate. Beware of mood swings

that could hamper your progress. You have a wonderful imagination, but practical though you are, it is easy for you to succumb to worry. If your imagination takes over, you can really work yourself into a frenzy.

Your emotional resources are considerable, and you should be able to find plenty of outlets for them in all areas of your life.

Romance
You will be a romantic, perhaps even sentimental lover, capable of expressing your feelings tenderly, and you will be sensitive and responsive to your partner's needs. It may, however, be difficult for you to come to terms with the circumstances of the breakup of a relationship.

Your well-being
The chest and breasts are the Cancerian body areas, but so, to a certain extent, is the digestive system.

The Moon in Cancer

Worry is likely to cause problems in the latter area and, as a Taurean, your liking for good food and wine can exacerbate them. You can put on weight all too easily and may well have to constantly discipline yourself to a very strictly controlled diet. The best forms of exercise for you are swimming and, as has already been suggested, dance.

Planning ahead

Taurean possessiveness and the Cancerian need to hoard things work in two ways. In the first instance you can be shrewd, intuitive, and practical. But in the second, you may hoard things, and your portfolio could become cluttered with unprofitable investments. Develop an enterprising spirit that will allow you to progress.

Parenthood

As a caring parent who wants the very best for your children, do not be over-protective or possessive. This could be very difficult for you, and at times you may tend to talk about life as it was when you were a child. Try seeing the world through your children's eyes, because it will help you to avoid the generation gap.

THE MOON IN
LEO

TAUREANS AND THOSE WITH THE MOON IN LEO LOVE COMFORT AND LUXURY. AS A RESULT, YOU MAY SPEND PLENTY OF MONEY IN ORDER TO ENJOY THEM. DEVELOPING YOUR NATURAL GOOD BUSINESS SENSE WILL HELP SUPPORT SUCH INDULGENCES.

Your powers of observation are enhanced by your Leo Moon, which gives you the ability to take command of almost any situation with only the briefest notice.

Self-expression
Your Taurean Sun makes you extremely reliable and full of common sense. People will take it for granted that you can cope well with any situation. In fact, they may easily tend to take advantage of these qualities – not that you will really mind. Knowing what your priorities are, you will rise above any pettiness and spend your time rewardingly.

Both Taurus and Leo are of the fixed quality, and as a result, not only can you be pretty stubborn at times, but you may also find it difficult to change your opinions.

Leo is a fiery, enthusiastic, and passionate sign, so your response to situations will be spiced with great emotion. Express your enthusiasm freely, especially in relation to your personal interests and hobbies.

Romance
When you are in love, your emotions should flow both positively and quite delightfully. You will be as lavish in expressing your feelings toward your partners as you will be in ensuring that you enjoy every possible luxury that you can, or perhaps really cannot, afford. Leos are naturally generous, and your Leo Moon makes you particularly responsive to such pleasures as beautiful, expensive evenings spent entertaining yourself and your lover.

Your well-being
The Leo body areas are the spine and back. If you have a sedentary job, get a well-designed chair to keep it in good order. The Leo organ is the heart. To benefit it, perhaps you

The Moon in Leo

should try walking or jogging regularly. Or you could work out at a pleasant, comfortable health club.

Your Taurean tendency to gain weight could be increased by the influence of Leo. If your Moon sign attracts you to exercise, it can only be a good thing.

Planning ahead
Where money is concerned, your needs are substantial. While you may be satisfied with a regular paycheck, you are unlikely to be very fulfilled by a lifestyle that does not allow you to enjoy your work and take pride in

it. Think about this carefully: Money is, indeed, important, but so is your inner contentment.

Parenthood
You will work hard for your children and do a lot for them, but you must ensure that you allow them to develop in the way that they want to. Do not be overpossessive, or try to make them into clones of yourself. Provided they have one or two compelling interests, that is all they need. If you also make an effort not to be bossy, you will minimize any problems associated with the generation gap.

THE MOON IN
VIRGO

WITH THE SUN AND MOON BOTH IN EARTH SIGNS, YOU ARE A VERY
PRACTICAL PERSON. DO NOT LET APPREHENSIVENESS OR
A LACK OF SELF-CONFIDENCE SPOIL YOUR TAUREAN ENJOYMENT
OF LIFE AND ITS SENSUAL PLEASURES.

The combination of your Sun and Moon signs makes you among the most practical of Taureans. Your Moon sign is, however, not noted for self-confidence, and this may have tended to inhibit you, especially when you were a child.

Self-expression

A certain shyness may have made you very quiet when you were young. Conversely, however, you may have become nervously talkative when you felt self-conscious. Attaining a balance and allowing the inner stability of your Taurean Sun to shine through may be something you have consciously had to develop.

Both Taurus and Virgo are of the earth element – hence your strong practical qualities. At the physical level, contact with the earth may mean a lot to you. Perhaps you love gardening, or can grow beautiful indoor plants. The countryside is probably important to you, so if your career holds you to a city center, try to live near a park, or escape out of town as often as possible.

Romance

You are a good communicator and must never hold back and fail to express your real feelings. This is especially true when you are in love. Do not cramp the wonderful Taurean way in which you express yourself, or your warm, tender passion.

You may also have an uncharacteristic tendency to be overly critical of your loved ones. Bear in mind that while well-founded constructive criticism may be helpful, carping and nagging are not.

Your well-being

The Virgoan body area is the stomach and, to some extent, the nervous system. When you are worried, it may be your stomach that reacts first.

The Moon in Virgo

You definitely need a high-fiber diet, to counter the effects of Taurean indulgence in rich food. If you suffer from a buildup of tension, you could find yourself prone to migraines.

Planning ahead

Virgoans are careful with money, and for you, that carefulness works at an instinctive level. This is helpful, since Taureans can be too generous. Virgoans often find it embarrassing to be generous. You will certainly find nothing ostentatious in owning property; Taurus will balance you in this respect.

Parenthood

You may well have a natural ability to teach your children, so that by the time they go to school they will be well on the way to reading. Be proud of their efforts. As in all of your dealings, remember that you have the capacity to be far more critical than you might realize.

THE MOON IN
LIBRA

AS THEY ARE BOTH RULED BY VENUS, LIBRA AND TAURUS HAVE
A GREAT DEAL IN COMMON. YOUR LIBRAN MOON WILL
ENCOURAGE YOU TO RESPOND VERY WELL TO EVERYTHING THAT
TAUREANS FIND ATTRACTIVE.

Although Taurus is an earth sign and of the fixed quality, and Libra an air sign and of the cardinal quality, they still have much in common. Above all, they share charm.

Self-expression
You find it very easy to convey the warmth of your Taurean personality with your instinctive and strong measure of tact and diplomacy. However, just because your Libran influence makes it easy to persuade people to your way of thinking, you must not stifle your Taurean common sense. Otherwise, you may end up using people. Anyone with a strong Libran influence also tends to be indecisive. When the occasion demands it, let Taurus take control.

Romance
With the Moon in Libra, you will possess a romantic air. You will express your feelings freely and

gracefully, without overwhelming your lover by too sudden an approach. Your courtship will lead gently but firmly from romance to passion.

Notorious Taurean anger is less likely to erupt openly in you than in many Sun sign Taureans. Your instincts incline you to peace at any price, and you will always try to resolve problems diplomatically.

Your well-being
The Libran body area is the kidneys, and any upsetting circumstances can cause a kidney imbalance that might lead to headaches.

The Taurean love of a relaxed lifestyle is echoed by your Moon sign – so you may need to be very strict with yourself if you start a new exercise program or a diet. It may pay for you to exercise at a good health club, where saunas and steam rooms offer both a relaxing and a sociable time. It would be best for you to avoid

The Moon in Libra

crash diets completely. Instead, very gradually teach yourself to stop eating any highly calorific foods.

Planning ahead

Compared to most Taureans, you may not have the same urge for making money. You will, however, enjoy spending it. Any spare money must therefore be invested wisely, so that as you get older, you will be able to afford more luxuries. If you are looking for extra money, selling beauty products might be a good idea.

Obtain sound professional financial advice before investing your savings, but do tell your advisor about any ideas you may have. You will learn a lot in the process and grow confident about managing your own affairs.

Parenthood

You could get a little tired of your children's demands for attention, so try to arrange to have a few hours away from them each week. Always make sure that your children know where they stand with you.

THE MOON IN
SCORPIO

TAURUS AND SCORPIO ARE POLAR OR OPPOSITE SIGNS, WHICH
MEANS THAT YOU WERE BORN UNDER A FULL MOON.
BEWARE OF RESTLESSNESS, AN UNCHARACTERISTIC TRAIT
AMONG TAUREANS, AND TRY NOT TO ACT JEALOUSLY.

Each of us is, in one way or another, apt to express the attitudes of our polar, or opposite, Zodiac sign. Each sign has its partner across the horoscope; for you this is Scorpio. Furthermore, as the Moon was in Scorpio when you were born, this "polarity" (as it is known) will emerge in a very interesting way.

Self-expression
Scorpio is very highly charged with emotional and physical energy. You will therefore react strongly when you meet with a challenge. Those born under Taurus are placid enough until rage gets the better of them, but your powerful polar qualities will join forces in your personality not only when you are angry, but also when you are moved in any way.

It is very important that you try to fill your days with tasks and events that make demands on your physical energy and also provide you with psychological fulfillment. Most people born at the time of the Full Moon tend to suffer occasionally from an element of restlessness or inner discontent. In your case, you must always be on guard against this.

Romance
The chief Taurean fault, possessiveness, is related to a Scorpio weakness – jealousy. In terms of your emotional relationships, this means that while they are likely to be highly charged (and you will no doubt contribute to that), jealousy can occur. It is always a good idea to discuss problems with your partners, but do not do this if your intuition leads you to explode into anger before you are sure of your facts.

Your well-being
The Scorpio body area covers the genitals, and these, along with your Taurean throat, are vulnerable. "Safe

The Moon in Scorpio

sex" and regular testicular exams for men or gynecological visits for women are important for you.

You may easily put on weight, especially if your metabolism is on the slow side. If this is the case, try to engage in some exercise.

Planning ahead

The Taurean business sense and liking for possessions and material security marries well with similar Scorpio qualities. In your case, however, because of the Moon's influence, you also have a considerable instinct for bargains and investments. You should follow it.

Parenthood

You will work hard for your family, but you could be more strict, and more insistent on somewhat harsh discipline, than you realize. Try to be aware of this, especially when your children want to move out and start living their lives in their own ways.

THE MOON IN
SAGITTARIUS

FACED WITH A CHALLENGE, YOU WILL FIND YOURSELF RESPONDING ENTHUSIASTICALLY. USE THIS ENTHUSIASM TO YOUR ADVANTAGE, AND DO NOT SUPPRESS IT WHEN YOUR TAUREAN CAUTION STRIVES TO TAKE OVER.

Your fiery Sagittarian Moon adds many contrasting facets to your steady, more cautious, earthy Sun sign. You respond much more quickly to situations than do many people of your Taurean Sun sign.

Self-expression
Your mind is always open to challenge, once excited by an idea or a project, you will immediately want to get involved. This can be a good thing, but it can also work slightly to your disadvantage: overoptimism is a Sagittarian problem that has to be contained. Luckily, in your case, after your initial enthusiasm, your Taurean caution usually takes over.

Romance
Your intense Taurean emotions are enlivened by your Moon sign, and while, like all Taureans, you need both emotional and material security, within a relationship you also need an element of independence. This sits uneasily with your Taurean tendency to be possessive. You may well resent your partners intensely for being possessive of you, but at the same time, act just as possessively toward them. If you are accused of this, take heed. Your Sagittarian enthusiasm and passion for life will color your attitude to love just as much as they do other areas.

Your well-being
The Sagittarian body area covers the hips and thighs. Sagittarius is yet another sign that enjoys rich food, in particular hefty casseroles, but the predilection for sweet desserts is less marked than in Taureans. Taurean women with a Sagittarian influence will have a tendency to gain weight on their hips and thighs.

The Sagittarian organ is the liver, and indigestion can be a problem. Upsets in this area are common

The Moon in Sagittarius

enough after a Taurean night out, but if you also have a Sagittarian Moon? No more need be said.

Sagittarians often enjoy sports with an element of daring. Fortunately, however, your Taurean caution will let you enjoy such activities safely.

Planning ahead

A similar sneaking regard for risk-taking can emerge in your attitude toward money, where your instincts can encourage you to invest too heavily. The thought of large spoils will attract you but, in the end, you might encounter disaster. Try not to learn the hard way. Think things out before you act. In this area, always rely on your Taurean nature.

Parenthood

You will be less conservative than many Taurean parents. Your lively response to your children's questions and demands will be gladly received, and you are capable of getting really enthused by their interests. Make sure that you take time out to have fun with your children, as well as spending your hard-earned money on them. For you, the generation gap should not prove to be a problem.

THE MOON IN
CAPRICORN

YOU HAVE AN AMBITIOUS STREAK AND SHOULD PURSUE YOUR
ASPIRATIONS AS FAR AS YOU CAN. USE YOUR TAUREAN
COMMON SENSE AND CAUTION, BUT DO NOT LET THEM CRAMP THIS
VITAL URGE — IT IS YOUR PATH TO INNER FULFILLMENT.

The earth element is important to your psychological makeup: Both Taurus and Capricorn are earth signs. So when you read about Taurean practical common sense and caution, you will immediately recognize these traits in yourself.

Self-expression

Are you ambitious and aspiring, or do you fail to progress in life as much as you would like to? The latter is fine if you are managing to achieve inner fulfillment; but surely you cannot be happy with simply trundling along in the same old rut, year after year. Of course, you could experience a mixture of times when you are successful, and others when you lack self-confidence and tend to hold back.

If you feel that other people are cramping your style – or for that matter, that you are doing so yourself – remember that caution and common sense are the best building blocks,

and that your Moon sign, while causing fluctuations in your responses to challenges, can also allow you to take steady strides toward bigger and better things.

Romance

Capricorn is a cool, unemotional sign, so some of your Taurean ardor will probably be stifled. Capricorn is, however, also a faithful sign, and therefore complements your Taurean qualities excellently.

One tendency of which you should be aware is a susceptibility to social climbing. This may not work well for your emotional life, whatever it does for your social position. Your heart should decide in these matters.

Your well-being

The Capricornian body area covers the knees and shins, and the bones. If you are sluggish and experience periods when you positively shun

The Moon in Capricorn

sports or other exercise, your joints could suffer. You should also make sure that you have regular dental checkups, especially if you have a Taurean sweet tooth, since Capricorn also rules the teeth.

Planning ahead
Taureans are generous, and love luxury and comfort. Capricornians are entirely the opposite. In fact, their tastes can be positively Spartan; this might cause some internal conflict that will need resolving. You should

be pretty good with cash, making wise investments that show a regular, steady growth.

Parenthood
Bringing work home from the office in order to make extra money for your children's education might not be a good idea. Your concern for their material well-being may mean that they lack both affection and pleasure. Also try not to be too much of a disciplinarian; you are fair, but you may be stricter than you realize.

THE MOON IN
AQUARIUS

YOUR AQUARIAN WISH TO BE UNCONVENTIONAL AND TO STAND
OUT FROM A CROWD COULD CLASH WITH A TAUREAN NEED
TO CONFORM. TRY TO UNDERSTAND THIS STRUGGLE; DEVELOP
CREATIVE ORIGINALITY AND CHECK STUBBORNNESS.

Although they are essentially very different, Taurus and Aquarius share the same fixed quality. Stubbornness, for example, is a characteristic common to all Taureans, and in your case it is exacerbated by your Aquarian Moon.

Self-expression
It is particularly important that you recognize your potential to be stubborn. Try to remember that firmness is one thing, but a closed mind is another.

Your Aquarian Moon also lends some unusual and lively qualities to your Taurean Sun. You are, for instance, among the least conventional of a sign that tends to adhere strictly to convention. You will often surprise your friends by reacting in ways that they do not expect. This is not a bad thing, since it gives you a certain attractive sparkle. Remember that your unconventional streak can,

however, make you unpredictable, and that your reactions may be inconvenient to other people.

Romance
Aquarius is not a highly emotional sign, and your Taurean passion will to some extent reflect this. However, an Aquarian enthusiasm for romance will reveal itself, to great effect, in your expression of love and sex.

You have an independent spirit and may need more freedom of expression than many Sun sign Taureans. Do not, therefore, rush into a permanent relationship or marriage. In fact, you could well have a lot to come to terms with in your love life.

Your well-being
The Aquarian body area is the ankles, so take extra care if you go skiing or skating, or decide to wear high-heeled shoes. Aquarius also rules the circulation and, while you will tend to

The Moon in Aquarius

enjoy cold, crisp weather, make sure that you keep warm; your circulation may not be too good. You could enjoy karate as a form of exercise.

Planning ahead
Financially, you may be less shrewd than many Taureans. You could be attracted to showy but not very sound investments, so be cautious, and do not gamble more than you can afford to lose. Furthermore, you are often drawn to buy interesting and unusual items for your home or wardrobe, which may be expensive and too fashionable to be wise investments.

Parenthood
It is important that your children know where they stand with you. If they do not, because you change your mind too often, you could end up causing a lot of family tension. Encouraging your children to be interested in unusual and intriguing hobbies comes easily to you.

THE MOON IN
PISCES

YOU ARE SYMPATHETIC, WITH A NEED TO OFFER OTHERS A HELPING
HAND. LET TAUREAN COMMON SENSE TAKE OVER, HOWEVER,
BEFORE YOU GIVE TOO MUCH MONEY AWAY. YOU ARE A WONDERFUL
LOVER, BUT BEWARE OF BEING TOO POSSESSIVE.

Your earth sign Taurean Sun and water sign Piscean Moon blend well. As a result, your reactions to situations are both sensitive and emotional; you respond in a very caring, sympathetic way.

Self-expression
While you are practical, your inner strength and toughness are less apparent. This is particularly true when you meet with a challenge, in that you are sometimes not as assertive or as determined as other Sun sign Taureans.

Beware of a tendency to take the easy way out of difficult situations, which could be caused by a lack of confidence. Should this be the case, think of all your past achievements and give yourself more credit.

Pisceans tend to put on rose-colored glasses at the least provocation, while Taureans usually face up to reality. A little dreaminess will not come amiss, especially when heightened by the imaginative creativity that could be an integral part of your potential.

Romance
Taurean affection and sensuality blend well with Piscean emotion, making you a wonderful lover. You should, however, beware of falling for someone too quickly, since when you meet with reality, you may come down to earth all too rapidly.

It should not be too difficult to keep Taurean possessiveness at bay, but your Piscean Moon could cause you to be deceitful in tricky situations, perhaps because you are choosing the easiest way out.

Your well-being
The Piscean body area is the feet. You may find it difficult to get shoes that fit well, or you might simply be glad to take them off and go barefoot

The Moon in Pisces

whenever possible. Like Taurus, Pisces is a sign prone to weight gain – perhaps because Pisceans get thoroughly bored when checking the calorie content of foods. Allow your gourmet tendencies their freedom, but do not fall back on junk food any more than is absolutely necessary.

Planning ahead

Kindness and sympathy, and a desire to help, may place a strain on your bank balance. Try to keep a practical outlook when someone tells you a heartrending story. Always discuss investments with an expert so that your rather impractical Piscean response to financial matters will not damage or smother your sound Taurean business sense.

Parenthood

You will make a wonderful, caring parent, who will be sensitive to your children's needs. Use your imagination not only to inspire and encourage the development of their potential, but also to help you express and develop your own. Any creative work that you do with them, for instance photography or dance classes, will be good for all of you.

SUN & MOON SIGNS

GEMINI

MAY 22 – JUNE 21

INTRODUCING
GEMINI

GEMINI, THE SIGN OF THE HEAVENLY TWINS, IS THE THIRD
ZODIAC SIGN. GEMINIAN SUBJECTS ARE NOTED FOR
THEIR DUALITY: THEY SELDOM RESTRICT THEMSELVES
TO DOING JUST ONE THING AT A TIME.

Being the first sign of the air element, Gemini bestows a light intellect. This is reflected in the fact that Geminians tend to know a little about a great range of subjects. Geminians must be aware that superficiality can lead to shallowness of character, and that restlessness may prevent them from ever managing to achieve their full potential. While recognizing that variety is essential for them, Geminians must try to develop continuity of effort if they are to achieve inner fulfillment.

Traditional groupings
As you read through this book you will come across references to the elements and the qualities, and to positive and negative, or masculine and feminine signs.

The first of these groupings, that of the elements, comprises fire, earth, air, and water signs. The second, that of the qualities, divides the Zodiac

into cardinal, fixed, and mutable signs. The final grouping is made up of positive and negative, or masculine and feminine signs. Each Zodiac sign is associated with a combination of components from these groupings, all of which contribute different characteristics to it.

Geminian characteristics
The Geminian ruling planet is Mercury, which often inclines its subjects to be good communicators. Gemini is also of the mutable quality, which heightens the properties of Mercury and the intellectual approach characteristic of the sign itself.

Gemini is a positive, masculine sign, and is regarded as the most youthful of all the 12 signs of the Zodiac. Although many different colors will no doubt appeal to individual Geminians, there is, overall, a tendency for them to favor shades of yellow.

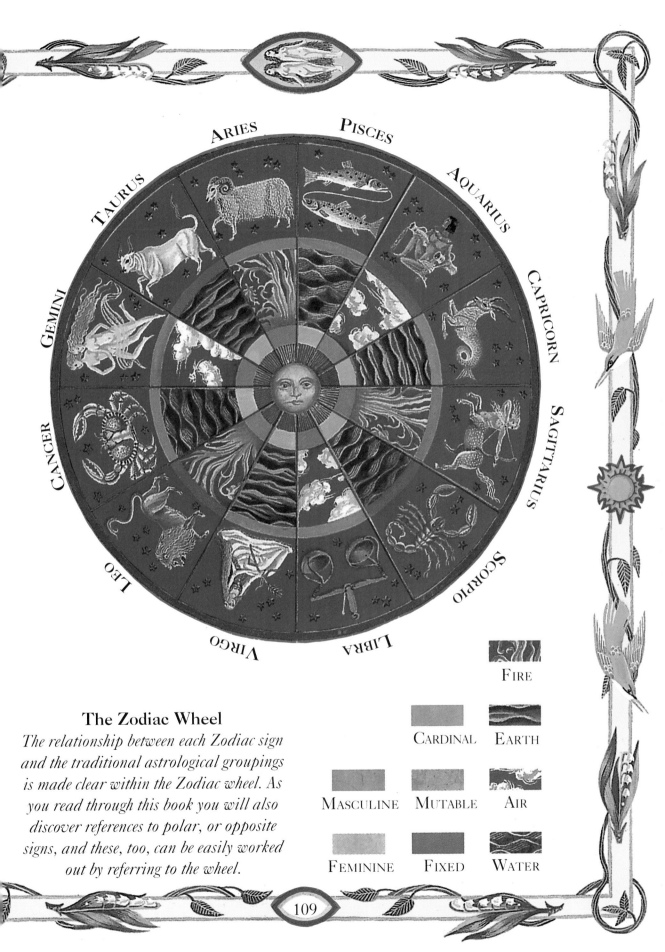

The Zodiac Wheel

The relationship between each Zodiac sign and the traditional astrological groupings is made clear within the Zodiac wheel. As you read through this book you will also discover references to polar, or opposite signs, and these, too, can be easily worked out by referring to the wheel.

FIRE

CARDINAL   EARTH

MASCULINE   MUTABLE   AIR

FEMININE   FIXED   WATER

MYTHS & LEGENDS

THE ZODIAC, WHICH IS SAID TO HAVE ORIGINATED IN
BABYLON AS LONG AS 2,500 YEARS AGO, IS A
CIRCLE OF CONSTELLATIONS THROUGH WHICH THE SUN
MOVES DURING THE COURSE OF A YEAR.

Gemini is one of only two signs whose myth has some pictorial connection with the pattern of stars that make up its constellation: it was so called because of the two bright stars it contains. The Babylonians called it the Great Twins in their Zodiac. The myth most strongly associated with the sign is that of Castor and Pollux, known as the Dioscuri, which means "the young sons of Zeus." The paternity of Castor and Pollux is in fact a complicated affair. While their mortal parents were Leda and Tyndareus, a union between Zeus,

Helmet cheekpiece
A typical Roman image of one of the Dioscuri.

the king of the gods, disguised as a swan, and Leda confuses the issue. Leda produced two eggs. From one came Pollux and Helen; from the other, Castor and Clytemnestra. Pollux and Helen (later to be known as Helen of Troy) were said to be the children of Zeus, and therefore immortal, whereas Castor and Clytemnestra were assumed to be the mortal children of Tyndareus. It was in fact quite common for people of ancient civilizations to claim that one child from a pair of twins was

of divine origin. Castor and Pollux were brought up in Sparta, where they formed a very close friendship.

Among their exploits together, Castor and Pollux rescued their sister, Helen, from an abductor, Theseus, and joined Jason and the Argonauts' expedition to recover the Golden Fleece. Afterward the two boys fell in love with two sisters, Hilaeira and Phoebe, who were already betrothed at the time. When the boys carried them off, Castor was tragically killed in the ensuing brawl. Pollux, the immortal, could not bear the thought of being parted from his brother and wept over his body. Touched by the sight of such brotherly devotion, Zeus allowed Pollux to share his immortality with Castor. As a result, the twins spent half their time in the Underworld with the spirits of the dead, and half with the gods on Mount Olympus.

Great athletes when on Earth, Castor and Pollux became patrons of all athletic contests. They were also said to protect sailors, to whom they still appear during storms as the lights of St. Elmo's fire. This belief dates back to the occasion when Zeus saved the Argonauts from a violent storm that was threatening to sink their ship, the Argo: Two flames came down from the heavens and hung above the heads of the Dioscuri, signaling the end of the storm. In later times, Castor and Pollux were regarded as divine and, according to legend, were supposed to ride through the sky on two white horses, carrying dazzling spears, each with a star above his brow. During the years of Imperial Rome, Castor and Pollux were believed to descend to Earth in order to fight at the head of the Roman army whenever it did battle with its enemies.

People who have a Geminian Sun sign tend to possess two distinct sides to their natures, enabling them to do two things at once. Duality is therefore very likely to constitute a strong part of your personality.

Roman Republican coin
This coin from 210 B.C. shows Castor and Pollux riding through the heavens.

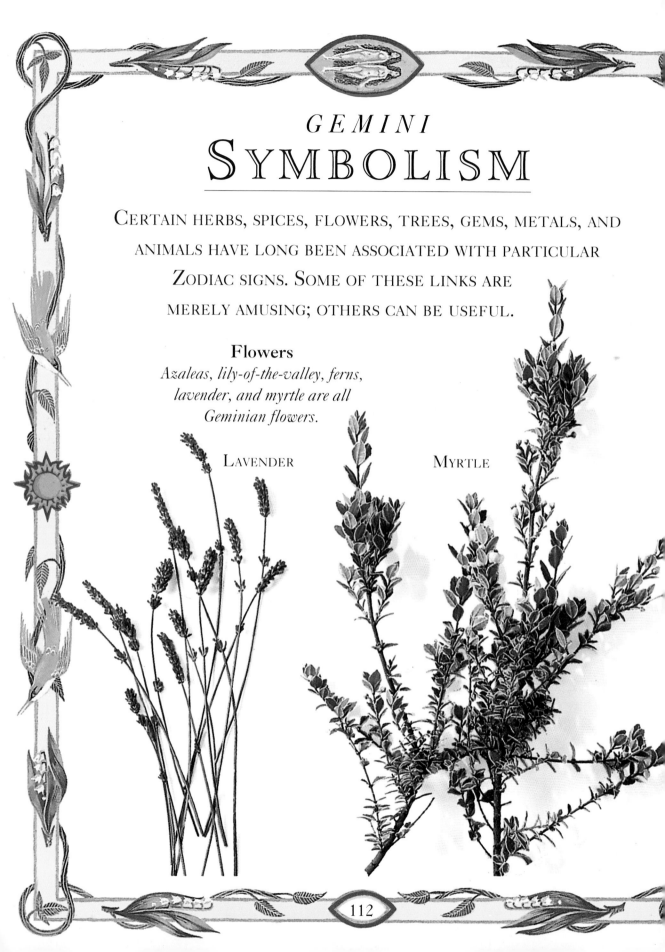

GEMINI
SYMBOLISM

CERTAIN HERBS, SPICES, FLOWERS, TREES, GEMS, METALS, AND
ANIMALS HAVE LONG BEEN ASSOCIATED WITH PARTICULAR
ZODIAC SIGNS. SOME OF THESE LINKS ARE
MERELY AMUSING; OTHERS CAN BE USEFUL.

Flowers
*Azaleas, lily-of-the-valley, ferns,
lavender, and myrtle are all
Geminian flowers.*

LAVENDER

MYRTLE

Trees
All nut-bearing trees are ruled by Gemini, but especially the hazel and walnut.

ANISEED

CARAWAY

HAZEL

Spices
No spices are particularly associated with Gemini, but many people of this sign tend to enjoy spicy food, perhaps seasoned with aniseed or caraway.

LEMON BALM

Herbs
Lemon balm is good for curing a stitch, and arrowroot can be applied to a blister. An infusion of nettles soothes a sore throat. All of these herbs are governed by Gemini.

MERCURY

Metal
Mercury is both the Geminian ruling planet and, as its popular name, quicksilver, suggests, the Geminian metal.

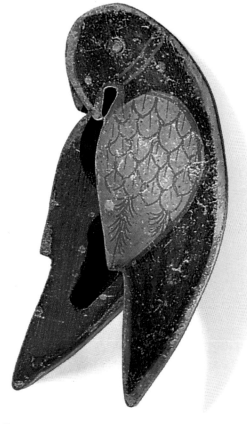

AGATE

INDIAN PARROT SPICE BOX

Gems
Agates and emeralds are Geminian stones. But Geminians like all colors, so most glittering gems will appeal to them.

WOODEN BIRD BROOCH

1920S CRÊPE PAPER BUTTERFLY FAN

BUTTERFLY BROOCH

CHINA MONKEY

Animals
The chattering monkey is certainly a Geminian beast, and so, traditionally, are small, swift, brightly colored birds and butterflies.

BRASS MONKEYS

GEMINI
PROFILE

THE OVERALL APPEARANCE OF A GEMINIAN IS USUALLY LIVELY, OFTEN REFLECTING RESTLESSNESS AND A KEENNESS TO BE UP TO THE MINUTE. GEMINIANS ARE OFTEN RECOGNIZED BY THEIR SPRIGHTLY, LIGHT-FOOTED WAY OF WALKING.

Geminians seem to hardly ever stand still. In a queue at a drinks party you will, for example, spend most of your time moving restlessly up and down, on and off the balls of your feet.

The body
The Geminian body is usually long and lean. Because you have a fast metabolism, you are not inclined to put on weight; so if you are tall and slender, the chances are that you will stay that way for the whole of your life. Your arms and legs may be long, and your hands prominent and flexible. Some Geminians give the appearance of being a little bony. Geminian shoulders are not wide, and may tend

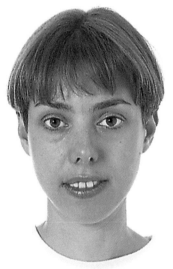

The Geminian face
You may have lively-looking features, and short, cropped hair.

to slope a little. It is very important for you to keep moving in order to burn up your high level of tense, physical Geminian energy.

The face
Many Geminians have fine hair that is cropped into an easily manageable style. Your forehead could well be rather broad, which will make you appear intelligent, and your eyes will be extremely alert, giving your whole face mobility and a bright expression. It is generally said that Geminians never stop talking, and it may well be the case with you that your lips do not seem to stop moving. You are also likely to have a particularly attractive mouth. The Geminian chin is

The Geminian stance

Many Geminians have a tendency to bob up and down on the balls of their feet whenever they have to wait for anything.

typically sharp, and sometimes pointed, which adds to the overall lively appearance.

Style

Geminians are fashionable, and like to wear the very latest styles – often favoring separates. Sometimes, through your need for variety, a "mix and match" policy may not pay off, and your appearance could become haphazard. However, with a little experience most Geminians can develop the gift of mixing separates in clever and interesting ways.

Accessories are very popular among Geminians, with trendy hats, sunglasses, belts, and fashion jewelry generally much in evidence. You may manage to accumulate quite a collection of these things. Most colors are popular among Geminians, but yellow particularly so.

In general

Even if you do not possess the typical Geminian physique, it is probable that you will still be be immediately recognizable, even from a distance,

because of your distinctive way of walking: Geminians seem to positively bob up and down, as much as they move forward.

Irrespective of your nationality, you probably gesticulate with your hands and arms more than people of other Sun signs. Every movement that you make is likely to be quick, rather sudden, and sometimes even a little twitchy or jerky.

GEMINI
PERSONALITY

GEMINIANS POSSESS NIMBLE MINDS AND BODIES. THE TWINS,
WHICH SYMBOLIZE THE SIGN, REPRESENT THE
GEMINIAN NEED TO BE ACTIVE IN A NUMBER OF DIFFERENT
FIELDS AT THE SAME TIME.

Simply because it is not in your nature, it would be wrong to urge you to do just one thing at a time. The rest of us must, however, see to it that in due course you get around to completing each project you start. This will probably subdue any restlessness and help you to achieve a sense of inner satisfaction.

At work

Geminians tend to function at a high level of nervous tension. If this is expressed positively, through work that you find rewarding, it will be burned off in a satisfactory way. On the other hand, if you are involved in repetitive work or are forced to tolerate stupidity, a great deal of stress can build up. In such cases it is very important that you find ways to ease the tension. A boring or undemanding job should be balanced with some stimulating continuing education courses. Alternatively, an exacting

intellectual job should perhaps be tempered by some form of lively competitive leisure activity, such as tennis or squash.

Geminians know a little about a lot of different subjects, and are often quite rightly accused of being superficial. This could be a difficult hurdle for you to overcome, although one way might be to develop variety within the confines of a few well-chosen subjects. This will ensure that your notoriously low threshold of boredom is not reached.

Your attitudes

You possess great cunning, and because you are recognized to be the communicators of the Zodiac, you will have no difficulty in expressing ideas and opinions to anyone who cares to listen. In doing so, you will manage to change people's ideas and opinions to match your own way of thinking. This will often be accomplished very

Mercury rules Gemini

Mercury, the messenger god, represents the ruling planet of Gemini. The influence of Mercury stimulates the mind, but it can also make its subjects critical, nervous, and tense.

artfully, without people realizing that you are doing it. Be careful, however, that your native cunning does not involve duplicity.

The overall picture

It must be remembered that the Geminian mind needs continual stimulation, and the Geminian body continual movement. Both physical and mental energy must be regulated like a well-oiled machine and released at a constant level.

Geminians are usually highly motivated and can end up being great achievers, especially if they are involved in the media or sales. The influence of your ruling planet, Mercury, will help you, since Mercury is the messenger god.

GEMINI
ASPIRATIONS

IDEALLY, GEMINI WOULD LIKE TO HAVE A NEW JOB EVERY DAY.
THE CHANCES ARE THAT A REGULAR ROUTINE WILL
BORE YOU STIFF. IF YOU DO HAVE TO PUT UP WITH ONE, A
VARIETY OF SPARE-TIME ACTIVITIES IS ESSENTIAL.

1920S OFFICE
INTERCOM
SYSTEM

Reception work
*Geminians usually
prosper in jobs related to
communications. This is
due to an association with
the planet Mercury,
which is linked
with activity.*

Teaching
*Geminians are not
known for their patience,
so if they become teachers –
a good choice given their
excellent communications
skills – they should
choose to
work with
older children
or teenagers.*

PENCIL SET

1920s
TELEPHONE
EXTENSION

OLD BANK NOTES

International banking

The wheeling and dealing and intense activity of either international banking or a stock exchange will suit many Geminians.

Telecommunications

This type of work will suit those who are fond of communication, especially conversation.

TOOLS USED IN
GRAPHIC DESIGN

MINIATURE CASH REGISTER

Media work

Many Geminians work in the media. This includes graphic design, public relations, and publicity.

Retail sales

Many Geminians have the ability to get along with anyone and to sell anything. You might enjoy the busy, lively atmosphere of a large department store.

GEMINI
HEALTH

GEMINI IS AN AIR SIGN, AND THIS INFLUENCES THE LUNGS.
FOR GEMINIANS LIVING IN AN UNPOLLUTED
ENVIRONMENT IS CRITICAL. THE ARMS AND HANDS
ARE ALSO VULNERABLE.

Geminians are usually fortunate enough to have a fast metabolic rate and are unlikely to put on weight. They have the reputation of being the most youthful of all the signs, never seeming to get old.

Your diet
The Geminian diet should be light, with plenty of fresh fruit and vegetables. You may need to supplement your diet with kali muriaticum (kali. mur.), which is essential for the formation of fibron. This will help prevent bronchial congestion and swollen glands.

Taking care
Gemini rules the lungs, and there is no doubt that Geminians can suffer from bad coughs. Remember that negligence may seriously weaken your lungs. You should also try not to smoke; the habit could prove to be even more dangerous for you than it is for other people.

Gemini partly rules the shoulders and many Geminians fracture collar bones, often while participating in a sport. The Geminian hands and arms are also extremely vulnerable; you may get a lot of cuts and splinters.

Walnuts
Most nuts, and many vegetables grown above ground, are traditionally regarded as Geminian foods.

Astrology and the body

For many centuries it was not possible to practice medicine without a knowledge of astrology. In European universities, medical training included information on how planetary positions would affect the administration of medicines, the bleeding of patients, and the right time to pick herbs and make potions. Each Zodiac sign rules a particular part of the body – from Aries (the head) to Pisces (the feet) – and textbooks always included a drawing of a "Zodiac man" (or woman) that illustrated the point.

GEMINI AT
LEISURE

THE SUN SIGNS TRADITIONALLY SUGGEST SPARE-TIME ACTIVITIES, HOBBIES, AND VACATION SPOTS. YOU SHOULD CONSIDER SOME OF THESE SUGGESTIONS – THEY OFTEN SUIT GEMINIAN TASTES AND INTERESTS.

GARLIC PRESS

GARLIC

Enjoying exotic food
While you may like to experiment with food and drink, you should bear in mind that a light diet usually suits Geminians best.

Amateur radio
Geminians are always trying to communicate more effectively, and you could be greatly attracted to the broad scope of ham radio.

1930S RADIO MICROPHONE

Massage

Geminians are traditionally very sensitive, so you may be attracted to massage. It is often used as a sensual means of expression between lovers.

MASSAGE OILS

POSTAGE STAMPS

Travel

Whichever destination you choose (and the United States, Belgium, Egypt, and Wales are all associated with Gemini) your main concern will be to get there quickly, so that you can enjoy yourself.

SEWING PINS

DRESSMAKING SCISSORS

Dressmaking

While many Geminians enjoy dressmaking, they do usually need quick results: "Make it tonight, wear it tomorrow" is usually their motto.

TAILOR'S CHALK

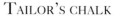

GEMINI IN
LOVE

WHEN GEMINI REALIZES THAT CUPID'S DART HAS HIT HOME,
A CAMPAIGN TO ATTRACT THE ATTENTION OF THE
ADMIRED ONE WILL IMMEDIATELY BE LAUNCHED. WHAT IS
MORE, THIS PLAN USUALLY WORKS.

You may not exactly overwhelm your lovers with passion early in an affair. However, they will no doubt enjoy themselves.

People with a Gemini Sun sign wallow in the exciting period when friendship is turning to love, and will often try to draw it out. In all Geminian relationships there are strong ties of friendship and intellectual rapport. Geminians are always happy to sing praises or indulge in a little flattery, so your lovers will always know where they stand. You will usually follow up a first flirtation with a suggestion for a date, and the occasion will never be dull or ordinary. You may decide on a rock concert or a picnic in the park.

As a lover
This sign is not as highly charged, emotionally, as some others, but Geminians enjoy a lively and very varied sex life. There is a vivacious freshness in their lovemaking, even if there is as strong a need for friendship as for passion. Despite what has been said, Geminians usually have what it takes to keep a relationship alive and flourishing. If a partner responds well to new developments and

changes within the relationship, everything should proceed smoothly. You will eventually develop constancy in love, but because of the low boredom threshold of all Geminians, you will have to think hard about this before making a final commitment. It can be all too easy for you to get bored with a relationship, and for restlessness to result in considerable unhappiness.

Types of Geminian lover

Some Geminians are demonstrative and passionate, but can express an element of selfishness in their relationships. While they are warm and sexy, they must learn to consider their partner's needs. Others, while being extremely affectionate and demanding an element of independence within a relationship, can turn out to be very possessive. A third type of Geminian will have a beautifully calm and tender side in the way they express love, and will be real romantics. Other people of this Sun sign like to show off. They can be generous to a fault, but may tend to overdramatize minor upsets. This type of Geminian is very easily hurt by even the most minor upsets in a relationship.

GEMINI AT
HOME

PLENTY OF LIGHT, A PLETHORA OF GADGETS, AND THE LATEST DESIGN FEATURES CHARACTERIZE THE TYPICAL GEMINIAN HOME. THE COLORS ARE BRIGHT, AND THERE IS A VARIETY OF PATTERNS IN THE WALLPAPER AND CURTAINS

Simple, uncluttered lines dominate the Geminian home, and yellow is often a favorite color choice for walls and furnishings. Glass and shiny chrome plate is popular among people of this sign, and may be combined to make a handsome dining table. As a Sun sign Geminian, you are likely to aim for an overall lightness in your decoration schemes.

Furniture
Most Geminians like to be up to date, and therefore choose the very latest styles of furniture for their homes. Your inner restlessness can, however, sometimes cause you to become dissatisfied with what you choose. After a year or two, you probably feel the need to acquire something newer and more fashionable.

Soft furnishings
You probably like to keep soft furnishings to a minimum, placing no great emphasis on heavy drapes. If you use cushions, they will be original

Workstation
A hectic workstation, with a telephone, notepads, and a fax machine, is likely to be a feature in any Geminian home.

Personal stereo and headphones
A love of gadgets is a typically Geminian trait. People of this Sun sign also enjoy loud music.

in design, and somewhat unusual in style. Lightweight blinds, as an alternative to drapes, are popular among Geminians. Since Gemini is an air sign, your choice of furnishing fabrics or rugs never provokes a feeling of claustrophobia.

Decorative objects

It is in the choice of objects that Geminians usually display most of their lively personality traits. Being the arch communicators of the Zodiac, Geminians usually place their telephones in prominent positions.

You probably possess a great many magazines on an equally wide range of subjects. This underlines your Geminian versatility, and a general desire to keep up with what is going on. Records and cassettes, and the means to play them, are in evidence, as is no doubt a good video recorder and possibly a camera. Your ideal choice of painting could be something fairly enigmatic; perhaps a print of a Kandinsky, Dufy, or a Klee – unless you are lucky enough to be able to afford the real thing. A picture by one of these artists, or similarly minded lesser-known painters, will leave you with enough space to come to your own conclusions about the artist's original intentions and then, perhaps after a while, to rethink your ideas again.

Delicate, bright fabric
A Geminian home will be incomplete without some light, bright fabrics.

THE
MOON
AND
YOU

THE SUN DECREES YOUR OUTWARD
EXPRESSION, YOUR IMAGE, AND MANY
IMPORTANT PERSONALITY TRAITS. THE
MOON, ALTHOUGH MERELY THE EARTH'S
SATELLITE, IS ASTRONOMICALLY THE
SECOND MOST IMPORTANT BODY IN THE
SOLAR SYSTEM. FROM THE SIGN THAT IT
WAS IN AT YOUR BIRTH, IT INFLUENCES HOW
YOU REACT TO SITUATIONS, YOUR
EMOTIONAL LEVEL, AND, TO A CERTAIN
EXTENT, WHAT YOU HAVE INHERITED FROM
YOUR PARENTS AND ANCESTORS. HAVING
FOUND YOUR MOON SIGN IN THE SIMPLE
TABLES ON PAGES 606 TO 609, TURN TO THE
RELEVANT PAGES AND TAKE A STEP
FORWARD IN YOUR OWN SELF-KNOWLEDGE.

THE MOON IN
ARIES

YOUR ARIEN MOON WILL HEIGHTEN YOUR EMOTIONS AND ENHANCE
YOUR NATURALLY RAPID GEMINIAN REACTIONS.
IMPATIENCE AND RESTLESSNESS COULD LEAD YOU TO MAKE
CARELESS MISTAKES ON IMPORTANT PROJECTS.

Sun sign Geminians are always alert, and your Arien Moon will speed up your already very swift reactions to situations, making you, in this respect, exceptionally Geminian. You will be extremely quick to answer back, and you always have an incisive, particularly slick response when challenged. Even more than most people of your Sun sign, you will love argument and debate.

Self-expression
You will always be in a hurry, but be careful: Undue haste could cause you problems. Also make sure that a quick response is not a selfish response.

Fire and air blend well, so your fiery Moon will help you not only to express your emotions freely, but also to feel far less anxious about them. Your characteristic Geminian versatility is often driven by a marvelous enthusiasm. But, as you know, you tend to get bored rather easily, and your Arien Moon will exacerbate this tendency. You must learn to keep it under control. Otherwise you will waste a great deal of energy on false starts.

Romance
You are more passionate than many Geminians, and tend to fall in love very quickly and easily. Although you may be familiar with the Geminian tendency to duality, this will be less characteristic of your personality. This does not mean that, over your lifetime, you are likely to have fewer partners than other Sun sign Geminians; only that a certain singularity of purpose is likely to deter you from having more than one lover at a time.

Your well-being
The Arien body area is the head, and there is a chance that you often bumped it when you were a

The Moon in Aries

youngster. This was because your instinctive hastiness, stemming from your Arien Moon, made you accident-prone. This could still be the case, and your hands and arms may get easily bruised, cut, or burned.

Planning ahead
You will not be particularly unhappy if you are presented with the opportunity to make money quickly. However, you should be careful when offered any kind of risky get-rich-quick scheme. You will probably do much better to encourage your instinct for investments that can be completely controlled.

Parenthood
You will be a very lively parent and will not find it difficult to keep up with, or indeed ahead of, your children's interests. You should have fun with your family, and they will enjoy your youthful, energetic approach toward them.

THE MOON IN
TAURUS

ALLOW THE STABILITY AND INNER CALM OF YOUR TAUREAN MOON
TO STEADY GEMINIAN IMPATIENCE AND RESTLESSNESS. IF
YOU THINK IDEAS THROUGH CAREFULLY, YOU WILL MAKE THE
MOST OF YOUR TREMENDOUS CAPABILITIES.

Your Taurean Moon will be very helpful in controlling your Geminian tendency to be a little reckless and superficial. It will stabilize your reactions and support them with a great deal of practical common sense. While it may slow down certain aspects of your behavior, it will add depth, kindness, and a warm sympathy to your dealings with other people.

Self-expression
You will be less inclined than many Geminians to talk about things that you are unsure of, and more ready to listen to others and empathize with them. Not only will you have more time for other people, but you will also be willing to use that time at a reasonable pace, without the haste and flurry of many Geminians.

Emotional and financial security may be far more important to you than you care to admit. You may need to consider this carefully when, for instance, you are choosing a career or thinking about changing your job.

Romance
It could be that your Moon sign will make you far less flirtatious and less likely to enjoy more than one partner at a time than is typical of your Sun sign. Your emotions are warmed and heightened by your Moon; you will trust them and will make an especially sensual lover. Take care, however, that you do not succumb to possessiveness, the worst Taurean fault. Some freedom is desirable for both you and your partner.

Your well-being
The Taurean body area covers the neck and throat. To a certain extent, these will be vulnerable, especially if you have been giving a speech or a lecture, or spiritedly arguing with friends. You may even lose your voice.

The Moon in Taurus

Needless to say, for you a cold will start with a sore throat. If this happens, do all you can to keep the cold from spreading to your lungs.

Planning ahead
You have a practical attitude toward finance and investment. Money is far less likely to burn a hole in your pocket than it is with most other Sun sign Geminians. You probably have a flair for selling and a strong instinct for business. You will invest wisely and, if you spurn any Geminian attraction toward quick financial growth, you will make your money work well for you.

Parenthood
You will work hard for your children, giving them a secure home, and encouraging mind-stretching interests and excursions in free time. While you are able to understand their enthusiasms and opinions, you can be quite strict at times. This is actually something that they will appreciate when they are older.

THE MOON IN
GEMINI

WITH BOTH THE SUN AND THE MOON IN GEMINI AT THE TIME OF YOUR BIRTH, YOU WERE BORN AT THE TIME OF THE NEW MOON. GEMINI IS AN AIR SIGN, SO YOU ARE VERY MUCH AN "AIR" PERSON – A DOUBLE GEMINI.

Reading a list of the characteristics of your very lively Geminian Sun sign, you will probably realize that a great many of them apply to you. On average, out of 20 personality traits attributed to a sign, most people recognize 11 or 12. For you the average will be considerably higher, since both the Sun and the Moon were in Gemini when you were born.

Self-expression
Your Sun and Moon combination make you eternally youthful and an excellent communicator. You will be forever talking and voicing your opinions and will have an instinctive urge to communicate with others. Of course, being so highly motivated in this way has its complications. Do you always give yourself time to think?

Superficiality, one of the more serious Geminian faults, could be a major stumbling block for you. Counter it not by suppressing your natural versatility, but by aiming to acquire a little more knowledge about the subjects you find interesting.

You could be very mistrustful about your feelings. But make sure that you do not rationalize your emotions out of existence, or suppress them so they are never freely expressed.

Romance
Geminian duality may well have an effect upon your love life. You could end up having two partners, both of whom you love, for quite different reasons. This can obviously cause complications and, while your Geminian ability to talk yourself out of difficult situations will certainly be useful, why treat anyone unfairly?

Your well-being
The comments concerning Geminian health (*see pages 122 – 123*) particularly apply to you. In addition, you may be exceptionally vulnerable

The Moon in Gemini

to anxiety and stress. It will be a very good idea for you to learn a relaxation technique such as yoga. This will help you to develop an inner calm – something that you may well need.

Planning ahead

Your attitude toward money may not be terribly sound. You will probably want to accumulate large amounts of it quickly, just so you can spend it. In fact, your general cleverness could actually lead to you being rather too clever in this area. Ensure that you do not invent money-making schemes that could end up collapsing like a house of cards.

Parenthood

You are among the most lively and forward-looking of all parents. In fact, you may even be ahead of your children's ideas and opinions. They will probably learn from you, but try to be consistent – and not too critical. As a double Gemini, both these tendencies could sometimes be a source of difficulty.

THE MOON IN
CANCER

YOU HAVE A WARM, CARING QUALITY THAT IS UNCOMMON AMONG SUN SIGN GEMINIANS. BUT YOU COULD BE A COMPULSIVE, EVEN OBSESSIVE, WORRIER. TO COUNTER THIS TENDENCY, DEVELOP YOUR GEMINIAN LOGIC AND SKEPTICISM.

Because the Moon rules Cancer, its influence from that sign is very powerful. While it will affect your responses to situations, it will also have a more general effect on your personality. It is likely to make you a very caring, protective, and sympathetic person.

Self-expression

You are sensitive, and could well suffer from rapid mood swings. While you are unlikely to become quiet or morose, you will sometimes shift between feeling very positive and extroverted, and being less confident and self-expressive. Your Geminian Sun will, however, see to it that you are always able to express your emotions verbally.

You have a very powerful imagination, and should use it both positively and creatively, perhaps through writing or craftwork. But do not let your imagination work overtime in negative ways, since you are far more prone to worry than most people of your Sun sign. It is in this sphere of your life that Geminian logic must come to your aid.

Romance

Your emotional resources demand positive expression through a meaningful relationship. This will involve a partner with whom you have an excellent rapport – especially sexually. Beware of the Geminian tendency to always question your emotions. All Geminians must accept that they have a tendency to rationalize their feelings out of existence, and work against that.

Your well-being

The Cancerian body area covers the chest and the breasts, so a vulnerability to Geminian breathing problems and to bronchitis is increased. If they linger, consult your

The Moon in Cancer

doctor. The digestive system is also Cancerian: Be careful what you eat. You could suffer from digestive problems, especially when you are at all worried. Resist the instinctive tendency to worry. Counter the impulse with Geminian logic.

Planning ahead

Your intuition can help you in relation to finance. You may well have a sound business sense, and you could make a lot of money – perhaps by building a collection of unusual articles or antiques. (Do you find it difficult to throw anything away?) On the other hand if you really feel that a certain investment would be good, rely on your intuition.

Parenthood

You will be very eager to have your own home and children, and could well be somewhat overprotective toward them. Take care not to create a claustrophobic atmosphere, and be very careful not to attempt to cling to your children. Because you have a nostalgic streak, you may not be as forward-looking as most Geminians. At times, this could widen the generation gap.

THE MOON IN
LEO

GEMINIANS ARE THE NATURAL COMMUNICATORS OF THE ZODIAC.
COMBINE THIS QUALITY WITH LEO CREATIVITY, AND YOU
COULD WELL HAVE LITERARY POTENTIAL. YOU WILL ALWAYS THINK
BIG, AND HAVE A WARM HEART.

Here is a vibrant, positive combination of Gemini, an air sign, and Leo, a fire sign. Just as air fans and feeds fire, your fiery Moon sign fans and feeds the intellectual approach of your Sun sign. It allows you both more emotion than the average Geminian, and the passion with which to express it.

Self-expression
Anyone with a Leo emphasis to their personality has a creative streak, and you may well have a great urge to express yourself imaginatively and creatively, perhaps through writing or painting. You need a creative hobby of some kind, although it need not be one directly related to the fine arts.

You could tend to be more fixed in your opinions than many Geminians. This may not be altogether a bad thing; it will add stability to your character and help to mitigate any Geminian superficiality. You will tend to organize your thoughts and to consider your conclusions. Make sure that you do not become dogmatic.

Romance
You make a wonderful lover, far more passionate than many people of your Sun sign are. You will lavish not only love and affection on your partner, but also a very varied and energetic form of sexual expression.

Elegance and comfort will be as important in this sphere of your life as in every other, and you will spend a lot of money in order to ensure it for you and your partner.

Your well-being
The Leo body areas are the spine and heart, and it is very important that you sit properly, especially if you spend hours at an office desk. A well-designed chair will be especially helpful to you. Make time to regularly exercise your spine. Equally, while

The Moon in Leo

you are no more prone to heart attacks than anyone else, it is obvious that you should exercise to keep that vital organ in good working order. You are easily bored with exercise, so vary your routine as much as possible. If you jog, cover a different route each day; alternatively, a health club, with all its varied activities, should keep you happy.

Planning ahead

Because of a liking for luxury and real quality, you probably need to make a lot of money. But you also need inner fulfillment from your work; if you do not get it you will tend to flit from one job to the next, and so never have enough cash to live in the style to which you aspire. You should be fairly good at investing.

Parenthood

You will want to encourage your children, urging them to enjoy a great variety of interests. You will take them on delightful and memorable outings, for example, to museums and theaters. They will be grateful for this and will enjoy your company as much as you enjoy theirs. However, try not to boss them around too much.

THE MOON IN
VIRGO

GEMINI AND VIRGO ARE BOTH RULED BY MERCURY, SO THERE IS A NATURAL EMPATHY BETWEEN THE TWO SIGNS. YOUR MIND IS VERY SHARP AND ANALYTICAL, BUT YOU EXPRESS YOUR EMOTIONS FREELY.

Here is an example of a positive air sign (Gemini) combining with a negative earth sign (Virgo). Both signs are, however, of the mutable quality, and also share Mercury as their ruling planet.

Self-expression
You are extroverted, and a wonderful communicator. Your instincts are very practical and, although you could well be overly talkative, you will make sure of your facts before expressing your opinion. You can be extremely critical, so make an effort to express your views constructively.

Do not dither or start too many jobs at the same time. You may need to develop better organizational skills.

Romance
Virgoan modesty and a rather low emotional level, together with Geminian shyness about the expression of emotion, may lead you

to mistrust your feelings and conceal them. If you lack confidence, you might benefit from counseling.

Your well-being
The Virgoan body area is the stomach, and in some cases this can become vulnerable, especially when you are worried. To overcome this, use your rational, logical approach to problems, instead of your intuition.

You need a high-fiber diet to keep your bowels in good order; many people with a strong Virgoan influence are successful on a vegetarian diet. All health foods can be beneficial to you, and you might consider investigating homeopathy and complementary medicine. With your Sun and Moon combination, you should respond very positively to them. Try to control restlessness and to develop a sense of inner peace: you will benefit from yoga or a similar discipline. If you allow tension to get

The Moon in Virgo

the better of you, there is a chance that you could become prone to migraines, which is a Virgoan ailment.

Planning ahead
Your Virgoan Moon will encourage you to be more careful with money than most Sun sign Geminians. Respond to the influence of your Moon sign, and keep a careful count of your money before you succumb to any Geminian frivolity. Mercury is the planet of trade and commerce, and

you are therefore in a good position to obtain excellent returns for any outlay. Just think carefully, critically, and practically when you invest.

Parenthood
You will be an energetic, hardworking parent, but do not allow yourself to be ruled by chores. Let your children persuade you to take them out. You will argue and discuss things with them in the best possible way, so avoid nagging them.

THE MOON IN
LIBRA

BOTH GEMINI AND LIBRA ARE AIR SIGNS, INCLINING THEIR
SUBJECTS TO BE UNDERSTANDING AND RATIONAL.
YOU MAY BE COMMUNICATIVE, BUT YOU COULD HAVE DEEP
EMOTIONS THAT ARE STILL WAITING TO BE EXPRESSED.

Your Geminian intellect is spiced with Libran charm, delicacy of approach, and love of balance, harmony, and comfort.

Self-expression
You are wonderfully diplomatic in a natural, instinctive way. Social intercourse is very important to you, and you probably show an automatic interest in everyone that you meet. No doubt you have a very wide circle of friends, among whom you give the impression that you know a lot about almost everything.

Geminian logic can be weakened by Libran indecisiveness. Do not be evasive or push decisions onto other people; be self-critical and you will manage to overcome the tendency.

Romance
While Libra makes you respond immediately both to the idea of romance and to romantic situations, it

may be that you tend to fall in love with love itself. In spite of a longing for romance, Libra is not really a very deeply emotional sign – and neither is Gemini. Do not let an idea be a substitute for reality.

Your well-being
You may be somewhat prone to headaches. These could relate to your kidneys – which are the Libran organ and therefore slightly vulnerable. You could, perhaps, suffer from some pain in the lumbar region of your back. This, too, may be attributable to your Libran Moon. In general make sure that you sit upright when working at a table or a desk.

Exercise will probably bore you even more than most Geminians. To keep in shape, devise a system of rewards for yourself – for example, a relaxed half hour in a sauna or steam bath, or a talk with friends at the salad bar after your workout. But be careful:

The Moon in Libra

Your Libran Moon may also give you more of a sweet tooth than most Geminians, and your waistline could suffer if you make that reward a slice of chocolate cake. The normally quick Geminian metabolism may, of course, be of some assistance here.

Planning ahead

Librans enjoy comfort and luxury. Beautiful clothes and expensive beauty products and treatments are therefore likely to cost you a lot of money. You will probably do well to take sound financial advice before investing, since you could instinctively fall for a whim that sounds good or glamorous, and end up losing in the long run.

Parenthood

You will be a kind, sympathetic parent, but might tend to bribe your children for the sake of peace and quiet. If you are too easy with them, they will soon learn to twist you around their little fingers. Use your Geminian astuteness.

THE MOON IN
SCORPIO

YOUR BASIC INSTINCTS ARE VERY PASSIONATE, AND YOU ARE
PARTICULARLY INTUITIVE. DO NOT ALLOW GEMINIAN
LOGIC TO SUPPRESS THESE TRAITS. YOUR INQUIRING MIND MAY LEAD
YOU TO BE SOMETHING OF A DETECTIVE.

A combination of Sun and Moon signs that is this dynamic is apt to make you a Geminian with a big difference. Your Scorpio Moon gives you a powerful emotional force that demands much positive expression if you are to achieve inner fulfillment.

Self-expression
If your general restlessness is not to be coupled with discontent and frustration, you must find work that is very satisfying. Go all out to achieve your aims, allowing your Geminian versatility full rein.

Unlike many Sun sign Geminians, you are not superficial; you need to get to the root of every problem.

Romance
Your emotional resources are so strong that you are unlikely to fall into the trap of letting them be dominated by your Geminian logic. Just as you need to be fulfilled in your career, so you

need fulfillment in an emotional relationship. Sexual satisfaction is of above-average importance to you, and you probably demand a great deal from partners in this respect. It is important that they respond positively, perceiving your needs and being sympathetic to them. Geminians like to experiment, and this, too, is vital for you.

Your well-being
The Scorpio body area is the genitals, and regular clinical checkups in this region are always a good idea. Safe sex is another obvious precaution that both sexes should consider.

Should a mysterious illness strike you down, it may be that, contrary to the instinct of most Geminians, you are denying a problem.

Scorpios love rich food and fine wine, and while many have a wiry build, if by chance you are thick-set or have a slower metabolism than

The Moon in Scorpio

average, you could suffer from obesity and a sluggish system. Try not to get bored with exercise – perhaps taking up judo or karate would be the solution. All kinds of sports can be enjoyable if approached correctly.

Planning ahead

Your shrewdness, intelligence, and cunning, enhanced by the influence of Gemini and Scorpio, will no doubt help you to make money, so act without hesitation. Your bank balance should grow steadily, even if you occasionally go wild on a case of wine or other expensive treats.

Parenthood

As a parent, you may be stricter than you realize, and could easily overreact to any misdemeanors. On the whole, however, your Geminian Sun keeps you very youthful and in no way pedantic. You should enjoy your role as parent and have time for fun with your children.

THE MOON IN
SAGITTARIUS

As Gemini and Sagittarius are polar or opposite Zodiac signs, you were born under a Full Moon. You may find it hard to control an inherent restlessness. Be versatile, but develop consistency of effort.

Each of us is, in one way or another, liable to express certain attributes of our polar, or opposite, Zodiac signs. For Geminians, the polar sign is Sagittarius, and as the Moon was in that sign when you were born, the polarity is powerfully emphasized. A great deal of sympathy and empathy exists between Gemini and Sagittarius: both are positive, mutable signs, and are complementary air and fire signs.

Self-expression
Your Geminian communicative ability is emphasized by an instinct that will help you get your ideas across to others with tremendous enthusiasm. Your natural optimism is very infectious, and you will easily win others around to your point of view.

Your life needs challenge, but do not start looking for alternatives just for the sake of it. Sagittarius, like Gemini, gives its subjects a versatility that needs to be expressed, but to get the best effect from it, you need to always be consistent in what you do. The worst Sagittarian fault is restlessness, and those, like yourself, who are born under a Full Moon are especially prone to it.

Romance
You make the liveliest of lovers, and possess a fiery passion. You need partners who, if anything, are ahead of you in their eagerness to experiment with, and enjoy, a physical relationship. It is, however, equally important that your partners have excellent minds; otherwise, you will be unlikely to develop any true and lasting friendship with them.

Your well-being
The Sagittarian body area covers the hips and thighs, and women with this sign emphasized tend to put on weight in these areas. You may well

The Moon in Sagittarius

enjoy rather heavier food than other Sun sign Geminians, and this could make matters worse. The liver is the Sagittarian organ, so hangovers may be something of a problem for you. Like all Geminians and Sagittarians, you need plenty of variety in anything that you do, to combat boredom.

Planning ahead

It is probably true to say that while, like everyone, you generally need money, it is usually there when you want it. You may not be very interested in investments, and could well have something of a gambling streak, which you should be wary of. If you enjoy rather risky deals or gambling on the stockmarket, do not invest more money than you know you can afford to lose.

Parenthood

Your children will find your natural enthusiasm for life infectious. Bringing them up should not prove to be too much of a worry or problem, since you are so young at heart yourself. You are also a natural teacher, and will keep their minds usefully occupied. For you, the generation gap simply does not exist.

THE MOON IN
CAPRICORN

GEMINI, WHICH IS AN AIR SIGN, IS NOT PARTICULARLY COMPATIBLE
WITH CAPRICORN, AN EARTH SIGN. THE DIFFERENT
CHARACTERISTICS THAT YOUR MOON SIGN ADDS TO YOUR
PERSONALITY ARE STILL VERY INTERESTING.

Your natural instincts tell you to be practical, aspiring, and ambitious. But to develop single-minded purpose may prove difficult for a versatile Sun sign Geminian. Try to compromise where and when you can.

Self-expression

You are among the most practical members of your Sun sign group, and need a secure base upon which to build your life. Gemini is a take-charge sign, and the influence of your Moon will be to urge you on.

Aspiring with determination, you know that you will achieve the ambition on which you have set your sights. That ambition is, however, just as likely to center on a contented family with an ideal home as on some professional aspiration.

You may be a little more susceptible to worry than other Sun sign Geminians. Should this lead to bouts of despondency, let your Geminian logic and optimism take control and rationalize any problems that you are having.

Romance

Your Moon sign does not increase your ability to express your emotions freely. While you are friendly and sociable, you may tend to distance yourself from your true feelings and, in doing so, suppress them.

You need a partner who is as ambitious as you are and capable of being a good friend within any emotional relationship. Sex may not be the main reason why you want to deepen a relationship, but sexual fulfillment is as necessary for you as it is for anyone else.

Your well-being

The Capricornian body area covers the knees and shins, which are therefore vulnerable. Fortunately, Geminians like to keep moving, so

The Moon in Capricorn

Capricornian stiffness of the joints should not be too much of a problem. The teeth are also ruled by Capricorn, so regular dental checkups are of paramount importance for you.

Planning ahead

As far as finances are concerned, your instinct is to save money and to be very careful with it. But when your Geminian Sun takes over, you will feel that you want to enjoy the fruits of your hard-earned cash. Consequently, you could be faced with something of a conflict. However, you should have a skill for budgeting and investment.

Parenthood

You may give the impression that you are a strict and rigid parent, but with your Capricornian sense of humor, your children will know that this is not entirely the case. If you make sure that you have time to enjoy their company and listen to their opinions, the generation gap should not be much of a problem for you.

THE MOON IN
AQUARIUS

MODERN, FORWARD-LOOKING GEMINIANS WITH A TRENDY IMAGE
WILL USE AN AQUARIAN URGE FOR GLAMOUR AND ORIGINALITY
TO GREAT EFFECT. DO NOT LET YOUR NEED FOR INDEPENDENCE
EXCLUDE MEANINGFUL EMOTIONAL RELATIONSHIPS.

You have an extremely interesting combination of intellectually inclined signs, both of which are of the air element. You are original and very logical, if slightly unpredictable.

Self-expression

You are among the most independent of Geminians, and many of you will build a lifestyle that could well have some unique features to it.

Aquarius is a sign of the fixed quality, so you may well have to bring your Geminian Sun into play if you have a tendency to be stubborn.

While Gemini has the reputation of being the most youthful of signs, Aquarius is high on the list of the most glamorous ones. Neither sign is very emotional. There is, in fact, a rather distant quality to many Aquarians. They tend to give the impression that while you may look at and admire them, you should also keep your distance.

Romance

It is very important for both you and your partner to recognize the fact that you will always need a considerable measure of independence. Perhaps contrarily, your Moon makes you a great romantic. You will no doubt love all the trimmings of romance, for example, bouquets of flowers, wonderful candle-lit dinners, and Valentine cards. Sexual fulfillment must, for you, be colored with romance – the atmosphere has to be just right. It should not be too difficult for you to persuade your partners to go along with this.

Your well-being

The Aquarian body area covers the ankles. If you like wearing high-heeled shoes, be careful. Aquarius also rules the circulation and, while most people with this sign emphasized in their birthcharts enjoy cold weather, their circulation is not

The Moon in Aquarius

always good. Perhaps you enjoy winter sports: these will be good for you, provided that you keep warm.

Planning ahead
You may not be very good with money. Gemini likes to keep up to date, especially in image, and Aquarius is easily attracted to rather glitzy, ephemeral things. You might, for example, want to back a theater show, but no quicker way of losing money has yet been invented.

Always talk potential investments over with a sound financial adviser. This will teach you how to handle your finances, and you will not have to learn the hard way.

Parenthood
You will be a typically forward-looking Geminian parent. You will sympathize with your children when they are upset, but sometimes in a too-adult way, discussing their problems when they need a cuddle.

THE MOON IN
PISCES

THE AIR ELEMENT OF GEMINI CAN CLASH WITH THE EMOTIONAL
CONTENT OF A PISCEAN WATER SIGN. ALLOW YOUR
EMOTION TO FLOW, PERHAPS THROUGH ARTISTIC APPRECIATION
OR EXPRESSION; DO NOT RATIONALIZE IT AWAY.

Although there is a clash of elements in this combination – Gemini is air and Pisces, water – both the Sun and the Moon work very well for you. On the whole, Pisces is a creative sign, and those in whose charts it is emphasized will long for some kind of creative expression.

Self-expression

You are, by nature, very versatile and probably like to have many tasks at hand at the same time. For all Geminians, developing consistency of effort and learning to finish all the tasks undertaken, is extremely important. If you do not do this, inner fulfillment will evade you.

You are likely to be very emotional. Because this trait is linked to your deepest instinctive level, you will tend to overrationalize a situation once you are aware that you are reacting emotionally to it. You will question yourself about your emotions, and may mistrust and even be inclined to suppress them. Be aware that by giving your emotions full rein, you will gain in the long run.

Romance

You make a delightful lover and are more caring of your partners – perhaps also more easily hurt, than many Geminians. Remember that Piscean and Geminian duality, plus a touch of deceit, could make for complications in your emotional life. Sexually, you enjoy variety as well as passion. But you do need to have a solid intellectual rapport and shared interests with any partners.

Your well-being

The Piscean body area is the feet, and they will be very vulnerable to blisters, corns, and cuts.

Even more than most Geminians, you are likely to worry or be apprehensive. If this is the case, let

The Moon in Pisces

your Geminian rationality take over. The best kind of exercise for you is likely to be swimming or any kind of dancing or skating.

Planning ahead
Financially, you should obtain professional advice regarding investment. As you can be a very soft touch indeed, you would be well advised not to lend money.

Parenthood
You will be a warm and loving parent, although you may sometimes have a tendency to spoil your children. You will also be very good at encouraging their interests, sometimes even getting yourself involved in things you never thought could possibly interest you. Your children will, of course, greatly appreciate this, and there is always the chance that they might even become hooked on a hobby or interest that particularly fascinates you.

The one thing that you should beware of is acting evasively toward them. It is always important for children to know exactly where they stand with their parents. In your case, the generation gap should not exist.

SUN & MOON SIGNS

CANCER

JUNE 22 – JULY 22

INTRODUCING
CANCER

CANCER, THE SIGN OF THE CRAB, IS THE FOURTH SIGN OF THE ZODIAC. WHILE A CRAB CAN SOMETIMES BE CRABBY, CANCERIANS PROJECT MANY EXTREMELY POSITIVE QUALITIES THAT MIGHT BE ASSOCIATED WITH THIS CREATURE.

Similarly to the way in which a crab's hard shell protects a soft interior, Cancer's subjects develop a hard psychological shell to protect themselves and their loved ones from the rigors of life. If you challenge or threaten a Cancerian in any way, you will see this self-defensive system spring into action at once.

Traditional groupings
As you read through this book you will come across references to the elements and the qualities, and to positive and negative, or masculine and feminine signs.

The first of these groupings, that of the elements, comprises fire, earth, air, and water signs. The second, that of the qualities, divides the Zodiac into cardinal, fixed, and mutable signs. The final grouping is made up of positive and negative, or masculine and feminine signs. Each Zodiac sign is associated with a combination of

components from these groupings, all of which contribute different characteristics to it.

Cancerian characteristics
Cancer is the first sign of the water element, and therefore has a very high emotional level and great intuition. Possessing an excellent memory, Cancerians sometimes recall minor injuries and slights best forgotten. As a sign of the cardinal quality, however, Cancer is outgoing toward loved ones, as well as being kind, helpful, and considerate.

The sign's ruling "planet" is the Moon. The changeability of the Moon is reflected in Cancerians: They are exceptionally prone to moodiness and sudden changes of outlook. Cancer is linked with silvery blue and smoky gray colors that reflect the colors of the Moon. It is a feminine, negative sign, which inclines its subjects toward introversion.

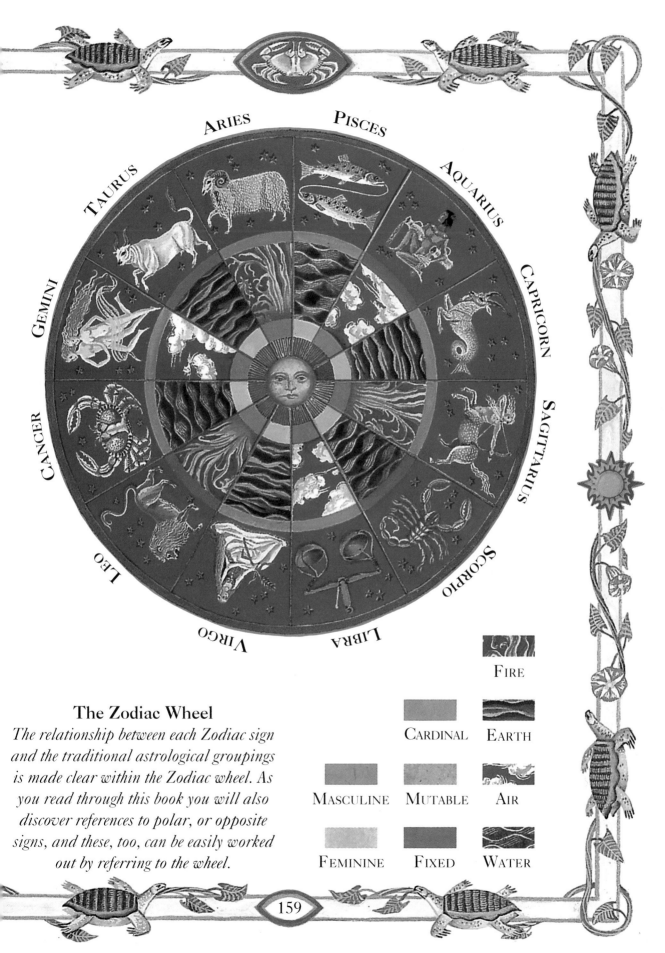

ARIES

PISCES

TAURUS

AQUARIUS

GEMINI

CAPRICORN

CANCER

SAGITTARIUS

LEO

SCORPIO

VIRGO

LIBRA

FIRE

CARDINAL

EARTH

MASCULINE

MUTABLE

AIR

FEMININE

FIXED

WATER

The Zodiac Wheel

The relationship between each Zodiac sign and the traditional astrological groupings is made clear within the Zodiac wheel. As you read through this book you will also discover references to polar, or opposite signs, and these, too, can be easily worked out by referring to the wheel.

159

CANCER
MYTHS & LEGENDS

THE ZODIAC, WHICH IS BELIEVED TO HAVE ORIGINATED IN
BABYLON AS LONG AS 2,500 YEARS AGO, IS
A CIRCLE OF CONSTELLATIONS THROUGH WHICH THE SUN
MOVES DURING THE COURSE OF A YEAR.

The sign of Cancer probably originated in Ancient Egypt, where the constellation was first known as the sign of the Stars of the Water and later as the Two Turtles (river turtles are found in the Nile and have a hard shell, like that of a crab). In Ancient Babylon, the sign was known not only as Al. lul, a water creature – "the wicked or rebellious one" – but also as bulug, the Crab or Crayfish. Much later, the Ancient Greeks named it the Tortoise.

Hercules and the Hydra
In this fourth-century image the crab is seen assisting the Hydra.

The labors of Hercules
Of all the Zodiac signs, this constellation is perhaps the least celebrated in myth and legend. The only association that has really been made is with one of the 12 labors that the hero Hercules was made to perform by King Eurystheus, the ruler of Greece, after he had murdered his own wife and children. Having consulted the Oracle at Delphi, Hercules learned that only by showing obedience to Eurystheus could he atone for his crime. The second labor consisted of the destruction of the Hydra, a monster specially reared by the goddess Hera to fight him. It had the body of a dog, and nine snaky heads – one of which was immortal. Furthermore, its breath was so poisonous that anyone unfortunate enough to be exposed to it fell dead instantly. From its den in a marsh

near Lerna in the Peloponnese, it would embark on great orgies of destruction and killing, devastating innumerable herds and crops.

Hercules battles the Hydra

Hercules forced the Hydra to leave its marsh by showering the beast in flaming arrows. At first his task seemed impossible; every time he struck off one of the monster's heads, two more grew in its place. Moreover, when Hercules eventually seemed to be gaining an advantage in his battle with the Hydra, Hera sent a great crab to help out, which it did by attacking the hero's foot. In the end, however, Hercules succeeded in stamping on it, disposing of it for good. Nevertheless, Hera was so grateful for the crab's assistance that she set it among the stars in a constellation of its own, which we call Cancer. Hercules went on to kill the Hydra by burning off its mortal heads with a red-hot branding iron, before slicing off its immortal head.

The characteristics of a crab can often be seen in people associated with this sign. Cancerians usually have a brittle protective shell, evident in an exterior gruffness; but this shell usually conceals a caring personality.

Egyptian mummy and coffin
This ancient wooden coffin, dating from the second century A.D., is decorated with the signs of the Zodiac.

CANCER
SYMBOLISM

CERTAIN HERBS, SPICES, FLOWERS, TREES, GEMS, METALS, AND ANIMALS HAVE LONG BEEN ASSOCIATED WITH PARTICULAR ZODIAC SIGNS. SOME ASSOCIATIONS ARE SIMPLY AMUSING, WHILE OTHERS CAN BE USEFUL.

Flowers

Plants that flower at night are connected with Cancer. Other Cancerian flowers include acanthus, honeysuckle, and white flowers such as the white rose and lily.

WHITE LILIES

WHITE ROSES

LAUREL

Trees
Cancer is said to have a special sympathy for all trees. This association is particularly strong with those trees that are rich in sap.

Herbs
Saxifrage, which calms the stomach, and purslane, good for liver ailments, are both Cancerian herbs.

SAXIFRAGE

NUTMEG

Spices
No particular spice is associated with Cancer, but coriander and nutmeg are sometimes mentioned in connection with water signs.

CORIANDER

CANCER
SYMBOLISM

Animals

The crab is, of course, associated with this sign; but so are all animals with shells or tough hides, such as the tortoise, crocodile, and armadillo.

TORTOISESHELL
COMB

TORTOISESHELL BOX

FAN WITH
MOTHER-OF-PEARL
STICKS

CRAB

Gems

The Cancerian gem is the pearl – its luster is closely associated with the Moon, which rules Cancer.

PEARL
NECKLACE

LOCKET DECORATED
WITH PEARLS

Metal

Silver is the Cancerian metal. Those born under this sign often like to wear silver jewelry.

SILVER FILIGREE SPOONS

ANTIQUE SILVER PICTURE FRAME

CANCER
PROFILE

THE APPEARANCE OF TYPICAL CANCERIANS OFTEN REFLECTS
THEIR HOARDING INSTINCTS. FAVORITE OLD JACKETS,
OR SOME REFERENCE TO THE PAST, ARE USUALLY IN EVIDENCE.
CARELESSNESS CAN SOMETIMES SPOIL THEIR IMAGE.

Many Cancerians fail to stand as straight as they should. They are often a little round-shouldered, which can tend to make them look rather fearful or apprehensive.

The body

Cancerians are generally good cooks. You may therefore tend toward being a little overweight if you are not careful about what you eat. Unless you are really keen on taking exercise you could be a little more prone to becoming flabby than many other Zodiac types.

You have a strong constitution, and will have excellent powers of resistance to illness. Many women of this sign have more than ample

The Cancerian face
Long red hair, and a pale and sometimes sensitive complexion, are both typically Cancerian characteristics.

bosoms, which can be an asset to their powers of attraction.

The face

Cancerians often have rather long hair, which can become a little untidy if it does not receive the appropriate amount of care. Red hair is very common among Cancerians. Your forehead is likely to be rather pale and pronounced, perhaps with frown lines between the eyes. The eyes themselves are usually on the small side; some Cancerians may have rather beady little eyes. Even among races with dark skin coloring, Cancerians tend to have pale skin that is rather sensitive to the sun. It is possible that scar tissue will show on

The Cancerian stance
Many Cancerians tend to hunch themselves up when they stand; this can make them look rather apprehensive.

your skin long after a wound has healed. As a Cancerian, your mouth is likely to be soft and flexible.

Style
The Cancerian style is often very distinctive. A particularly smart image is often spoiled by choosing the wrong accessories or by sheer carelessness: you may for example sometimes leave a shoulderstrap showing, or wear an untidily knotted tie. Because of this tendency you need to take great care over the way you decide to dress – more, in fact, than members of any other sign. You could have a preference for antique clothes, which can be very attractive.

You are likely to have a very good sense of color. Soft shades of blue or gray often complement the Cancerian personality. Many Cancerians also choose the fabric for their clothes extremely skillfully.

In general
Your overall appearance may be marked by a tendency to stoop, and glance furtively around you to make sure that you are not about to be challenged. As a Cancerian, you are probably also likely to pay an unusual amount of attention to the weather. In your efforts to pre-empt and cater for every type of weather condition you may sometimes appear exaggeratedly swathed in heavy layers of warm clothes and thick scarves when it is cold, but also dress extremely lightly when it is hot.

CANCER
PERSONALITY

KINDNESS AND SENSITIVITY ARE DOMINANT FEATURES OF THE
CANCERIAN PERSONALITY. WHILE THEY THEMSELVES
ARE EASILY HURT, CANCERIANS ARE OFTEN UNAWARE THAT THEY
CAN BE HARSH IN THEIR RESPONSES TO OTHERS.

The first time that someone meets you, it may be easy for them to get the wrong impression. This is because you can tend to act a little defensively toward people you do not know; you develop your own hard shell in order to protect yourself. Underneath this, however, you probably feel very vulnerable.

If others are tactful to you and take their time in getting to know you, it should not be too difficult for them to break through your defenses. When this happens, your deeply caring and understanding nature will shine through. Those who succeed in gaining your friendship will discover that you have the capacity to be a really good friend.

At work
You have a marvelously fertile imagination and should aim to use it positively and creatively under all circumstances. This applies to the way you approach your work. Only then will you be able to express your potential in the best possible way.

Your attitudes
You are probably the most tenacious of all Zodiac types, and you hang on tightly to your friends and loved ones. While you are tremendously faithful and want to do as much as possible for your family, it can be extremely difficult for you to accept the fact that your children will want to leave home and build their own lives once they grow up.

The overall picture
One of the most common character traits shared by all Cancerians, which is linked to your tenacity, is a strong tendency to hoard. You will hardly ever throw anything away – so much so that you and your home will inevitably become surrounded by clutter. If, however, you decide to

The Moon rules Cancer

The Moon, represented here by the goddess Diana, is usually shown as feminine. It encourages Cancerians to act instinctively, and influences the emotions and the digestive system.

take a serious interest either in antiques or in collecting articles that you find fascinating, this tendency will be put to good use.

By rechanneling your Cancerian hoarding instinct into a love of collecting things, you will be able to avoid having much of your space consumed by ugly heaps of newspapers, battered pots and pans, and any old junk – for example, pieces of string that are too short to be of any possible use to anyone.

Having said this, many Cancerians do have extremely good taste, and when this is fully developed, it really shows in every aspect of their lives. You are more than likely to have a great appreciation of, and sensitivity toward, everything that is beautiful.

CANCER
ASPIRATIONS

CARE-GIVING PROFESSIONS OFFER IDEAL WORK FOR CANCERIANS.
YOU WILL PARTICULARLY ENJOY WORKING WITH
YOUNG CHILDREN. AND SINCE YOU MAY BE THE BEST COOK IN
THE ZODIAC, CATERING COULD ALSO APPEAL TO YOU.

Flight attendant
*Working as a flight
attendant or a courier
involves a strong element of
service, and you will
therefore probably enjoy
either profession.*

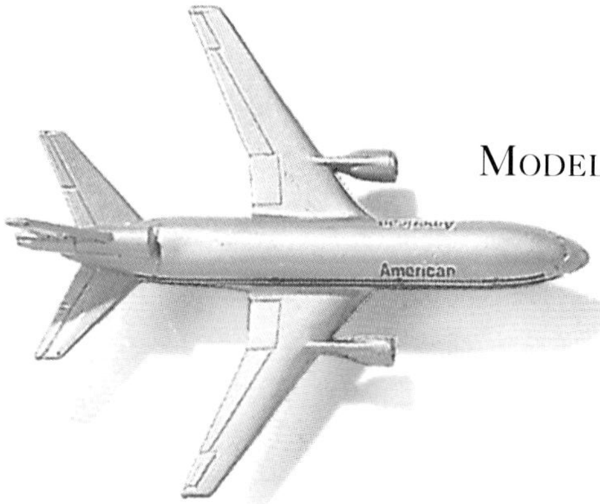

MODEL JET

WHISK

SAUCEPAN

EGGS

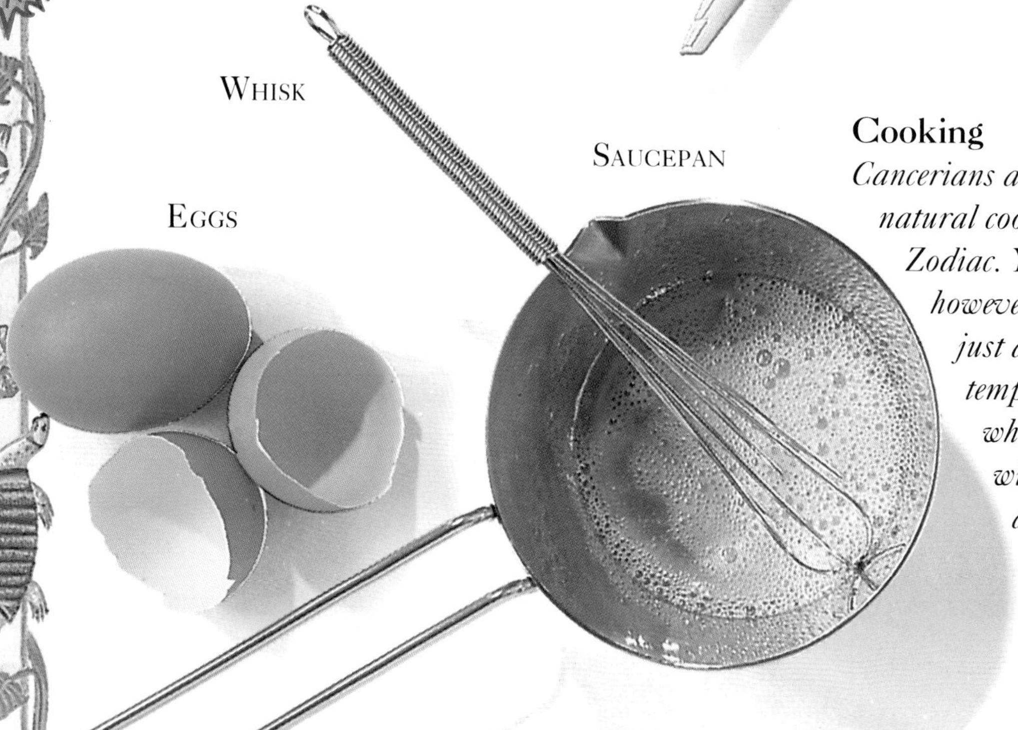

Cooking
*Cancerians are the
natural cooks of the
Zodiac. You may,
however, be
just a little
temperamental
when working
with others in
a kitchen.*

QUILL PEN

Author

Many Cancerians are inspired
by history and romance. You could
be successful as a fiction writer in
either of these areas.

1920s GLASS
INKWELL

Caring professions

Caring for children may
come naturally to you. You
could find working in the social
services particularly rewarding.

MERCURY THERMOMETER

BLOTTING PAPER

Teaching

You could well receive pleasure
from inspiring young children
and helping them to develop their
minds. Your powerful
imagination will be a great asset
to you in this profession.

ABACUS

CANCER
HEALTH

THE PREVAILING ATMOSPHERE WILL HAVE A PHYSICAL, AS
WELL AS AN EMOTIONAL, EFFECT ON A SENSITIVE
CANCERIAN. YOUR RESPONSES TO THIS ATMOSPHERE ARE
LIKELY TO BE HIGHLY INDIVIDUAL.

Sun sign Cancerians usually have somewhat pale complexions, irrespective of their background. This is not, however, a clue to how healthy or unhealthy they may be. In fact, you have a fairly strong constitution.

Your diet
As long as you beware of consuming too much cholesterol, you will benefit from a diet that includes a lot of dairy products. You may need to supplement your diet with calcium fluoride (calc. fluor.). This is considered to be important for the health of the teeth, fingernails, and bones.

Of all the 12 Zodiac signs, Cancerians are particularly prone to worrying. When you become upset, you may find yourself suffering from digestive problems.

Taking care
The traditional Cancerian body area is the breasts. Although this sign has no connection at all with breast cancer, it is sensible for all women to perform regular self-examinations. The sensitive Cancerian skin is a problem area. Protect yourself against the strong rays of the sun, as you are prone to sunburn.

Melon
Fruit and vegetables with a high water content, such as melons and pumpkins, are among the foods associated with Cancer.

Astrology and the body

For many centuries it was impossible to practice medicine without a knowledge of astrology. In European universities, medical training included information on how planetary positions would affect the administration of medicines, the bleeding of patients, and the right time to pick herbs and make potions. Each Zodiac sign rules a particular part of the body, and textbooks always included a drawing that illustrated the point.

CANCER AT
LEISURE

EACH OF THE SUN SIGNS TRADITIONALLY SUGGESTS SPARE-TIME
ACTIVITIES, HOBBIES, AND VACATION SPOTS.
CONSIDER SOME OF THESE SUGGESTIONS — THEY OFTEN SUIT
CANCERIAN INTERESTS.

Writing
*Cancerians often have
fertile imaginations,
and these can be
expressed through
creative writing.*

POSTAGE STAMPS

Travel
*Although a nervous traveler, you may
enjoy a cruise. Your ideal location could
be near a lake or the sea. Try Scotland,
Holland, New Zealand, Paraguay, and
North Africa as vacation destinations.*

1920S FOUNTAIN PEN

Cookery
*It is typical for Cancerians
of either sex to find cooking
for their friends and family
very fulfilling.*

WOODEN SPOONS
FOR COOKING

174

SAILOR'S SHACKLE
FOR SECURING ROPE

SILVER
PERFUME
BOTTLE

Sailing

Since Cancer is a water sign, many of us subjects are never happier than when enjoying themselves in boats. Some become skillful sailors.

Silverwork

Silver can be quite important to Cancerians, so much so that they often enjoy silverwork. It is the metal associated with the Moon, which rules Cancer.

Sewing

This is often a Cancerian hobby. Making children's clothes can be a particular specialty.

TOY SEWING MACHINE

COLLECTION OF
SHELLS AND CORAL

Collecting

Cancerians are the hoarders of the Zodiac. If this tendency is directed toward forming an unusual collection of some kind, it can be most rewarding.

CANCER IN LOVE

MANY OF THE BEST CANCERIAN QUALITIES SPRING INTO ACTION
WHEN CANCER FALLS IN LOVE. THOUGH YOU ARE ROMANTIC
AND PASSIONATE, YOUR REACTIONS TO BOTH THE GOOD AND BAD
THINGS IN A RELATIONSHIP CAN BE EXTREME.

While Cancerian emotions find a wonderfully positive outlet when you fall in love, it is also very easy for you to express certain traits that can have a negative effect on a relationship. If, however, you are conscious of the fact that you can create a more unpleasant atmosphere for your partners than you realize, you will be able to correct yourself before anything goes drastically wrong.

You have a very powerful motivation to love, cherish, and protect your loved ones. Unless you are careful, you may end up taking this tenderness too far and create a claustrophobic atmosphere within your relationship. Many people are unable to cope with this, finding it too confining, so this tendency to limit independence or freedom of expression may sometimes come between you and your lover.

As a lover
You are likely to take your love life very seriously, and while this does not mean that you do not enjoy – indeed revel in – love and sex, it does mean that due to a strong homemaking and family-raising instinct, you may tend to look upon all relationships with this in mind.

You should be aware that many prospective partners may not be so interested in a serious commitment. You are, no doubt, a wonderful lover, since you are both sensuous and in possession of a great instinct for the kind of things that are likely to make your partners happy.

Types of Cancerian lover

When Cancerians are young, it is a good idea for them to play the field. This way, they will gain experience with the opposite sex, and later, they are experienced and mature enough to cope with a stable, long-term relationship.

The influence of other planets will produce some subtle differences from one Cancerian to the next. Some of the more clinging members of the sign will be warmly affectionate as well as passionate, but can be very possessive. Others have a wonderfully flirtatious streak, which lightens their Cancerian intensity in love; yet another group has a lot of style and elegance, and will put partners on a pedestal. Some people of this Sun sign group display a sense of modesty that often intrigues prospective partners.

CANCER AT
HOME

A CANCERIAN'S DWELLING PLACE IS, ABOVE ALL, A HOME. THE
LOOK OF THE ROOMS USUALLY TAKES SECOND PLACE TO
CONVENIENCE, WHICH IS OFTEN THAT OF THE CHILDREN. THIS
CAN LEAD TO SUPREME UNTIDINESS.

When choosing a place to live you would do well to remember that Cancerians need a degree of peace and tranquility, perhaps in the form of a beautiful view, close at hand. This does not mean that you will feel unhappy living anywhere other than the heart of the country; a tiny balcony, or a corner filled with flowers, will provide you with a quiet, calming focus. The Cancerian home will ideally be quite close to a water source such as a slow-moving river, the sea, or a lake.

Wicker sewing basket
A sewing basket, knitting, or toys may be scattered around your home.

or, if you can afford it, quality antique furniture. You may become so fond of articles such as favorite armchairs that you will cling to them until they eventually begin to fall to pieces.

With well-developed Cancerian taste you may, however, choose quite beautiful, extremely comfortable furniture. Since your home is likely to be so important to you, the overall effect and atmosphere may be a joy to experience.

Furniture
Cancerians love the past, and hate to throw anything away. You are likely to choose either very traditional designs

Soft furnishings
Cancerians look to the past when deciding on drapes. Your choice may veer either toward heavy silk brocades in pale silvery gray, or pastel colors, or alternatively Victorian chintz. When

Jug and fabric
These objects reflect the Cancerian colors and metal.

choosing new drapes, make sure that they are not too heavy, and try not to create a claustrophobic atmosphere. A Cancerian will have no desire to be overlooked by neighbors, but if you happen to live near the sea or a river, you will certainly want to see it clearly. If this is the case, drapes will definitely take a back seat.

Many Cancerians enjoy creating their own cushions, perhaps using petit point or some other form of decorative needlework.

Decorative objects

The tendency to hoard can ruin the effect of the Cancerian home. It may become extremely cluttered. If, however, your tendency to hoard can be controlled, and expressed through

Armchair and doll
A comfortable, well-worn armchair may be a much-loved item in your home.

showing off an interesting personal collection of some kind, this will obviously enhance the overall appearance of your home.

You may choose to display a painting of your children, or perhaps a seascape. If you are fortunate enough to own some silver, or perhaps some family heirlooms, these are likely to be prominently displayed. Cancerians should accept the fact that sentimentality about old things can tend to be rather counterproductive.

THE
MOON
AND
YOU

THE SUN DECREES YOUR OUTWARD
EXPRESSION, YOUR IMAGE, AND MANY
IMPORTANT PERSONALITY TRAITS. THE
MOON, ALTHOUGH MERELY THE EARTH'S
SATELLITE, IS ASTRONOMICALLY THE
SECOND MOST IMPORTANT BODY IN THE
SOLAR SYSTEM. FROM THE SIGN THAT IT
WAS IN AT YOUR BIRTH, IT INFLUENCES HOW
YOU REACT TO SITUATIONS, YOUR
EMOTIONAL LEVEL, AND, TO A CERTAIN
EXTENT, WHAT YOU HAVE INHERITED FROM
YOUR PARENTS AND ANCESTORS. HAVING
FOUND YOUR MOON SIGN IN THE SIMPLE
TABLES ON PAGES 606 TO 609, TURN TO THE
RELEVANT PAGES AND TAKE A STEP
FORWARD IN YOUR OWN SELF-KNOWLEDGE.

THE MOON IN
ARIES

JUST AS CANCER IS THE FIRST WATER SIGN, SO ARIES IS THE FIRST
FIRE SIGN. BOTH SIGNS HAVE HIGH EMOTIONAL LEVELS. YOUR
ARIEN MOON ADDS ENTHUSIASM TO YOUR CHARACTER, WHICH YOU
ARE LIKELY TO EXPRESS AT A MOMENT'S NOTICE.

You will be eager to surge ahead with projects and to accept challenges. Cancerians are noted for being both brave and protective, and these qualities are strongly emphasized in your personality.

Self-expression

In some respects a combination of fire and water elements is not an easy one. But your fire sign Moon works positively: you will be far less apprehensive, and less introverted, than some Cancerians.

You are one of the tougher types of Cancerian and will be able to cope extremely well during demanding and strenuous periods. Perhaps your instinctively adventurous spirit will encourage you to be something of an explorer, with a penchant for visiting unusual places.

Cancerian moods, spiced with sudden emotional flare-ups, could make you a force to be reckoned with.

You should try to control these impulsive outbursts; they might be more potent than you realize.

Romance

You are extremely passionate, and it is in your love life that your very high emotional level will be best expressed. However, while your Cancerian Sun makes you somewhat clinging, your Arien Moon dictates that you need an element of independence and freedom.

Your well-being

The Arien body area is the head: If you are worried, you may tend to get unpleasant headaches. These may also be due to slight kidney upsets.

Planning ahead

As well as having plenty of Cancerian shrewdness and a good business sense, you react extremely well to enterprising schemes and suggestions.

The Moon in Aries

You should, however, always think carefully before becoming involved in them, in order to avoid disappointment later.

Parenthood

A great sense of fun and a marked sentimental streak color your attitude to life – this will certainly rub off on your loved ones. Like all Cancerians, you will be eager to have children, but you will be less prone to worry about them than most people of your Sun sign. But make sure that you recognize the fact that, in due course, they will want to move away from home and live their own lives. Your Aries Moon should help you to understand this and to ensure that you do not feel life is too empty once they are gone. Try to always look to the future and to see life through your children's eyes; otherwise, your Cancerian nostalgia and sentimentality could create a generation gap.

THE MOON IN
TAURUS

AS AN EARTH SIGN, YOUR TAUREAN MOON WILL STABILIZE YOUR
CANCERIAN QUALITIES AND ADD A PRACTICAL INSTINCT,
AS WELL AS AN APTITUDE FOR MAKING MONEY. BEWARE OF
ACTING TOO POSSESSIVELY TOWARD LOVED ONES.

Earth and water signs complement each other well, and while the Moon, which rules Cancer, exerts a very powerful influence over all Cancerians it is, by tradition, well placed in Taurus. As a result you will share many of the qualities commonly attributed to Taurus.

Self-expression
It is extremely important for you to feel both materially and emotionally secure. Provided you can do this, you will flourish and be able to express many fine positive qualities.

Through Taurus, you are warm and affectionate, and will not find it difficult to combine these traits with your caring, protective Cancerian traits. But you must ensure that possessiveness, which is the worst Taurean fault, does not obscure your warmth and kindness. On another level, your Cancerian instinct toward hoarding things, together with your

instinctive love of possessions, will make it difficult for you to throw anything away.

Romance
You have the capacity to love both deeply and very passionately. Cancerians are noted for the sensual expression of their emotions, and when this is combined with the warm passion of a Taurean Moon, your partners may consider themselves very fortunate indeed. You have the ability to make and maintain a long-lasting relationship.

Your well-being
The Taurean body area is the throat, so yours could be vulnerable. More importantly, if you happen to be one of those great Cancerian cooks, the likelihood is that you will specialize in making very rich desserts with lots of cream, chocolate, and liqueurs. Many Cancerians tend to put on weight

The Moon in Taurus

easily, and Taurean good looks are often endangered by their fondness for good food. In short, be careful. If you have a slow metabolism, try to speed it up a little by getting some sensible exercise.

Planning ahead

Cancerian shrewdness combines extremely well with the Taurean ability to make money. You have very valid instincts in this area. There should be no problems when you have money to invest. In fact, if you

discuss your finances with professional advisers, you could end up advising them.

Parenthood

Given the Cancerian tendency to cling, and Taurean possessiveness, you should be constantly aware of the problems that can arise when you are bringing up children. Still, you have the potential to be a wonderful parent. You will be sensitive to your children's needs, giving them much love and affection.

THE MOON IN
GEMINI

YOU ARE PROBABLY ABLE TO COME UP WITH PERTINENT AND WITTY COMMENTS WITH VERY LITTLE EFFORT. GEMINIAN LOGIC COMES IN HANDY WHEN YOUR CANCERIAN IMAGINATION GETS THE BETTER OF YOU.

The elements – Cancer is a water sign and Gemini, air – add a variety of interesting facets to your personality. You are quick to respond to situations and are able to act rationally under stress. Your Cancerian tendency to worry will probably be filtered by an ability to look at problems very objectively.

A powerful Cancerian trait is moodiness. Here, however, your Geminian Moon helps to steady you; it will influence your reactions and create a balance.

Self-expression

Cancerians usually have very powerful imaginations, but sometimes this potential is not quite as well developed as it should be. Your Geminian Moon will help, since it will intellectualize this area. You may have an ability for storytelling or writing, or for using your hands creatively in craftwork of all kinds. Geminians can be restless and inconsistent. Always make sure that you go on to complete every project that you begin, and counter any restlessness and inconsistency in your personality.

Romance

You may not be quite as easily overwhelmed by emotion as many people of your Sun sign. Like all of them, however, you are a genuinely caring and protective lover.

It is also very important for you to have a good tie of friendship within your relationship and to share common interests with your partner. You should consider this very carefully before deciding to deepen an emotional relationship.

Your well-being

The Geminian body area covers the arms and hands; if you are a Cancerian cook or work with metals or tools, these may be especially vulnerable.

The Moon in Gemini

The Geminian organ is the lungs. Anytime you get a cold, that settles in your chest, seek medical advice as soon as possible.

Planning ahead
Although you will probably possess Cancerian shrewdness and instinctively sound business sense, you may be attracted to get-rich-quick schemes. If this is the case, be wary of your initial reactions; they could let you down. Always take your time when making decisions of this kind.

You may have the ability to sell and will get a good price for anything you can bring yourself to part with. Cancerians are collectors and you may be attracted to gadgets of some kind, such as animated toys.

Parenthood
You are more modern in outlook, more logical, and far less clinging than most other Cancerian parents. Being less sentimental and nostalgic than many Cancerians, the generation gap should not be a problem for you.

THE MOON IN
CANCER

WITH BOTH THE SUN AND THE MOON IN CANCER ON THE DAY OF YOUR BIRTH, YOU WERE BORN UNDER A NEW MOON, AND ARE KNOWN AS A DOUBLE CANCER. SINCE THE MOON RULES CANCER, YOU MAY BE VERY CANCERIAN INDEED.

Reading a list of the characteristics of your sensitive, caring Sun sign, you will probably recognize that a great many of them apply to you. On average, out of a list of 20 personality traits of any particular Sun sign, most people will identify with 11 or 12. Because the Moon was also in Cancer when you were born, for you the average increases considerably.

Self-expression
Your Sun sign makes you caring; you will like to cherish and look after people. Your Moon sign accentuates this primary motivation. You will tend to be both moody and changeable, and it is necessary that you recognize these tendencies.

It is also important for you to realize that, like the crab which is the symbol of your sign, you can easily become rather "crabby," expressing your feelings in a remarkably terse, sharp, and hurtful way.

You should find some way of positively expressing your powerful emotions. It is an excellent idea for you to have at least one compelling interest aside from your career or home and family.

Romance
You have a great deal of love to give to your partner; this is probably the most important area of emotional expression for you. But it may well be that your imagination will need to find expression. It can make you a stunning lover, capable of giving great pleasure to your partners, but it could mean that you will always be worried about them. You may find yourself either becoming jealous or thinking that the worst has happened to them.

Your well-being
As far as your health is concerned, if you read pages 172 to 173 you will probably agree that you suffer from

The Moon in Cancer

most Cancerian ailments. Many of these relate to the tendencies to worry that have been described here.

Planning ahead
You will often read that Cancerians are very shrewd in business. Because both your Sun and your Moon signs are in Cancer, you rightly conclude that you would be wise to follow your instincts in this area.

Even more than many people, you like to feel the security of a healthy bank balance, although Cancerians sometimes tend to be a little tightfisted when it comes to actually spending their money. You probably know that Cancerians are the collectors (and also the hoarders!) of the Zodiac. Any unusual articles that you care to collect may well become valuable assets in the long term.

Parenthood
You will be eager to have children and should make an excellent parent. Recognize that your children are individuals who will want to create their own lifestyles and eventually start families. If you avoid being sentimental and nostalgic, the generation gap will not be a problem.

THE MOON IN
LEO

CANCER AND LEO ARE NEIGHBORING ZODIAC SIGNS AND OFFER
THEIR SUBJECTS CONTRASTING CHARACTERISTICS. IF YOU
HAVE AN INSTINCTIVE URGE TO BE CREATIVE, DO NOT LET ANYONE,
INCLUDING YOURSELF, CRAMP YOUR STYLE.

Your Cancerian caution contrasts vividly with the nature of your Leo Moon, which is a fire sign. You will therefore respond to most things with greater enthusiasm than many Sun sign Cancerians, and you will be less apprehensive, not so prone to worry, and much better organized.

Self-expression
The Cancerian tendency toward untidiness will be considerably mitigated by your Leo Moon; it gives you a certain style and elegance that many Cancerians lack. Leo creativity blends well with the Cancerian instinct for imaginative design, and finding some form of creative expression could be of great importance to you.

The worst Leo fault is bossiness. If you are accused of this, take heed. You respond extremely quickly to other people's remarks and actions, and when this trait is combined with the Cancerian tendency to be critically aggressive, you will see how, for you, sparks might occasionally fly.

Romance
Your Leo Moon gives you very warm and passionate emotions that will be beautifully expressed toward your loved ones. Sexually, you are probably quite assertive, and perhaps more willing to take the lead than many other Sun sign Cancerians.

Because Cancerians are sensitive, you could easily be hurt if difficulties arise within a relationship. In spite of the fact that your Leo Moon makes you brave and assertive in this area, when hurt you will creep into your Cancerian shell and lick your wounds.

Your well-being
The Leo body area is the spine, and you really need to indulge in a little exercise to keep it in good condition. If you have a sedentary job, make

The Moon in Leo

sure you have a good chair that supports your spine properly.

The Leo organ is the heart: if you follow the suggestions for exercising your spine, you will automatically be strengthening your heart, too.

Planning ahead

It is very likely that, although you have a shrewd Cancerian business sense, you will enjoy luxury and real quality more than many people of your Sun sign. In order to keep your Cancerian conscience happy, it might be wise to consider quality when you go shopping – that way you will get more value for your money and thoroughly enjoy what you may consider to be slightly extravagant. Do not be afraid to think big where investment is concerned.

Parenthood

You will be a very active, positive, and encouraging parent. If you keep the negative side of your imagination under control, you will not worry unduly about your children. Try to avoid any stubborn or dogmatic reactions to their ideas and suggestions, and you will also avoid the development of a generation gap.

THE MOON IN
VIRGO

CANCER AND VIRGO ARE THE TWO ZODIAC SIGNS MOST PRONE TO WORRY. CANCERIAN WORRY IS INTUITIVE AND IMAGINATIVE; VIRGOAN, MORE INTELLECTUALLY ORIENTED. TRY TO BALANCE ONE WITH THE OTHER.

Your Sun sign is of the water element, and Virgo is of the earth element. Since water and earth are complementary elements, the influences of your Sun and Moon signs generally work well together.

Self-expression
Cancer and Virgo certainly share some positive common attributes, but the signs also vie with each other to be the worst worriers of the Zodiac. Cancerian worry is emotional; Virgoan worry is illogical. But Cancerians are cautious, and Virgoans are practical. These traits will help to counter the difficulty. Try to be more logical, and bolster this with Cancerian caution.

Romance
Your Cancerian emotions may be slightly inhibited when you need to express your feelings toward lovers. Virgoans are very modest, and when someone declares their affection for you, your immediate reaction may well be to recoil a little. Try to recognize the tendency, because it could limit your delightfully sensitive, sensual, and caring qualities.

You will tend to be very critical of your partners and may nag them. If you are accused of this, take heed.

Your well-being
The Virgoan body area is the stomach; your digestive system is related to your Cancerian Sun. As a result worrying can upset your stomach. Virgoans are also prone to nervous tension and stress, which can lead to migraines. Try to develop a sense of inner calm. Perhaps a relaxation technique such as yoga will be of help to you.

Planning ahead
Your Cancerian Sun sign makes you careful with money; your Virgoan Moon sign makes you even more

The Moon in Virgo

cautious. You therefore have the ability to save wisely. Just be sure to remember to enjoy the fruits of your labors. When investing, look for slow, steady growth.

Parenthood

Although Cancerians generally make warm, caring, and protective parents, you may tend to criticize your children a little too easily. This can be far more damaging than you might realize, especially if you have energetic, exuberant children. If you criticize them too much, they will probably lose their self-confidence. In the long term, this could lead to problems, so guard against it.

Your creative imagination will stand you in good stead with your children. You are less likely than most people to have difficulty with the generation gap, since you will keep a keen and attentive eye on the values and opinions of the younger generation, encouraging lively discussions.

THE MOON IN
LIBRA

IF YOUR INSTINCT TELLS YOU TO SWITCH OFF, CALM DOWN
AND RELAX. BY FOLLOWING THAT INSTINCT, YOU WILL
MAKE THE MOST OF YOUR FINE, DIPLOMATIC MOON IN LIBRA,
AND KEEP YOURSELF IN BALANCE.

The cardinal quality is shared by both Cancer and Libra , and this gives you some very interesting personality traits.

Self-expression
No matter how busy you may be, the chances are that you will always have time for others. As a result, you may give the impression that you spend most of your time doing nothing. That is not, of course, the case. You will work hard to achieve whatever you set out to do.

You are diplomatic, and probably less likely than most Cancerians to give in to moodiness. You also have a natural instinct for beautiful things, and will want your environment and personal appearance to be pleasing.

Romance
A natural indecisiveness may make committing yourself more difficult for you than for many people. Once that

commitment has been made, however, your Cancerian need for home and family life will be satisfied, and you will become a wonderful, loving partner.

You have a strong inclination toward romance, and this does a great deal to enhance both your love and sex lives. There is an air of calm and serenity about you – but this will not inhibit passionate Cancerian emotion.

Your well-being
The Libran organ is the kidneys. Recurrent headaches could indicate that you have a minor kidney disorder. On the other hand, headaches could also be the result of the Cancerian tendency to worry. Your Libran Moon will work in your favor in this area, telling you to calm down, switch off, and relax.

Bearing in mind that you could well love gourmet cooking and delicious food, and remembering that Librans

The Moon in Libra

often have a sweet tooth, there is obviously a danger that you may put on weight easily. Attend regular exercise classes at a large and friendly health club where there is the possibility of socializing after class.

Planning ahead

Cancerian financial caution could dampen a luxurious, pleasure-loving instinct bestowed on you by your Libran Moon. Look at it this way: You are clever with money, and have no lack of shrewdness, so why not give in to your love of luxury? It will make life fun and far more enjoyable, and will certainly help you relax.

Parenthood

You will probably have a more relaxed attitude about parenthood than many other Sun sign Cancerians, but you should be very careful that you do not confuse your children by being indecisive. You will always be happy to listen to your children, so in that respect there should be no difficulty with the generation gap.

THE MOON IN
SCORPIO

CANCER AND SCORPIO ARE BOTH SIGNS OF THE WATER ELEMENT.
YOUR MOON GIVES YOU A TERRIFIC SOURCE OF EMOTIONAL
ENERGY; CHANNEL THIS WISELY, AND DO NOT RESORT TO BEING
JEALOUS OR VINDICTIVE.

Because both Cancer and Scorpio are water signs, you are likely to have tremendous resources of emotional and physical energy. You must find fulfilling ways of expressing these, because inner satisfaction and psychological wholeness are of above-average importance to you.

Self-expression
Your work must satisfy you. If its demands are not enough for you and your lifestyle is equally unengaging, then develop a compelling spare-time interest. This should consume either your emotional or physical energy – or ideally, both. Cancerian tenacity and your urge to get to the bottom of every problem will blend well, whatever you do.

Romance
You have a great deal to contribute to a long-term relationship. As an extremely passionate lover, you can,

however, be very demanding both sexually and in more general matters. You need an understanding partner, who is as eager as you are to live an active and full life. Should any Cancerian moods catch up with you, your partner will have to be considerate enough to understand.

The worst Scorpio fault is jealousy. If you allow your Cancerian imagination to work overtime, you could build up the most terrible tension in a relationship. Try to accept rational explanations and recognize that logic can escape you.

Your well-being
The Scorpio body area is the genitals, so regular health checks of this area are most advisable. You could be more prone to worry than is usual for Cancerians, and this could also have an effect upon your health. Remember, too, that a boring job will leave you lacking inner satisfaction.

The Moon in Scorpio

Planning ahead

You may have a really good business sense and perhaps a desire to set up and develop your own company. You are shrewd; your Cancerian Sun sees to that. But your Scorpio Moon will also stand you in excellent stead here.

Parenthood

Your Cancerian Sun makes you a good, but demanding, parent – it could be that you are considerably stricter than you may realize. You will be eager to spur your children into action, but be careful not to be too dogmatic. Encourage them, but remember that finding the appropriate kind of encouragement for each child may be difficult. Try not to push your children into following in your footsteps; they may find their own paths more rewarding. If you allow them the freedom of expression that is so necessary to young people, you will avoid problems with the generation gap.

THE MOON IN
SAGITTARIUS

YOUR SAGITTARIAN INSTINCT IS FOR FREEDOM OF EXPRESSION
AND INDEPENDENCE, BUT YOU ALSO VALUE CANCERIAN
EMOTIONAL SECURITY AND YOUR FAMILY. LEARN TO COMPROMISE
WHILE RETAINING YOUR OWN VALUES.

The combination of a Cancerian Sun and a Sagittarian Moon gives your personality some contrasting and very unusual aspects. It may even be that when you read descriptions of your Sun sign, you think some of the statements hold little or no truth at all for you.

Self-expression
You are likely to have a wider-ranging mind than other Sun sign Cancerians, incorporating qualities that differ from those normally associated with your Sun sign. While, for instance, you love and need the security of your home and family, claustrophobic feelings – brought on either by the physical layout of your home, or more psychologically, because of the pressures of family life – are something that you cannot cope with. It is important that you respond freely to the outgoing, extrovert levels of your personality. Do not let Cancerian sensitivity or inhibition cramp the open expressiveness of your Moon sign qualities.

Romance
Your attitude toward love is very positive. You will like to have fun and enjoy your relationships. Sagittarius is an emotional sign, and as a result you have abundant resources of outgoing emotion and passion.

It may be that you will take longer than many people of your Sun sign to settle into a permanent relationship. Before you do so, remember that you really need an intelligent partner, who will be equipped to stretch your mind.

Your well-being
The Sagittarian body area covers the hips and thighs. If you are a female Cancerian cook or simply love good food, you will tend to put on weight very easily around these areas. Male Cancerians can, all too easily, develop

The Moon in Sagittarius

paunches. Fortunately, you probably love many sports and participate in several. If this is not the case, try some kind of freely expressive dance. In complete contrast, horse-riding may appeal to you.

Planning ahead
A tendency to take risks can make you a little foolhardy when dealing with money. Remember, however, that Cancerians are usually shrewd and clever both in business and when dealing with cash. Try, therefore, to get the best of both your Sun sign and your Moon sign, and learn to enjoy the challenge of making money grow without letting a deep-rooted gambling instinct overpower you.

Parenthood
You will have a very positive attitude toward your children and, unlike many Cancerians, will probably not worry if they are a few minutes late getting home from school. You can inspire them, and if you allow an instinctive and very natural sense of enthusiasm full rein, you will gain their love and respect. You should have few problems with the generation gap.

THE MOON IN
CAPRICORN

CANCER AND CAPRICORN ARE OPPOSITE OR POLAR ZODIAC SIGNS,
SO YOU WERE BORN UNDER A FULL MOON. YOU ARE
INHERENTLY PRONE TO RESTLESSNESS AND AN INNER DISCONTENT;
TRY TO COUNTER ANY TENDENCY TO COMPLAIN.

You will probably be more ambitious, and aspire to greater achievements, than other Sun sign Cancerians. But because Capricorn is not particularly emotionally oriented, it may be that this ambition, which is usually so strong, will remain subdued. It is important that you do not suppress it.

Self-expression

Both Cancer and Capricorn are of the cardinal quality, and as a result, you possess the ability to use your energies freely and willingly for the benefit of others. For yourself, you have the capacity to achieve great pinnacles of happiness both at home and at work.

Be careful of one thing: You may have a tendency to grumble, especially when presented with challenges or suggestions that do not precisely fit in with your plans. This will not make you popular with other people. Be aware, too, that because you were born under a Full Moon you could tend to suffer from restlessness.

Romance

While Cancerian warmth and tenderness will color your attitude toward your partners, your first reaction when approached by a prospective lover could be slightly cool. They may well have to break through that initial chilliness, and perhaps get past the self-defensive Cancerian protective shell that could easily manifest itself if you begin to feel vulnerable or insecure. But your lover, having gained your confidence, does have someone very special, and you are more than likely to remain faithful forever.

Your well-being

The Capricornian body areas are the shins and knees. These, and your joints in general, are prone to stiffness

The Moon in Capricorn

and rheumatic pain. It is vital for you to find a form of exercise that will help you to keep mobile.

Planning ahead

One way in which the Cancerian and Capricornian "polarity" emerges is through the fact that both signs are known to be very careful with money. A little more generosity may create a more enjoyable lifestyle for you.

Your Capricornian Moon gives you a natural inclination and taste for real quality. You like to buy things that will really last – partly because you hate waste and probably loathe throwing things away. You will invest very wisely and, in general, will always aim for steady growth.

Parenthood

Avoid the tendency to distance yourself from your children. Make sure that you have fun, and that the quirky sense of humor which comes from your Capricornian Moon finds plenty of expression. By doing so, you will bridge the generation gap.

THE MOON IN
AQUARIUS

TRY NOT TO BE AFRAID OF EXPRESSING YOUR UNCONVENTIONAL ORIGINALITY: IT OFFERS YOU THE CHANCE TO FIND CONSIDERABLE INNER SATISFACTION AND FULFILLMENT. AVOID DISTANCING YOURSELF FROM OTHERS.

Your air sign Aquarian Moon and water sign Cancerian Sun are not the best of bedfellows. You will, however, have some extremely interesting and unusual qualities that make you a truly fascinating person.

Self-expression
Your reactions to situations are somewhat unpredictable. On some occasions you can be sympathetic, but on others, shocked. Your Cancerian kindness and sensitivity are, however, complemented by some very humanitarian qualities. You will give both time and energy, as well as money, when and where you come across need – it will be this sense of need that instinctively motivates you. Having taken action, you will freely express your caring, protective Cancerian spirit.

Your Cancerian emotions are somewhat cooled by your Moon sign influences. You are able to rationalize your feelings and, if it becomes necessary, should be able to distance yourself from them.

Romance
At heart, you are very romantic, but it could be that an inner need for independence clashes with a desire to have your own home and family. You may be attracted to a lifestyle that is individual in some way.

A love of romance is never too far from the surface, and because of it, you are likely to enjoy love and sex in a romantic atmosphere. It should not be difficult for you to persuade your partner to go along with this. Since you have an intriguing air of glamour, and are attractive to the opposite sex, you should enjoy yourself.

Your well-being
The Aquarian body area is the ankles, and these are very vulnerable. The circulation is also governed by

The Moon in Aquarius

Aquarius, so you must be careful to take care of yourself when the weather is cold.

Planning ahead
Of all the Cancerian Sun and Moon sign combinations, yours may be the least practical when it comes to money. Of course, you have Cancerian shrewdness and business sense lurking somewhere in your personality, and you may be wasting your potential. Can you see yourself owning your own business? If you do, remember that you do not lack originality, and stand an excellent chance of finding a gap in the market.

Parenthood
As a parent, your tendency to be unpredictable, plus Cancerian changes of mood, may cause difficulties. Keeping abreast of your children's ideas and concerns will help you to come to terms with any generation gap problems.

THE MOON IN
PISCES

A TENDER AND LOVING CANCERIAN, WITH THE POWERFUL, FORCE OF PISCES, HAS A TORRENT OF EMOTIONAL ENERGY. USE THAT ENERGY AND NEVER UNDERESTIMATE YOURSELF OR YOUR ABILITIES.

While the combination of two water signs will serve to integrate your instincts and self-expression successfully, you should be careful that you are not entirely swayed by your reactions to people and by the power of your emotions.

Self-expression
You will automatically follow your intuition and natural instincts. Remember, though, that because you are so very kind, helpful, and charitable, and always ready to part with time, energy, and cash, people could take advantage of you all too easily. You may consciously have to develop your protective Cancerian shell, and at times you will have to be very firm with yourself if you wish to have complete control over your life.

Your Cancerian Sun gives you inner strength and tenacity, but a very tender and ultrasensitive Piscean Moon could sometimes tend to undermine your more powerful characteristics, especially when you are moved in some way.

Romance
If you get caught up with a partner who does not allow you the freedom to develop your potential and use your vivid imagination, think again.

You need a strong partner who will encourage you in all your efforts and take some of the strain, should an area of your life fall under pressure. There is a romantic, almost poetic, side to you, which colors your expression of love and sex – your partners should really enjoy it. Be careful that you do not delude yourself when you are in love, seeing every partner as your ideal, and try not to be deceptive.

Your well-being
The Piscean body area is the feet. These could cause you a lot of trouble. On the other hand, as can be

The Moon in Pisces

the case with astrology, the reverse could be true, and your feet may be healthy and problem-free.

The Cancerian tendency to worry will certainly affect you. Make sure that this does not become irrational and that your very powerful imagination does not take over. Be guided by your intuition and control any exaggerated reactions.

Planning ahead
Your Piscean Moon may overcome your practical, cautious Cancerian qualities when it comes to dealing with money. If you are aware of this,

then perhaps, over a period of time, you will learn not to be a financial soft touch. Take advice from your financial consultant, accountant, or some other professional.

Parenthood
Children are bright and, from an early age, yours may know how to handle you. It may be necessary for you to act strictly from time to time.

Try not to be too clinging and sentimental, and remember that if you do not keep up with your children's way of thinking, you may have generation gap problems.

SUN & MOON SIGNS

LEO

JULY 23 – AUGUST 23

INTRODUCING
LEO

LEO, THE SIGN OF THE LION AND KING OF BEASTS, IS THE
FIFTH SIGN OF THE ZODIAC. LEOS USUALLY MANAGE
TO ACQUIRE THEIR OWN INDIVIDUAL KINGDOMS OVER WHICH
THEY CAN RULE SUPREME.

The Zodiac lion or lioness rules skillfully, tactfully organizing others and always expressing creativity in one form or another.

This sign is ruled by the Sun. In fact, it is almost as if the generous, bright Leo personality radiates from some inner sun. When such a forceful personality fails to shine through, one can tell that something is seriously wrong. Leos who suppress their inner glow will be unhappy and unable to fully express their potential.

Traditional groupings
As you read through this book you will come across references to the elements and the qualities, and to positive and negative, or masculine and feminine signs.

The first of these groupings, that of the elements, comprises fire, earth, air, and water signs. The second, that of the qualities, divides the Zodiac into cardinal, fixed, and mutable signs. The final grouping is made up of positive and negative, or masculine and feminine signs. Each Zodiac sign is associated with a combination of components from these groupings, all of which contribute different characteristics to it.

Leo characteristics
Leo is of the fixed quality, which means that while Leos are generally stable people, they can also be very stubborn. They work hard to curb any tendency toward being bossy or pompous, and limit their urge to overdramatize every problem.

Because Leo is a masculine, positive sign, it inclines its subjects to be extroverted. Another characteristic that makes Leos easy to identify is their enthusiasm. This is, in fact, indicative of the sign's element: fire.

Most Leos will prefer, and perhaps enjoy wearing, the opulent colors of the Sun, their ruling "planet."

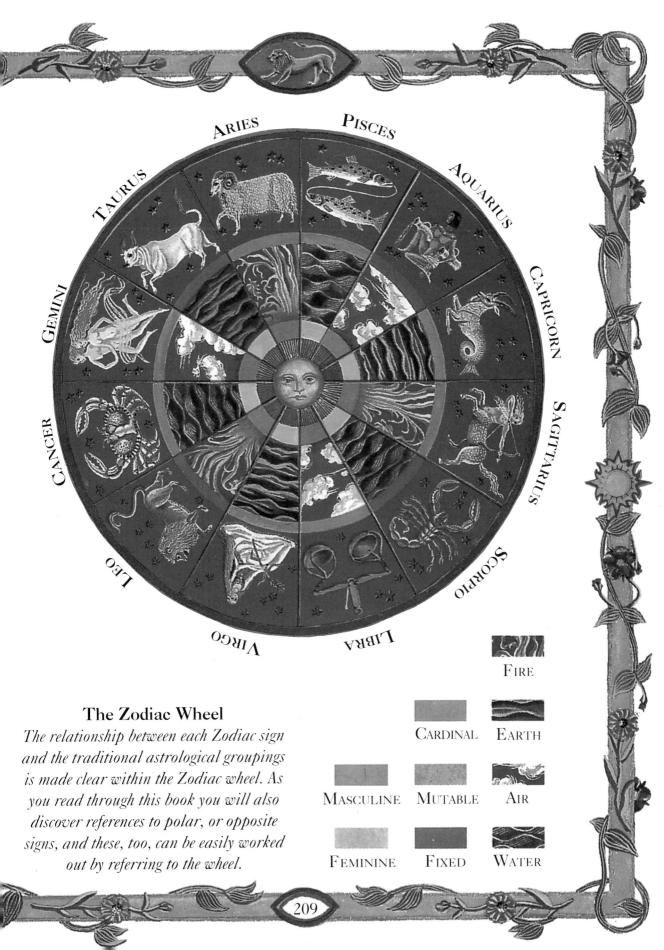

ARIES

PISCES

TAURUS

AQUARIUS

GEMINI

CAPRICORN

CANCER

SAGITTARIUS

LEO

SCORPIO

VIRGO

LIBRA

FIRE

CARDINAL

EARTH

MASCULINE

MUTABLE

AIR

FEMININE

FIXED

WATER

The Zodiac Wheel

The relationship between each Zodiac sign and the traditional astrological groupings is made clear within the Zodiac wheel. As you read through this book you will also discover references to polar, or opposite signs, and these, too, can be easily worked out by referring to the wheel.

Myths & Legends

THE ZODIAC, WHICH IS BELIEVED TO HAVE ORIGINATED IN BABYLON AS LONG AS 2,500 YEARS AGO, IS A CIRCLE OF CONSTELLATIONS THROUGH WHICH THE SUN MOVES DURING THE COURSE OF A YEAR.

When the major stars of the constellation Leo are joined together, they do actually resemble a crouching beast. The ancient Babylonians called the constellation Great Dog. At least 5,000 years ago, the Egyptians gave it the name that is familiar to us today.

The Labors of Hercules

Like the Crab of Cancer, the Lion is associated with one of the 12 labors that the hero Hercules was made to perform by King Eurystheus, the ruler of Greece, as an atonement for slaughtering his own wife and children. After consulting the Oracle at Delphi, Hercules learned that only by showing obedience to King Eurystheus could he ever be forgiven for his dastardly crime.

Hercules's first labor involved killing and flaying an enormous lion, whose pelt was so tough that it could turn aside all weapons.

The Nemean lion

The lion, which lived at Nemea, in the Peloponnese, was born of Echidna the snake-woman and Typhon, a monster with a hundred eyes. The goddess Hera had sent it to wreak havoc upon the neighborhood of Nemea, the plain of which was sacred to Zeus, king of the gods.

Meeting the lion on the slopes of Mount Tretus, Hercules first shot at it with arrows (it merely yawned as they rebounded from its skin), then attacked it with his sword, and finally struck it with his club. At this point, irritated by a headache, it bit off one of Hercules's fingers.

Hercules eventually resorted to the novel idea of choking the lion to death while it was resting in its cave. On trying to skin it, however, he found that its hide resisted all knives, so that he eventually had to use its own claws – the only instruments sharp enough. Hercules subsequently

Hercules and the Nemean Lion
This Greek vase, which dates from 510 B.C., shows Hercules struggling to overcome the seemingly invincible Nemean lion.

wore the lion's impenetrable skin as armor, with the head as a helmet. The lion itself was set in effigy among the stars by Zeus.

Leo characteristics

It is, of course, virtually impossible to determine how various human qualities became associated with a particular sign of the Zodiac. It can, however, be said that those born with the Sun in Leo are extremely likely to possess the unmistakably proud demeanor of lions, and that they seem to be just as invulnerable to attack. Indeed, bravery, strong leadership, and forcefulness of personality are all definite Leo characteristics. However, when Leos find themselves troubled, they will retire to some private place in order to recover from their wounds in solitude.

LEO
SYMBOLISM

CERTAIN HERBS, SPICES, FLOWERS, TREES, GEMS, METALS, AND ANIMALS HAVE LONG BEEN ASSOCIATED WITH PARTICULAR ZODIAC SIGNS. SOME ASSOCIATIONS ARE SIMPLY AMUSING, WHILE OTHERS CAN BE USEFUL.

Flowers
The sunflower, marigold, and celandine, all of which reflect the vibrant colors of this sign, are ruled by Leo.

MARIGOLDS

SUNFLOWERS

Herbs

All herbs are believed to be ruled by Leo. This is particularly true of angelica, which "comforts the heart"; eyebright, which is good for eye ailments; and pimpernel, which alleviates toothache.

BAY

ANGELICA

Trees

The bay, palm, and walnut are traditionally Leo trees. The same is true for the orange, lemon, and all other citrus trees.

Spices

No spices are specifically connected with Leo. As a fire sign, however, Leo surely rules pepper and mustard.

ARECA PALM

MUSTARD

PEPPER

LEO
SYMBOLISM

BRASS LION'S-HEAD DOOR KNOCKER

Animals
*The lion is, naturally, the Leo
animal, but all other big cats are also
ruled by this sign.*

DIAMANTÉ TIGER BROOCH

Metal
*Gold is the Leo metal, not only
because of its association with the
Sun, but also because of Leo's
unquestionable taste for riches.*

WOODEN TIGER
FOLK CARVING

GOLD

LEOPARD CIGARETTE LIGHTER

RUBY EARRINGS

RUBY BROOCH

TOY TIN LION

RUBY NECKLACE

Gem
The dark red, glowing ruby, the color of the Sun at dusk, is ruled by this sign.

LEO
PROFILE

THE LION'S MANE OF HAIR, THE UPRIGHT STANCE, AND A RATHER CONVENTIONAL, BUT VERY DASHING IMAGE, CHARACTERIZE THIS DRAMATIC ZODIAC SIGN. LEOS MAY SOMETIMES CONVEY AN IMAGE OF HAUGHTINESS TO OTHERS.

Sun sign Leos stand with their feet placed slightly apart and their legs held straight. They tend to make strong, meaningful gestures that are carried through in a distinctive and often dramatic way.

The body

Generally speaking, the Leo spine and back are erect, which gives people of this sign the appearance of height even if they are not tall. Leos are typically broad shouldered, and most have admirably slim waists. This can be a decided asset when fashion decrees an emphasis on that area. Leos usually move well, and should aim to keep their elegant, cat-like agility well into old age. Your feet and hands are unlikely to be large,

The Leo face
You are likely to have a noble face, with bright, clear eyes.

and you will probably be small boned in comparison to members of most other Zodiac sign groups.

The face

You will hold your head high. If you leave your hair to grow long it will probably become as luxuriant and flowing as a lion's mane, although it may sometimes be equally untamable. Most Leos have clear complexions, and are likely to tan well. There is a striking nobility about the Leo forehead and face that you may well possess. Your eyes are likely to be very bright and clear, with perhaps slightly drooping eyelids, and your nose may be large and prominent. Some Leos develop a habit of occasionally looking down

The Leo stance

In keeping with their outgoing manner, Leos stand well, and are prone to making bold, meaningful gestures.

their noses at other people. You will not find it hard to break into a wide, sunny smile.

Style

Of all the Sun signs, Leo probably has the best sense of style. Since most Leos enjoy making a dramatic impact, there is often something eye-catching or spectacular about the things that they decide to wear.

Designer jeans and designer labels are very popular among Leos. However, people of this sign should make sure that they control their showiness, since too much glitter can ruin their image. Similarly, although Leos are generally inclined to buy high-quality, slightly conservative clothes, many of them will rashly spend enormous sums of money on dazzling but terribly impractical outfits that they can only wear once. Most Leos learn with experience.

People of your Sun sign usually look marvelous in the colors of the Sun, from palest lemon and pink to darkest orange, with younger people liking the brightest colors.

In general

Because the Leo body reflects the Leo psychology, it is not difficult to tell how happy a Leo is. It is obvious that a round-shouldered, stooping Leo, with eyes dimmed, is burdened with problems. On the other hand, if Leos are upright and smiling, their psychological Sun, which is so much a part of every Leo, is quite clearly shining, and all is well.

LEO
PERSONALITY

GENEROSITY AND ENTHUSIASM ARE BOTH DOMINANT LEO TRAITS. WHILE LEOS ENJOY TAKING CENTER STAGE, THEY WILL ALSO ENCOURAGE THEIR LOVED ONES AND FRIENDS TO GET THE MOST OUT OF LIFE.

Being positive and enthusiastic in outlook, Leos have a great zest for life, and if only because they put so much into it in the first place, they will get a great deal out of it. Every day has to be lived to the fullest. Inner satisfaction comes when you settle down to relax at the end of the day and realize that not only has each of your tasks been well and truly completed, but also that there is something to show for all your efforts.

At work

As a Sun sign Leo, your organizing ability is almost certain to be excellent. You can, however, sometimes express your love for organization in an extremely bossy way. This tendency to become too dominant over people must be controlled if it is not to be a source of embarrassment to your family and friends. Should you find yourself in charge of a situation (as Leos so often are), you should make sure that you hand out instructions with as much charm and warmth as you can. Bear in mind that other people thrive on receiving encouragement and praise, just as you do.

Your attitudes

Leos are known to hate pettiness of any kind. You will be very good at comprehending the overall plan and concept of a project, but will then willingly leave the smaller, fussy details to other people. Small-minded behavior and nit-picking arguments will no doubt infuriate you. When you encounter these, what might very accurately be called your "lion's roar" will be heard, and you will put the culprits in their place.

Leos usually have a well-developed sense of drama, which definitely needs to be tempered with a little restraint. At its best, however, it will provide you with a great

The Sun rules Leo

Apollo, the Greek Sun god, represents the Sun that rules over Leo. The Sun inclines its subjects to be generous, affectionate, and creative.

awareness of occasion. You will have no trouble making something special out of every get-together that you are party to, and you will really love to entertain extravagantly.

The overall picture

Firmness, determination, and decisiveness are marvelous qualities. Dogmatism and stubbornness are, however, just the opposite. You must tread very carefully in this area. Although it can be very difficult for you to develop an ability to be flexible, it will help if you consciously remember that the best rulers are those who are understanding, reasonable, and fair – especially when they are pronouncing judgment on other people.

LEO
ASPIRATIONS

FLAIR, ENTHUSIASM, AND SHOWMANSHIP MUST FIND A PLACE IN ANY LEO CAREER. MAKE SURE THAT YOU WILL BE ABLE TO USE YOUR EXCELLENT ORGANIZATIONAL ABILITIES, WHATEVER YOUR CAREER ASPIRATIONS ARE.

Fashion and jewelry design
Leo is the most creative of all the signs. You may love high fashion and could design and make your own jewelry.

WATERCOLOR
PAINTS

DESIGNER EARRINGS
AND BROOCH

Teaching
Since they are so creative, Leos often make fine teachers of the arts. Their natural enthusiasm inspires their students.

ARTIST'S PALETTE

SABLE PAINTBRUSHES

VENETIAN FESTIVAL MASK

The theater

A career in the theater, which would combine a number of the qualities traditionally associated with Leo, may strongly appeal to you.

1912 FOOTBALL MEDAL
REFEREE'S WHISTLE

Professional sports

Leos find sports and exercise important, and like to take a pride in their bodies. You could therefore find the idea of a career in professional sport attractive.

LEAD SOLDIERS

The armed forces

Leos have great powers of leadership. You may do well in the armed services and could rise to a position of authority.

Illustration

Leos often turn their artistic talents to illustrative drawing or painting.

CHARCOAL

HEALTH

MORE THAN ANY OTHER ZODIAC TYPE, LEO NEEDS TO BE SOUND IN
BOTH MIND AND BODY; THEY ARE UNIQUELY CONNECTED
IN THIS SIGN. FOR EXAMPLE, AN INJURED BACK COULD LEAD TO
DEPRESSION, OR A PRESSING PROBLEM, A HEADACHE.

The lions of the Zodiac will rapidly fall into black moods if some injury threatens to cramp their action-packed lives. You will become angry with yourself if such an injury forces you to stay away from your health club, and your irritation with an injury may far outweigh your pain or discomfort. This is because you really do not like wasting time or neglecting something you love doing. Rather fortunately for you, and perhaps for those who know you, such situations do not arise all that often.

Your diet

Mineral salts are considered to be a necessary part of the human diet. Because of modern eating habits, however, our supply of them is often unbalanced. As a Sun sign Leo you may benefit from supplementing your diet with the cell salt magnesium phosphate (mag. phos.). This is good for the heart, and helps to aid relaxation. You should also make sure that you control the amount of cholesterol you consume.

Taking care

The Leo body area is the spine and back. Chairs that offer good support are an excellent idea. So are exercises geared to strengthening the back; these will help you to avoid backache – often just a sign of stress. The Leo organ, the heart, also needs to be exercised if it is to be kept in good shape like the rest of the body.

Leos are usually strong and healthy, with mind and body at one with each other. You must be careful that you do not use up your energy – you might be forced to take a rest. Maintaining a balance is therefore of above average importance for you. Of course, you should be careful not to lose sight of the fact that when you do set aside some time to relax, you will enjoy it with all of your Leo panache.

Astrology and the body

For many centuries it was impossible to practice medicine without a knowledge of astrology. In European universities, medical training included information on how planetary positions would affect the administration of medicines, the bleeding of patients, and the right time to pick herbs and make potions. Each Zodiac sign rules a particular part of the body, and early medical textbooks always included a drawing that illustrated the point.

LEO AT
LEISURE

Each of the Sun signs traditionally suggests spare-time activities, hobbies, and vacation spots. Here are a few suggestions that reflect Leo's interests and inclinations.

Astrology
Due to their eagerness to help other people make the most of their potential, Leos often make enthusiastic astrologers.

TOOLS FOR ASTROLOGICAL CALCULATIONS

Amateur theater
Leos generally enjoy amateur theater. It gives them an opportunity to express their natural dramatic flair and allows them to show off a little.

GREASEPAINTS

PLASTER IMAGE
OF THE SUN

POSTAGE STAMPS

Travel

*Comfort, even luxury, should be the
hallmark of your holiday. You would
rather spend a day in a five-star hotel
than a month in a tent. Italy, Iraq,
the South of France, and the Alps
all appeal to Leo.*

The Sun

*Leos love enjoying the Sun. Its
light and warmth give them a sense
of well-being, making them feel
positive and optimistic.*

NAPKIN
AND CUTLERY

Eating out

*You no doubt have a great
sense of style and occasion,
and therefore only the best will
be good enough for you when
you choose to eat out.*

LEO IN
LOVE

WHEN LEO FALLS IN LOVE, THE WORLD TAKES ON A GOLDEN GLOW – BUT WHEN LEO IS REJECTED OR UNLUCKY IN LOVE, THE STORM CLOUDS GATHER. ANY WOUNDS ARE LICKED IN THE PRIVACY OF THE LAIR.

Sun sign Leos tend to put their partners on pedestals. You may be the king or queen of the Zodiac, but you will also enjoy playing consort to your partners. This means that when things go wrong, you may suffer more than most Zodiac types. Disillusion and heartbreak are common, and are sometimes followed by a loss of self-confidence that only time can heal. Unfortunately, some Leos are psychologically less developed than others and will tend to dominate a weak partner. At times this may work, if that partner is the type who needs a great deal of support, but both parties must aim to achieve a balanced relationship based upon sharing.

The generosity attributed to Leo will certainly be expressed when you are in love. The wrong partner may feel that you are showing off or trying to impress. This is not the case: with you "celebration" is the key word, and to blazes with the cost.

As a lover
The fire element of Leo burns strongly and brightly when you realize that you are in love. You will want your partner to share the sheer joy and exuberance of your

positive expression of emotion, through psychological rapport and friendship as well as through rewarding and fulfilling sex. It is equally important for all Leos to have partners who are able to share an enthusiasm for their interests.

expression of love: When in love, life for them becomes one huge, romantic musical, opera, or film. Some other Leos display, very surprisingly, a certain modesty in this sphere of their lives. Finally, there are those Leos who are never really psychologically whole until they are sharing their life with a partner. Premature commitment can be a real danger for these types.

Types of Leo lover
Many Leos are flirtatious, enjoying a powerful bond of friendship as well as love and romance. They need partners who are their intellectual equals. Other Sun sign Leos are very sentimental. They may tend to create a claustrophobic atmosphere within a relationship and, should a partner decide to break away, will find it difficult to accept the fact that the romance has ended. Many Leos are totally leonine in their

HOME

A LEO'S WARM AND WELL-LIT HOME WILL REFLECT THE HIGHEST STANDARDS OF COMFORT. ELEGANCE, STYLE, AND BEAUTY ARE THE KEYNOTES AND, EVEN ON SLENDER MEANS, THEY WILL USUALLY BE ACHIEVED.

Wherever Sun sign Leos end up living, they always strive to make their homes very special places. You will probably spend a great deal of money on beautiful things, and on improving your home, for precisely this reason. If you have a garden, you have probably filled it with many different types of colorful flowers, and if the climate permits, attractive exotic fruits and vegetables. Your entire home is likely to have a warm and glowing atmosphere.

Classical sculpture
Leos often own a copy of an ancient sculpture.

Furniture
When it comes to choosing furniture for your home, your decisions are probably based around elegance and comfort. Leos like to relax in

beautiful surroundings that are stylish, luxurious, and easy on the eye. You take great pride in your home, and will, as has already been said, spend a lot of money on it, making sure that the furniture and decor you choose is unlikely to become boring after a year or two. In this way you will avoid the disruption of the constant necessity for change. Quality is likely to be very important to you, and Leos sometimes have a marked tendency toward showiness that should be controlled. You may, for instance, overdo a room by placing too much elaborate and obviously expensive furniture together, and perhaps in inappropriate places.

Exotic wallpaper
Leo furnishings are often striking, like this wallpaper in the style of William Morris.

Soft furnishings

Texture and warm, glowing color are both important: many Leos favor rich silks and brocades, or velvet which will deepen and enhance the colors that they choose. Although you may be very much attracted to fur rugs, Leos are among the leaders in the conservation of wildlife, and are especially sympathetic toward the big cats. No self-respecting Leo would decide to own a real lion- or tiger-skin rug; it will have to be a very high-quality imitation.

Decorative objects

Only the best is good enough for Leos, whatever decorative objects they may choose. Therefore one finds ornaments in the Leo home that are as near to perfection as can be afforded, and some that may have strained the individual's purse-strings.

Your glass will be the finest crystal, and the paintings, will be beautifully framed. Leos like classical things, so a reproduction of a Greek sculpture or a miniature copy of some noble Roman emperor sitting in triumph on his horse may also make an appearance.

Colorful armchair and cushion
The golden colors of this chair and cushion reflect the colors of the sun, which are so dear to Leos.

THE
MOON
AND
YOU

The Sun decrees your outward expression, your image, and many important personality traits. The Moon, although merely the Earth's satellite, is astronomically the second most important body in the Solar System. From the sign that it was in at your birth, it influences how you react to situations, your emotional level, and, to a certain extent, what you have inherited from your parents and ancestors. Having found your Moon sign in the simple tables on pages 606 to 609, turn to the relevant pages and take a step forward in your own self-knowledge.

THE MOON IN
ARIES

A COMBINATION OF TWO FIRE SIGNS GIVES YOU A HIGH LEVEL OF
PHYSICAL AND EMOTIONAL ENERGY, BUT YOU MUST LEARN
TO CURB HASTINESS AND SELFISH REACTIONS TO PARTNERS. YOU
ARE MORE CASUAL THAN MOST LEOS.

Basically, you are a very energetic person with a powerful motivation to win, and your Leo organizational ability will enable you to take over any critical situation at the drop of a hat.

Self-expression
You will, unfortunately, express Leo bossiness from time to time. But the lively, positive influence of your Arien Moon makes it unlikely that you will come to annoy other people too much. Your Arien Moon will also mitigate any Leo pomposity.

You should avoid being too hasty, since this could lead you into premature and ill-considered action. Learn from your past mistakes and pace yourself. You may not be too good at coping with detail; perhaps you need the help of others once you have mapped out an overall plan. You have formidable resources of energy, and could easily have a hot temper.

However, neither Aries nor Leo harbors resentment, and Leo magnanimity usually emerges soon after any explosion of anger.

Romance
Your Arien Moon makes you a very passionate and lively lover, and your natural *joie de vivre* is both infectious and attractive. The worst Arien fault can be selfishness, and this trait is not at all endearing.

You are among the most highly sexed of Leos and will probably fall in love at first sight. You will expect an equally positive and immediate response from prospective partners. Remember that not everyone is as sure of their feelings as you, and try to develop patience.

Your well-being
The Arien body area is the head, and you may suffer from an above-average number of headaches. Often these

The Moon in Aries

will be caused by other people. Arien headaches may also sometimes be caused by slight kidney disorders.

You are probably somewhat accident-prone, because of hastiness and your quick reactions. Take care in dangerous circumstances.

Planning ahead
Your Arien Moon can make you somewhat impulsive financially, and you may tend to put too many eggs in one basket if you are convinced that an investment will be lucrative. A little caution is advisable, since over-enthusiasm could be your downfall.

Parenthood
You will be among the most enthusiastic and encouraging of parents, making time to enjoy your children and seeing to it that their out-of-school life is full of activity. Learn to enthuse about their projects, and you will have fun. You should have no generation gap problems.

THE MOON IN
TAURUS

LEO LIKES THE BEST AND MOST EXPENSIVE OF EVERYTHING. YOUR
TAUREAN MOON IS IN SYMPATHY. SINCE YOU NEED MONEY
FOR ALL THOSE LUXURIES, TRY TO DEVELOP YOUR BUSINESS SENSE.
MAKE AN EFFORT NOT TO BE FLASHY.

You are lucky, since in astrology the Moon is said to be "well placed" in Taurus. This means that it will exert a strong influence upon you. Your Moon sign will make you very reliable and dependable.

Self-expression
You need an above-average sense of emotional and financial security; if you have both, you will flourish.

Your Leo liking for luxury and quality will certainly be enhanced by your Taurean Moon since, after Leo, Taurus is the sign of the Zodiac most inclined toward such pleasurable things. Your Taurean Moon makes you practical and down-to-earth, and you will work hard and persistently to achieve your objectives.

Romance
Your Leo passion is enhanced by Taurean sensuality, and you are usually faithful. But you must remain aware that the worst Taurean fault, possessiveness, can very easily overcome you. Try to counter this negative trait with Leo magnanimity.

Your well-being
The Taurean body area is the throat. If your particular love is singing, you will really have to cosset it, since colds will at once settle in that area.

Very often, Taureans have a fairly slow metabolism. To prevent excessive weight gain, make sure that you exercise regularly. It is important to remember, too, that Taurus may have given you a sweet tooth, so control your intake of heavy, rich cakes and chocolates.

Planning ahead
Your luxury-loving instincts will decree that you need to earn a lot of money. Fortunately, your Moon sign endows you with a very good financial instinct, and you should follow it. You

The Moon in Taurus

will probably know intuitively when to invest and what to invest in, and will not overextend yourself in any one area.

A credit balance on your bank statement will give you much satisfaction (and proof of hard work well done); you will also be anxious to make your money work for you.

Parenthood

You will make a good parent, but will not allow your children to waste time. Both Leo and Taurus are disciplined signs, so you will be fairly strict with your offspring – at times, you may even be a little hard on them. Your children will certainly know where they stand with you: What you say is exactly what you mean. There will be no nonsense. But think carefully about this; sometimes you might just be too inflexible. Try to keep abreast of your children's opinions, and make sure that you try to move with the times. Otherwise, in spite of an excellent set of values, you may encounter great difficulties.

THE MOON IN
GEMINI

YOUR LEO CREATIVITY COULD BLEND WITH YOUR GEMINIAN GIFT
FOR COMMUNICATION AND MAKE YOU A WRITER. DO
NOT QUESTION YOUR EMOTIONS OR TALK SO MUCH THAT
THERE IS NO TIME FOR ACTION.

The fire of your Leo Sun is fanned and encouraged by your air sign Geminian Moon, which makes you respond to situations in a powerful, rational, and intellectual way. You are very quick-witted, and always ready with some clever and original remark. The Leo tendencies to formality and pomposity are unlikely to emerge in your personality.

Self-expression

You are extremely versatile and may tend to flit – perhaps too readily – from one interest or project to the next. Try to avoid superficiality and falling into the trap of leaving a clutter of unfinished tasks and abandoned hobbies in your trail.

Your Leo creativity could find expression through writing or perhaps in some glamorous craftwork – using, for instance, precious or semiprecious stones, crystals, metals, or fabrics. You do not lack enthusiasm, but may have to make a conscious effort to keep it on the boil, since boredom and that uniquely Geminian fault, restlessness, could overtake you.

Romance

You may question or rationalize your emotions, especially when you first realize that they are awakened. Make quite sure that you do not suppress your emotions altogether, since your whole personality will suffer if you do.

In love, you can be both lighthearted and passionate. When friendship embraces full, physical love, all the notes of your Leo personality will be sounded.

Your well-being

The Geminian body area covers the hands and arms, which may be particularly vulnerable to accidents; the Geminian organ is the lungs. It is absolutely vital that anyone with a Gemini emphasis who is a smoker

The Moon in Gemini

should try to limit or stop the habit. Consult your doctor right away if a cough settles on your lungs.

Planning ahead
Leos love quality goods, and need to earn as much money as possible. You may be attracted to moneymaking schemes with speedy and generous returns on capital. Be cautious: You could lose more than you gain. Take professional advice in these matters. Because you are among the most versatile of Leos, you may want to organize your life to ensure that you have two different sources of income. You could, for instance, take a hobby to professional standards and then go on to market it in some way.

Parenthood
You will probably be among the liveliest of Leo parents, since Gemini has the reputation of being the most youthful sign of the Zodiac. You will be young at heart (and probably body), and your children will appreciate the fact.

THE MOON IN
CANCER

THE SUN AND MOON ARE IN THE SIGNS THAT THEY RULE, AND
YOU THEREFORE HAVE A PERFECT BLEND OF POSITIVE AND
NEGATIVE ELEMENTS. USE YOUR LEO SELF-EXPRESSION, AND
FOLLOW YOUR CANCERIAN INTUITION AND INSTINCTS.

The Sun and Moon, the two most powerful bodies in the Solar System, work very strongly and well for you; their influences combine to give you some excellent personality traits that you should always aim to use to your full advantage.

Self-expression
Your Cancerian Moon adds a very potent intuition to your Leo Sun sign characteristics and powerful instincts that you should nurture. If you instinctively feel that you should take a certain line of action, then go ahead and do so. Your Moon sign also gives you a very powerful and vivid imagination that should be expressed creatively in some way.

By harnessing this quality, you may well produce some great work in arts and crafts. But take care that you do not let your imagination get out of hand, since you have a tendency to worry unnecessarily.

Romance
Your emotions are highly charged: The fiery, assertive, and enthusiastic emotion of Leo is joined by the more tender, sensitive emotion of the Moon in Cancer. You will not find it difficult to express your feelings to your loved ones, be they lovers, children, or a household pet. Your protective instinct is also very strong, and while you are a wonderfully exuberant and passionate lover, you may at times tend to smother your partners. Be careful, because you may create a claustrophobic atmosphere within your relationships.

Your well-being
You are far more prone to worry than most Leos. To counter any unnecessary anxiety, allow your Leo optimism plenty of free expression.

The Cancerian body area covers the chest and breasts. Women with this emphasis should examine their

The Moon in Cancer

breasts regularly – although it is important to realize that it is mere coincidence that the name of the sign is the same as that of the disease.

Planning ahead

Your Cancerian Moon gives you an instinctive business sense. You are able to invest wisely and shrewdly, although you could feel a certain amount of conflict in this area. The Leo you is very generous and enjoys spending money on pleasure and beautiful things, while your Cancerian instinct tends to make you more careful with money. A fascinating and very lucrative hobby for you could be to start an unusual collection of some kind, of objects that will increase in value over the years. This will make positive use of your Cancerian hoarding instinct.

Parenthood

You will be a very sensible and enthusiastic parent, and will encourage your children to express their own potential as fully as possible. Try not to be overprotective toward them, and allow them to leave the nest and make their own lives when they feel the need.

THE MOON IN
LEO

BECAUSE BOTH THE SUN AND THE MOON WERE IN LEO ON THE DAY OF YOUR BIRTH, YOU WERE BORN UNDER A NEW MOON. LEO IS A FIRE SIGN, AND THIS ELEMENT POWERFULLY INFLUENCES YOUR PERSONALITY AND REACTIONS.

Should you study a list of your enthusiastic, optimistic, and positive Sun sign, you will realize that a great many apply to you. On average, out of a list of, say, 20 Sun sign characteristics, most people will identify with 11 or 12. For you the average increases considerably, because the Sun and Moon were both in Leo when you were born.

Self-expression
Your Sun sign makes you very positive in outlook and gives you exceptional organizing ability, plus a great deal of creative potential. Your Moon influence adds a powerful instinctive urge to express these qualities fully. Bear in mind also that since there is an additional emphasis on the fixed quality of Leo, you may sometimes be inflexible.

You will react to most situations in a very Leo way, expressing the ability to take over at a moment's notice –

especially in a crisis. You can also be extremely bossy and dogmatic. Pay attention if you are accused of these unattractive characteristics.

Romance
You have a great deal of positive, fiery emotion that you express with great intensity in your relationships. Your zest for love and sex is great, but you will see to it that both you and your partner also enjoy a lifestyle highlighted by as many enjoyable events as you can (or possibly cannot) afford. Be careful not to dominate your relationships too powerfully.

Your well-being
Everything that has been said about Leo health on pages 222 to 223 really does apply to you. Make sure that you take enough exercise to keep your system, and especially your spine and heart, in good working order. Your liking for rich living could cause

The Moon in Leo

weight gain, so keep moving. This will also help to ensure that your circulation remains good. You no doubt love sunshine and warm weather, and hate the cold. While you will probably tan well, remember to protect your skin with a powerful sunscreen cream or makeup.

Planning ahead

Because you like to do things in a refreshingly extravagant way, you will spend a lot of money, and so you need to earn plenty of it. Let your financial motto be "great oaks from little acorns grow," and get pleasure from small investments. Financial security is important to you, and although you tend to be extravagant you probably do not lack business sense.

Parenthood

Leo is the sign of parenthood and children, and you will make an excellent parent provided that you avoid being too dogmatic in your attitude. Your interest, encouragement, and enthusiasm will help build a really good relationship between you. You should try to keep abreast of your children's ideas, and you will minimize the generation gap.

THE MOON IN
VIRGO

A CAUTIOUS, SOMEWHAT DAMNING INNER VOICE MAY CRITICIZE YOUR ACTIONS AND SAP YOUR SELF-CONFIDENCE. YOUR INNER LEO SUN MUST COMBAT THIS INFLUENCE TO ALLOW YOUR VIRGOAN MOON TO BE CONSTRUCTIVE AND HELPFUL.

Your earth sign Moon, while not particularly in harmony with your fire sign Sun, gives you a marvelously practical instinct that can stabilize the exuberance of your Leo Sun.

Self-expression
Your natural caution acts as a brake when you are tempted to show off or behave raucously. However, when confronted with a challenge, you sometimes feel a certain apprehension or lack of self-confidence. This is uncharacteristic for most Sun sign Leos, but it could happen in your case due to the influence of your Moon sign. If such a situation occurs, think of your achievements and allow yourself some pride.

You are very logical, with a powerful critical streak, and can cope better with detail than most Sun sign Leos. You will, however, have a tendency to be swamped by the minutiae of a project. Your Leo creativity may well find expression through gardening or craftwork involving natural materials.

Romance
Your Virgoan Moon will cool your Leo emotions and add a refreshing modesty to your personality.

Despite a passionate Leo nature, caution will be your key word in a developing relationship. Anyone who is attracted to you will be critically dissected before you make a date, and certainly before they are allowed to deepen the relationship.

Your well-being
Virgo is a sign prone to worry, and more than many Sun sign Leos, you may suffer from this. Your approach should be an analytical one; always assess your problems logically.

The Virgoan body area covers the stomach, and you may have a digestive problem that tends to recur

The Moon in Virgo

when you are under stress. You will have a great deal of nervous energy, and should this result in tension, you may be prone to migraines. If this is the case, a relaxation technique such as yoga could be of help.

Planning ahead
Your Virgoan Moon will be a vital influence when it comes to finance. Leo extravagance is less likely to affect you than other Sun sign Leos. Sometimes you will be better off than you realize; while you should not waste money, do not deny yourself things that make life enjoyable.

Parenthood
While all Sun sign Leos have fun with their children, be careful that you are not too critical of their efforts. Such criticism can lead to ebbing self-confidence in a youngster. If you respond to the younger generation's opinions and attitudes, you will not suffer from generation gap problems.

THE MOON IN
LIBRA

WITH YOUR MOON IN LIBRA, YOU MAY SEEM LAZY OR DISTANT
TO CASUAL OBSERVERS, BUT A LEO SUN NEEDS
TO LIVE EVERY DAY TO THE FULL. YOUR MOON WILL
ALSO HELP YOU TO ENJOY LIFE.

The combination of the fire element of your Sun and the air element of your Moon add some fascinating aspects to your personality.

Self-expression

You will respond to challenges with typical Leo enthusiasm. Your Libran Moon will ensure that this enthusiasm will be governed and controlled in a calm, relaxed, and diplomatic way.

With indecisiveness being the worst Libran fault, you may have uncharacteristic second thoughts, especially under pressure or in a stressful situation. At such times, use your Leo organizing ability. It will enable you to take control of your thinking processes.

Both Leos and Librans love the good life, comfort, and luxury. In this area you will experience no conflict between your Sun and Moon signs; you have the ability to sit back, relax, and simply enjoy being sociable.

Romance

You make a wonderful lover, and are, no doubt, very considerate of your partner's needs. In some respects you may not feel psychologically whole until you are settled in a permanent relationship. Be careful: in your desire to relate in depth, you may have a tendency to commit yourself prematurely. At times you could expect too much from your partner, simply because you, yourself, have so much to give.

Your well-being

The Libran body area covers the kidneys and the lumbar region of the back. Because Leo rules the spine and back, you may well be subject to pain in that area. The quality of the mattress you sleep on is important. You may also tend to get a lot of headaches, which could be due to slight kidney upset. Seek medical advice whenever necessary.

The Moon in Libra

Good food is another luxury enjoyed by both Leo and Libra; Librans tend to put on weight more easily, since many have a fairly slow metabolism. If you tend to move in a languid way and walk slowly, make an effort to speed up your metabolism through frequent exercise.

Planning ahead
Leo extravagance and love of quality will certainly eat into your finances. Since you may be bored by bookkeeping and investing, you would be wise to seek sound financial advice from an expert and to embark on a sensible saving plan.

Parenthood
Do not allow Libran indecisiveness to undermine your positive Leo qualities in your role as a parent. Your Leo Sun sign will ensure that you enjoy parenthood, and your enthusiasm for your children's interests will spur them on to greater effort. Be aware of their concerns and opinions in order to avoid the generation gap.

THE MOON IN
SCORPIO

LEO QUALITIES GAIN DEPTH, INTENSITY, AND A POWERFUL, EMOTIONALLY ORIENTED DRIVING FORCE BY A SCORPIO MOON. YOU MUST BE TRULY INVOLVED IN YOUR WORK AND ENJOY A FULFILLING RELATIONSHIP.

You are likely to have very strong resources of both physical and emotional energy and, for the sake of your inner fulfillment, it is vital that your life is rewarding enough to allow them full rein.

Self-expression

You must be mentally involved in your work. If this is not the case, you will probably feel discontented and growing dissatisfaction will get the better of you.

Both Leo and Scorpio are of the fixed quality, so you may well have to consciously develop the art of being flexible. Try to keep an open mind, and take heed if someone accuses you of being dogmatic or stubborn. Be firm, but not intractable.

Romance

Possessing both the fiery emotion of Leo and the deep, intense emotion of Scorpio, you will express your feelings very fervently. You will be among the most passionate of lovers and will have a great need for a responsible partner who is as highly sexed as you are. The worst Scorpio fault is jealousy, which is not something that is usually felt by Sun sign Leos. Should you fall prey to it, try to be rational and to allow Leo magnanimity full expression.

Your well-being

The Scorpio body area is traditionally said to cover the genitals. Regular gynecological examinations are advisable for women and men should examine their testicles regularly, as good preventive measures.

While some people with a Scorpio emphasis are lean and wiry, others tend to be stocky. If you fall into the latter category you may have a slightly slow metabolism. Try to speed it up through exercise. Both Leo and Scorpio like to live life to the full, and

The Moon in Scorpio

enjoy quality food and wines. These can, of course, adversely affect your body shape. If you need to lose weight, gradually adjust your general food intake and develop a more sensibly balanced diet.

Planning ahead

You have excellent business instincts. When investing, you will probably do well by following them. Your Leo and Scorpio fondness for quality and beautiful things is likely to cost you a great deal of money. Therefore a lot of your energy should be geared to making as much money as possible.

Parenthood

You may be a strict parent. While you will enjoy being with your children, you may be a little too demanding. If you are not dogmatic, you will share a good relationship. As your children grow up, they will develop different opinions to yours, and you should try to accept them.

THE MOON IN
SAGITTARIUS

YOUR SUN AND MOON SIGNS OFFER A LIVELY COMBINATION, WITH
THE SAGITTARIAN MOON ADDING A CASUAL STREAK
TO THE LEO SUN. YOU NEED ADVENTURE IN STUDY AND TRAVEL,
AND YOU WILL COPE WITH DAUNTING CHALLENGES.

Provided that you are consciously aware of one or two negative tendencies, you should be able to make your Leo Sun and Sagittarian Moon work together for you.

Self-expression

You have great positive spirit that surfaces as soon as you are challenged in any way. When someone makes a suggestion that pleases you, you will want to encourage them. As long as you keep your enthusiasm burning bright you will ensure that, together, you will achieve every one of your goals. It is easy for you to grasp the overall picture of any situation immediately, but you should accept the fact that you are rather easily bored by detail.

You are very versatile, and for you to be really happy with this area of your personality you should have a variety of physical, mental, and creative interests. Your emotions are powerful, and it is good for you to involve yourself in a cause about which you feel strongly.

Romance

It is in the area of love and relationships that your powerful feelings can be most fully expressed. You may fall in love very quickly – perhaps even at first sight – and your love of life, enthusiasm for love and sex, and warm, affectionate nature will soon break down your prospective partner's defenses. Although you are eager for a permanent relationship, you also have a greater need for freedom of expression than most Sun sign Leos.

Your well-being

The Sagittarian body area covers the hips and thighs, where most women of this sign tend to put on weight. It is advisable for you to have a fairly light diet. The Sagittarian organ is the

The Moon in Sagittarius

liver; as a result you may suffer from hangovers rather more than most Leos if you overindulge.

Planning ahead

You may be fascinated by financial risk-taking, or even gambling. Your Leo Sun gives you extravagant tastes, so be careful. Do not risk more money than you can afford to lose, and do not be tempted by get-rich-quick schemes. You could, all too easily and all too quickly, lose a great deal of money. Always be prepared to seek sound professional advice in this area of your life.

Parenthood

Although most Leos enjoy parenthood, some tend to be rather formal in their relationships with their children. This is less likely in your case, and you will not find it difficult to enjoy their enthusiasms.

Similarly, while you will not want your children to be clones of yourself, they should not, on the whole, be bored by your own varied interests; Try to develop any creative talent that they inherit. You will be able to keep abreast of their opinions, and should suffer very few problems with the generation gap.

THE MOON IN
CAPRICORN

YOU WILL BE AMBITIOUS AND WILL SUCCEED IN WHATEVER YOU
PUT YOUR MIND TO. ALLOW YOUR EARTH SIGN MOON TO
TELL YOU INSTINCTIVELY WHEN TO MAKE IMPORTANT MOVES,
BUT DO NOT LET IT COOL YOUR WARM LEO SUN.

Your Capricornian Moon endows you with qualities that contrast strongly with those of your Leo Sun, but you should be able to blend them and make them work for you.

Self-expression
Caution and a serious, well-considered response to most situations are characteristic of you, and your Leo enthusiasm will be controlled by a practical and cool approach to important issues. But your Leo love of life will always shine through, and it is extremely likely that you have an instinctive, dry sense of humor that is more amusing than you think.

Your Capricornian Moon may have a slight dampening effect on the warmth of your Leo Sun, making you feel somewhat gloomy and depressed at times. Clouds may darken your psychological landscape until the influence of your Leo Sun takes over.

Leos are generally very ambitious and like to have their own tiny kingdoms to rule. Capricornians can also be extremely ambitious and are always aspiring to rise to greater things. If all goes well, this combined attitude will help you achieve whatever you set your heart on.

Romance
Your Capricornian Moon will make you cautious in your attitude and approach to the opposite sex. Once committed, both Leos and Capricornians are usually faithful. But you may not be averse to a little social climbing, and you should curb any tendency to show off.

Your well-being
The Capricornian body area covers the knees and shins. If you suffer from stiffness of the joints, exercise may help. The teeth are also Capricorn-ruled, so make sure you

The Moon in Capricorn

have regular dental checkups. Your skin may tan less easily than that of most Leos, so wear a good sunscreen.

Planning ahead

While your Leo Sun urges you to spend and enjoy your money, your Capricornian instincts will encourage you to take a practical line and make you a wise investor. You probably have good business sense, and could do well if you start your own business. For you the most important thing is to enjoy your money. Do not waste time

and energy spending it simply to impress other people. Spend it, instead, on your loved ones. Your Moon will work for you and prevent you from spending unwisely.

Parenthood

If your children ever accuse you of being pompous or a fuddy-duddy, be sure to take note. Avoid being so involved with making money for them and trying to provide everything they need, that you miss out on really knowing them.

THE MOON IN
AQUARIUS

LEO AND AQUARIUS ARE POLAR OR OPPOSITE ZODIAC SIGNS, SO YOU WERE BORN UNDER A FULL MOON. YOU COULD SUFFER FROM PERIODS OF RESTLESSNESS, AND YOU MUST AVOID BEING STUBBORN. LET AQUARIAN ORIGINALITY IGNITE LEONINE CREATIVITY.

Each of us, in some way, expresses elements of our polar or opposite sign, the sign that lies across the Zodiac from our Sun sign.
For Leo, the polar sign is Aquarius, and because the Moon was in that sign when you were born, the polarity is emphasized in a most striking way.

Self-expression
You have a very independent streak and like to do things in a way that is just right for you. It may be that you have evolved a unique lifestyle that you guard jealously.

You will express your originality in a variety of ways. Perhaps you like to look a little different, or maybe your job is an unusual one. Your Leo creativity could be spiced with originality, and that will make inner fulfillment even more likely for you.

It is important that you develop flexibility; since both Leo and Aquarius are of the fixed quality, that tends to make you stubborn. Always aim to complete projects, or you will feel dissatisfied and restless. This is one effect of being born at the time of the Full Moon.

Romance
You may tend to distance yourself from prospective partners, feeling that you are not yet ready for total commitment. However, anyone with an Aquarian influence is also very romantic, and once a partner has paved the way for you, you are capable of very faithful love and a rewarding sex life – if you are given enough room to breathe, and allowed some independence.

Your well-being
The Aquarian body area covers the ankles, and you may easily twist yours. The circulation is also Aquarius-ruled, and since this is so strongly related to the heart, the Leo

The Moon in Aquarius

organ, you should make sure that your blood flows freely. You probably like cold, crisp weather more than most Leos, and may enjoy winter sports.

Planning ahead
You could be attracted to very glitzy things, such as unusual mirrors, vases, executive toys, high-fashion clothes, and jewelry. These can prove expensive and not very durable and, as a result, your finances may suffer. Try to develop a practical attitude toward money, and seek professional financial advice when you have any cash to invest.

Parenthood
You will be a lively parent, but your unpredictability may leave your children uncertain where they stand with you. You may want to test new theories by bringing them up in an unusual way. This may work well, but some children feel more secure with a strict set of rules to live by.

THE MOON IN
PISCES

YOUR HIGHLY EMOTIONAL LEO FIRE SIGN IS SENSITIZED BY THE EMOTION OF YOUR WATER SIGN PISCEAN MOON. IF YOU ARE DISCIPLINED AND CHANNEL YOUR SUPERB RESOURCES, YOU WILL ACHIEVE A GREAT DEAL IN CREATIVE OR CARING WORK.

While your Sun and Moon signs suggest very different qualities, there is also great sympathy between them, which is emphasized by emotion and creative potential.

Self-expression

At times you could feel pretty unsure of yourself. It is very important for you to realize that you could deceive yourself. Do not doubt yourself, or resort to putting yourself down. Allow your Piscean Moon to be a source of inspiration and imagination; channel its force creatively. However you do this, express your abundant potential with all the Leo confidence in the world. Be bold, and you will achieve inner fulfillment.

Romance

You have a very powerful emotional energy that you may, to an extent, express toward humanitarian causes and in the relief of suffering, but it will mostly be directed toward your partner. You are capable of a really grand passion, reaching heights of happiness and the depths of despair.

There is a great dramatic sense in your attitude toward your lover – this is present in most Sun sign Leos, and in your case is made even more colorful by your Piscean Moon. You will be very sensitive to your partner's needs. Learn to be open about your own needs, since you know the things that give you pleasure, and you should not hold back.

Your well-being

The Piscean body area covers the feet. Do not hesitate to spend money on visits to the podiatrist if you have problems with your feet.

It can be difficult for those with a Piscean influence to be disciplined. When it comes to exercise and regular meals you may, for instance, simply not bother if you are alone. Try to get

The Moon in Pisces

into and stick to a regular routine; the Leo in you really needs it, if you are to express your potential fully. Any exercise that inspires you will do you good in both body and soul, and by exercising you will overcome a Piscean vulnerability to flabbiness.

Planning ahead

Being both very generous and something of a soft touch, you are probably less talented with money than many Leos. Remember, however, that some people will take advantage of you, so be firm if they ask for a loan. While you should seek financial advice before investing, you may wish to put money into building a specific collection of some kind. This will be fun and, if properly managed, it could be a good investment in itself.

Parenthood

You will be a sympathetic, enthusiastic, and encouraging parent, but do not allow your sensitive reactions to your children's needs and suggestions to get the better of you. Keep in tune with their ideas and concerns, and you will be able to bridge the generation gap.

SUN & MOON SIGNS

VIRGO

AUGUST 24 – SEPTEMBER 22

INTRODUCING
VIRGO

VIRGO, THE SIGN OF THE VIRGIN, IS THE SIXTH SIGN OF THE ZODIAC. SINCE IT IS RULED BY THE PLANET MERCURY, VIRGOANS OFTEN TEND TO BE EXCELLENT, IF SOMETIMES HYPERCRITICAL, COMMUNICATORS.

Modesty is a common Virgoan trait, and Virgoans often express themselves in a self-effacing manner. You must be careful not to underestimate your capabilities and should constantly try to build up your self-confidence. While Virgoans achieve inner satisfaction by helping and serving others, this can lead to your being imposed upon.

Virgoans tend to be practical and hardworking, but the influence of the planet Mercury can make you restless, and you may tend to do too much. You should plan your days well in advance, so that there is time for relaxation. This will also help counter stress, to which you are prone.

Traditional groupings
As you read through this book you will come across references to the elements and the qualities, and to positive and negative, or masculine and feminine signs.

The first of these groupings, that of the elements, comprises fire, earth, air, and water signs. The second, that of the qualities, divides the Zodiac into cardinal, fixed, and mutable signs. The final grouping is made up of positive and negative, or masculine and feminine signs. Each Zodiac sign is associated with a combination of components from these groupings, all of which contribute different characteristics to it.

Virgoan characteristics
Virgo is a sign of the earth element, and earth is often of importance to Virgoans. You may find close contact with it to be restorative; many Virgoans are superb gardeners.

Virgo is also a sign of the mutable quality, which bestows a flexible mind and a good intellect. Because it is a negative, feminine sign, its subjects tend to be introverts. The Virgoan color is navy blue.

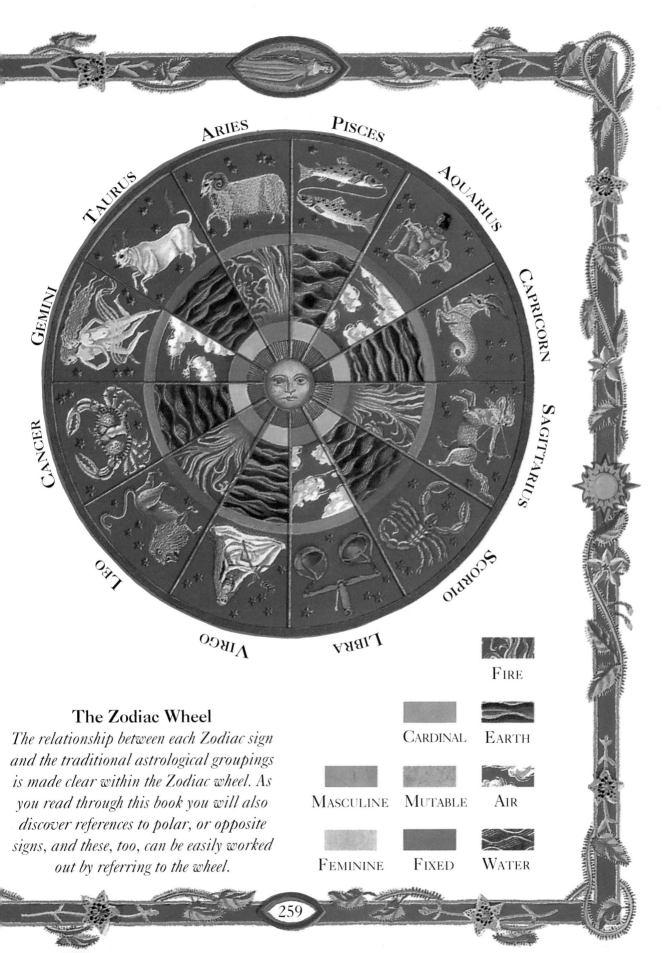

ARIES

PISCES

TAURUS

AQUARIUS

GEMINI

CAPRICORN

CANCER

SAGITTARIUS

LEO

SCORPIO

VIRGO

LIBRA

FIRE

CARDINAL

EARTH

MASCULINE

MUTABLE

AIR

FEMININE

FIXED

WATER

The Zodiac Wheel

The relationship between each Zodiac sign and the traditional astrological groupings is made clear within the Zodiac wheel. As you read through this book you will also discover references to polar, or opposite signs, and these, too, can be easily worked out by referring to the wheel.

VIRGO
MYTHS & LEGENDS

THE ZODIAC, WHICH MAY HAVE ORIGINATED IN BABYLON
AS LONG AS 2,500 YEARS AGO, IS A CIRCLE
OF CONSTELLATIONS THROUGH WHICH THE SUN MOVES
DURING THE COURSE OF A YEAR.

The sign Virgo is thought to have been named in ancient Babylon, or perhaps Sumeria, and the original Virgin that represents the sign is considered to have been Nidaba or Shala, a grain goddess. In one ancient tablet she is described as having "a star on her head and a whip in her right hand, the thong of which stretches out over the tail of Leo." (Similarly, in an ancient Egyptian zodiac, at Esna, Virgo is shown holding Leo by the tail.) As time passed, however, the conception of a matronly goddess slowly evolved. She was gradually rendered as more youthful, and she is perceived in modern representations as being a beautiful young maiden.

Elizabeth I (1533–1603)
Those who surrounded this English queen kindly compared her to the "starry maiden."

In the first century B.C., the famous Roman writer Marcus Manilius set out an early account of astrological mythology in his *Astronomica*. He mentions two myths in relation to Virgo. In the first myth he claims that the original virgin was a young girl named Erigone, the daughter of Icarius, king of Attica and the first mortal maker of wine. Unfortunately, his gift led to Icarius's downfall: he unwisely gave some liquor to a party of shepherds, who then drunkenly murdered him. His faithful dog, Maera, took Erigone by the hem of her gown and led her to his grave, above which she hanged herself in

Ancient Map of the Heavens
This early astrological chart, Atlas Coelistis Hemisphaerium Stellatum Boreale, *dates from 1660. On it can be seen representations of each of the constellations.*

grief. Zeus, king of the gods, set Maera in the skies as the Dog-star, and Erigone as Virgo.

The starry maiden

As an alternative figure for Virgo, Manilius offers Astraea, the "starry maiden," who has long been identified with Justice and was the last of the gods to leave the Earth. Astraea lived among men in the Golden Age, but fled to heaven when mankind grew to unwisdom. The English queen Elizabeth I, also known as the Virgin Queen, was often referred to as Astraea by the sycophants who surrounded her.

It is important to remember that the earliest associations of Virgo had far more to do with beauty and kindness than with virginity and coldness. Indeed, the modern emphasis on the cool frigidity of the sign is quite ridiculous.

VIRGO
SYMBOLISM

CERTAIN HERBS, SPICES, FLOWERS, TREES, GEMS, METALS,
AND ANIMALS HAVE LONG BEEN ASSOCIATED WITH
PARTICULAR ZODIAC SIGNS. SOME ASSOCIATIONS ARE SIMPLY
AMUSING, WHILE OTHERS CAN BE USEFUL.

BLUE
BUTTERFLY

Flowers
*Red, pink, bright yellow, and bright blue
flowers, particularly the cornflower,
are associated with Virgo.*

CORNFLOWER

Trees

Nut-bearing trees are associated with the planet Mercury, which rules Virgo.

OAK

BEECH

Spices

No spice is traditionally associated with Virgo, but cinnamon and cardamom are sometimes mentioned.

CARDAMOM

CINNAMON

Herbs

Any herb that has a red or a pink flower comes under the rulership of Virgo.

LEMON BALM

VIRGO
SYMBOLISM

Gems
*The Virgoan stone is sardonyx,
which is composed of onyx, a kind of
quartz, layered with sard, the yellow
color of which no doubt led to
the association.*

SARD SEALS

Metal
*As with Gemini, Mercury is a Virgoan
metal. So is nickel, with its silvery
white, lustrous quality.*

NICKEL

EBONY MOUSE

CERAMIC RABBIT

PORCELAIN
HARE

TOY METAL RABBIT

Animals

Small cats and most domestic pets come under the dominion of Virgo. All female animals are, however, to some extent ruled by Virgo.

CERAMIC CONTAINER
DECORATED WITH
RABBITS

VIRGO
PROFILE

QUICK, SLIGHTLY JERKY MOVEMENTS OF THE HEAD AND HANDS, A
VERY NEAT IMAGE, AND AN OVERALL AIR OF ACTIVITY ARE
TYPICAL OF THIS ZODIAC GROUP. AS A VIRGOAN, YOU ARE ALWAYS
LIKELY TO BE "ON THE GO."

Some Virgoans have a tendency to stoop. If this is the case with you, make every effort to ensure that you do not become round-shouldered. As a Virgoan, you probably keep your feet close together, and your hands clasped in front of you. While you release your hands frequently in order to gesticulate, they are usually quickly and firmly clasped again. When kept waiting, you strum your fingers impatiently. Virgoans usually have no time to waste, after all.

The Virgoan face
Virgoans often possess very quizzical expressions. You rarely miss a thing.

The body
Virgoans tend to have rather elongated bodies and limbs; their bone structures are also usually very prominent. However, because they can be very well-proportioned people, this can make them look extremely photogenic, as opposed to awkward.

The face
Your hair is likely to be well cut and cared for. In the case of many Virgoans it will also appear sleek, and people of either sex may have "widow's peaks." Virgoan eyes are usually very clear, alert, and bright, and tend to dart from side to side with curiosity – Virgoans can sometimes be a little too curious. Your nose might be rather sharp, as could your chin, and your mouth is probably quite small. You may purse your lips when you are worried. Many Virgoans have an

The Virgoan stance

Many Virgoans tend to stand with both of their feet placed close together, and their hands clasped in front of them.

extremely quizzical appearance. In fact, you might give the impression of never missing a single thing.

Style

You are likely to favor navy blue and rather dark colors, or small floral patterns that are sometimes quite brightly colored. The neat Virgoan businessman often wears a colorful floral tie, and his white collars and cuffs will stay pristine all day. Virgoan women often choose a Victorian look, and may dress in country styles, using natural fabrics.

The majority of Virgoans enjoy searching for high-quality clothes that have a long life ahead of them, as opposed to fashion items that become redundant after being worn only once.

Virgoans usually like wearing high-quality leather gloves, and beautifully made belts. However, a hat is something that you are likely to wear only for practical reasons. Overall, your image is likely to reflect Virgoan modesty, and to be extraordinarily neat, but it has a very special, alluring charm all of its own.

In general

Your bright personality is probably reflected in the quick movements that you make, and through a fast, rather bouncy walk. You sometimes tend to be rather fussy, and may be prone to flicking imaginary bits of lint from your clothes or playing with a string of beads. Due to slight nervousness, you may sometimes blink a lot.

VIRGO
PERSONALITY

VIRGOANS ARE THE WORKERS OF THE ZODIAC AND ALWAYS ENJOY WORKING FOR OTHER PEOPLE IN ONE WAY OR ANOTHER. WHILE PRACTICAL, WITH PLENTY OF COMMON SENSE, THEY ARE NOT VERY GOOD ORGANIZERS.

All Virgoans need to keep busy. In fact, many never seem to stop, and find it hard to even sit and listen to a conversation.

At work
The need to serve, or to work for other people, is a very important part of the Virgoan psychological motivation. As a direct result of this, many Sun sign Virgoans make excellent secretaries, or they may find themselves positions in which they are either helping or perhaps serving other people.

You will like to know what you have to do and when you have to do it by. It may be that your tendency to be a poor organizer stems from a certain lack of self-confidence. This, in turn, is frequently outwardly expressed through what can sometimes be a delightful, if often overplayed, modesty. You will feel, and perhaps say, that you cannot do something, and then go on to give many reasons why, and name a lot of other people who, in your opinion, could do it better. It is at times like this that friends and family are in a position to help Virgoans most. Self-effacement has charm, but it can go too far.

Your attitudes
The influence of Virgo's ruling planet, Mercury, is interesting. It is liable to make you an exceptionally good communicator, and usually pretty talkative. You are excellent at expressing your opinions, and do not need much encouragement to do so.

Mercury's influence is apt to make you very critical and could give you the ability to analyze problems in detail. As a result, Virgoans are often able to carve out successful careers for themselves in the media. However, if you feel a need to be critical in the context of personal relationships, you would be wise to exercise a little

Mercury rules Virgo

*Mercury, the messenger god, represents the ruling planet of Virgo.
The influence of Mercury stimulates the mind, but it can also
make its subjects critical, nervous, and tense.*

restraint. No one will appreciate a person who is frequently prone to nagging and criticizing their partners and friends. You do not want to obtain a reputation for being too fussy.

The overall picture

Virgoans are, for all of the reasons that have been mentioned, exceptionally prone to worry. If, however, you put yourself into a position in which you approach whatever it is that happens to be bothering you using your natural logic and analytical acumen, you will no doubt come up with some really practical answers. Making comprehensive lists of the pros and cons of a difficult situation could help you to assess and analyze it in the necessary detail.

VIRGO
ASPIRATIONS

YOU COULD EASILY BE AN EXCELLENT SECRETARY OR ASSISTANT, BUT REMEMBER THAT YOU ARE CAPABLE OF MORE THAN MERE SUBSERVIENCE. TO SATISFY YOUR NEED FOR SECURITY, YOU SHOULD MAKE YOURSELF INDISPENSABLE.

Agriculture
Because earth is the Virgoan element, working in agriculture or horticulture may come naturally to you.

MODEL TRACTOR

Library work
A career that combines serving the public and working with books could prove to be very satisfying. Similarly, you may find bookshop work appealing.

INK PAD, DATE STAMP, AND BOOKS

Detective's Magnifying Glass

Police work
Virgoans can be strongly drawn to the detection and investigation of crime.

Communications
A natural enthusiasm for detail, and a skill for research of all kinds, may lead to your forming some kind of career in the media.

Photographic Film

Medicine
Virgoans respond well to alternative medicine, and often thrive on vegetarian diets. An enthusiasm for either may may lead to successful careers in these areas.

Pestle and Mortar

VIRGO HEALTH

A STEADY OUTLET FOR NERVOUS AND PHYSICAL ENERGY IS VITAL TO KEEP THE VIRGOAN SYSTEM IN GOOD ORDER. FRUSTRATION AND WORRY WILL LEAD TO PHYSICAL PROBLEMS, PLUS PSYCHOLOGICAL AND MENTAL STAGNATION.

The high level of nervous energy that most Virgoans have needs to be worked off through really satisfying work. The discipline of a relaxation technique, like yoga or meditation, can also sometimes help to calm Virgoans and get their nervous energy under control.

Your diet
Virgoans benefit from a diet that is high in fiber. It is worth noting that, before vegetarianism was fashionable, Virgoans were most inclined to it, as well as to homeopathy and complementary medical techniques.

You may benefit from the cell salt kali sulphicurum (kali. sulph.), which is said to help prevent bronchitis.

Taking care
The Virgoan body area is the stomach. Because of this many Virgoans find themselves suffering from stomach complaints when they are forced to bear strain or nervous tension. The whole nervous system is actually related to Virgo, so the fact that it is very easily upset by external influences is hardly surprising. If Virgoans become tense, there is also a good chance that they might end up succumbing to migraines.

Hazelnuts
As with Gemini, most nuts are traditionally considered to be Virgoan foodstuffs.

Astrology and the body

For many centuries it was impossible to practice medicine without a knowledge of astrology. In European universities, medical training included information on how planetary positions would affect the administration of medicines, the bleeding of patients, and the right time to pick herbs and make potions. Each Zodiac sign rules a particular part of the body, and early medical textbooks always included a drawing that illustrated the point.

VIRGO AT
LEISURE

EACH OF THE SUN SIGNS TRADITIONALLY SUGGESTS SPARE-TIME
ACTIVITIES, HOBBIES, AND VACATION SPOTS.
ALTHOUGH THESE ARE ONLY SUGGESTIONS, THEY OFTEN WORK
OUT WELL FOR VIRGOANS.

POSTAGE STAMPS

Sports
*Outdoor sports of all
kinds, like cycling or
golf, will probably
appeal to you.*

CIGARETTE CARDS
SHOWING CYCLING

Travel
*As a Virgoan, you will like
visiting mountainous places.
A trip to Syria, Brazil,
Iraq, the West Indies, or
Czechoslovakia may
also appeal to you.*

Gardening
*Virgo is an earth sign, and
many Virgoans
specialize in
growing
vegetables or
small, brightly
colored
flowers.*

GARDENING
GLOVES AND
PRUNING
SHEARS

Pottery

You may obtain pleasure from working with natural materials, for example, clay or wool.

POTTER'S
TOOLS

BOOKS AND
READING GLASSES

Reading

Virgoans often like to read biographies and critical essays. Some may enjoy family sagas.

Knitting

Handicrafts that require meticulous attention to detail, such as knitting, crochet work, intricate sewing, and tailoring, are often popular with Virgoans.

WOOL AND
KNITTING NEEDLES

VIRGO IN LOVE

MODESTY AND SHYNESS, PERFECTIONISM AND A CRITICAL EYE, ARE ALL CHARACTERISTIC OF THE VERY INDIVIDUAL VIRGOAN ATTITUDE TO LOVE. VIRGOANS WILL PONDER LONG AND HARD BEFORE COMMITTING THEMSELVES TO SOMEONE.

Having such an inquiring, questioning mind, plus modesty and a certain apprehensive shyness, will tend to make loving rather tricky for many Virgoans. Their reactions will often be to question their feelings, or to try and figure out why someone finds them attractive.

The celebrated Virgoan modesty is, in fact, often a most attractive feature. If a prospective partner proceeds slowly and with care, and develops a good degree of friendship and intellectual rapport with you, there is a high chance that a rewarding bond of affection, love, and sexual fulfillment will develop. You must, however, also play a part in a relationship. Most importantly, you should not look for excuses to criticize your partner.

As a lover
In extreme cases, some Virgoans can develop a very clinical attitude to sex. They may even consider it to be "dirty" in some way. If this is the case, professional counseling should be sought. On a more positive note, because Virgoans are likely to have inquiring minds, many are extremely curious about sex from a very early age and could indulge in considerable

experimentation in this sphere. The emotions of Virgo are not normally highly charged and, while Virgoans are generally verbally skillful and charming, they may not always express their feelings in a deeply passionate way.

Types of Virgoan lover

Many Sun sign Virgoans make really tender and caring partners. They can, however, sometimes create a claustrophobic atmosphere within a relationship. Other Virgoans have a fine sense of drama and display a warm, fiery passion toward their partners. A third type will agree with all that has been said about Virgo in love: if they can increase their self-confidence and relax, they will enjoy rewarding relationships. Some people in this Sun sign group have a surprisingly relaxed attitude to love and a powerful romantic streak. Their only problem is likely to be an unfortunate tendency to rush into a relationship because they feel incomplete without a partner. A final group consists of those Virgoans who have strong emotional and sexual feelings. The majority of people in this group are very demanding of their partners.

VIRGO AT
HOME

NEATNESS AND PERHAPS AUSTERITY CAN MAKE THE TYPICAL
VIRGOAN HOME A LITTLE TOO CLINICAL FOR COMFORT.
ENDEARINGLY, HOWEVER, A CLUTTER OF SMALL ORNAMENTS
CAN HUMANIZE IT. THERE WILL BE PLENTY OF PLANTS.

The typical Virgoan home is pretty and neat. The colors are often very cheerful, and the rooms full of detail and clutter, as a result of your diverse and plentiful interests. If you were able to live in the ideal place of your choice, you would probably choose the country. However, as city careers are common among Virgoans, unless you feel able to face long, and often tiring, hours spent commuting you may have to make do with a home in town.

It would probably be wise for you to look at a few properties located near parks or some other form of open space whenever you are deciding where to live.

Furniture
Virgoans are usually very attracted to natural materials, so wood, particularly wood that has been treated so that its richness and natural beauty show to full advantage, is favored. This rich effect is usually enhanced by either wool or linen covers, since showy brocades or silks, and lavish or elaborate furniture, are not to the Virgoan taste. The Virgoan home

Potted plants
A selection of fascinating plants are likely to be very much in evidence in a typically Virgoan home.

sometimes has a rather ethnic look to it and, because Virgoans are practical people, durability is also very important.

You will find space in your living room for a writing desk or some kind of work table if you do not have a studio or workshop in which to relax and practice your favorite hobbies.

Soft furnishings

Checks and spots, and above all small floral patterns, are especially popular with Virgoans. It is very common to discover chintzes with a tiny flower or leaf design in either the kitchen or the living room, and the impression given is of neatness combined with a certain prettiness. This can occasionally translate into overfussiness. The cushions in a Virgoan home can sometimes be rather hard, since most Virgoans are not that keen on really relaxing. They do not always list comfort very high among their priorities.

Decorative objects

On the whole, Virgoans tend to like tiny objects and rather unusual curios, such as miniature vases, small silver boxes, and tiny, neatly framed pictures of the family. Your choice of paintings will usually be taken from schools that work in great detail. Dutch interior paintings, particularly domestic scenes, often enhance Virgoan walls. Tidiness and neatness are qualities attributed to Virgoans and, on the surface, this is true. Chaos is normally reserved for cupboards, where it cannot be seen. A sunny corner in your home, such as a windowsill, usually sports some plants that have spectacular foliage as well as flowers.

Dressmaker's dummy

Virgoans take great pride in their hobbies, and evidence of them (in this case sewing) is often visible in their homes.

279

THE
MOON
AND
YOU

THE SUN DECREES YOUR OUTWARD EXPRESSION, YOUR IMAGE, AND MANY IMPORTANT PERSONALITY TRAITS. THE MOON, ALTHOUGH MERELY THE EARTH'S SATELLITE, IS ASTRONOMICALLY THE SECOND MOST IMPORTANT BODY IN THE SOLAR SYSTEM. FROM THE SIGN THAT IT WAS IN AT YOUR BIRTH, IT INFLUENCES HOW YOU REACT TO SITUATIONS, YOUR EMOTIONAL LEVEL, AND, TO A CERTAIN EXTENT, WHAT YOU HAVE INHERITED FROM YOUR PARENTS AND ANCESTORS. AFTER FINDING YOUR MOON SIGN IN THE SIMPLE TABLES ON PAGES 606 TO 609, TURN TO THE RELEVANT PAGES AND TAKE A STEP FORWARD IN YOUR OWN SELF-KNOWLEDGE.

THE MOON IN
ARIES

YOUR ALERT AND CRITICAL VIRGOAN CHARACTERISTICS ARE SPICED
WITH VERY QUICK RESPONSES TO SITUATIONS. YOU ARE
EXCELLENT IN EMERGENCIES, BUT SHOULD ALWAYS BEWARE OF
TAKING PREMATURE, ILL-CONSIDERED ACTION.

Your Arien Moon adds many contrasting characteristics to your practically inclined Sun. You are able to react rapidly to most situations and are good at grasping the immediate essentials of any set of circumstances.

Self-expression
You are always on the ball. There is, however, a drawback to this, since you may sometimes be impatient and too hasty. You will probably be far less cautious than many Sun sign Virgoans and should always think twice before you commit yourself.

The greatest contrast between Aries and Virgo is an emotional one. You have powerful emotional resources, and will probably be able to express them freely and rewardingly.

Romance
You have a passionate side to your nature, and characteristic Virgoan modesty will be unlikely to inhibit your approach to sex. If you manage to follow your basic intuition and impulses, you should enjoy a truly rewarding love and sex life.

When you become involved in a relationship, you may find Virgo prompting you to have second thoughts. You may ask yourself whether you are good enough for your partner. Try to ignore such doubts – they are the product of your Virgoan Sun, which will be trying to put a brake on the forthright and passionate response of your Arien Moon.

Your well-being
Ariens often suffer from headaches, and Virgoans are prone to migraine. The cause will probably be a buildup of tension, to which you will be very prone. All Virgoans have a busy lifestyle that allows little time for relaxation, and your Arien Moon chimes in with this. You need to learn how to relax, and a discipline like yoga will help. It should, however, be

The Moon in Aries

noted that headaches are sometimes the result of slight kidney disorders.

You probably have a very fast metabolic rate and will therefore be unlikely to put on excess weight.

Planning ahead
You may be far less careful with money than many people of your Sun sign. Try to control your Arien response to so-called bargains. If you are attracted to some big purchase, ask yourself if you really need it. This whole area is one that demands Virgoan caution.

Parenthood
The chances are that you will be less overtly critical of your children than many Virgoans, and this is not a bad thing. If you get really involved in their hobbies, you will develop a marvelously positive rapport with them. You should have no problems with the generation gap.

THE MOON IN
TAURUS

YOUR SUN AND MOON SIGNS ARE BOTH OF THE EARTH ELEMENT, AND YOU ARE THEREFORE A PRACTICAL PERSON. ALLOW YOUR SLOW, CAREFUL RESPONSES TO SITUATIONS TO GUIDE YOU WHEN DISTURBED BY VIRGOAN TENSION AND WORRY.

Both Virgo and Taurus are earth signs, and bestow practical common sense upon their subjects. Try, however, not to be overcautious.

Self-expression

The elements of shyness or inhibition that can be a part of every Virgoan character could prompt you to develop a safe and predictable routine, which may allow little or no scope for adventure. Always aim to consider situations constructively, as challenges, taking each development step-by-step, with confident assurance. In this way you will make the most of your best qualities.

You have marvelous potential that needs to be positively expressed, perhaps through craftwork or music.

Romance

Your Taurean Moon gives you a tender and affectionate emotion that enhances your attitude to, and expression of, love. If you allow it some freedom, an instinctive sensuality, which will no doubt delight your partner, should emerge.

The worst Taurean fault is possessiveness. Virgoans are extremely rational and logical, and it is this area of your personality that you should tune into if possessiveness becomes a problem. Remember also that you can be rather critical. If you avoid carping, and allow your love room to breathe, you will enjoy a rewarding relationship.

Your well-being

The Taurean body area is the throat, and yours could be vulnerable. Always keep a remedy on hand, especially during the winter or if there is an influenza bug going around.

Your Virgoan metabolism may be somewhat slower than average, as Taureans tend to move slowly, consequently putting on weight quite

The Moon in Taurus

easily. You could also have a high regard for chocolate and most rich foods. If you are at all worried or upset, a burst of "comfort eating" may need to be resisted.

Planning ahead

You have an excellent business sense, and should be able to make good, sound investments. Taurus enjoys luxury and every creature comfort, and is very attracted to quality. On the whole, Virgo goes for economy and good value. Here, therefore, is a possible source of conflict that only you can resolve. Why not enjoy those quality luxuries, and feel no guilt?

Parenthood

You will work extremely hard in every way, but especially to give your children a good life. Make sure that you have time for fun and outings with them, and that you do not miss out on their company. You may tend to be strict and discipline them firmly. Do not overdo this, and try not to be too critical of their efforts.

THE MOON IN
GEMINI

BOTH VIRGO AND GEMINI ARE RULED BY THE PLANET MERCURY,
SO THERE IS GREAT EMPATHY BETWEEN THESE SIGNS.
YOU HAVE A SHARP MIND, BUT DO NOT LET GEMINIAN LOGIC BE
DAMAGED BY VIRGOAN CRITICISM AND NAGGING.

The planet Mercury rules over both Virgo and Gemini, and these two signs are of the mutable quality. You therefore like variety and change, and are extremely versatile.

Self-expression
Mercury is regarded as the planet of communication, so it is likely that you are an excellent communicator. You may be a good teacher, or perhaps you work in the media.

The worst Geminian faults are restlessness and superficiality. While you could juggle many tasks at the same time, remember that you will get far more inner fulfillment if you complete everything you begin.

Romance
You may tend to fight showing your true feelings. Once in love, however, your partner could well receive sackfuls of letters, postcards, poems, and the like from you. Try to relax

into your relationships, and be aware that while Virgoan modesty can be charming, it should not prevent you from enjoying a rich and rewarding sex life.

It is important for you to have a high level of friendship within any emotional relationship. Seek partners who are at least your intellectual equals, and who can challenge your extremely lively mind.

Your well-being
The Geminian body areas are the arms and hands: be extra careful when using tools or when cooking. The body organ is the lungs, and it is therefore inadvisable for anyone with a Geminian influence to smoke.

You may be quite highly strung, since you have a great deal of nervous energy. This must be burned off through exercise that is both physically and mentally stimulating, for instance fast games such as

The Moon in Gemini

badminton, squash, or tennis. As a result of tension, you may suffer from migraines even more often than many Virgoans. Try to cultivate your sense of inner calm by learning some kind of relaxation technique.

Planning ahead

Mercury is the planet most closely associated with buying and selling. If you have something to sell, you will almost always contrive to get the best possible price for it. You may need to get professional advice when investing, because there is a chance that your cautious, practical Virgoan Sun could sometimes fail you.

Parenthood

You will be a very lively parent, and will not find it difficult to keep well up with, or ahead of, your children's current crazes, ideas, and opinions.

You are, however, very critical, and may tend to deflate your children by being too critical of their efforts. Be careful: such put-downs can, in the long run, be very damaging.

THE MOON IN
CANCER

VIRGO AND CANCER ARE THE TWO SIGNS OF THE ZODIAC MOST
PRONE TO WORRY. VIRGOAN WORRY IS INTELLECTUAL;
CANCERIAN, INTUITIVE AND IMAGINATIVE. YOU SHOULD AIM
TO BALANCE THESE TRAITS AGAINST EACH OTHER.

The Moon rules Cancer, and its influence over you is therefore very powerful, perhaps even to the point where you will show rather less than the average number of characteristics said to be typical of your Sun sign.

Self-expression
Your practical Virgoan Sun and extremely intuitive Moon suggest that you might possess a number of admirable virtues.

You have a very vivid and powerful imagination, which is probably highly spiced with creative potential. Try to express it whenever you can. For example, if you have a sneaking feeling that you would like to write, do not hesitate to do so.

Where your Sun and Moon signs meet all too well is in relation to anxiety. These signs seem to fight for first prize in the Zodiac where the tendency to worry is concerned. It will

work at two levels, and you can fight it in two ways. The Virgoan way is to make lists of all the pros and cons of a situation; the Cancerian way is to follow your instinct and intuition.

Romance
You no doubt possess a rather high emotional level and are able to express it much more freely than many Virgoans. You also have the wonderful capacity to live a rich and fulfilling love and sex life, and the ability to contribute a great deal to a happy relationship. You must, however, recognize the fact that you can sometimes be too protective.

Your well-being
The Cancerian body area covers the chest and breasts. The sign has nothing to do with the disease of the same name, but women should, of course, check their breasts regularly. Because of your tendency to worry,

The Moon in Cancer

you may, at times, be subject to stomach (from Virgo) and digestive (from Cancer) problems. Aim for inner calm and peace, and avoid flapping about pointlessly.

You may be an excellent cook, but should watch how much you eat. You could be more prone to weight gain than most Virgoans. If your metabolism is slow, try to speed it up a little, perhaps through exercise.

Planning ahead

You will be very careful, perhaps even overly cautious with money. However, you certainly have what it takes to make money: a really shrewd and intuitive business sense, which should enable you to invest wisely.

Parenthood

You make a marvelous, caring parent, and will want to "mother" your children. Try to accept the fact that they will eventually leave home and make their own lives. It is particularly important for women with this Sun and Moon combination to develop new interests at such times. Try not to be too sentimental, recalling "the old days" too relentlessly, or the generation gap will loom large.

THE MOON IN
LEO

GIVE YOUR LEO MOON ROOM TO BREATHE. IT WILL PROVIDE
YOU WITH THE CONFIDENCE TO DO WHAT YOU WANT,
BECAUSE IT IS RIGHT FOR YOU. DO NOT LET SHYNESS CRAMP
YOUR STYLE OR INHIBIT YOU IN ANY WAY.

Your Leo Moon creates some very striking qualities that contrast strongly with those of your Virgoan Sun. Try to become more aware of them, and allow them to work for you.

Self-expression
You have greater self-confidence than many people of your Sun sign, and if you can combine this with the Virgoan ability to communicate your ideas, emotions, and opinions, you cannot fail to make excellent progress.

Should you be someone who initially seems to accept challenges and copes positively with situations, but then retreats on second thought, try to reach a better balance. Your Leo Moon is there to push you forward and boost your self-confidence.

In addition, in contrast to most Virgoans you have very good organizing ability. You do not need to be told everything that is expected of you, and you can cope well in a crisis.

You may have creative potential and should try to fit time in which to express this into your busy schedule.

Romance
You have warm, fiery emotions and, because you are such a good communicator, should not find it difficult to express your feelings. You certainly have the capacity to love deeply and passionately, but must consciously dispel any typically Virgoan feelings of inferiority.

You will want to look up to your partners and do everything possible to please them, but remember that relationships should be partnerships.

Your well-being
The Leo body area is said to cover the back and spine. These are therefore vulnerable, so make sure that you take enough exercise to keep them in really good condition. Many Virgoans love walking and jogging. If you feel that this applies to you,

The Moon in Leo

remember to make sure that you walk well, with a straight back.

The Leo body organ is the heart, and this organ, like all the others, needs regular exercise. You will probably be less prone to worry than most people of your Sun sign, and this characteristic is therefore less likely to affect your health.

Planning ahead

The contrast between Leo and Virgo will emerge in your attitude toward money. Your Moon sign instinct veers toward generosity, extravagance, and quality. Your Virgoan Moon encourages a taste for simple things, of good value. Somewhere between the two is the point of balance.

You will probably invest soundly, provided your Leo Moon does not encourage you to put all your financial eggs in one basket.

Parenthood

Your natural enthusiasm will make you a lively parent. You will be less critical, and more encouraging, than most Virgoans. Take into account your children's opinions, and encourage debate among them.

THE MOON IN
VIRGO

BECAUSE BOTH THE SUN AND THE MOON WERE IN VIRGO ON THE DAY OF YOUR BIRTH, YOU WERE BORN UNDER A NEW MOON. SINCE VIRGO IS AN EARTH SIGN, THIS ELEMENT POWERFULLY INFLUENCES YOUR PERSONALITY AND REACTIONS.

Should you study a list of your Sun sign characteristics, you will probably recognize that a great many of them apply to you. On average, out of a list of perhaps 20 traits of a Sun sign listed in books or magazines, most people will strongly identify with 11 or 12. In your case, however, the average increases considerably because the Sun and Moon were both in Virgo when you were born.

Self-expression
Your Sun sign will tend to make you lively and talkative, but rather cautious and, sometimes, perhaps lacking in self-confidence; your Moon sign causes you to react to challenges in the same way.

You have an alert mind, and your responses tend to be critical. Be careful that you do not get too bogged down in detail, and try consciously to develop the ability to grasp the overall concept of a suggestion or project.

Romance
Your Sun and Moon signs are not very highly charged with emotion and, when you are in love, you could well be a little apprehensive about expressing your feelings. Remember that you are good with words, and do not be afraid to say what you feel. Take your time, however, since nervousness can make you overly talkative. Do not allow yourself to be rushed into a relationship, but do not make excuses, either, in order to avoid committing yourself.

One area in which you should hold back is in being critical of your partners. Try to accept them for what they are.

Your well-being
Everything that has been said about health on pages 272 to 273 probably applies directly to you. You are possibly one of the great worriers of the world, and this could affect your

The Moon in Virgo

digestion. You probably respond very well to most homeopathic and complementary medical treatments, in particular reflexology.

Your very high nervous energy can lead to a buildup of tension. Like many Virgoans, you may therefore benefit from yoga.

Planning ahead

You will not be very adventurous when it comes to money and will spend carefully and wisely. Go for investments that show slow but steady growth. You may need professional guidance when you wish to invest or save some money.

Parenthood

You will stimulate your children's minds, but may be a little cool. They will benefit from sound explanations, but a hug is often more reassuring. Try not to be too critical. This will not be easy for you, although keeping up with your children's concerns will.

THE MOON IN
LIBRA

VIRGO IS ALL ACTION, WHILE LIBRA IS MORE RELAXED. IT IS IMPORTANT FOR YOU TO KEEP YOUR PHYSICAL AND INTELLECTUAL ENERGIES IN BALANCE. A LIBRAN MOON GIVES YOU A DIPLOMATIC STREAK THAT YOU MUST NOT SUPPRESS.

Your Libran Moon lightens your personality and helps you to take a rather more relaxed attitude to life than many Virgoans.

Self-expression
When confronted by problems, you may respond with "Que sera, sera" and, while for some Zodiac types this could prove a negative or complacent reaction, for you it is actually fitting, since it allows you breathing room before your more energetic, tense nervous energy springs into action. One word of warning: you could be rather indecisive in certain situations and, to counter the tendency, should bring your marvelously logical and critical Sun sign qualities into play.

Romance
You are very romantic at heart, and should not find it too difficult to relax into emotional and sexual relationships. In fact, your response to people of the opposite sex is probably far more outgoing than that of many Sun sign Virgoans.

Be careful that you do not rush into marriage or a permanent relationship, only to find that the man or woman of your choice is terribly irritating or does not come up to your standards.

You are probably more tactful and diplomatic toward your partners than most Virgoans. Shyness and modesty will be less dominant in you, and you should have no problem enjoying a rich and fulfilling love and sex life.

Your well-being
The Libran body organ is the kidneys. Virgoan headaches and migraines, which are due to stress and tension, may be exacerbated by your Libran Sun, since there is a possibility that slight kidney upsets could also give you headaches. However, your Moon sign should help to prevent too much tension from building up.

The Moon in Libra

You may have a slower metabolism than many Sun sign Virgoans, and could enjoy rather rich food. If you are at all prone to weight gain, try to adjust your diet, and do not allow yourself to get lazy about exercise.

Planning ahead

You may well be conscience-stricken when you have been extravagant. Try not to get too concerned about such things. You may not be terribly good at handling your finances and should seek professional advice in this area, especially if you want to buy stock or are considering an investment or some form of savings plan.

Parenthood

While you will be a fine parent, it is possible that your children may not always know precisely where they stand with you. Be careful, since this can cause problems. Aim to keep a balance. Remember, too, to keep abreast of your children's opinions and concerns, in order to avoid problems with the generation gap.

THE MOON IN
SCORPIO

YOU NEED TO GET TO THE BOTTOM OF ANY PROBLEM THAT YOU
ENCOUNTER AND TO DELVE INTO IT IN GREAT DETAIL.
YOU HAVE MORE EMOTIONAL FORCE THAN MOST VIRGOANS, AND
YOU SHOULD USE THIS POSITIVELY.

The earth element of a Virgoan Sun blends well with the water element of your Scorpio Moon, for in many respects these influences have certain qualities in common.

Self-expression
You will find research compelling and should get involved in a subject into which you can delve in real depth.

You also have great determination and sense of purpose, and need to be emotionally involved with any work that you do. The inner psychological fulfillment that you will get out of this is essential to you, but you must learn to develop breadth of vision. While your flair for detail is marvelous, you may not always grasp overall concepts very well.

Romance
You need really rewarding sexual expression and fulfillment. This may not be simple, because you will be a demanding partner and, while capable of giving great sexual pleasure, you may well have special needs. Choose your partners with all the discrimination and care bestowed by your Virgoan Sun and Scorpio Moon.

The worst Scorpio fault is jealousy, and the worst Virgoan fault, that of being overly critical. Clearly, these can marry in an unfortunate way, so consciously guard against them.

Your well-being
The Scorpio body area covers the genitals. Scorpio women should make sure they have regular checkups, and men should regularly examine their testicles for irregularities. With your Sun and Moon combination, your throat may also be open to infections.

You may be very prone to Virgoan worry, as your Scorpio Moon gives you an active, fertile imagination that can sometimes prompt you to worry over nothing. This may lead to an upset

The Moon in Scorpio

stomach and minor ailments that are difficult to pin down. At such times, try to let Virgoan logic dominate.

Planning ahead

You are likely to have an instinctive business sense and a natural ability to for making money.

You will probably also have much more expensive tastes than other Virgoans, and you will need to earn a good salary in order to allow for some costly indulgences.

Parenthood

You may be a far stricter parent than you realize, but in many ways this is not a bad thing at all. You are aiming to make your childern grow up to be decent and considerate people. It may, however, be necessary for you to achieve a little more balance. Let yourself go, and allow yourself to express your enjoyment of life in your relationship with your children. In this way, you will have real fun and reduce generation gap problems.

THE MOON IN
SAGITTARIUS

Do not underestimate your own intelligence; you may have a great capacity for study. Be careful that your Sagittarian Moon does not give others the impression that you are uncaring.

Both Virgo and Sagittarius offer a good intellectual capacity, and make you adaptable to changing atmospheres and conditions. Your Sagittarian Moon makes you respond optimistically to challenges and gives you a positive outlook. As a result, you should, in theory, be far less of a worrier than most Sun sign Virgoans.

Self-expression
You are always happy to become involved in the details of an argument but, because of your Sagittarian Moon, you have the breadth of vision and the ability to take in the overall situation as well. The worst Sagittarian fault happens to be restlessness; try to avoid it by developing consistency of effort.

There is an element of the "eternal student" about you. You can cope well with intellectual challenge, so it is quite important

that you always have a challenging project on hand. If your work constantly taxes your brain, make sure that you spend some of your spare time involved in a physically demanding interest.

Romance
You have a fine, positive, fiery emotional force that will find its most positive expression in your love and sex life. You are unlikely to be shy or modest; your attitude to love is lively, and you have a great capacity to enjoy sexual relationships. You need partners who understand your need for an element of freedom and independence within a relationship. An even vaguely claustrophobic atmosphere will not suit you at all.

Your well-being
The Sagittarian body area covers the hips and thighs. Women who have this sign emphasized will tend to put

The Moon in Sagittarius

on weight in those areas. Only exercise and a very controlled, regular diet will help. The Sagittarian organ is the liver, and it is surprising how easy it is for you to feel unwell. Your body and mind must be kept in good running order, like a well-oiled machine. If they are not, you will suffer far more than most people.

Planning ahead
You have something of a gambling spirit, and it could well need careful control. It is related to a love of taking risks. If you are attracted to get-rich-quick schemes, always make sure that you allow your more cautious Virgoan self to have its say before embarking on them.

Parenthood
Your children will appreciate your enthusiastic responses to their suggestions, and you will not find it difficult to stimulate their minds and keep them active. They are unlikely to turn into couch potatoes, slumped in front of the television set for hours on end. If you can control any overtly critical qualities that spring from your Virgoan Sun, you ought not to experience generation gap problems.

THE MOON IN
CAPRICORN

YOUR CAPRICORNIAN MOON WILL EITHER HELP YOU TO SCALE THE
HEIGHTS OR HOLD YOU BACK. PRAISE YOURSELF AS OFTEN AS
POSSIBLE AND YOU WILL GET TO THE TOP. FALL INTO INHIBITING
SELF-CRITICISM AND YOU WILL NOT.

You are a very practical, sensible, and dependable person. Your Capricornian Moon can work for you in one of two ways. You will either respond well to challenge and be very ambitious to succeed, stepping with great agility over every difficulty that crosses your path and eventually reaching the top; or you will respond very negatively, declining to accept responsibility on the grounds that you cannot cope, or do not have the brains, the stamina, or the self-confidence. It is even possible that you may recognize both of these tendencies in yourself.

Self-expression

If you are rather timid, ask yourself whether this is due to the influence of your Virgoan Sun. The blending of the influences of your Sun and Moon is, in many ways, a great help in countering this tendency, and provides sound building blocks for your personality. You can build a reputation for reliability and common sense, and your truly practical outlook on life is enviable.

Romance

Capricorn is a cool, unemotional sign, and so is Virgo. You may therefore be inclined not to show your feelings all that readily. You will take your love and sex life very seriously, and may need to learn to relax more into your relationship if you are to experience a rewarding partnership.

Your well-being

The Capricornian body area covers the knees and shins, so if you enjoy long country hikes or jogs, you should make sure that your knees are well protected.

The skin, teeth, and bones are also Capricorn-ruled, so use good-quality, natural skin products, and do not miss out on regular dental checkups.

The Moon in Capricorn

Planning ahead

Because you are practical and cautious, you will no doubt be extremely careful with money. You probably enjoy putting carefully calculated sums aside regularly in some safe investment, for instance savings bonds or CDs.

You may also have a liking for quality, and will discreetly go for the best whenever you can. There is a chance, however, that you may not always enjoy the fruits of your labors. You should find time to relax with a few well-chosen friends, and forget about entertaining only those people that you feel obligated to.

Parenthood

You may need to modify your conventional outlook by seeking other people's opinions. Do not be too critical of your children. Always make time for them, and do not present them with logical arguments if they are upset. Give them a hug instead. Listen to their opinions, and you will avoid the generation gap.

THE MOON IN
AQUARIUS

VIRGOANS ARE PRACTICAL, AND OFTEN CONVENTIONAL. WITH AN AQUARIAN MOON YOU ARE LIKELY TO RESPOND WELL TO NEW, INVENTIVE, AND ORIGINAL IDEAS. IF YOU HAPPEN TO BE INTERESTED IN UNTRIED CONCEPTS, DO NOT DISMISS YOUR INTUITIONS.

Your Aquarian Moon and your Virgoan Sun give you an intriguing and perhaps even somewhat enigmatic personality.

Self-expression
You have a very independent streak, and will often react to situations and to the suggestions of other people in a very individual way. More than this, when it comes to helping other people, you are all kindness.

You have plenty of originality and probably a great deal of creative, artistic flair. Make sure that you have time to express this fully, as it will give you a great deal of satisfaction.

While your Virgoan Sun makes you practical and conventional, your Aquarian Moon attracts you to less conventional things. Beware of responding a little unpredictably at times; while surprising other people is great fun, unpredictability can sometimes be embarrassing.

Romance
Both Virgo and Aquarius are emotionally cool, and it may not be very easy for you to show your true feelings. However, your Aquarian Moon shines brightly for you, giving you a very romantic streak and making you a faithful lover once committed. It can also bestow a film-star glamour that is devastatingly attractive. However, like a magnet, you can distance yourself from what you attract, and may at times appear entirely out of reach. If you relax and allow your romantic side to take over, you will enjoy a very rewarding love and sex life.

Your well-being
The Aquarian body area covers the ankles. Be very careful, as they are vulnerable when you are exercising or involved in sports. The circulation is also Aquarius-ruled, so even if you enjoy bracing, cold weather, keep

The Moon in Aquarius

very warm. Your whole well-being may otherwise suffer, and you could feel uncomfortably stiff and aching.

You are less inclined to worry than many Virgoans, and the effect of worry on your health is not as bad as it can be for other Sun sign Virgoans.

Planning ahead
You are attracted to glamorous and expensive things, especially for your home and wardrobe. These will certainly eat into your finances and,

while you are as practical as the next Virgoan, you could consider seeking professional financial advice.

Parenthood
Your Aquarian Moon gives you a modern outlook that your children will really appreciate. You will keep up with their ideas and should not suffer generation gap problems. You may, however, consciously need to express a little more emotional warmth from time to time.

THE MOON IN
PISCES

VIRGO AND PISCES ARE POLAR OR OPPOSITE ZODIAC SIGNS, SO YOU
WERE BORN UNDER A FULL MOON. RESTLESSNESS AND
INNER DISCONTENT COULD BOTHER YOU. BE RATIONAL, AND DO
NOT BE SWAYED BY NEGATIVE EMOTIONS.

We all commonly express certain attributes of our polar or opposite sign (the sign that is across the Zodiac circle from our Sun sign). For Virgoans, the polar sign is Pisces and, because the Sun was in that sign when you were born, the polarity is expressed in a particularly interesting way.

Self-expression
You will be very sensitive to other people's suggestions and actions, and could be more easily hurt than most Virgoans. The kindness of Virgo is powerfully emphasized in your personality; you instinctively know when help is needed, and will respond immediately.

Neither Virgo nor Pisces is basically very self-confident. You have great potential and, if there is something that you long to do or wish to study, you should give yourself the opportunity to do so. Try not to give up too quickly or easily, and develop your powers of concentration and persistence of effort.

Romance
You are among the more emotional of Virgoans, and this is good. Being practical, and not lacking in common sense, you are also able to respond to lovers in a tender, warm, and sensual way. You need to feel secure in emotional and sexual relationships; then you make a wonderful partner.

The worst Piscean fault is deceptiveness. Your Piscean Moon may also make you self-deceptive. If you remain level-headed, you will find a partner on whom you can rely.

Your well-being
The Piscean body area covers the feet, and you may have difficulty in obtaining comfortable shoes. Foot exercise sandals are very good for you, and far preferable to bare feet.

The Moon in Pisces

Your feet are particularly susceptible to blisters, cuts, and so on. Regular visits to the podiatrist are advisable.

Your Virgo and Pisces polarity increases your inclination to worry, which will, undoubtedly, affect your health. When worried, try to follow your Piscean intuition, be logical and, like most Virgoans, practical. Keep calm, perhaps by practicing a relaxation technique.

Planning ahead
You are generous and could give a great deal of money to charity. This is fine if you manage to balance the books. Do examine sob stories with a critical Virgoan eye. You have the tendency to be too soft-hearted. Do not lend money, and seek professional advice when you wish to invest.

Parenthood
You will be a kind and sympathetic parent, tending to spoil your children one moment but, perhaps, being over-critical the next. An awareness of this will help you to keep your attitude to your children in balance. Listen to their opinions and views, and you should not suffer too many problems with the generation gap.

SUN & MOON SIGNS

LIBRA

SEPTEMBER 23 – OCTOBER 23

INTRODUCING
LIBRA

LIBRA, THE SIGN OF THE SCALES, IS THE SEVENTH SIGN OF THE ZODIAC. LIBRANS NEED HARMONY AND BALANCE IN THEIR LIVES. THE RULING PLANET OF THE SIGN IS VENUS, NAMED AFTER THE GODDESS OF LOVE — AND TO LIBRANS, LOVE IS ALL.

Peace is important to Librans, and they will sometimes try to obtain it at any price. Although they often have a reputation for laziness, it is generally undeserved. They usually have the motivation to work hard, but always make time to listen to others. Decision-making is hard for them as they always see both sides of a problem and tend to procrastinate.

Librans must be careful not to be overindulgent, since this may lead to weight gain that will spoil their natural good looks.

Traditional groupings

As you read through this book you will come across references to the elements and the qualities, and to positive and negative, or masculine and feminine signs.

The first of these groupings, that of the elements, comprises fire, earth, air, and water signs. The second, that of the qualities, divides the Zodiac into cardinal, fixed, and mutable signs. The final grouping is made up of positive and negative, or masculine and feminine signs. Each Zodiac sign is associated with a combination of components from these groupings, all of which contribute different characteristics to it.

Libran characteristics

Libra is a sign of the air element, and there is a certain light airiness to the Libran personality. People born under this sign are usually able to communicate with ease and are pleasantly sociable.

The sign is of the cardinal quality, which makes its subjects agreeable, outgoing, warm, and charming. It is a positive, masculine sign, and is therefore likely to incline you toward being extrovert. Venus is the sign's ruling planet, and Libran colors include pink, pale green, and different shades of blue.

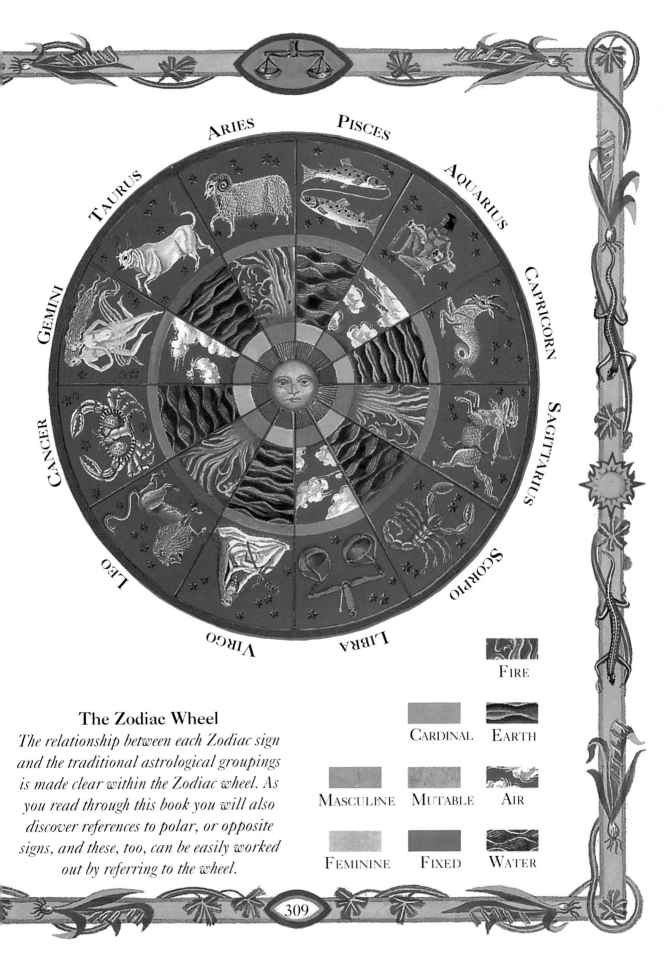

The Zodiac Wheel

The relationship between each Zodiac sign and the traditional astrological groupings is made clear within the Zodiac wheel. As you read through this book you will also discover references to polar, or opposite signs, and these, too, can be easily worked out by referring to the wheel.

CARDINAL

MASCULINE   MUTABLE

FEMININE   FIXED

FIRE

EARTH

AIR

WATER

LIBRA
MYTHS & LEGENDS

THE ZODIAC, WHICH MAY HAVE ORIGINATED IN BABYLON
AS LONG AS 2,500 YEARS AGO, IS A CIRCLE OF
CONSTELLATIONS THROUGH WHICH THE SUN MOVES
DURING THE COURSE OF A YEAR.

The constellation of Libra was celebrated in Babylon at least two thousand years before Christ, where it was connected to the myth of the last judgment and the weighing of souls. This is the earliest Libran association with scales. Later, the ancient Egyptians also weighed their harvest and assessed their taxes in autumn, at the time when the Babylonian judgment ceremony is believed to have taken place.

The Scorpion
In ancient times the claws of the Scorpion were recognized as occupying some of the area of the sky that is now set aside for Libra.

An ancient Babylonian name for Libra, ziba. anna, means the "horn" of a scorpion, which must actually be a reference to the creature's claws. Pictorially, these horns later developed into the scales of the balance that symbolizes Libra.

Weighing the soul
No myth is directly associated with Libra, but a single idea has been connected with the sign since at least ancient Egyptian times – that of a person's soul being weighed in the balance, after death.

The scene is shown in many illustrations in the Egyptian Book of the Dead. It features a man standing, often with his wife, beside the scales on which his heart is being weighed against a feather representing Truth. Anubis, the jackal-headed god of the dead, also known as Lord of the Mummy Wrappings, was believed to open up the roads to the afterlife for those who had died; the ancient Greeks associated him with their god, Hermes, the "Conductor of Souls." He often stands close to the scales, watching the judgment occurring. Thoth, the ibis-headed Egyptian moon-god, patron of science and literature, and of wisdom and

Judging the Dead

*This scene from the Egyptian Book of the Dead, dating from
1100 B.C., shows Anubis, the jackal-headed god, and Thoth, the god of
scribes, weighing a soul against Truth.*

inventions, can also be seen nearby, meticulously noting down a faithful record of events.

The Bible
The conception of all the good in one's life being weighed against the sum of the evil, established by the ancient Egyptians, persisted into early Jewish culture. It is clearly reflected in the writings of what has come to be known as the Old Testament. In one passage from the Old Testament, the prophet Job asked that God "weigh him in the scales of justice," while Belshazzar was "weighed in the balance and found wanting."

Those people who are lucky enough to be born with the Sun in Libra are traditionally considered to have a particularly strong sense of justice and fairness.

LIBRA
SYMBOLISM

CERTAIN HERBS, SPICES, FLOWERS, TREES, GEMS, METALS, AND ANIMALS HAVE LONG BEEN ASSOCIATED WITH PARTICULAR ZODIAC SIGNS. SOME ASSOCIATIONS ARE SIMPLY AMUSING, WHILE OTHERS CAN BE EXTREMELY USEFUL.

Flowers
Large, opulent roses and those flowers which, like Taurus, are ruled by Venus – for example, violets, foxgloves, and daisies – are all loved by Librans.

WHITE ROSE

DAISIES

CYPRESS

Trees

The ash, the cypress, all vines, and those trees governed by Taurus, which shares the same ruling planet as Libra, are Libran trees.

SORREL

Herbs

Sorrel, which alleviates skin disorders, and figwort, which prevents blood clots, are all ruled by Libra.

Spices

No spices are particularly associated with Libra, but mace, and sometimes cloves and ginger, are generally popular among Librans.

CLOVES

GINGER

LIBRA
SYMBOLISM

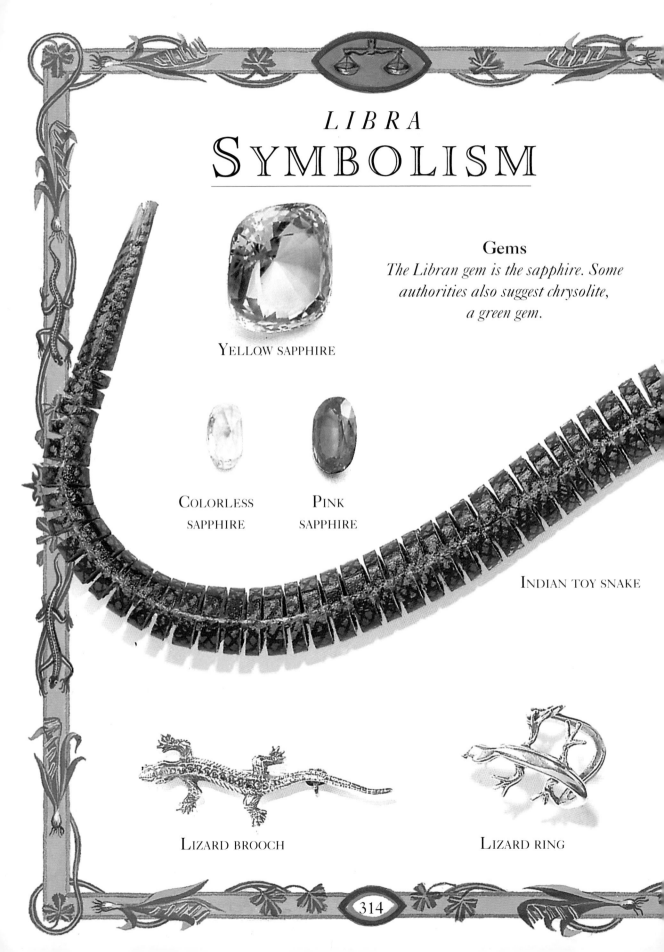

YELLOW SAPPHIRE

Gems
The Libran gem is the sapphire. Some authorities also suggest chrysolite, a green gem.

COLORLESS
SAPPHIRE

PINK
SAPPHIRE

INDIAN TOY SNAKE

LIZARD BROOCH

LIZARD RING

Metal

Copper is a Libran metal, associated, like Taurus, with Venus. Bronze, an alloy of copper and tin, is also sometimes associated with the sign.

MIDDLE EASTERN COPPER COFFEE POT

Animals

Lizards and small reptiles are traditionally associated with Libra. Snakes and many small domestic animals, such as mice and hamsters, are also sometimes linked with the sign.

SILVER SNAKE BROOCH

LIBRA
PROFILE

THERE IS AN ATTRACTIVE SOFTNESS TO THE LIBRAN IMAGE. THE
FEATURES MAY NOT BE VERY CLEAR-CUT.
PEOPLE OF THIS SIGN ARE USUALLY WELL DRESSED IN
THE CONTEXT OF THEIR PEER GROUP.

You might sometimes see Librans walking along, holding hands with their partners and looking affectionately at them, rather than at the road ahead. This invariably means that everything is right with their world. If, on the other hand, you see people of this sign slumping along the road, with their heads down and their hands deep in their pockets, you can assume that they lack love and affection. These signs of despondency usually mean that they are at a psychological low point.

The Libran face
*Librans often appear
gentle, and full of kindness
and understanding.*

well-proportioned body and natural good looks, which contribute greatly to the enhancement of your charming personality. You may move gracefully, with a swinging gait, but are usually in no hurry. This explains your tendency to gain weight and your hesitancy in starting a diet.

The face
Libran men are inclined to have rather fine hair, and some of them are particularly prone to baldness. Your eyes are likely to show a capacity for kindness and understanding, and your nose is probably well proportioned in relation to the rest of your face. There is a tendency for the Libran chin to become less well defined with

The body
Provided you do what you can to increase your often rather slow metabolism, you will not lose your

The Libran stance

Librans often betray their uncertainty by shifting their weight from one foot to the other when in conversation.

increasing age and weight gain. You easily break into a gentle, sympathetic smile. Overall, the Libran expression often conveys a certain feyness. This usually has the effect of making the individual appear rather gentle.

Style

Librans generally have good taste in fashion. Pastel colors often suit both sexes. The women's image is rather pretty, with sexual allure, but not overt or vampish. An asymmetric line is sometimes favored, as are draped skirts. Rather light, delicate fabrics in pastel colors are often worn. These enhance the gentleness in the Libran image. Libran men, too, love to introduce a little romance into their clothes. They particularly like attractive, elaborately decorated shirts and unusual waistcoats. Hats are also very popular.

In general

The Libran stance can sometimes betray a degree of uncertainty. You may sometimes have a tendency to shift your weight from one foot to the other when you are speaking to someone. Similarly, when in conversation, you could sometimes hold your head first to one side, and then to the other. Bear in mind that people will not be slow in reading such body language.

In general, the gestures that you make tend to be quite slow, but they will always be meaningful and relatively uncomplicated.

LIBRA PERSONALITY

LIBRANS ARE BOTH KIND AND WARMLY AFFECTIONATE. THEY HAVE TIME FOR OTHER PEOPLE AND ARE NATURALLY GENEROUS. THEIR NEED TO RELATE TO OTHERS CAN, HOWEVER, SOMETIMES DRIVE THEM TO BUY FRIENDSHIP.

The Libran motivation might be summed up as a desire to keep life in balance and to relate in depth to another person.

Most Librans find loneliness almost intolerable and, until they are able to form a permanent relationship with someone, they are unlikely to be psychologically whole.

When you find yourself settled into a steady partnership, you will undergo a considerable blossoming of your Libran personality. It is, however, important for you to remember that a successful partnership is all about sharing. You must strive to keep the necessary balance and harmony that is typical of the Libran lifestyle.

At work
Librans are often lucky enough to possess the very pleasant ability to calm others and to help them unwind, giving the impression that time is no problem for them.

It is this tendency that has unfortunately given Librans in general a reputation for laziness. In fact, many of you are great achievers, who may well have reached top jobs in government, or perhaps the armed services. While Librans can sometimes be aggressive, they are also known to be peacemakers.

Your attitudes
Most Librans have the remarkably clever knack of seeing both sides of every problem. Because you understand your opponents' opinions, you may find it very difficult to draw final conclusions and come to constructive decisions. This is something that may cause you a variety of problems.

On the one hand, avoiding decisions can become so common for you that problems go away before they finally have to be faced. On the other hand, the same tendency can

Venus rules Libra

Venus, the Roman goddess of love, represents the ruling planet of both Libra and Taurus. The influence of Venus extends to art and fashion, and relates to the feminine side of a Libran's nature.

lead to immeasurable inconvenience to friends and family, who may never know quite where they stand, or what you actually plan to do and whether or not it will eventually be done.

The overall picture

While Librans are kind and do good things for others, it cannot be denied that they also enjoy receiving profuse thanks. Librans themselves are usually very forthcoming in this respect, so perhaps it is only natural that they expect the same reaction from other people. Some Zodiac types find it difficult to be even marginally gushing, but if a Libran merely receives a quiet "thank you" or, much worse, no thanks at all, resentfulness will soon set in.

LIBRA
ASPIRATIONS

YOU ARE A GREGARIOUS PERSON AND NEED COMPANY, SO WORKING IN AN OPEN-PLAN OFFICE WILL HOLD NO TERRORS. A POSITION OF AUTHORITY MAY NOT SUIT YOU; YOU COULD FIND IT TOO LONELY.

Agent
Librans have the ability to see both sides of a situation, and therefore make excellent agents in any area.

APPOINTMENT DIARY

The legal profession
Provided that they can come to terms with their indecisiveness, Librans are people who are able to ensure that justice will be done.

JUDGE'S GAVEL AND BLOCK

Receptionist

Libran charm will be a considerable asset to any firm that decides to employ a person of this sign to greet its clients.

RECEPTIONIST'S HEADPHONES

MAKEUP BRUSHES AND
FACE POWDER

Diplomacy

Tact and diplomacy often come naturally to Librans. Their love of socializing helps make them natural diplomats.

The beauty trades

The Libran ruling planet, Venus, encourages Librans to make the most of their own, and other people's, looks.

DIPLOMAT'S LEATHER CASE

LIBRA
HEALTH

IN ORDER FOR LIBRANS TO BE PHYSICALLY WELL, THEY NEED TO
LIVE WELL-BALANCED LIVES. UPSETTING ARGUMENTS AND
UNCOMFORTABLE LIVING CONDITIONS CANNOT BE TOLERATED
AND MUST BE AVOIDED AT ALL COSTS.

The delicate Libran system will be thrown into disarray by almost any kind of imbalance. This will often result in both mental and physical exhaustion, leading to headaches.

Your diet
As a Sun sign Libran you may need to supplement your diet with natrum phosphate (Nat. Phos.), which reduces acidity in the stomach. It

Red currants
Berry fruits such as red currants are strongly associated with Libra.

prevents and helps to dissolve gallstones, and sometimes soothes an inflamed throat.

Many Librans have a rather slow metabolism. This, coupled with a preference for rich and often sweet food, can often lead to weight gain. Regular exercise is the solution to this problem.

Taking care
The Libran body area covers the kidneys. Should a headache strike unexpectedly, and if nothing has upset you, it may be that you are suffering from a slight kidney disorder. Perhaps, as with any unexpected health problem, you would be wise to receive a medical checkup. The lumbar region of the back can be somewhat vulnerable, and people in this Sun sign group would be wise to invest in a back-rest chair if they expect to spend a lot of time sitting at an office desk.

Astrology and the body

For many centuries it was impossible to practice medicine without a knowledge of astrology. In European universities, medical training included information on how planetary positions would affect the administration of medicines, the bleeding of patients, and the right time to pick herbs and make potions. Each Zodiac sign rules a particular part of the body, and early medical textbooks always included a drawing that illustrated the point.

LIBRA AT
LEISURE

EACH OF THE SUN SIGNS TRADITIONALLY SUGGESTS SPARE-TIME
ACTIVITIES, HOBBIES, AND VACATIONS. ALTHOUGH
THESE ARE ONLY SUGGESTIONS, THEY OFTEN WORK OUT
WELL, AND REFLECT LIBRAN INTERESTS.

Dressmaking
*Librans who express their creativity
through dressmaking may use their
intuition to divine precisely the styles
and colors that will be popular in
the next season.*

POSTAGE
STAMPS

Travel
*You will spend much time anticipating a
month spent in Austria, Egypt, Burma,
Japan, or even Tibet.*

DRESSMAKING EQUIPMENT

Playing music

*Some Librans obtain a lot of pleasure
from playing a musical instrument
with small amateur groups
or by accompanying singers.*

Competitive games

*It is surprising how
aggressive normally passive
Librans can be when they are
involved in competitive
games and sports.*

FLOWER-ARRANGING TOOLS

BLACK BELT
WON IN THE
MARTIAL ARTS

Flower arranging

*The Libran love of harmony and
balance is often borne out in the
creation of wonderful floral displays.*

LIBRA IN
LOVE

FOR LIBRANS, LIFE IS AT ITS MOST BEAUTIFUL WHEN THEY FALL IN LOVE. THEY SHOULD, HOWEVER, ALWAYS REMEMBER TO STOP AND CONSIDER WHETHER THEY ARE IN LOVE WITH THEIR LOVER, OR WITH LOVE ITSELF.

The basic Libran motivation is to relate to another human being. Sharing, keeping life in balance, and living a harmonious life are all essential to you. More so than any other Zodiac type, a Libran who is alone will probably find life difficult to cope with and incomplete.

Although it might seem that a Libran's very indecisive nature could prevent commitment, this is in fact not usually the case. Librans are so eager to share and to relate that they often rush prematurely into a permanent relationship or marriage. Very often, of course, all is well, but if things go wrong, the resulting disruption to their lives can be far worse than it would be for people of any of the other Sun signs.

While in reality you are greatly in need of peace and harmony, many of you will try to pick fights with your partner just because it is so nice to kiss and make up afterward. Try not to take this too far, since such an attitude could be intensely wearing for your partners.

As a lover
It is the warmth and expression of really sincere affection that makes life with a Libran worthwhile.

Most of the time you will be in possession of the natural ability to create a delightful atmosphere that will doubtless enhance and color almost every aspect of the loving relationship which you enjoy with your partner.

Types of Libran lover

Some Librans have a great sense of drama. They enjoy making love in glamorous surroundings and have a tendency to look up to their partners. A second group is somewhat apprehensive about sex. These individuals are modest and romantic, but do not find it easy to relax into a relationship and can sometimes be very critical. The third group will agree with all of the comments made here. Their enjoyment of sex will develop gradually. Other Librans are deeply passionate, with a great need for sexual fulfillment. They can make very demanding partners, and must be careful not to act jealously. The final group is lively and enthusiastic about sex, and gets a great deal of sheer fun and pleasure from it. People in this group have a positive attitude, although they can be very flirtatious at times, and may even attempt dual relationships.

LIBRA AT
HOME

LIBRAN ROOMS ARE USUALLY HANDSOME, AND ENHANCED BY
FULL, HEAVY CURTAINS AND HANGINGS, PERHAPS IN
SHADES OF WARM PINK AND PALE BLUE. COMFORT IS A KEYNOTE,
AND IT IS BORNE OUT BY HUGE, WELCOMING CHAIRS.

Most Librans are very adaptable people who could probably set up a happy home in just about any kind of environment. The one place that is unlikely to appeal to them is a run-down district with very obvious signs of poverty and ugliness. Librans may also experience a great deal of unhappiness if they end up living miles from their nearest neighbors. No matter how happy they may be with their partners, loneliness could be a problem.

Elegant portraits
*You may choose to display
some elegantly framed
antique photographs*

not popular, since furniture like this often looks, and may even be, less than comfortable. There is no lack of elegance in the overall appearance of the home, or in individual pieces. For instance, fine legs will support occasional tables, as opposed to anything too heavy or solid. Few Librans like housework, but their sense of pride in their homes encourages them to get on with it.

Furniture
Many Librans tend to favor traditional styles of furniture, and if some sweeping, well-balanced curves are integrated into the design, so much the better. Harsh, angular designs are

Soft furnishings
Libra is a sign that positively wallows in soft furnishings. Cushions abound – they may even have been made by yourself. Curtains and drapes are of really lavish, rich velvet or lovely, printed floral satin with huge designs of roses. Austrian blinds are popular,

and rugs will appear to be ankle deep. The colors are usually pastel, echoing those of Venus, the Libran ruling planet. A rich red or dark blue often makes an attractive contrast to these pale colors, and ensures that the overall effect is not too insipid.

Decorative objects

Librans are romantic, so objects that hint at love, for example heart-shaped pictures of your children, or of wedding groups, may be prominently displayed. The romantic theme often extends to your choice of paintings, and may be reflected in their soft colors or subject matter.

The emphasis that you will want to place upon stylish, cultured living will also be reflected in your paintings. A typical Libran choice might be a print of one of Gainsborough's portraits of beautiful women, an elegant painting of some flowers, or a set of prints depicting rare and exotic birds. If you actually collect prints or pictures, they will probably focus on fashion or on trades and professions from the past. A great many Librans like to collect

china or porcelain figures. These need not necessarily be antiques; they could just as easily be very attractive, but relatively inexpensive, graceful modern pieces. Even if you are not directly creative (and many Librans are) you are likely to have a great love of music and a highly developed appreciation of the arts. A musical instrument, most probably of the woodwind kind, may therefore provide the focal point of a decorative scheme in your home, even if you decide to simply leave it lying around until you can persuade someone else to play it.

Cushions and curtains
The Libran home will contain plenty of cushions and curtains made from sensuous velvets and satins.

THE SUN DECREES YOUR OUTWARD
EXPRESSION, YOUR IMAGE, AND MANY
IMPORTANT PERSONALITY TRAITS. THE
MOON, ALTHOUGH MERELY THE EARTH'S
SATELLITE, IS ASTRONOMICALLY THE
SECOND MOST IMPORTANT BODY IN THE
SOLAR SYSTEM. FROM THE SIGN THAT IT
WAS IN AT YOUR BIRTH, IT INFLUENCES HOW
YOU REACT TO SITUATIONS, YOUR
EMOTIONAL LEVEL, AND, TO A CERTAIN
EXTENT, WHAT YOU HAVE INHERITED FROM
YOUR PARENTS AND ANCESTORS. AFTER
FINDING YOUR MOON SIGN IN THE SIMPLE
TABLES ON PAGES 606 TO 609, TURN TO THE
RELEVANT PAGES AND TAKE A STEP
FORWARD IN YOUR OWN SELF-KNOWLEDGE.

THE MOON IN
ARIES

LIBRA AND ARIES ARE POLAR ZODIAC SIGNS, SO YOU WERE BORN
UNDER A FULL MOON. RESTLESSNESS CAN SOMETIMES
BE A PROBLEM FOR YOU. WHEN YOU MEET WITH A CHALLENGE,
ALLOW YOUR ARIEN MOON TO STIR YOU TO ACTION.

Each of us, in one way or another, tends to express attributes of our polar sign (the opposite sign across the Zodiac circle from our Sun sign). For Librans, this is Aries, and since the Moon was in Aries when you were born, this "polarity" is emphasized in a very interesting way.

Self-expression
The typical indecisiveness of Libra is mitigated by your Arien Moon. Provided that you consciously control the tendency to act too quickly, your first reactions will often be correct. Therefore do not change your mind, however badly you are tempted.

Romance
Your Arien Moon bestows a wealth of positive emotion, which you no doubt express freely and passionately toward your partner. You are a romantic Libran, and your tendency to rush into a relationship is heightened by your impulsive Moon.
You make a very rewarding partner, provided that you control selfishness, which is the worst Arien fault.

Your well-being
The fact that Libra and Aries are polar signs means that the relationship between the head (Aries) and the kidneys (Libra) is strongly emphasized. There are therefore two reasons why you may sometimes suffer from headaches. One may be psychologically based, while the other may be due to a mild kidney problem.
   Aries is also prone to minor accidents, particularly cuts and burns. As a result you would be extremely wise to wear protective clothing whenever it is required.

Planning ahead
You have a wonderfully enterprising spirit, and provided that you do not allow your natural energy and

The Moon in Aries

enthusiasm to flag, you have what it takes to run a successful "sideline" business in addition to your main career. You will find such an interest extremely rewarding.

While you will be anxious to make your money work for you, make sure that you control impulsiveness when investing. You could, at times, get a little carried away. Remember, too, that it is not a good idea for you to put all your eggs in one basket just because of a burst of enthusiasm.

Parenthood

You respond positively and well to your children. You must, however, try very hard to be faithful to any decisions or opinions that you express. Otherwise they will be uncertain where they stand with you.

Your Arien Moon gives you the happy ability to tune into your children's ideas and interests. If you express its lively qualities toward them, you will avoid problems with the generation gap.

THE MOON IN
TAURUS

LIBRA AND TAURUS ARE RULED BY THE PLANET VENUS, SO
THERE IS A NATURAL SYMPATHY BETWEEN THEM.
YOU LOVE COMFORT AND LUXURY, AND SHOULD USE YOUR
INTUITIVE BUSINESS SENSE TO PAY FOR THEM.

You have the ability to take life as it comes and to deal easily with worries, tension, and stress, giving others the impression that you are totally laid back. In many respects, you probably are. You certainly do not lack common sense, you pace yourself well, and you are less likely to get agitated than almost any Sun and Moon combination.

Self-expression

You may consciously have to nudge yourself when a swift answer or an immediate reaction is necessary. You much prefer to work deliberately through a problem, approaching it in a step-by-step fashion.

A slight problem is that while your Libran Sun encourages you to be fond of achieving peace at any price, your Taurean Moon inclines you to a predictable routine. When combined, the two influences may manage to edge you into a rut.

Romance

You are a very romantic, emotional Libran, and your Taurean Moon adds a warm sensuality and underlying passion to your personality that should be beautifully expressed toward your partners. You do, however, need a secure relationship; if you do not know where you stand with your partner you will not function well.

The worst Taurean fault is possessiveness. If this is combined with a Libran tendency to be slightly resentful, it could sometimes mar this vital area of your life. Let your Libran qualities give your partner the chance to breathe freely, and you will achieve a very rewarding life together.

Your well-being

The Taurean body area is the throat. With the onset of a cold, you could lose your voice and will certainly get a sore throat. A worse problem may be a slow metabolism and a love of rich

The Moon in Taurus

food. Try to regulate your eating habits and to discover some form of exercise that you enjoy.

Planning ahead

You should have excellent intuition where money is concerned, and will probably be able to watch the figures in your bank book grow steadily and satisfactorily. However, the luxuries that you enjoy so much will be expensive. Go all out for a regular pay check, and invest when you can. Use your great intuition in these matters.

Parenthood

Do not let Libran indecision and Taurean possessiveness encroach on your relationship with your children. You will work hard for them, but you could be rather conservative in your attitude to their opinions and concerns. Make a conscious effort to understand their problems and you will avoid the generation gap. You will certainly give your children a good, secure background and will be kind and thoughtful. You must, however, remember to have fun, too.

THE MOON IN
GEMINI

BOTH LIBRA AND GEMINI ARE AIR SIGNS, SO IN ADDITION
TO BEING SYMPATHETIC AND CHARMING, YOU ARE A
GOOD COMMUNICATOR. BE CAREFUL, HOWEVER, THAT
YOU DO NOT SUPPRESS YOUR DEEPER EMOTIONS.

The air element forms a large part of your personality. You have a lightness about you; a certain breezy but logical approach to problems. When challenged, you will always have flip, off-the-cuff verbal responses on hand.

Self-expression
You find conversation and social intercourse even more rewarding and entertaining than most Sun sign Librans and may well make a real hobby of entertaining your friends.

To prevent Geminian restlessness, try to develop a compelling and rewarding interest. Take care that you do not simply glide over the surface of important problems because you do not wish to get too involved.

Romance
Your love of romance will be very well expressed verbally, and to a certain extent you need a high level of

friendship within an emotional relationship. While you are as romantic as any Libran, you may not be able to allow your deepest feelings to flow as freely as would be ideal.

Aim for partners who will be intellectually challenging to live with, so that your extremely lively mind will be kept active.

Your well-being
The Geminian body area covers the arms and hands, and yours may be somewhat vulnerable to accidents. The Geminian organ is the lungs, and anyone with this sign emphasized should try not to smoke.

Usually, Moon sign Geminians tend to be restless, but you should suffer less than most in this respect because of your Libran Sun. You may well enjoy exercise more than most Sun sign Librans, and this could take the form of tennis, badminton, or some other fast game. Because you

The Moon in Gemini

probably have a higher metabolic rate than many Librans, and may not have the typical taste for sweet food, you are less likely to incur excessive weight gain.

Planning ahead
As far as coping with money is concerned, you may not be terribly practical. You love luxury and are generous, but money could very easily burn a hole in your pocket, and you may be attracted to get-rich-quick schemes. Take professional financial advice in this area, and make sure that you never lay out more money than you can afford to lose.

Parenthood
You have a modern outlook, of which your children will no doubt thoroughly approve. Keeping up with their opinions and concerns will therefore be no problem for you. Provided you are firm and decisive, so that your children know where they stand, you will have no problems with the generation gap.

THE MOON IN
CANCER

YOU ARE VERY GOOD AT LISTENING TO PEOPLE, BUT COULD
THROW YOUR SYSTEM OUT OF BALANCE BY TAKING ON
OTHERS' BURDENS. WATCH OUT FOR STRESS, AND BE AWARE
THAT YOU MAY BENEFIT FROM PHYSICAL EXERCISE.

Both Libra and Cancer are of the cardinal quality, which means that you have the ability to sympathize and empathize with others, and will give of yourself to help and comfort them. Your instinct is to protect and care for your family and friends, and you do more than your fair share to help people feel good. Do not burn yourself out, emotionally or intellectually.

Self-expression
In spite of having a great deal of inner strength, you can be very easily hurt. Although you can be extremely kind, you can sometimes express yourself rather sharply, and say things that insult others. Be aware of this. It would be a pity to let such a negative trait mar your finer qualities.

You are probably very prone to worry – far more, in fact, than most Librans. You do, however, have very powerful instincts, and can use them to counter this problem. If you feel that you should take a certain line of action, go ahead and do so.

Romance
You are a wonderfully romantic and sensual lover, and should enjoy a rich and fulfilling sex life. Try, however, not to be overprotective of your partners. You may well create a rather claustrophobic atmosphere, which some people will find hard to cope with. Whether you are a man or a woman, you may occasionally tend to "mother" your partners.

Your well-being
The Cancerian body area covers the chest and breasts. Although there is no connection between this sign and the disease of the same name, regular checkups are always a good idea.

The Cancerian tendency to worry may have a negative effect on your health. Your food could tend to

The Moon in Cancer

disagree with you when you are worried. If you can keep this negative emotion under control, your digestion will be far less likely to suffer.

Planning ahead

Like all people of your Sun sign, you like luxury and creature comforts, but you are less extravagant than many Librans and have a natural instinct to be careful with money. You also have a shrewd business sense that will work well for you whether you have your own business or have merely collected a little spare money that you want to invest.

Parenthood

You make a wonderfully caring parent and will enjoy bringing up your children, although their natural exuberance and energy may tend to deflate you at times.

If you make a conscious effort to be decisive, and do your best to avoid sentimentality or dwelling on the past, you will have few problems with the generation gap. You must try not to get too upset when your children leave home to build their own lives. Rather than moping, take the opportunity to become involved in some new interests.

THE MOON IN
LEO

YOU LIKE EVERYTHING THAT IS EXPENSIVE. YOU ARE ALSO WARM,
SYMPATHETIC, BIG-HEARTED, AND GENEROUS, BUT IF YOU
ACT ON YOUR IMAGINATIVE IDEAS WITHOUT SERIOUSLY COUNTING
THE COST, YOU COULD GET INTO TROUBLE.

The combination of Libra and Leo is a good one. It makes your outlook very positive and optimistic. Much more so than many of your Sun sign compatriots, you will "think big" and be magnanimous.

Self-expression

Anyone with an emphasis on Leo has creative potential and, while this is not always expressed through the fine arts, it is nevertheless present. It is important to your sense of inner fulfillment that some form of creativity play a part in your life.

You are an excellent organizer and can readily take over in a crisis. You should enjoy work that gives you the chance to show off a little and, if Libran diplomacy is combined with Leo warmth, you can probably cope well with people and their problems.

Your Leo Moon gives you a sense of drama, but be careful not to overstep the mark. Do not make a

dramatic scene over something trivial that displeases or upsets you. Calm authority is more effective.

Romance

You have a wealth of positive emotion to express toward your partners, and you want to feel proud of them.

Beware of the tendency to fall in love with love. You can be very easily hurt and, when you are, you will retire to a private lair to lick your wounds.

Your well-being

The Leo body area covers the spine and back. You must therefore make sure that you always sit correctly. A support chair is advisable for desk workers, and back-strengthening exercises are good for anyone with this emphasis.

The Leo organ is the heart, and it must be kept well toned. Therefore take regular exercise; dancing is excellent if you hate the thought of

The Moon in Leo

sports or health clubs.

Both Libra and Leo like to live the good life. This all too often means lots of rich food and, in turn, a weight problem. Try to ration the sauces and elaborate desserts.

Planning ahead

You are more than likely to be both very generous and very extravagant. It should therefore come as no surprise for you to realize that you will consequently need to earn a lot of money in order to support such habits. Quality is also important to you, so at least the things that you buy will last a long time. You could tend to over invest at times, and you may benefit from professional advice.

Parenthood

You will probably be an enthusiastic and very encouraging parent, and will be constantly delighted with your children's efforts. Spurred on by your encouragement, they will want to do even more to please you.

Be careful that you do not to change your mind too often, once you have told your children something. It is extremely important for them to know where they stand with you.

THE MOON IN
VIRGO

YOUR MOON SIGN CAN CAUSE YOU TO BE MORE SPONTANEOUSLY
AND HARSHLY CRITICAL OF OTHERS THAN YOU MAY
REALIZE. WHILE IT MAKES YOU PRACTICAL, IT CAN ALSO MAR
SOME FINE LIBRAN QUALITIES.

You may express your Libran loving-kindness very well, but you will, under some circumstances, also respond in a very critical manner. Perhaps you should try to be a little more tactful and diplomatic.

Self-expression

Your Virgoan Moon certainly gives you a lot more energy than many Sun sign Librans, and you are unlikely to waste much time.

Your initial reaction to a difficult situation may be to worry about it. Very soon, however, your attitude will take a turn toward being much more relaxed and philosophical.

You can use your Virgoan Moon to help you overcome Libran indecision. You could, for instance, analyze problems by making comprehensive lists of their positive and negative aspects, and then considering them in as detached, logical, and unemotional fashion as you are able.

Romance

Although you will certainly work very hard for your partners, and give them excellent backup, you may not find it easy to unlock your emotions and really relax. Although you are as romantic as anyone of your Sun sign, it may not be easy for you to enjoy love and sex wholeheartedly. Be very careful not to overcriticize your partner or to nag.

Your well-being

The Virgoan body area is the stomach, and it is possible that this reacts very quickly to the least worry or concern. You probably need a high-fiber diet.

Many people with this combination of signs have a fast metabolism; in these cases the tendency to put on weight is minimized. If you do move rather slowly, be careful not to eat too much heavy food. Conversely, if you are working very hard, try to make sure that you have a well-balanced

The Moon in Virgo

diet, and do not eat too much junk food. Aim for a fairly light diet that contains salads and fresh fruit.

Like many people with a Virgoan emphasis, you may be a vegetarian. If this is the case, make certain that your vitamin intake is adequate.

Planning ahead

You love your Libran luxuries, but will not waste money and will generally have enough for your needs. Making investments could, however, be rather boring for you, so keep them simple and take professional advice if you wish to invest a large sum of cash.

Parenthood

As a parent you are kind and generous, but you must watch a tendency to sometimes speak to your children rather harshly.

You are a good communicator and find it easy to get your ideas across. Listen to your children, and you will avoid generation gap problems.

THE MOON IN
LIBRA

BOTH THE SUN AND THE MOON WERE IN LIBRA AT THE TIME OF
YOUR BIRTH, AND YOU WERE THEREFORE BORN UNDER A NEW
MOON. YOU HAVE MANY LIBRAN CHARACTERISTICS AND RESPOND
TO MOST SITUATIONS IN A BALANCED AND HARMONIOUS WAY.

Should you read a list of the characteristics of your Libran Sun sign, you will probably realize that a great many of them apply to you. On average, out of a list of around 20 personality traits attributed to a sign, most people accept 11 or 12. For you the average will be much higher, since both the Sun and the Moon were in Libra when you were born.

Self-expression
You need to lead a well-balanced, harmonious life, and find quarrels very upsetting.

You always respond to situations by first considering the other people involved, and never give priority to your own considerations or opinions. This can make you very indecisive and, at times, you may well avoid a commitment simply by mulling over a situation for so long that a decision becomes unnecessary. You are very diplomatic, and respond kindly and

affectionately to people around you. They will love you for your natural charm and delightful personality.

Romance
Your need to relate to another person is instinctive and runs very deep. You will be psychologically whole only when settled in a permanent relationship or marriage. It is in this area that Libran indecision can totally desert you, and you can very easily rush prematurely into a relationship just because you feel that you need one badly. A degree of objectivity could well save a lot of heartache.

Your well-being
Everything that has been said about Libran health on pages 322 – 323 will probably apply to you. You must keep your whole system balanced with steady exercise, and should refrain from overindulgence in food or drink. Your thoughts and emotions must

The Moon in Libra

remain at one, and you should try to avoid arguments. Learn to have your say calmly and effectively.

Planning ahead

Your creature comforts are important to you, and you will spend a lot of money on them.

You are inclined to be naturally generous and may not be terribly practical when it comes to handling money. You will probably do well to consult a professional adviser if you have money to invest.

Parenthood

You will enjoy a warm, affectionate rapport with your children and will be very kind to them. Force yourself to be decisive, and do not spoil your children for the sake of peace and quiet. They need a constructive framework and fair discipline. If you make sure that your children know where they stand with you, you will be an excellent parent.

As long as you remain interested in your children's ideas and concerns, you will bridge the generation gap.

THE MOON IN
SCORPIO

YOU RESPOND TO MOST SITUATIONS WITH GREATER EMOTIONAL
FERVOR AND INTENSITY THAN MANY LIBRANS, AND YOU
HAVE IT IN YOU TO TAKE STRONG, DECISIVE ACTION. DO NOT
SUPPRESS THIS QUALITY; LISTEN TO YOUR INTUITION.

Your Scorpio Moon gives you more determination and a stronger sense of purpose than many Sun sign Librans. You have a powerfully inquiring mind and, when challenged, strong forces immediately come into play in order to help you combat opposition.

Self-expression
Your opponents will get as good, or better, as they give, but it is important that you do not later backtrack and overapologize to them. This can upset the status quo, and lead to disruption and even quarrels, which your Libran Sun sign positively hates.

You must also aim to be emotionally involved in your work. An "ordinary" job, or drifting from one job to the next in an aimless fashion, will not do at all. Go all out for what you want to do, and do not let Libran hesitancy or indecision bog you down. You have powerful reserves of emotional energy and the ability to express them very positively through your chosen career or some other compelling interest.

Romance
You will be a demanding partner, but one who contributes greatly to a relationship. Like all Librans, you are a romantic, but you are far more passionate and highly sexed than many people of your Sun sign.

The worst Scorpio fault is jealousy. Be very careful, as you could become a victim of this very negative emotional expression.

Your well-being
The Scorpio body area is the genitals, and both men and women should pay attention to the health of that area.

You may have a tendency to bottle up your problems. When worried, make sure that you unburden yourself to a sympathetic friend.

The Moon in Scorpio

Planning ahead

Your Scorpio Moon is beneficial to you when it comes to dealing with money. It is likely to make you a shrewd and clever investor.

Anyone with a strong Scorpio influence will, however, want to both get a lot out of life and put a lot into it. This usually means resorting to heavy spending. Therefore look for savings schemes that make your money grow and work for you. You are clever enough not to make many mistakes, even if you do not take professional advice, but you may well need to curb extravagance.

Parenthood

You will have strong views about bringing up your children, but your more placid, Libran qualities could persuade you to spoil them.

Make sure that you keep up with your children's opinions and concerns. Otherwise you may encounter problems with the generation gap.

THE MOON IN
SAGITTARIUS

YOU ARE EASYGOING AND HAVE MUCH INTELLECTUAL POTENTIAL.
TO MAKE IT WORK FOR YOU, YOU SHOULD KEEP MOVING,
BOTH PHYSICALLY AND MENTALLY. DO NOT IMMEDIATELY BRUSH
ASIDE OTHER PEOPLE'S SUGGESTIONS.

The two elements of your Sun and Moon signs, air and fire, respectively, will work to your benefit. You will always have a very positive and philosophical outlook on life, and will not, on the whole, be plagued by worry or tension.

Self-expression

You like to be challenged and, upon encountering difficult situations or problems, you are always optimistic about their outcome. Your Moon sign gives you a very natural, instinctive optimism that harmonizes extremely well with your Libran qualities, but be careful not to be too laid back.

You may have a natural flair for study and could actually need this particular kind of challenge.

Romance

You have very lively and fiery emotions, and are capable of a marvelously exuberant enjoyment of love and sex. You may not always take this sphere of your life very seriously and, unlike many people of your Sun sign, you will have a strong need for independence within a relationship. As a result, you will be far less likely to rush into a commitment, in spite of all your buoyant enthusiasm. You also have something of a roving eye, and should remember that this is not necessarily a very good thing, especially in relation to love.

Your well-being

The Sagittarian body areas are the hips and thighs, and women with this sign emphasized may put on weight easily in these areas. You need more exercise than most Librans, and will perhaps enjoy the challenge of keeping fit. Maintain a steady exercise routine.

The Sagittarian organ is the liver, and anyone with a Libra and Sagittarius combination will enjoy

The Moon in Sagittarius

their food. Therefore be careful, since you are no doubt very prone to overeating and hangovers.

Planning ahead

Your Sagittarian Moon gives you a powerful gambling instinct, so beware of casinos and racetracks.

You may also be very attracted to investments that make promises of high returns on your capital. Control your enthusiasm, or you could well lose out. The same applies when a get-rich-quick scheme is put to you. Develop skepticism and always seek professional advice.

You are very generous, but should remember that it is better to give someone a few dollars than to lend them a lot, since the chances are that you will not see your money again.

Parenthood

Your Sagittarian Moon will make it easy for you to encourage your children in all their interests and studies. You will enjoy their company, and there will be an element of fun in your relationship. You will not find it difficult to keep up with your children's views and opinions, and will thus avoid the generation gap.

THE MOON IN
CAPRICORN

YOU HAVE AN INNER DESIRE TO REACH THE TOP, BOTH SOCIALLY AND IN YOUR CAREER. TRY NOT TO SHOW OFF. ALLOW YOUR PRACTICAL, EARTHY MOON SIGN INSTINCTS TO STEADY YOU AND KEEP YOUR PERSONALITY IN BALANCE.

Both Libra and Capricorn are of the cardinal quality and, as a result, you may use your energies to encourage others. You will respond practically to their problems, and will cope extremely well in emergencies.

Self-expression
You may take life more seriously than many Librans. Some of the time you will feel positive and optimistic; at other times you may succumb to negative feelings.

You are probably very ambitious and a hard worker, even if you give the impression of being relaxed. You will pack a lot into the working day and, with persistence of effort, will achieve a great deal.

Romance
Libra is a warm, romantic sign, while Capricorn is rather unemotional and cool. You cope well with solitude; better, in fact, than most Librans.

When you share your life with a partner, you may need to spend some time alone.

Once committed to a partner you will be faithful, but may be a little grudging in expressing your affections. Allow your Libran Sun to counter this tendency, and relax.

Your well-being
The Capricornian body area covers the knees and shins, which are therefore vulnerable.

The skin and teeth are also ruled by Capricorn. Your skin may be more sensitive to the sun than most people's, so wear a protective cream in summer. Do not neglect your regular dental checkups, either.

You may be less attracted to sweet food than many Librans and will therefore be less prone to weight gain. A tendency to incur stiffness of the joints means that you will probably benefit from exercise.

The Moon in Capricorn

Planning ahead

You are likely to be more careful when it comes to handling money than many Librans, and will no doubt tend to opt for quality in what you buy. You may spend a lot of money on impressing other people, perhaps by entertaining them lavishly.

Social climbing may be something of a hobby with you. This is fine, but it could cost you dearly and will not always have the desired effect. You will invest wisely and probably have a sensible attitude to finance in general.

Concentrate on maintaining steady growth from sound, even unadventurous, investments.

Parenthood

Although you are in many ways warm and affectionate, there will be periods when you may not have time for your children. You could find it difficult to keep up with their ideas, perhaps because you are rather conventional in outlook. Try to counter this tendency, or it could well cause generation gap problems.

THE MOON IN
AQUARIUS

BOTH LIBRA AND AQUARIUS ARE AIR SIGNS. TOGETHER THEY GIVE YOU ORIGINALITY AND CHARM. YOU MAY, HOWEVER, NEED TO DEVELOP A MORE PRACTICAL AND SERIOUS APPROACH TO SOME SPHERES OF LIFE.

There is a delightful friendly and lighthearted area of your personality that immediately rises to the surface whenever you come into contact with other people.

Self-expression

Your manner is open and positive, and you are very gregarious. More than most Librans, you possess an independent streak which ensures that you do things in your own way. You have a great deal of individuality, which may be expressed creatively.

Surprisingly, you could sometimes react to situations rather stubbornly and can be very unpredictable. Try to control these tendencies, for while they can be amusing, they can also cause disruption and annoyance.

Romance

Libra and Aquarius are the two signs with the greatest inclination for real romance. Your Aquarian Moon will contribute glamour, but will also cool the emotions. You are attractive to the opposite sex, but may tend to keep people at a distance. In doing so, you will be expressing Aquarian independence, but also acting against your Libran need to relate. You need a partner who understands these areas of your personality, and who will encourage you to express your emotions freely.

Your well-being

The Aquarian body area is the ankles. You may find yourself turning your ankle all too often, which will cause you considerable discomfort.

Aquarius also rules the circulation, and you may well feel the cold very badly. Conversely, you may suffer when it is hot. Exercise is necessary to keep your circulation in good order. You could get bored with many forms of it, but should enjoy tennis, dance, or winter sports. You could

The Moon in Aquarius

participate in a variety of physical activities, changing them according to the different seasons.

Planning ahead
You have an eye for beautiful things and may end up spending a lot of money on them. Do, however, choose carefully. Many things increase in value and therefore make good investments; others lose their value. Because you are attracted to the unusual and glamorous, you could invest your funds unwisely. Always obtain financial advice when you have money to put aside, and try to save regularly.

Parenthood
You should not suffer from the generation gap as your children grow up, because you are always attracted to the new. Do, however, make a solid effort to curb unpredictability, since it is vital that your children know where they stand in relation to you.

THE MOON IN
PISCES

YOUR RESPONSE TO DIFFICULT SITUATIONS MAY BE TO TAKE THE
PATH OF LEAST RESISTANCE. DOING SO COULD, HOWEVER,
HURT OTHERS FAR MORE THAN YOU REALIZE, THEREBY UPSETTING
YOUR PRIZED HARMONIOUS LIFESTYLE.

The combination of your Sun and Moon signs makes you an extremely kind, gentle, and magnanimous person.

Self-expression

Without hesitating, you will offer help as soon as you see that it is needed and will often inconvenience yourself in order to do so. You must try to distance yourself from emotional and psychological involvement in such cases, while at the same time retaining your sympathetic and understanding rapport.

You may need to develop a sense of purpose and greater determination if you have an inclination to drift. The real reason for this tendency may be a certain lack of self-confidence.

Romance

You have a high emotional level that you will be able to express in your relationships. You will make a wonderfully caring partner, but may become a far too willing slave. Remember that partnership is about sharing. Keep your balance, and try to develop a relationship with someone who will be strong enough to lean on, but who will also recognize your talents, encourage your efforts, and help you to organize your life.

Your well-being

The Piscean body area is the feet. Your feet are therefore vulnerable to blisters, corns, and other ailments.

You are also sensitive to prevailing atmospheres. Bad ones could cause stomach upsets, as will worry, to which you may be more susceptible than many Sun sign Librans.

Planning ahead

You really are a soft touch where money is concerned. You need someone to control your finances with a rod of iron; otherwise you may end

The Moon in Pisces

up being too generous. There are, however, certain things that you can do for yourself. You can take part in a savings plan in which the contributions are taken out of your paycheck. You would be wise never to lend money and should try not to give too much of it away.

Your artistic and creative potential could well prove to be exceptionally lucrative. You should, however, concentrate on producing the raw product, and leave the difficult and specialized task of balancing the books to someone who is much more proficient at it than you.

Parenthood

As a parent, you may tend to spoil your children badly when they are young. This could be partly to buy yourself peace and quiet. Be decisive, and do not keep changing your mind when your children need direction from you. It is important for them to know where they stand with you.

You will not find it too difficult to enjoy your children's interests, and as a result you should not incur problems with the generation gap. However, never let your children twist you around their little fingers, as they will certainly try to do.

SUN & MOON SIGNS

SCORPIO

OCTOBER 24 – NOVEMBER 22

INTRODUCING
SCORPIO

SCORPIO, THE EIGHTH SIGN OF THE ZODIAC, IS A SIGN OF THE WATER ELEMENT. IT BESTOWS ON ITS SUBJECTS DEEP, PENETRATING, AND INTENSE PERSONALITIES, AND GIVES THEM GREAT RESOURCES OF EMOTIONAL AND PHYSICAL ENERGY.

The qualities of Scorpio must be channeled positively to prevent jealousy and resentfulness from leading to inner dissatisfaction that can badly mar its subjects' characters.

Scorpio has the reputation for being the sexiest of the 12 Zodiac signs. Like most popular astrological beliefs, this is often unjustified. Scorpios need sexual fulfillment, but their energy can be expressed in many other ways.

Pluto, the sign's ruling planet, underlines a characteristic sense of purpose. For Scorpios to be psychologically fulfilled, every single day must have its own full and demanding schedule.

Traditional groupings
As you read through this book you will come across references to the elements and the qualities, and to positive and negative, or masculine and feminine signs. The first grouping, the elements, comprises

fire, earth, air, and water signs. The second, the qualities, divides the Zodiac into cardinal, fixed, and mutable signs. The final grouping consists of positive and negative, or masculine and feminine signs. Each Zodiac sign is associated with a combination of components from these groupings, all of which add different characteristics to it.

Scorpio characteristics
The sign is of the fixed quality, which indicates stubbornness – something of a contradiction in terms when one thinks of the ebb and flow of water, the Scorpio element. The sign is also feminine and negative, which signifies introversion. There is a traditional association between Scorpio and dramatic deep shades of red and maroon.

Scorpios often have incisive minds, and sometimes a great desire to get to the bottom of every problem.

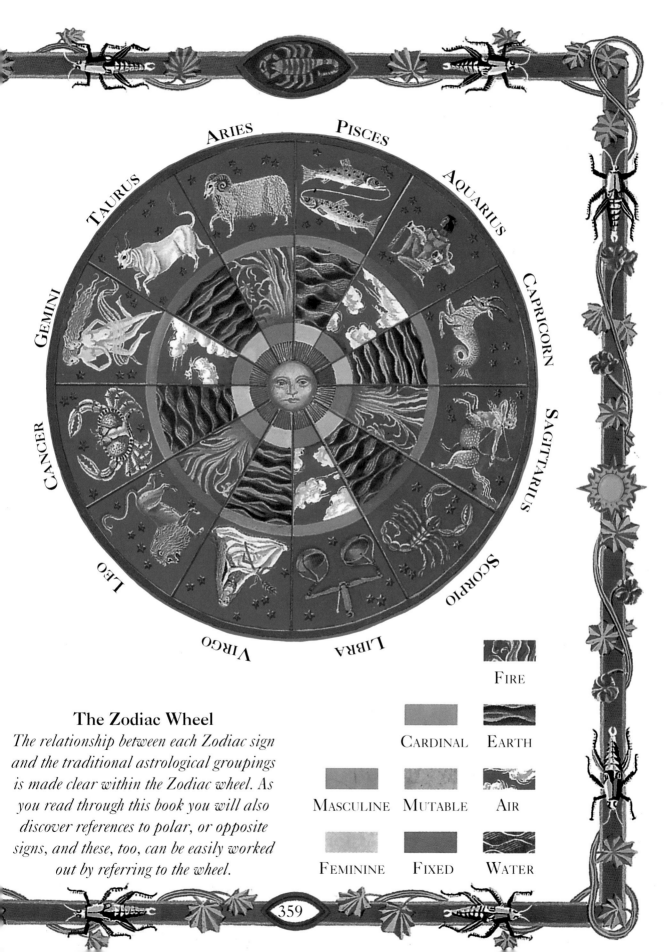

The Zodiac Wheel is shown with the twelve signs arranged around a central sun:

ARIES · PISCES · AQUARIUS · CAPRICORN · SAGITTARIUS · SCORPIO · LIBRA · VIRGO · LEO · CANCER · GEMINI · TAURUS

The Zodiac Wheel

The relationship between each Zodiac sign and the traditional astrological groupings is made clear within the Zodiac wheel. As you read through this book you will also discover references to polar, or opposite signs, and these, too, can be easily worked out by referring to the wheel.

FIRE

CARDINAL · EARTH

MASCULINE · MUTABLE · AIR

FEMININE · FIXED · WATER

SCORPIO
MYTHS & LEGENDS

THE ZODIAC, WHICH IS SAID TO HAVE ORIGINATED IN BABYLON AS LONG AS 2,500 YEARS AGO, IS A CIRCLE OF CONSTELLATIONS THROUGH WHICH THE SUN MOVES DURING THE COURSE OF A YEAR.

Fairly often, it takes a very great leap of the imagination to see any definite likeness between the "shape" of some constellations and the 12 different Zodiac symbols that have come to be associated with them. A case does, perhaps, exist for saying that the constellation of Scorpio has a tail that resembles a scorpion's. In the case of Scorpio, however, the obscure link between its Zodiac symbol and the pattern in the stars that constitutes the Scorpio constellation is quite hard to explain.

Evidence suggests that the Scorpio symbol initially had no link with a constellation. A scorpion-man, apparently not based on any group of stars, appears as a fully developed

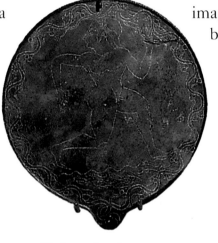

Orion the hunter
This image, cut into the back of an Etruscan mirror, shows Orion crossing the sea.

image on many Babylonian boundary stones. On the majority of these boundary stones, he is depicted with a scorpion's tail, and drawing a bow, as though he were a combination of the figures for Scorpio and Sagittarius, the Archer. This scorpion figure appeared in Babylon at least 1,000 years before he finally took his place in the Egyptian Zodiacs that were created in the ancient cities of Denderah and Esna, as the image we know today.

Orion and Eos
Manilius, the Roman writer who, in the first century B.C. set down several astrological myths, suggested that the original scorpion was

connected with Orion. A Greek giant (it was said that his stature was so great that he could walk on the bottom of the sea without getting his head wet), hunter, and the handsomest man alive, he was by no means impervious to female charms.

When the dawn-goddess Eos, an inveterate collector of handsome young men, invited him to bed, he happily accepted the invitation. But Orion bragged of the conquest and also boasted that he was so great a hunter that he would exterminate all of the wild beasts.

The God Apollo, responsible for guarding herds, therefore persuaded Gaia, the Earth goddess, to send a giant scorpion with impenetrable armor to sting him to death.

Artemis's mistake

Some variations of this myth say that it succeeded, others that Orion tried to escape by swimming out to sea, only to be accidentally shot by Artemis, the goddess of the hunt and Apollo's sister. Artemis, who, unsurprisingly, was very attracted to Orion, actually fired her arrow in an attempt to kill the scorpion that was molesting him. Being a magnificent shot, she struck the black head that she saw bobbing in the water with her

The goddess Artemis
This gold plaque, dating from the seventh century B.C., shows Artemis in her role as goddess of the animals.

first arrow. Tragically, however, her target turned out to be Orion's head, rather than the scorpion, and the hunter died instantly.

According to this latter version of the story, the grief-stricken Artemis then placed Orion as a constellation among the stars, where he is eternally pursued by the giant scorpion. The constellation of Orion, incidentally, sets in the sky just as the constellation of Scorpio rises.

SCORPIO
SYMBOLISM

CERTAIN HERBS, SPICES, FLOWERS, TREES, GEMS, METALS, AND
ANIMALS HAVE LONG BEEN ASSOCIATED WITH PARTICULAR
ZODIAC SIGNS. SOME ASSOCIATIONS ARE SIMPLY AMUSING, WHILE
OTHERS CAN BE USEFUL.

WILD
THISTLE

Flowers

*Those flowers ruled by Aries, like the
spiky thistle, and most dark red
flowers, such as some geraniums,
are governed by Scorpio.*

GERANIUMS

Trees

The blackthorn has always been associated with Scorpio, but so are all bushy trees, such as the hawthorn, and trees that are used for hedging, like the macrocarpa.

HAWTHORN

Spices

No spices are specifically linked with Scorpio, but red or hot spices such as cayenne pepper, paprika, and chili are sometimes associated with the sign.

PAPRIKA

Herbs

Scorpio rules the same herbs as Aries, such as peppermint. It is most strongly associated with herbs that have very dark red flowers. These include figwort, which quells itching, and dovesfoot, which is good for colic and for expelling kidney stones.

PEPPERMINT

CHILI

SCORPIO
SYMBOLISM

RAW IRON

CUT STEEL
BROOCH

SCORPION

STEEL DOUBLE-
AX BROOCH

JAMESI SCARAB

WEST AFRICAN
SCARAB

STEEL BRACELET

Metal
*The Scorpio metal is
traditionally said to be
either steel or iron.*

AMBER JEWELRY

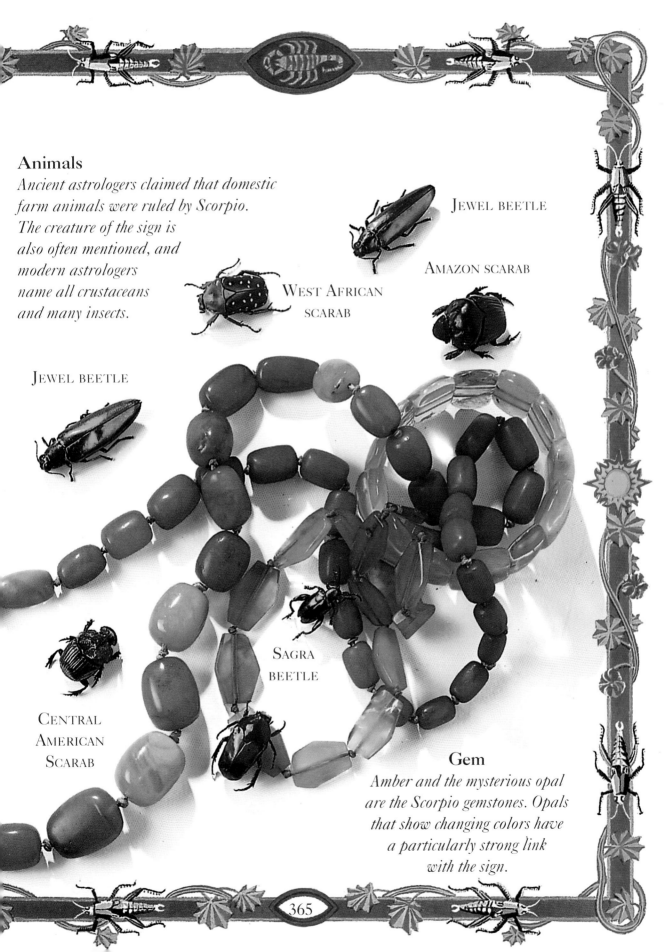

Animals

Ancient astrologers claimed that domestic farm animals were ruled by Scorpio. The creature of the sign is also often mentioned, and modern astrologers name all crustaceans and many insects.

JEWEL BEETLE

AMAZON SCARAB

WEST AFRICAN SCARAB

JEWEL BEETLE

SAGRA BEETLE

CENTRAL AMERICAN SCARAB

Gem

Amber and the mysterious opal are the Scorpio gemstones. Opals that show changing colors have a particularly strong link with the sign.

SCORPIO
PROFILE

THE INTENSITY OF THE SCORPIO PERSONALITY IS USUALLY VISIBLE IN THE INDIVIDUAL'S APPEARANCE AND EXPRESSION. SHARP-EYED, THEY DO NOT MISS A THING, AND ARE THE NATURAL DETECTIVES OF THE ZODIAC.

Your determination is usually evident in your stance. You stand with your head jutting forward in a sleuth-like manner, as though you are peering through some fascinating keyhole.

The Scorpio face
An obvious characteristic of the Scorpio face is an intent and piercing gaze.

The body
There are two distinct Scorpio body types. The first is heavy, giving the impression of a certain world-weariness, as if the individual has been around for a long time, and enjoyed every minute of it. The other is very lean and wiry, probably as a result of slogging it out in a health club, and burning up all that Scorpio energy. In general, Scorpios are rarely above medium height, and some can be rather short. Female Scorpios can become very buxom if they gain weight, but they rarely lose their figures or become any less active. They tend to swing their hips as they walk.

The face
A typical Scorpio has a fairly large forehead, and deep-set, piercing eyes. Comparisons are often drawn with the eagle, a bird that is connected with this sign. The chin is usually well formed, unless the individual is overweight, and the mouth is often extremely sensual and full lipped. A typical Scorpio will have somewhat large ears, high cheek-bones, a full neck, and a wide, strong jaw. Many Scorpios have strong, but often rather coarse hair.

The Scorpio stance
You probably possess a determined stance that has your head jutting forward as if peering through a keyhole.

Style
Leather and the color black are popular among Scorpios, even when they are not particularly fashionable. You will probably favor an image that enhances sexiness, and if this is not overdone it works well. Many Scorpios like wearing tight jeans, leather trousers, and severely plunging necklines; not everyone is suited to each of these.

The texture of your clothing may be very important to you. Scorpios usually like the smoothness of satin and pure silk. Velvet is also popular. Any sharp, or remotely coarse material, such as wool, will probably hold no appeal for you.

On formal occasions Scorpios usually look extremely smart in somewhat severe clothes. You will not submerge your personality by dressing conventionally. All that has to be done is for you to study how to make fashion work for you. You will instinctively want to exploit your own personal image as far as you possibly can, and there is no reason why you should not do so.

In general
Many Zodiac types consciously or unconsciously tend to aspire to the image of their sign, and in Scorpios this can be very much the case. This can be amusing, but it may also be overdone at times. Sun sign Scorpios like a sense of mystery, and in extreme cases the women can be femmes fatales. Keep a sense of humor and all will be well.

SCORPIO
PERSONALITY

YOU ARE LIKELY TO HAVE A STRIKING, INTENSE PERSONALITY, AND THE POTENTIAL TO BE A GREAT ACHIEVER. IF, HOWEVER, THIS POTENTIAL IS NOT FULLY EXPRESSED, YOU CAN BECOME NEGATIVE IN OUTLOOK.

Having a strong, passionate belief in whatever you do will lead to a full expression of the remarkable resources of both physical and emotional energy that you possess, which are characteristic of all Scorpios.

At work
It must be said that Scorpios with no clear objective in life, who are uninvolved in their work or in any other activity worthwhile for them, can be difficult, uncooperative, stubborn, and impervious to reason. In all, they will be a complete pain to the people around them.

It is worth remembering that while Pluto, Scorpio's ruling planet, can enable its subjects to overcome obstacles, it can also encourage a host of negative tendencies, for instance slyness, cruelty, and an urge to be somewhat overly critical. These negative characteristics, which can sometimes constitute a fairly

considerable force, may make Scorpios illogically jealous of other people's achievements, especially their partners'. It may even come to the point where they will start to act in an underhanded and vindictive fashion, even scheming toward their rivals' downfall, and often giving way to outbursts of unpleasant, illogical rage when others offer help or advice.

Your attitudes
When all is well with you, however, you will know exactly what it is that you want to do in life, and will certainly see to it that whatever this is gets done. When it is properly fulfilled, this powerful and demanding motivation will lead to your finding that vital sense of inner satisfaction upon which so much of life can rest. The urge to move ambitiously forward will then follow from it, encouraging you to better and greater achievements. You will no

Pluto rules Scorpio

Pluto, god of the underworld, represents the ruling planet of Scorpio.
The influence of Pluto can encourage its subjects to overcome obstacles,
but may also make them critical, cruel, and secretive.

doubt value your friends highly and are likely to strive very hard in order to make your relationships work.

The overall picture
Scorpios tend to fling themselves straight into projects, whether these involve starting a business venture or embarking on demanding intellectual study. You will probably work very hard on any project for some time and achieve many of the goals that you set for yourself. Then, for no apparent reason, you will give up the whole venture and start again from the bottom of another hill.

Having said all of this, for the most part, Scorpios enjoy life, living it to the full and encouraging their friends and loved ones to do the same.

SCORPIO
ASPIRATIONS

YOU ARE HAPPY DOING HARD WORK, PERHAPS INVOLVING DETAILED RESEARCH, BUT NEED TO BE REALLY INVOLVED WITH THE TASK AT HAND. A GOOD BUSINESS SENSE SHOULD HELP YOU MAKE MONEY, AND YOU WILL ENJOY ORGANIZATIONAL WORK.

BOTTLE STOPPERS AND CORKS

The wine trade
The Scorpio love of food and wine means that you could obtain a great deal of satisfaction from working in the wine trade.

POLICEMAN'S HANDCUFFS AND NIGHTSTICK

Police work
A career on the police force, especially as a detective, could prove to be an excellent choice for you. Scorpios will love searching for the facts of a crime.

1930s MINING AND ENGINEERING CIGARETTE CARDS

RIFLE BULLETS

Mining and engineering

Many Scorpios enjoy examining the Earth's resources. An interest in ecology often persuades them to discover positive ways of exploiting them.

The armed forces

Scorpio is a water sign, and many of its subjects join the navy. The army may, however, also prove attractive. Many famous generals share a Scorpio Sun sign.

CLAY PIGGY BANK AND BANK NOTES

Banking

A fascination for making money and seeing it grow can lead to careers in banking and the stock exchange.

HEALTH

THE SCORPIO BODY AREA IS THE GENITALS, AND IT IS THIS RELATIONSHIP THAT HAS GIVEN THE SIGN ITS OFTEN UNJUSTIFIED REPUTATION FOR OVERT SEXINESS. MANY OTHER FACTORS SHAPE THE SCORPIO CHARACTER.

Scorpio can, in a number of ways, be considered the most powerful sign of the Zodiac. Its subjects are often fortunate enough to possess tremendous resources of both physical and emotional energy. In order for you to be both psychologically whole and in the best physical shape, you must be prepared to shape your life in such a way that both of these areas manage to find some form of positive expression.

Tomatoes
The foods ruled by Aries, like tomatoes, are also associated with Scorpio.

Your diet
For most Scorpios, food is something that has to be enjoyed. You may, for instance, like a lot of rich food and wine, and dieting may prove to be difficult. You might benefit from supplementing your diet with the cell salt kali muriaticum (Kali. Mur.).

Taking care
When lacking any real objective in life, or suffering from a lack of physical exercise, a Sun sign Scorpio will become discontented, depressed, and unwell. Brooding on the situation is only likely to make matters worse. All Scorpios must realize that they need demanding projects in life, of both an intellectual and physical nature. You require goals toward which you can aim and direct your abundance of energy, and if all is well you will achieve them.

Astrology and the body

For many centuries it was impossible to practice medicine without a knowledge of astrology. In European universities, medical training included information on how planetary positions would affect the administration of medicines, the bleeding of patients, and the right time to pick herbs and make potions. Each Zodiac sign rules a particular part of the body, and early medical textbooks always included a drawing that illustrated the point.

SCORPIO AT
LEISURE

Each of the Sun signs traditionally suggests spare-time activities, hobbies, and vacation spots. Although these are only suggestions, they reflect Scorpio's tastes and interests.

Postage stamps

Motor racing
The speed and great risk involved in fast motorcycling and driving can prove compulsive for many Scorpios.

STANLEY WOODS

Travel
You will enjoy visiting exotic locations such as Morocco, Syria, and Uruguay. Bavaria and Norway may have appeal.

1930s cycle
racing cards

Trout-fishing fly

1920s magnifying glass

Fishing
Water sign Scorpios often love sitting on a riverbank with a fishing rod.

Detective fiction
With their inquiring minds, Scorpios will enjoy unraveling the plot of a good detective novel.

Sailing

The fact that Scorpio is a water sign could mean that you are drawn to all kinds of aquatic sports, including sailing.

SAILOR'S KNOT

HOTEL BELL

Hotel holidays

Scorpios enjoy life, so the luxury and comfort of expensive hotels with excellent facilities may well appeal to you.

Beach holidays

A beach holiday will offer you the opportunity for water sports, such as scuba diving, which are usually enjoyed by Scorpios.

RED ROSE

SEASHELLS AND SAND

Seduction

Scorpios take their love and sex lives very seriously, but there is no doubt that seduction can become a hobby for some of you.

SCORPIO IN
LOVE

THE PASSIONATE EMOTION OF SCORPIO IS AT ITS MOST POTENT IN LOVE AND IN SEXUAL RELATIONSHIPS. THE NEED FOR SEXUAL FULFILLMENT IS IMPORTANT FOR THIS ZODIAC TYPE, BUT MANY ASTROLOGICAL WRITERS TEND TO OVERSTATE IT.

You may find it difficult to unburden yourself by talking things through with a sympathetic friend, let alone your partner. Therapy may provide a solution.

Scorpios have a great capacity for true love and are therefore able to contribute much to the success of a long-term relationship. The worst Scorpio fault is jealousy, and if this occurs, it can really spoil your happiness. Being aware of this tendency can help to counter it.

As a lover

Despite the traditional emphasis on Scorpio sexuality, it is wrong to think that all members of this sign are always on the rampage, moving from one conquest to the next.

Much of a Scorpio's abundant resources of emotional and physical energy are oriented toward their sex life. However, once you have found a responsive mate, with an equal level of need, fulfillment is not hard to find. Your sexual needs will take their place in a balanced life.

Types of Scorpio lover

Scorpios are capable of expressing desire in one of at least five different ways. One group takes a somewhat clinical view of love, in extreme cases suspecting that there is something "dirty" about sex. People in this group are very discriminating, can be critical, and must be helped to relax if their inhibition is not to spoil things. A second group is romantic, with a liking for glamorous settings. Members of this group usually enjoy a slow build up to love making, and are probably eager to enter into a permanent relationship, but may be indecisive about entering a long-term commitment. Another group consists of those who may be called "pure Scorpios." These people are generally capable of loving both deeply and passionately, but must learn to guard against jealousy and emotional outbursts. A fourth group of Scorpios is lively and enthusiastic about sex, but may sometimes take it rather less seriously than other Scorpios. Finally, there are those Scorpios who are somewhat cooler in their responses than the rest. They are usually very faithful once they are committed to a partner and may end up sharing a relationship with someone who is wealthier than they are.

SCORPIO AT
HOME

SCORPIO ROOMS CAN BE ALMOST TOO COMFORTABLE. THEY MAY
HAVE A SEDUCTIVE AIR THAT WILL BE ACHIEVED THROUGH
DARK COLORS AND SUBDUED LIGHTING. THIS CHARACTERISTIC
MAY APPLY TO ALL THE ROOMS IN YOUR HOME.

Your ideal home would be placed on the edge of an idyllic lake. However, you will probably have to compromise over this, so some form of water garden, or perhaps a well, might provide a pleasant alternative. You are also likely to feel very much at home in the city. One important factor to consider might be the need for privacy that many Scorpios have. A private study could be the answer.

Furniture
There is a certain slickness in the furniture Scorpios choose and, most often, it will be covered in leather;

Stuffed alligator
An article like this will enhance the overall air of mystery that many Scorpios are attracted to.

black is popular. Comfort is important, so while settees may be bold in appearance, they will actually be soft and seductive.

You will spend a great deal of money on furnishings, and are unlikely to take risks when choosing items that will have to be lived with for a long period of time. A classic Barcelona chair is very popular, combining as it does style, tradition, and a smart, expensive elegance. Scorpios are very image conscious in their choice of furniture as well as their clothes.

Soft furnishings
The Scorpio color is basically deep crimson, which is the color of Pluto, the Scorpio ruling planet, and the overall effect of your furnishings can tend to be rather dark. It will, however, be very rich, and there will be no lack of

cushions to enhance comfort. These will often match the upholstery itself or be printed in an exotic pattern such as paisley. Dark shades of heavy satin can be popular, because texture is often important for Scorpios. Rugs will have a heavy pile, and curtains will be well lined and contribute to a somewhat seductive atmosphere.

Decorative objects

A visitor's eye will be drawn very quickly to the decorative objects that you choose. They will be very striking and will make definite statements. Your choice of paintings will be dramatic and colorful; Gauguin is often a popular choice because of his sensual colors and subject matter. You

Wine and grapes
The richnes of dark red grapes and wine boldly reflects the intensely seductive Scorpio image.

may also like surreal and imaginative paintings, or energetic and aggressive works. Young Scorpios could favor posters of hard rock bands. A bowl of luscious fruit, and perhaps some splendid wine may be in evidence – they will blend beautifully with the appearance of the overall scheme. Something in metal, such as a pot or an antique weapon, could also be present, or perhaps some decorative colored glass.

The lighting in your home is probably rather subdued. A spotlight may be used to enhance one of your favorite objects, such as vases, or an unusual antique that is dear to you.

Barcelona chair
Combining style, tradition, and expensive elegance with the texture of leather, this chair is a clear choice for the Scorpio home.

THE
MOON
AND
YOU

THE SUN DECREES YOUR OUTWARD
EXPRESSION, YOUR IMAGE, AND MANY
IMPORTANT PERSONALITY TRAITS. THE
MOON, ALTHOUGH MERELY THE EARTH'S
SATELLITE, IS ASTRONOMICALLY THE
SECOND MOST IMPORTANT BODY IN THE
SOLAR SYSTEM. FROM THE SIGN THAT IT
WAS IN AT YOUR BIRTH, IT INFLUENCES HOW
YOU REACT TO SITUATIONS, YOUR
EMOTIONAL LEVEL, AND, TO A CERTAIN
EXTENT, WHAT YOU HAVE INHERITED FROM
YOUR PARENTS AND ANCESTORS. AFTER
FINDING YOUR MOON SIGN IN THE SIMPLE
TABLES ON PAGES 606 TO 609, TURN TO THE
RELEVANT PAGES AND TAKE A STEP
FORWARD IN YOUR OWN SELF-KNOWLEDGE.

THE MOON IN
ARIES

THE FIERY EMOTIONAL ENERGY OF YOUR ARIEN MOON IS BACKED UP BY THE INTENSE ENERGY OF SCORPIO. YOU NEED BOTH PHYSICAL AND PSYCHOLOGICAL FULFILLMENT IN LIFE, AND SHOULD NEVER ALLOW YOURSELF TO STAGNATE.

Scorpio and Aries are both very powerful Zodiac signs, bestowing on their subjects a high level of emotional and physical energy. Your Scorpio intensity is heightened by your Arien sense of immediacy and instinct to be first.

Self-expression
With this Sun and Moon combination you will not be prepared to allow opponents to get the better of you. Inner fulfillment is essential to you, and your way of achieving it is to fill every day with work. Avoid time-filling jobs, or a career in which you have no real interest but pursue solely for money. If you have a job that is dull, make sure that your leisure hours are challenging and lively.

Romance
You have a high emotional level, and are very passionate. This passion will find its best expression within your relationships. You will possess a somewhat less smoldering intensity than many Sun sign Scorpios and will approach love and sex with an uncomplicated enthusiasm.

The worst Arien fault is selfishness. If anyone accuses you of this, listen to them, as they will probably be right.

Because of a tendency to act prematurely, you may feel inclined to deepen an emotional relationship too early. When this appears likely to happen, allow the critical faculties of your Scorpio Sun extra expression.

Your well-being
The Arien body area is the head, and you may therefore suffer from headaches, perhaps because of the way other people are acting. On the other hand, they may sometimes stem from slight kidney upsets. Because Aries promotes hastiness, you might be rather accident-prone and could often incur minor cuts and bruises.

The Moon in Aries

Planning ahead

Your Scorpio business sense is spiced with the Arien spirit of enterprise. Should you start a business venture, you will find it not only enjoyable, but also probably very financially rewarding. You are shrewd and capable with money, but may need to stop and think twice before investing, since you could be a little too enthusiastic about schemes that seem solid, but may in fact be hollow. If you give yourself time to think, your Scorpio shrewdness will come into its own and you will manage to avoid coming to grief.

Parenthood

You will make an energetic and lively parent and will expect a lot from your children. You will discipline them in a positive way and will not find it difficult to keep up with their concerns and opinions. This should avoid any problems with the generation gap.

THE MOON IN
TAURUS

SCORPIO AND TAURUS ARE POLAR ZODIAC SIGNS, SO YOU WERE BORN
UNDER A FULL MOON. AVOID RESTLESSNESS
BY ALLOWING YOUR PRACTICAL MOON SIGN TO STEADY YOUR
POWERFUL EMOTIONS AND CONTROL JEALOUSY.

Everyone, in one way or another, expresses elements of their polar or opposite sign: the sign that lies across the Zodiac circle from their Sun sign. For Scorpios, this is Taurus and, as the Moon was in that sign when you were born, this polarity is emphasized in an interesting way.

Self-expression
The Moon is, traditionally, "well placed" in Taurus. This means that its psychological effect on you is somewhat above average.

In order for you to develop your full potential and live life in a satisfying and rewarding way, you need great emotional and financial security. When you have it, you flourish and are capable of great achievements. Without it, your lifestyle suffers.

Even more than many Sun sign Scorpios, you must always have an objective in view and should carve your way toward it constructively.

Romance
Both Scorpio and Taurus are of the fixed quality and, as a result, you can be rather stubborn. Taurus, like Scorpio, is a passionate sign. It will therefore increase the smoldering intensity that your Sun sign gives you.

You will express your feelings in a warm and affectionate way, and are capable of giving great sexual enjoyment. However, the worst Taurean fault is possessiveness and, if this is ignited by Scorpio jealousy, you could well have problems. Be aware that these negative emotions could spoil your relationships.

Your need for emotional security could cause you to create something of a claustophobic atmosphere, which some partners might resent.

Your well-being
The Taurean body area covers the neck and throat. Colds will almost certainly settle in that area, so take

The Moon in Taurus

care of it, especially in winter. Taurus likes good food, and so does Scorpio. Living it up can therefore mean considerable weight gain, unless you have a high metabolic rate. Moderation and exercise will help.

Planning ahead

You will be good with money and have a great instinct for investment. Therefore your bank balance and portfolio of stocks, however small, will grow to your satisfaction. However, you certainly love luxury and will therefore also spend freely. You will probably be able to cope with your finances without professional advice.

Parenthood

You are conventional and may be somewhat conservative in outlook. Be careful: your children could accuse you of being old-fashioned. You will work hard for them, but might be stricter than you realize. If you try to keep up with all their concerns, you should have few problems with the generation gap.

THE MOON IN
GEMINI

YOU ARE MORE LOGICAL AND LESS INTUITIVE THAN MANY SCORPIOS. IT IS PROBABLE THAT YOU CAN USEFULLY RATIONALIZE YOUR EMOTIONS AND INTELLECTUALIZE ANY DEEP-ROOTED PSYCHOLOGICAL PROBLEMS OR WORRIES.

The combination of two very different signs makes for a dynamic influence on your character. Gemini is an air sign and is intellectually oriented; it therefore adds a lightness and inquisitiveness to your Scorpio Sun, which makes you intense and pushes you to get to the root of every problem.

Self-expression
When challenged in any way, you will at once respond with lively, searching questions. You will be very skeptical of every theory put to you.

It may be that you are attracted to the media, and all kinds of research could well fascinate you. You are an excellent communicator, and this can be of advantage not only in your career, but also on a personal level.

When moved, you will probably try to rationalize your emotion. By all means go in for self-analysis, but remember that in the process you can rationalize away a lot of pleasure. Like many Sun sign Scorpios, you may tend to bottle up your problems. You should not, however, suffer badly from this tendency, due to the communicative nature of your Geminian Moon.

Romance
In addition to expressing Scorpio passion and achieving sexual fulfillment, you also find it very rewarding to enjoy a high level of intellectual rapport and friendship within an emotional relationship.

It is particularly good for you to have a partner who is at least your intellectual equal, if not considerably ahead of you in this area.

Your well-being
Scorpios tend to go whole hog, liking a lot of everything. If you smoke, you will probably smoke heavily, and this is inadvisable given that the Gemini

The Moon in Gemini

organ is the lungs. You have quite a high level of nervous energy, and should aim to burn that and your Scorpio physical energy positively, in sports or through demanding exercise.

Planning ahead
You may be somewhat less skillful with money than many Sun sign Scorpios. You have a natural selling ability and are capable of organizing profitable deals. Are you, however, perhaps a little too easily attracted to get-rich-quick schemes that, in the long run, turn into get-poor-quickly disasters? When tempted, remember to ask questions.

Parenthood
You probably find it easy to keep up with your children and enjoy discussing their opinions. At times, you could even be ahead of them and may surprise them with your knowledge of current trends. You should have few problems with the generation gap, especially if you maintain your acidic sense of humor.

THE MOON IN
CANCER

YOUR CANCERIAN MOON INCREASES YOUR SENSITIVE AWARENESS
OF OTHERS' NEEDS. YOU HAVE A PROTECTIVE INSTINCT
AND GREAT EMOTIONAL ENERGY. CHANNEL THESE POSITIVELY,
AND BEWARE OF IRRATIONAL WORRY.

Because Scorpio and Cancer are both water signs, the level of your emotional energy is very high. You should always be sure that you have positive and demanding ways of expressing it. You are a powerhouse of strong feeling and, for your psychological comfort, must be intensely involved in work that you find totally rewarding.

Self-expression
Your Cancerian Moon is likely to make you very intuitive, and you have an active imagination that you should make every effort to express creatively. If this does not happen, you will worry irrationally and could spend too much time waiting for the worst to happen. Also try to recognize the fact that, perhaps as the result of your sensitivity to atmospheres and other people's reactions, you may sometimes be prone to bouts of moodiness. Aim to keep your outlook

positive, and endeavor to be more optimistic than you may naturally be inclined to feel.

Romance
You are a wonderfully sensual and highly sexed lover, good at assessing your partner's needs. You are also demanding and need a partner who is not only active but also sympathetic. Watch out, though, for a tendency to "mother" your partners. This can create a rather claustrophobic atmosphere, which more freedom-loving partners may resent.

Your well-being
The Cancerian body area covers the breasts and chest. While there is absolutely no connection between this sign and the disease that bears the same name, Cancerian women should be as diligent as all their sisters in regularly examining their breasts. To some extent the digestive system

The Moon in Cancer

is also Cancer-ruled and, when you are worried, you could find your stomach giving you trouble. Cancerians and Scorpios enjoy their food, which will not help. You may need strenuous exercise to keep any flab at bay.

Planning ahead

There is a fair chance that you could be something of a financial wizard. You possess Cancerian shrewdness, with the additional business acumen that springs from your Scorpio Sun. This gives you the capacity to make a lot of money, provided that you do not give in to the Scorpio tendency to suddenly stop what you are doing and begin a new project.

Parenthood

You will enjoy the responsibilities of family life and may well be eager to have your own home and children.

You will be pretty strict with your children, which is fine. Do, however, allow them the freedom to express themselves. Avoid being sentimental and harking back to the past, when you were a child. If you get involved in your children's interests, you will bridge the generation gap.

LEO

YOU ARE INTENSE, AND YOUR SCORPIO ENERGY IS SPICED WITH
A POWERFUL CREATIVE INSTINCT THAT YOU SHOULD
EXPRESS AS FREELY AS YOU CAN. BE AWARE, HOWEVER, THAT
YOU ARE PRONE TO STUBBORNNESS.

Your Scorpio personality is exaggerated by the fiery emotion and energy of your Leo Moon. You have a great deal of inner strength and determination, and marvelous organizing ability. However, you should be very careful not to become autocratic and domineering.

Self-expression

Your Scorpio passion and powerful motivation are enhanced by your instinct to do your very best and to develop every hobby and interest, as well as your career, to the highest standard. The result is that you are probably very good at everything you do. You are one of the world's workers and will like to fill every day with useful activity.

Both Scorpio and Leo are signs that are highly charged with emotion, and Leo emotion is warm, fiery, and enthusiastic. It will make you look at life in a positive, optimistic way.

Romance

Your lovemaking has style, elegance, and more than a hint of glamour, and you will see to it that your partners enjoy life as much as you do, both in and out of bed.

Both Scorpio and Leo are of the fixed quality, which means that you can be very stubborn at times. Make an effort to reassess your opinions from time to time, and never mind admitting your mistakes.

The worst Leo fault is bossiness, so be careful that this unpleasant trait does not mar your relationships.

Your well-being

The Leo body area is the spine and back, so you need exercise to keep these in good working order. A back-support chair is also an excellent idea if you work long hours at a desk.

The Leo organ is the heart, and this needs regular exercise. You may find exercise rather boring, so aim to

The Moon in Leo

find a good health club, or perhaps dance or movement classes, where some of your dramatic qualities can find creative expression.

Scorpio and Leo could encourage you to have an all-too-rich diet. Try to keep this in check; otherwise you may well put on weight.

Planning ahead

You need to earn a lot of money to cater to what are probably expensive tastes. Your financial flair and potential for success should, however, enable you to do this. You will enjoy keeping an eye on your bank statements and seeing your money grow and will usually invest wisely, but resist any tendency to put too many financial eggs in one basket.

Parenthood

You will enjoy your children, but could sometimes seem rather pompous to them, and perhaps conventional. Try to see life through their eyes, and you will avoid problems with the generation gap. If you use your lively, enthusiastic Moon qualities and are encouraging rather than critical, you will certainly win your children's love and respect.

THE MOON IN
VIRGO

YOUR VIRGOAN MOON WILL ENSURE THAT YOU WILL NOT BE
SATISFIED UNTIL YOU HAVE GOTTEN TO THE ROOT OF EVERY
PROBLEM. BE CAREFUL, SINCE YOU COULD BECOME OBSESSIVE,
AND TRY NOT TO GET TOO BOGGED DOWN IN DETAIL.

Your water sign Sun and earth sign Moon combine well and share several complementary characteristics. Scorpio enjoys mystery and getting to the root of problems; your Virgoan Moon will encourage you to analyze them.

Self-expression
You are among the natural sleuths of the Zodiac and will therefore enjoy any kind of research. Be careful, however, that in examining the minutiae of a problem you do not miss seeing the overall pattern, and try to develop breadth of vision.

You have a great deal of common sense and a very practical approach to life. However, you must keep a tendency to worry under control.

Romance
The influence of Virgo is unlikely to be highly charged, emotionally. Some of your Scorpio passion will therefore

be moderated by your Moon sign. You will work hard to make your relationships work, possibly rather gradually overcoming any Virgoan timidity in your response to sex. As your tension eases and your Scorpio Sun takes over, you will find yourself enjoying an ever-increasing richness in this sphere of your life.

Your well-being
The Virgoan organ is the stomach, and you may suffer from stomach disorders when you are worried. You need a high-fiber diet.

A Virgoan influence brings with it a great deal of nervous energy. This can sometimes lead to a buildup of stress and tension, which may result in migraines. Try to relax. Outdoor exercise may help you, and so will talking things over with a friend. A relaxation technique such as yoga may prove to be useful, as will walking, cycling, and jogging.

The Moon in Virgo

Planning ahead

You may be far less of a big spender than many Scorpios, and will probably be good at balancing the books. There is even a chance that you could feel slightly guilty whenever you are extravagant. Do your best to ensure that you do not, and enjoy yourself. In particular, make sure that you do not hesitate when it comes to spending money on a favorite hobby, and go wild on good fabric, materials, tools, and machines.

If you are at all apprehensive about how to invest your money, seek financial advice.

Parenthood

Be careful not to be too critical of your children's efforts. You could deflate them far more than you realize.

Scorpios are usually fairly strict, but always retain the capacity for fun. If you listen to your children's opinions, you will encounter very few problems with the generation gap.

THE MOON IN
LIBRA

You sometimes appear a little lazy because your Libran Moon encourages you to relax and study every aspect of a problem. You are more considerate of other people than many Sun sign Scorpios.

The charm of your Libran Moon softens the powerful intensity of your Scorpio personality, and you always respond warmly and sympathetically to other people.

Self-expression
It may be that you are rather slower to come to decisions than many Scorpios, because your immediate reaction is to hesitate; you usually want to think at least twice before committing yourself.

You are tactful and diplomatic, especially when put on the spot in a bad situation, and you can produce the right answer at the right time. The influence of your Libran Moon will encourage you to always have time for other people.

Romance
You are among the more romantic of Scorpios, and enjoy the relaxed development of a relationship almost as much as a passionate scene. You will be considerate of your partners and will understand their needs.

A serious Libran fault is resentment, and you must guard against a tendency to cling to past differences or minor misdemeanors that your partner may have made.

Your well-being
The Libran body area is the lumbar region of the back. If you are prone to back pain, consider purchasing a back-support chair. The Libran organ is the kidneys and, as the result of a slight imbalance in that area, you may suffer from headaches.

Unless you are a quick-moving, wiry Scorpio type, your Moon sign may give you a rather slow metabolism. This can mean that with a Libran emphasis on good, rich, and sometimes sweet food, you may put on weight all too easily. Vigorous exercise will help, but you will

The Moon in Libra

probably find that physical activity will need to be accompanied by another, perhaps philosophical, element. Yoga, tai chi, and tantra are worth considering.

Planning ahead

You are more generous than the average person, and the immediate attraction of expensive clothes or fine items for the home may prove so tempting that your excellent Scorpio financial good sense could suffer. It might be advisable for you to seek professional advice when investing. Regular, steadily growing savings plans are good for you.

Parenthood

You will alternate between being a strict parent and a bit of a softy. Make certain that your children know where they stand with you, and you will develop an affectionate rapport. If you keep up with their ideas and always try to be aware of their problems, you will avoid difficulties with the generation gap.

THE MOON IN
SCORPIO

WITH BOTH THE SUN AND THE MOON IN SCORPIO ON THE DAY
OF YOUR BIRTH, YOU WERE BORN UNDER A NEW MOON.
SINCE SCORPIO IS A WATER SIGN, THIS ELEMENT IS IMPORTANT,
AND YOU WILL HAVE MANY SCORPIO CHARACTERISTICS.

Should you read a list of the characteristics of your Scorpio Sun sign, you will probably realize that a great many of them apply to you. On average, out of a list of, say, 20 personality traits of any particular Sun sign, most people will identify with 11 or 12. However, because the Moon was also in Scorpio when you were born, for you the average increases considerably.

Self-expression
You will react to most situations with a keen incisiveness, getting to the root of a matter and thrashing out every detail in the most searching way.

It is essential for all Scorpios to be emotionally involved in their work, but for you this is even more the case.

Romance
You are highly sexed and very passionate, and it is as important for you to share a rewarding relationship with someone as it is to have a satisfying job. You will contribute a great deal toward the success of your relationship, but must be aware that you are a very demanding partner. You need to share your life with someone who both realizes and understands this.

You would also do well to remember that you can sometimes be extremely susceptible to jealousy, and that this tendency can often cause problems between you and your lover.

Your well-being
As far as your health is concerned, you stand a good chance of being particularly vulnerable to Scorpio ailments (*see pages 372 – 373*). Bear in mind that Sun sign Scorpios can go hog-wild, and this applies to you more than to most people of your Sun sign. Try to keep your food intake in balance, and aim for a certain amount of moderation.

The Moon in Scorpio

You will probably enjoy all kinds of winter sports, and perhaps serious team games. It is more than likely that you will want to become very involved in whatever sport you decide to take up, and that you will be capable of great dedication to it.

Planning ahead
You should have considerable financial flair and plenty of intuition when it comes to investment. You may find a career in big business or banking rewarding. Be careful to spread your investments – while you are very capable of making a lot of money, do not overinvest.

Parenthood
You will be very anxious for your children to make good progress, and may consequently tend to push them a little too hard, and be rather strict with them. Try to make a conscious effort to be sympathetic toward their ideas and problems.

THE MOON IN
SAGITTARIUS

YOUR SAGITTARIAN MOON MODERATES THE INTENSE SIDE OF
YOUR PERSONALITY. YOU CAN GRASP AN OVERALL
SITUATION FAR MORE EASILY THAN MOST SCORPIOS AND
ARE NOT AS OBSESSED WITH DETAIL.

The qualities attributed to Scorpio and Sagittarius are very different. As a result you have some contrasting facets to your personality. You possess natural optimism and enthusiasm, which surfaces as soon as a project is given to you, or whenever you meet with a challenge.

Self-expression

Many Scorpios are properly described as "deep." Such a description is less applicable to you, and you do not find it difficult to be open and frank.

Your capacity to enjoy life, especially when you are confronted by challenge, is wonderful. You will hate the thought of wasting time even more than others of your Sun sign.

Romance

As well as burning Scorpio passion, you have a fiery liveliness in your expression of love and sex. You will probably enjoy many relationships during the course of your life and, once you are committed to a partner, you will still need a certain amount of freedom of expression.

Be careful that Scorpio jealousy does not complicate your life. Despite your instinct for independence, you will not be very happy if your partner shows signs of being even mildly flirtatious. Remember that you are sometimes capable of similar behavior, and relent a little.

Your well-being

Scorpios usually love rich and often expensive food. Sagittarians are not averse to it, either, and also love good wines and beers. The Sagittarian organ is the liver, so that in your case excesses of wining and dining may easily cause problems.

The Sagittarian body area covers the hips and thighs, and women with this sign emphasized have a tendency to put on weight in that area.

The Moon in Sagittarius

Moderation does not come naturally to either Scorpio or Sagittarius; both types find it very boring. Self-discipline is therefore important. On the plus side, Sagittarians usually like energetic exercise, so you should not find it too difficult to get involved in an appealing exercise regimen.

Planning ahead
Although you will, no doubt, have the Scorpio ability to make money, you may enjoy gambling, and could find risky financial schemes attractive. Be careful, since you could lose a lot of hard-earned money in this way.

You may do well as an investor, as long as you do not take undue risks. Be aware of the extremes to which you may succumb, and maintain a balanced outlook.

Parenthood
You will be among the most lively and positive of Scorpio parents. You have the ability to share a lot of fun with your children and will encourage them in their efforts, both intellectual and physical. You will not find it too hard to understand your children's problems, and the generation gap should hold no terrors for you.

THE MOON IN
CAPRICORN

YOUR OBJECTIVES ARE IMPORTANT TO YOU, AND YOU WILL SEIZE
EVERY OPPORTUNITY TO ACHIEVE YOUR GOALS. DO NOT
MISS OUT ON THE LIGHTER SIDE OF LIFE OR ALLOW YOUR
AMBITION TO INTERFERE WITH YOUR RELATIONSHIPS.

The water element of your Scorpio Sun and the earth element of your Capricornian Moon blend well, giving you the potential to be among the most successful of Scorpio Sun and Moon combinations.

Self-expression
You take life very seriously, but have an unusual and very offbeat sense of humor that emerges naturally and often very unexpectedly.

Your objectives and ambitions are very important to you, and you get a great deal of fulfillment from pursuing them, but you should take care that you do not miss out on enjoying life – you may veer toward becoming a workaholic. Try to avoid bringing too much work home from the office.

Romance
Your powerful Scorpio emotions are calmed by your Capricornian Moon. Your reactions to situations are logical and practical, and you are rather less likely to be emotionally moved than many Scorpios. Sometimes, you may even give the impression that you are slightly aloof.

Your approach to your love and sex life is less passionate than that of many Scorpios, and you are likely to be very faithful once committed.

Your well-being
The Capricornian body area covers the knees and shins, and yours are therefore more vulnerable than other people's. It is essential that you keep moving, because people with an emphasis on Capricorn are prone to stiffness of the joints, and rheumatic and arthritic pain.

It is unlikely that you will have a weight problem, since your Capricornian Moon has probably given you a rather lean frame, and you are possibly less attracted to heavy, rich food than is the case with many

The Moon in Capricorn

Scorpios. The teeth are also ruled by Capricorn, so be careful not to neglect to have regular dental checkups.

Planning ahead

You are, or have the potential to be, something of a financial wizard. Capricornians are often good at business, as are Scorpios. If you are self-employed, you should be able to build up your business extremely well, provided you pace its development. The same applies if you have cash to invest.

Parenthood

Perhaps you need to reassess your attitude to your children, since you may be far stricter than you realize. Most children thrive when they have a secure structure to their lives, but try to avoid damaging put-downs. Also make sure that you have time to enjoy their company as opposed to just working hard to ensure that they have all the material needs of life. Consciously tune in to their opinions and concerns. Otherwise you might experience generation gap problems.

THE MOON IN
AQUARIUS

STUBBORNNESS CAN BE A PROBLEM FOR YOU, BUT YOU ARE
ABLE TO DETACH YOURSELF RATIONALLY FROM
DIFFICULTIES AND TO BE VERY OBJECTIVE IN ASSESSING THEM.
LOOK AHEAD AND TRY TO KEEP AN OPEN MIND.

Your Aquarian Moon enables you to approach problems in an unusual way. Your reaction to situations is usually logical, and you can detach yourself from your emotions and see any difficulties from various angles, quickly focusing on each before reaching practical and often unique conclusions.

Self-expression
Lateral thinking comes naturally to you, and colleagues and friends often have cause to be very grateful for your originality. Because both Scorpio and Aquarius are of the fixed quality, you may tend to be very stubborn at times. Be aware of this tendency; otherwise you may be accused of being willfully obstinate.

Romance
Life may not be particularly easy when you are beginning to solidify a personal relationship. You are a passionate Scorpio, but may, early on in a relationship, send out signals warning people to keep their distance.

You need sexual fulfillment as much as, or perhaps more than, anyone else. However, your independence will be important to you, and you must try to find partners who will not resent this need. You may delay a long-term commitment or marriage, which is no bad thing: take your time if you feel that you should.

Your well-being
The ankles are the Aquarian body area, and yours are likely to be vulnerable, especially if you enjoy wearing some types of fashionable shoes. The circulation is also Aquarius-ruled, so take care that you look after yours. Obviously, all exercise regimens and sporting activities are a help, and you shoul find time for them. Scorpios usual enjoy swimming and other water

The Moon in Aquarius

sports, but you may also be attracted to winter sports and could be particularly good at them.

Planning ahead

While Sun sign Scorpios are usually very smart about money, your originality may sometimes get the better of you, and you could end up committing yourself without due thought to some exciting but not very practical scheme that catches your imagination. Financial loss may follow. Aim for conventionality where finance is concerned. Express your originality in other ways, for example in your image or in creative work.

Parenthood

Although you will initially respond well to your children's more extreme ideas and suggestions, you may end up backtracking. Try to avoid this. Make a conscious effort to see life through their eyes and you will not be troubled by the generation gap.

THE MOON IN
PISCES

YOUR POWERFUL SCORPIO CHARACTERISTICS ARE SOFTENED BY THE TENDER EMOTION OF YOUR PISCEAN MOON. YOU ARE KIND AND MORE SENSITIVE THAN MANY SCORPIOS, BUT THIS WILL NOT PREVENT YOU FROM TAKING ASSERTIVE ACTION WHEN NECESSARY.

Both Scorpio and Pisces belong to the water element and, as a result, there is a very natural sympathy between the two signs.

Self-expression
You have extremely powerful instincts and intuition, and should follow these. You also have an active imagination, and this, too, can work positively for you. However, if your imagination is operating negatively, you are capable of supposing that all sorts of things have gone wrong when, in fact, they probably have not. Try to avoid this by finding rewarding ways of expressing your imagination.

It may be that you have psychic ability. If you have premonitions or if strange things seem to happen to you from time to time, do not be worried. If, however, you want to develop your psychic powers, get special training from a psychic society of some kind. You have a powerful emotional level

and may often be swayed by your emotions. This need not be a negative trait, as long as you listen to your intuition, which will guide you in the direction that you should take.

Romance
You will get much pleasure from your love and sex life, and can give a great deal of yourself to your partners. However, you can be easily hurt and, if this occurs, it may be because you have not faced up to reality.

Your well-being
The Piscean body area covers the feet. Yours are vulnerable, and you probably find it difficult to get really comfortable shoes.

Many people with a Piscean emphasis tend to put on weight relatively easily, and Scorpios love good food. It is better for you to discipline your eating habits than to go on a crash diet.

The Moon in Pisces

Planning ahead

Although your Scorpio Sun gives you a good basic financial sense, your Piscean Moon succeeds in removing rather a lot of it. You have such a sensitivity to suffering, and identify so strongly with it, that you may be over-generous to charities. It could be that you also tend to lend money far too freely. Avoid this whenever possible, and remember that it is usually much better to give a few dollars to someone than to loan them money.

You should probably take financial advice when you are thinking of investing. Should you want to start a business, it is advisable for you to work with a partner, unless you feel that you really can control your Moon in Pisces weak approach to finance.

Parenthood

You are likely to have a great understanding of human nature, and it could well be of enormous help to you in your relationship with your children. You will sometimes be very strict with them, and at others times may tend to spoil them. If you manage to succeed in keeping these two extremes in balance, you will be a splendid parent.

SAGITTARIUS

NOVEMBER 23 – DECEMBER 21

INTRODUCING
SAGITTARIUS

SAGITTARIUS, THE SIGN OF THE CENTAUR, THE ARCHER WHO IS
HALF MAN AND HALF BEAST, IS THE NINTH SIGN OF THE
ZODIAC. YOU NEED DEMANDING PHYSICAL OR INTELLECTUAL
EXERCISE IN ORDER TO FULFILL YOUR POTENTIAL.

Being a Sagittarian, you should guard against restlessness, and develop a sense of purpose. This will ensure that you possess the continuity of effort required for a full expression of your potential, and thus your psychological fulfillment.

You are likely to be one of the explorers and travelers of the Zodiac – both in mind and in body. You are willing to take risks, but must control a gambling spirit that can occasionally get out of hand.

Traditional groupings

As you read through this book you will come across references to the elements and the qualities, and to positive and negative, or masculine and feminine signs.

The first of these groupings, that of the elements, comprises fire, earth, air, and water signs. The second, that of the qualities, divides the Zodiac into cardinal, fixed, and mutable signs. The final grouping is made up of positive and negative, or masculine and feminine signs. Each Zodiac sign is associated with a combination of components from these groupings, all of which contribute different characteristics to it.

Sagittarian characteristics

Being a sign of the fire element, Sagittarius bestows great natural enthusiasm upon its subjects. This often extends to a fondness for demanding physical or intellectual exercise. Since Sagittarius is also a positive, masculine sign, you are liable to be one of the optimistic extroverts of the Zodiac. Being of the mutable quality, Sagittarius is a "dual" sign, and its subjects are therefore versatile.

The ruling planet of Sagittarius is Jupiter, the giant of the Solar System, and a great god in Roman mythology. The Sagittarian colors are rich purples and dark blues.

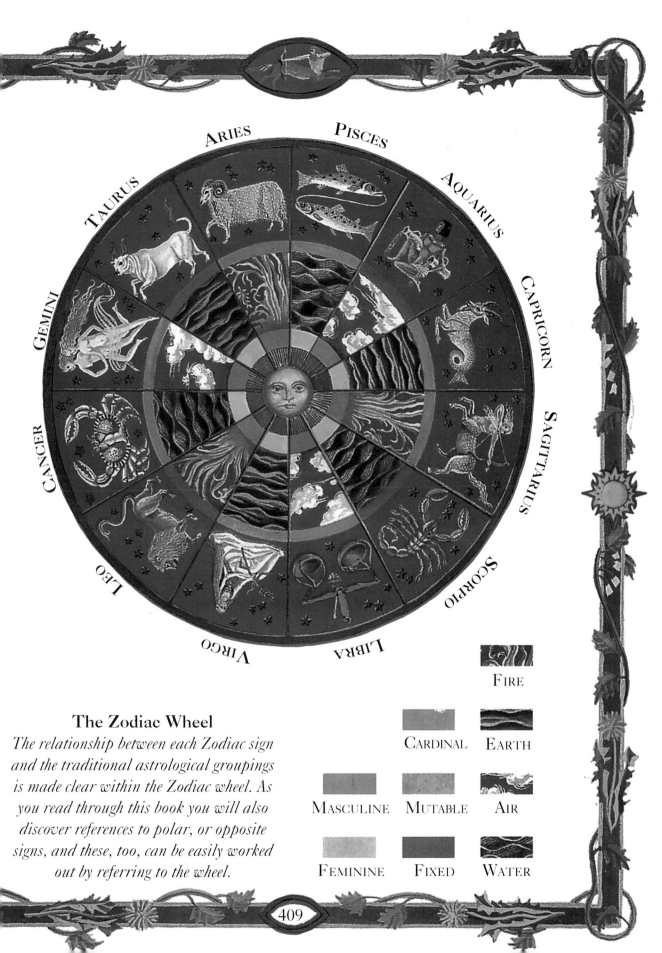

The Zodiac Wheel

The relationship between each Zodiac sign and the traditional astrological groupings is made clear within the Zodiac wheel. As you read through this book you will also discover references to polar, or opposite signs, and these, too, can be easily worked out by referring to the wheel.

ARIES

PISCES

TAURUS

AQUARIUS

GEMINI

CAPRICORN

CANCER

SAGITTARIUS

LEO

SCORPIO

VIRGO

LIBRA

FIRE

CARDINAL   EARTH

MASCULINE   MUTABLE   AIR

FEMININE   FIXED   WATER

MYTHS & LEGENDS

THE ZODIAC, WHICH IS BELIEVED TO HAVE ORIGINATED IN
BABYLON AS LONG AS 2,500 YEARS AGO, IS A
CIRCLE OF CONSTELLATIONS THROUGH WHICH THE SUN
MOVES DURING THE COURSE OF A YEAR.

The constellation of Sagittarius first seems to have been identified and named in Babylon. The symbolic centaur with his bow began to appear in ancient Egypt much later than the time when he was carved on Babylonian boundary stones. The origin of the sign is, however, shrouded in considerable mystery, and there is no myth firmly associated with it.

Ancient Greece and Rome
In ancient Greece, Sagittarius seems to have been a satyr: in particular, one called Crotus, who lived on Mount Helicon with his foster sisters, the Muses. The satyrs were attendants of the god Dionysus; they had goats' legs and the tails of horses, and were much given to riotous living. In those days, Sagittarius had only two legs.

Later on, Manilius, the Roman writer who in the first century B.C. set down several astrological myths, and the great astronomer Hipparchus saw him as a four-footed centaur. The centaurs, who were also attendants of Dionysus, lived in Thessaly. Their heads and torsos were human, but the rest of their bodies were those of horses. It seems likely that the legend of the centaurs arose around a tribe of cow herders who lived in Thessaly. Indeed, the name "centaurs" can be translated as "those who round up bulls." Like the American cowboys, the Thessalonian herders rode on horseback when they were attending to their livestock.

In general, centaurs were thought to revel in cruelty and to indulge frequently in bouts of frenzied lechery and drunkenness.

Chiron the centaur
Some astrologers like to insist that the original Sagittarius was a centaur named Chiron, who seems to have had nothing in common with the

Achilles and Chiron, the Centaur

This late-Roman image shows Chiron schooling Achilles in the art of riding. Chiron was responsible not only for the education of Achilles, but also that of another great hero, Jason.

ordinary centaurs except his body. Although the centaur was generally considered to be a barbarous beast, his human association made Chiron kindly, learned, and a good friend to many gods and heroes.

Tutor of Jason and Achilles

Skilled in many arts, including that of prophesy, Chiron taught such famous heroes as Jason, who captured the Golden Fleece, and Achilles, who was killed by a fatal arrowshot to his legendary vulnerable heel during the capture of Troy. Chiron fed the young Achilles on a diet that consisted of the entrails of lions and the marrow bones of bears in order to give the boy courage, and taught him the valuable arts of riding, healing, hunting, and playing the pipes.

Chiron was an immortal but, after being accidentally injured by one of the hero Hercules's deadly poisoned arrows, he was in such profound pain, and was so afraid that his wound would never again heal, that he gave away the gift of his immortality to the suffering Prometheus, father of all the arts and sciences.

Zeus, the king of the gods, wanted so fine a creature as Chiron to be remembered. He therefore decided to set him in the sky as a constellation, bearing the same arrow that Hercules had used to defend Prometheus.

SAGITTARIUS
SYMBOLISM

CERTAIN HERBS, SPICES, FLOWERS, TREES, GEMS, METALS, AND ANIMALS HAVE LONG BEEN ASSOCIATED WITH PARTICULAR ZODIAC SIGNS. SOME ASSOCIATIONS ARE SIMPLY AMUSING, WHILE OTHERS CAN BE USEFUL.

Flowers
Dandelions, lime-flowers, carnations, and pinks are all flowers traditionally associated with Sagittarius.

DANDELION FLOWER

DANDELION SEED

CARNATIONS

Trees

Sagittarian trees include the oak, birch, lime, mulberry, chestnut, and ash.

BIRCH

OAK

Herbs

Lemon balm is a Sagittarian herb. A syrup made from it, with sugar added, was once kept in every house to relieve a weak stomach and general sickness.

LEMON BALM

Spices

No spices are particularly associated with Sagittarius, but allspice is sometimes mentioned in connection with this sign.

ALLSPICE

SAGITTARIUS
SYMBOLISM

GUN DOG
BROOCH

DEER BROOCH

INDIAN HORSE
SPICE BOX

BRONZE STAG'S HEAD

Gems

Topaz is the Sagittarian gem. To be used as a talisman, it should always come from Spain, a Sagittarian country.

TOPAZ

ANCIENT GREEK
BRONZE HORSES

Animals

All animals related to hunting, including big and small game and horses, fall under the dominion of Sagittarius.

Metal

The Sagittarian metal is traditionally said to be tin; it is especially relevant to the sign when it is highly polished and shining.

SAGITTARIUS PROFILE

HAPPY-GO-LUCKY SAGITTARIANS GIVE THE IMPRESSION THAT THEY HAVE NOT A CARE IN THE WORLD. THEY ARE ALWAYS READY TO OFFER A FRIENDLY SMILE AND A WORD OF ENCOURAGEMENT TO LESS POSITIVE PEOPLE.

You are likely to possess a very firm stance, with your feet apart and your hands on your hips. You probably hold your head high, seeming to peer toward some distant horizon.

The body

The Sagittarian body is often somewhat thick-set, and usually very muscular. It is, perhaps, a body designed less for office work than for sports and physical activity. There have been many great Sagittarian dancers and basketball players.

Your legs are likely to be long. The Sagittarian hips and thighs are particularly strong, but sometimes a bit too prominent, much to the annoyance of many women of the sign. If you spend all of your time

The Sagittarian face
Wavy hair and, in men, a beard are typical of the Sagittarian face.

following intellectual pursuits, you may develop a rather round-shouldered stoop.

The face

A number of distinctive features characterize the Sagittarian face. Your hair could be wavy and thick, and perhaps a little difficult to control. A broad, open forehead is likely to enhance your generally optimistic expression, and your eyes will probably be set wide apart, beneath straight eyebrows. Your lips are likely to be firm, and will easily break into a relaxed smile.

Style

Sagittarians often tend to cling to a "student" image, and may sport a college ring long after they are well

The Sagittarian stance

A firm stance, with feet spread wide apart, hands placed on hips, and head held high, is typically Sagittarian.

established in the world. You are very likely to hate wearing formal clothes and, whenever possible, will dress as casually as you possibly can. Polo-neck sweaters are very popular among Sagittarian men and women.

Clothing that permits ease of movement is advisable for you. It is, in fact, extremely important for your clothing to be comfortable, since anything restrictive will leave you feeling intolerably claustrophobic. Perhaps your clothes will be in royal blue or purple, which are favorite Sagittarian colors.

In general

Sagittarians are not too concerned about their appearance; their outlook on life usually leads them to concentrate on other, more interesting things. Even those who are fashion-minded like to choose a number of garments at one session, so that they can then forget about clothes and get on with their lives. Similarly, you will no doubt want to be able to put on your clothes first thing in the morning, and then not have to worry about them again until the evening. You may be perfectly happy wearing comfortable jogging clothes or track-suits most of the time, and they can sometimes be quite fashionable.

The independent Sagittarian spirit does not encourage conformity. You should therefore be careful if you decide to bend the rules when, for instance, deciding what clothes to wear for work.

SAGITTARIUS
PERSONALITY

SAGITTARIANS ARE AT THEIR BEST WHEN CHALLENGED. YOUR POSITIVE MIND WILL ALLOW YOU TO GRASP THE OVERALL STRUCTURE OF A SITUATION AND ASSESS THE BEST WAY OF SOLVING A PROBLEM, WHATEVER THE DIFFICULTIES.

People of your Sun sign sometimes seem to possess the secret of eternal youth and may appear to be perpetual students. If you are asked what you are planning for the coming months, you will almost certainly mention some study group, class, or series of lectures that you are planning to attend. If you are not the kind of person to become involved in intellectual pursuits, you will be eager to talk about the new health club that you have just joined.

At work
The duality of Sagittarius makes for an interesting influence, since it accentuates versatility. Many people of your Sun sign are likely to enjoy two quite separate occupations, or at least a rather considerable amount of variety within one.

You are often at your best expressing a number of varied talents. You may complete a task and then turn to something that puts a very different set of demands on other skill that you might have.

Your attitudes
Sagittarians usually need to be stimulated both mentally and physically. There are, however, certain types of Sagittarian who are attracted almost exclusively to either physical or mental activities.

There are the bookish types who do not care for anything resembling physical exercise, and there are the sports fiends who enjoy participating in intense team sports, even when they are well past their prime. Both types of Sagittarian may tend to hang on to their youth.

Most Sagittarians obtain a great deal of pleasure from traveling and, if it is not possible for you to do so, you will probably turn to travel books and videos as an alternative. You may have a flair for languages, and could

Jupiter rules Sagittarius

*Jupiter, the Roman god of philosophy and languages,
represents the Sagittarian ruling planet. It can make
its subjects optimistic and loyal, but sometimes conceited.*

do far worse than to invest some of
your time and money in refining this
particular skill.

The overall picture

Sagittarian enthusiasm is usually
boundless and infectious, and it is
often expressed through risk-taking,
often of a physical nature. You must
be careful to ensure that such risks are
always extremely carefully calculated.
You may also enjoy taking a small
gamble from time to time, and some
Sagittarians may even be unlucky
enough to find the idea thoroughly
irresistible. If such a tendency is not
controlled, it can cause problems for
weaker-minded Sagittarians.

SAGITTARIUS
ASPIRATIONS

YOU WILL BE HAPPIEST IN A CAREER THAT CAN BE PLANNED IN ADVANCE. PREDICTABILITY DOES NOT HAVE OTHER APPEAL, HOWEVER, AND YOU MUST BE FREE TO DO THINGS IN YOUR OWN WAY. IT IS EXCELLENT IF YOUR WORK INVOLVES TRAVEL.

Veterinarians

A love for animals, especially horses and dogs, is a powerful Sagittarian trait. It encourages many Sagittarians to become dedicated veterinarians and trainers.

VETERINARY MEDICINES

Teaching

The centaur, which symbolizes this sign, was at one time the symbol of education. Many Sagittarians occupy teaching posts, often specializing in languages.

BLACKBOARD AND CHALK

The travel industry

Sagittarians enjoy traveling and like to broaden their horizons both intellectually and physically. They therefore make excellent couriers and guides.

The law

Because most Sagittarians enjoy argument and debate, and usually have no difficulty in expressing their opinions, they make excellent attorneys.

HARDBACK
BOOKS

Publishing

To expand their own knowledge, and to encourage others to do the same, is a powerful Sagittarian motivation. Many people of this Sun sign are therefore attracted to publishing.

LEGAL
DOCUMENTS

SAGITTARIUS
HEALTH

YOUR DUAL SAGITTARIAN NATURE INCLINES YOU TO BE PHYSICALLY ACTIVE, AS WELL AS STUDIOUS AND INTELLECTUAL. IDEALLY, YOU SHOULD AIM TO KEEP THESE CHARACTERISTICS IN BALANCE.

Sagittarians need to exploit their physical and intellectual energy. They have excellent resources of both, and it is a great pity if they are not fully developed. Because your outlook is generally positive and enthusiastic, you respond well when you are challenged.

Your diet
The Sagittarian body area is traditionally said to cover the hips and thighs, and because a fairly rich, somewhat heavy diet is preferred by people of this sign, weight gain can sometimes be a problem for them.

You are likely to benefit from the cell salt Kali Muriaticum (Kali Mur.), which may help prevent bronchial congestion and swollen glands.

Taking care
The Sagittarian body organ is the liver. You should therefore make an effort to learn what does and does not agree with you, and find out exactly what your food and drink limits are. It is therefore a good idea for you to always have supply of hangover remedies in the medicine cabinet; you might even develop one of your own. Restlessness can be a problem for Sagittarians. You may find it hard to really relax; a complete change of occupation usually works well in these cases.

Asparagus
Onions, asparagus, and tomatoes are all foods linked to this sign.

Astrology and the body

For many centuries it was not possible to practice medicine without a knowledge of astrology. In European universities, medical training included information on how planetary positions would affect the administration of medicines, the bleeding of patients, and the right time to pick herbs and make potions. Each Zodiac sign rules a particular part of the body – from Aries (the head) to Pisces (the feet) – and textbooks always included a drawing of a "Zodiac man" (or woman) that illustrated the point.

SAGITTARIUS AT LEISURE

Each of the Sun signs traditionally suggests spare-time activities, hobbies, and vacation spots. Although these are only suggestions, they often work out well for Sagittarians.

POSTAGE STAMPS

Travel
Hungary, Australia, and Spain are among the countries ruled by Sagittarius. Spain is a big favorite for Sagittarian vacations.

Reading
Sagittarians are eternal students who love to study – especially foreign languages. You will therefore enjoy reading.

BOOKS

INDIAN SHAWL

ARROWS AND QUIVER

Hunting curios
As the hunters of the Zodiac, Sagittarians often enjoy searching for bargains and for unusual or exotic articles.

Archery
The mortal half of the centaur that represents Sagittarius is an archer. Sagittarians who become interested in archery are often exceptionally good at it.

MODEL PORSCHE COUPE

Driving
With their fondness for travel, Sagittarians like to be constantly on the move, and usually make excellent drivers.

SAGITTARIUS IN
LOVE

TRADITIONALLY, SAGITTARIANS ARE THE HUNTERS OF THE
ZODIAC. IN LOVE, AS IN OTHER AREAS OF THEIR LIVES,
THE CHALLENGE OF THE CHASE IS ALL-ENGROSSING, AND
MAY EVEN BE MORE EXCITING THAN THE CAPTURE.

The Sagittarian love of challenge can be ignited if the object of your affection plays hard to get. This may be very exciting for you.

As a lover
A Sagittarian's natural enthusiasm for love and sex is very infectious, and it is not difficult for people of your Sun sign to attract partners. Your need for your own space, and for a relationship without even a hint of claustrophobia, is very important. You really cannot bear to feel restricted, and your partners must realize this and allow you a measure of independence if the relationship is to last.

Once they have tamed their coltish attitudes, Sagittarians make very rewarding partners because of their love of life, optimism, and ability to encourage partners to pursue their own interests.

Types of Sagittarian lover
The influence of other planets encourages every Zodiac type to express love in one of five different ways, and it is usually fairly easy to recognize the group to which you belong. Some Sagittarians are really romantic, and go for affairs with all the memorable trimmings. They either rush into

relationships because they are a little in love with love itself, or procrastinate because they cannot decide which partner they should settle for. A second group loves passionately and very emotionally. Uncharacteristically, these individuals are sometimes prone to bouts of jealousy, in spite of the fact that they usually want to have the same amount of independence as that desired by their partners.

There are also those Sagittarians who will end up loving in a truly Sagittarian manner. They will readily agree with the general comments that have already been made.

Others of this Sun sign will be surprisingly cool and far more cautious in their attitude to love. They are less likely to play the field and, once committed to a stable and permanent relationship, are usually faithful to a single partner. The final group consists of those Sun sign Sagittarians who need a considerable measure of independence within a partnership, and who enjoy their love and sex lives to the full. They are, perhaps, likely to delay making a serious commitment to a relationship because of their strong need to achieve their own highly individual lifestyles.

SAGITTARIUS AT HOME

ANY SAGITTARIAN HOME WILL FEEL VERY ROOMY, PERHAPS BECAUSE OF A CLEVER USE OF MIRRORS. THIS IS JUST AS WELL, BECAUSE FURNITURE, BOOKS, ORNAMENTS, AND CHINA WILL OCCUPY EVERY SPARE CORNER.

The Sagittarian home is usually marked by a definite tendency to steer clear of anything that might result in a rather claustrophobic atmosphere. Large windows, and spacious, open-plan living are therefore given substantial priority.

Globe of the world
A love of travel is often reflected in the Sagittarian choice of objects or pictures.

Furniture
You are one of the hunters of the Zodiac, and probably love to visit street markets and antique shops in search of bargains that suit your taste and practical needs. Sagittarians usually choose furniture that is not particularly adventurous, but that is built to last. While you like to be reasonably comfortable, space for bookshelves, or simply piles of books, and places to keep the articles of sports equipment that are so much a part of the Sagittarian lifestyle are just as important, or perhaps even more so.

Soft furnishings
The cushions in your home may appear somewhat crumpled and well used, but they will invite people to sit down. Many items, such as oriental rugs, will have originated overseas, and the fabric for the curtains will sometimes have a rather unusual design. Sagittarians often favor the strong, energetic, perennial designs of William Morris, which reflect Sagittarian energy and a liking for warm color. Dark blue and purple are popular, and those of this

Either books or sporting trophies, or perhaps even both, may be present, depending on whether you are a bookish or an athletic type of Sagittarian. There may also be a fair variety of objects scattered around your home that represent your own religious faith, such as a crucifix or some kind of icon.

Tidiness is not a characteristic that one would immediately associate with a Sagittarian home; you are very likely to position the objects in it quite indiscriminately, and then to shuffle them around continually.

sign usually like the yellows, reds, and golds of the fire element that influences their personalities.

Decorative objects

Because most Sagittarians have lively minds, the decorative items that enhance your home, and certainly the overall effect, will often arouse interest and intellectual discussion among those who come to visit. The pictures that you choose are often open landscapes, since Sagittarians cannot bear anything claustrophobic.

There will almost certainly be interesting, rather than purely beautiful, travel souvenirs. Many Sagittarians enjoy playing the guitar, and one may be given an honored place in your home.

Guitar, rug, and chest
Sagittarian homes may display a guitar; a Spanish influence may also be evident.

THE
MOON
AND
YOU

THE SUN DECREES YOUR OUTWARD EXPRESSION, YOUR IMAGE, AND MANY IMPORTANT PERSONALITY TRAITS. THE MOON, ALTHOUGH MERELY THE EARTH'S SATELLITE, IS ASTRONOMICALLY THE SECOND MOST IMPORTANT BODY IN THE SOLAR SYSTEM. FROM THE SIGN THAT IT WAS IN AT YOUR BIRTH, IT INFLUENCES HOW YOU REACT TO SITUATIONS, YOUR EMOTIONAL LEVEL, AND, TO A CERTAIN EXTENT, WHAT YOU HAVE INHERITED FROM YOUR PARENTS AND ANCESTORS. AFTER FINDING YOUR MOON SIGN IN THE SIMPLE TABLES ON PAGES 606 TO 609, TURN TO THE RELEVANT PAGES AND TAKE A STEP FORWARD IN YOUR OWN SELF-KNOWLEDGE.

THE MOON IN
ARIES

BOTH THE SUN AND THE MOON WERE IN FIRE SIGNS AT THE TIME OF YOUR BIRTH. IT IS THEREFORE LIKELY THAT YOU HAVE AN ENTHUSIASTIC AND OPTIMISTIC OUTLOOK ON LIFE, AND IMMEDIATE REACTIONS TO SITUATIONS.

Some aspects of your character may have been tempered by a number of strong influences in your birth chart. Otherwise you are likely to be a lively, extroverted person.

Self-expression
You are always ready to accept daunting challenges at a moment's notice. In fact, you often throw yourself in at the deep end, without thinking about the consequences.

Perhaps even more than most Sagittarians, you have breadth of vision and the ability to grasp the essentials of a situation. But having done so, the details may defeat you; therefore either make sure that you leave them to someone else, or discipline yourself to cope with them.

Romance
Your fiery enthusiasm for love and sex should ensure that you obtain a lot of pleasure out of this sphere of your life. You may not always take your relationships too seriously, since your passion has a lighthearted air.

Be aware that the worst Arien fault is selfishness, and that you may sometimes react to your lovers in a somewhat selfish way. You certainly need a partner who can match your abundant Sagittarian and Arien emotional and physical energy, and sheer enjoyment of love and sex.

Your well-being
The Arien body area is the head, and you could be rather prone to headaches. Perhaps these are due to your frustration at other people's incompetence or their slowness to respond to you. Alternatively, you may suffer from a slight kidney problem. If your headaches persist, get a medical checkup.

Anyone with an Arien influence may, because of a tendency to be too hasty, be somewhat accident-prone.

The Moon in Aries

Minor cuts and burns, even fender benders, can easily occur. An awareness of this tendency will help you to combat it. You are pretty energetic, physically, and should have a fairly fast metabolism.

Planning ahead
Sagittarians love a gamble, and with an Arien Moon this tendency is exacerbated. While you could well enjoy investment, your enterprising spirit may be marred by this gambling streak. Therefore resist seductive schemes that may well be far less rewarding than they sound, and take professional advice in this sphere.

Parenthood
You make an excellent parent and will be as young at heart as your children, encouraging them greatly in all their interests. You should have few generation gap problems. In fact, the reverse may be true; you might have to remind yourself of your age.

THE MOON IN
TAURUS

YOUR TAUREAN MOON STABILIZES YOUR FIERY CHARACTERISTICS, ESPECIALLY WHEN YOU ARE CONFRONTED BY CHALLENGES. IT ALSO HELPS TO CURB UNNECCESSARY RISK-TAKING AND A TENDENCY TO BE BLINDLY OPTIMISTIC.

The Moon is, according to traditional astrology, "well placed" in Taurus. As a result, its influence on you is rather stronger than it is on other Sagittarians.

Self-expression

Like Sagittarius, Taurus is an earth sign. It prevents you from taking premature action, and instills caution, common sense, and even a good measure of patience – not a quality that one naturally associates with Sun sign Sagittarians. Your response to most situations is not to get immediately involved. You will give yourself time to assess a situation before allowing your natural verve and enthusiasm, springing from your Sagittarian Sun sign, to emerge.

Romance

You have the warm affection usually associated with Taurus, and it is this that will first emerge when you

develop an emotional relationship. Your Taurean Moon adds a great deal of natural charm to your personality, while removing nothing of the sexiness of your Sagittarian Sun.

Bear in mind that the worst Taurean fault is possessiveness. As a Sagittarian with an instinctive love of freedom, you detest this unacceptable trait, but your Moon can edge you toward it. Recognize the fact, and watch for the signs.

Your well-being

The Taurean body area is the throat, and you probably find that colds start there. You may also have trouble with your tonsils.

Those with a Taurean emphasis tend to put on weight easily, often because they have a sweet tooth. Sagittarians like rich, hearty food, so you may need to keep a constant calorie check if you want to retain your good figure. Do not let the

The Moon in Taurus

relaxed attitude of your Taurean Moon get the better of you where exercise is concerned. Sagittarians must never stagnate.

Planning ahead

You are cautious and have good business sense. As a result you can cope with money far better than many Sun sign Sagittarians. Even if you do succumb to your Sagittarian gambling instinct, the chances are that you will not fritter away more money than you can afford to lose.

Parenthood

As a parent, you no doubt get things just about right, and will discipline your children in precisely the right way, so that they know exactly where they stand with you.

The power of your Sagittarian Sun makes you an optimistic and very encouraging parent, and your children thrive on your constructive comments and warm affection. You do not find it difficult to keep up with their ideas and are unlikely to incur problems with the generation gap.

THE MOON IN
GEMINI

SAGITTARIUS AND GEMINI ARE POLAR OR OPPOSITE ZODIAC SIGNS,
SO YOU WERE BORN UNDER A FULL MOON. RESTLESSNESS IS A
GEMINIAN CHARACTERISTIC, AND YOU SHOULD TRY TO FIGHT IT.
BE VERSATILE, BUT DEVELOP CONSISTENCY OF EFFORT.

Each of us is, in one way or another, likely to express the attributes of our polar, or opposite, Zodiac sign. Each sign has its partner across the horoscope; for Sagittarians, this is Gemini and, because the Moon was in Gemini when you were born, this polarity is emphasized in an interesting and powerful way.

Self-expression
Sagittarius and Gemini are both mutable signs, which means that you are flexible and intellectual in character, and have a versatile mind. These signs are also traditionally dual in nature, and you may therefore have a tendency to do more than one thing at a time. This is probably very natural to you, and it is something that you should not try to curb. You must, however, work to avoid superficiality, which may also result from your dual nature. Always make a special effort to complete everything

that you undertake. Also remember that restlessness is the worst fault of both Gemini and Sagittarius. This characteristic is further emphasized in people born under a Full Moon.

Romance
You have all the passion of your Sagittarian Sun to express in your love and sex life, added to which your Geminian Moon will make you very flirtatious. Some duality can obviously find a place in this area of your life, and it is worth remembering that you could encounter problems if you do not keep these tendencies under control. Even more than most Sagittarians, you require a good level of intellectual rapport with a lover.

Your well-being
Gemini rules the arms and hands, so yours may be vulnerable to injury. It also rules the lungs, so you could be susceptible to bronchitis and should

The Moon in Gemini

beware of a cough that will not go away. If you smoke, break the habit as soon as possible.

Your Geminian Moon gives you a great deal of nervous energy, which must be positively expressed through lively physical exercise.

Planning ahead

You should probably always seek professional advice when you have money to invest. Your Sagittarian gambling spirit may combine with a Geminian liking for get-rich-quick schemes and, as a result, you could end up losing far more money than you are really able to afford.

Parenthood

As a parent, you may even be ahead of your children in relation to the most modern trends.

It is, however, possible that a tendency to be inconsistent may damage your relationship. Make sure that your children always know where they stand with you. In this way you should avoid the generation gap.

THE MOON IN
CANCER

YOU REALLY NEED INDEPENDENCE, FREEDOM OF EXPRESSION, AND EMOTIONAL SECURITY. YOUR URGE FOR THESE IS INSTINCTIVE AND POWERFUL. YOU ARE PROTECTIVE TOWARD THOSE YOU LOVE, AND VALUE SOLIDARITY.

The combination of Sagittarius, a fire sign, and Cancer, a water sign, makes for some contrasting characteristics that you should use to full advantage. Because the Moon rules Cancer, the influence of your Moon sign is very powerful.

Self-expression
You are much more sensitive than many Sagittarians, and can be more easily hurt, too. You are also prone to changes of mood. While you will have plenty of Sagittarian optimism and enthusiasm, your immediate reaction to any situation will be cautious. You have an instinctive self-defensive system that immediately springs into action when you are challenged.

Romance
You express love very sensually and have many desirable qualities that should enable you to maintain a stable, yet exciting, relationship.

Your emotional level is very high, for you have all the powerful, fiery emotion of Sagittarius, which will spur you into passionate expression of love and sex. You also have the more tender emotion of Cancer, which should enable you to tune into your partner's needs on all levels.

You are probably less happy-go-lucky in your relationships than many Sun sign Sagittarians, but should be careful not to let Cancerian moodiness and a tendency to react very sharply mar so much that is positive.

Your well-being
The Cancerian body area covers the breasts and, although Cancerians are no more likely to contract cancer than anyone else, Sagittarian women should obviously make the usual regular checks.

Sagittarians are among the people who are least likely to worry when confronted with problems, whereas

The Moon in Cancer

Cancerians are among those most prone to it. The positive areas of your personality should enable you to deal with worry, although your digestion may sometimes trouble you under difficult circumstances.

Cancerians are usually good and enthusiastic cooks, and Sagittarians like tasty, rich food. If you are overweight, you may not be getting enough exercise.

Planning ahead

You are very lucky where finance is concerned. Your Sagittarian gambling spirit is mitigated by a shrewd and instinctive business sense, stemming from your Moon sign. If you are investing, follow your intuition; when you are in doubt, you would be wise to seek professional advice.

Parenthood

You are probably a far more caring and protective parent than most Sagittarians. Do not take this too far, though, and allow your enthusiasm to encourage your children. If you are not too sentimental, and manage to keep abreast of your children's thoughts and ideas, you will have few problems with the generation gap.

THE MOON IN
LEO

YOUR LEO MOON PROMPTS A WELL-ORGANIZED, RATHER FORMAL APPROACH TO MOST SITUATIONS. YOUR ACCEPTANCE OF CHALLENGE IS ENCOURAGED BY AN ABILITY TO TAKE COMMAND, BUT YOU MUST TAKE CARE TO AVOID BEING BOSSY.

Your Sun and Moon signs are both of the fire element, so you have great natural enthusiasm and optimism, and an extremely positive outlook on life.

Self-expression
You may tend to be marginally more conventional than most Sun sign Sagittarians, but this only serves to make you naturally elegant and gives you a powerful instinct for real quality. Your Sun sign, on the other hand, endows you with a good mind, and you may have very considerable creative potential.

You are able to cope well with people and very possibly have excellent organizing ability. Generally speaking, your Sagittarian Sun prevents you from becoming pompous or bossy, but should you be accused of these traits, take note. You are extremely magnanimous, and never harbor a grudge.

Romance
You are a very passionate and demonstrative lover, and probably have a stylish approach to a prospective partner. You will create an expensive, romantic atmosphere, and will do everything in your power to make life happy, enjoyable, and even blissful for your lovers.

You will be a very supportive partner and, because loyalty is important to you, once you are committed you have less of a roving eye than many Sagittarians.

Your well-being
The Leo body area covers the back and spine. You will do well to remember this, and to gear part of your exercise schedule toward that area. If you have to spend a lot of time sitting at an office desk, consider getting a back-support chair. The Leo organ is the heart, and it too must be kept in good condition.

The Moon in Leo

Most Sun sign Sagittarians not only need, but also enjoy, physical exercise. Keeping fit through sports and exercise should therefore be no real problem for you. Your Leo Moon may attract you to all kinds of dance, and this is something that you should consider as an alternative to health clubs or participating in team sports.

Planning ahead

You need to earn a lot of money in order to enjoy a comfortable lifestyle; you have big ideas and may well be very extravagant. But you are not without financial flair and can be good with investments, provided that you remember to control your Sagittarian gambling spirit and the tendency to put too many eggs in one basket. Aim to have one or two really sound, secure savings plans.

Parenthood

You are a very encouraging and enthusiastic parent, and your children will thrive on your positive, lively comments on their interests. At times your children may see you as slightly pompous, but if you keep a sense of humor you should not have many problems with the generation gap.

THE MOON IN
VIRGO

Do not hesitate when confronted by tricky situations; you have a tendency to underestimate yourself. Guard against tension and restlessness. You are a good communicator and can cope well with detail.

Both Sagittarius and Virgo are mutable signs and, as a result, you have a flexible mind and great intellectual capacity.

Self-expression
While most Sagittarians find detail boring and difficult to deal with, you respond differently. You react well to it and may look at details even before looking for a broad overview.

You are critical and analytical in your approach to problems, and will probably express your Sagittarian versatility within the broad confines of one or two large subjects. Your ability to get your ideas across to other people is excellent, since you communicate fluently.

Romance
Your Sagittarian passion is somewhat moderated by your Virgoan Moon, which may inhibit you in the area of love and sex. An instinctive modesty

can make you feel a little inferior in this field. In fact, you have much to offer, so try not to put yourself down.

A serious Virgoan fault is to nag and to criticize partners, often for no good reason. Your Sagittarian Sun sign will loathe this tendency and help you to bite your tongue if you find yourself beginning to complain.

Your well-being
The Virgoan body area is the stomach and, while Sagittarius is not prone to worry, Virgo certainly is. Interestingly, your stomach may react before your mind. You need a high-fiber diet and will perhaps incline to vegetarianism, to which Virgoans tend to be particularly attracted.

You have a great deal of nervous, tense energy, and periods of stress can wreak havoc with you. A calming, centering discipline such as yoga could well be of considerable benefit to you. Also think about sports and

442

The Moon in Virgo

exercise regimens, which could include pursuits such as walking, rambling, cycling, and gardening.

Planning ahead
You are more careful with your finances than most Sagittarians, and find it fairly easy to save money and to avoid unnecessary extravagance. Your ability to cope with detail may incline you to keep careful accounts and to watch the stock market. Do, however, guard against your Sagittarian gambling spirit, and be self-critical if it seems likely to run away with you. This will be the time to seek professional advice.

Parenthood
All your Sagittarian enthusiasm will color your attitude to your children. However, that Virgoan critical response may be far harsher in your children's eyes than it seems to you. Keep up with their concerns, and you will avoid the generation gap.

THE MOON IN
LIBRA

YOUR REACTION TO ALMOST ANY SITUATION IS LIKELY TO BE VERY
CALM. ALWAYS MAKE SURE THAT YOU EXPRESS YOUR
SPLENDID SAGITTARIAN POTENTIAL, AND NEVER ALLOW
YOUR MIND AND BODY TO STAGNATE.

The fire of your Sagittarian Sun and the air of your Libran Moon blend well. You have a warm-hearted and attractive personality, and respond well to people, showing sympathy and understanding.

Self-expression

Because of their characteristic haste, Sagittarians sometimes tend to lack tact. This is not so in your case; your Libran Moon helps you to control the tendency and, in many ways, makes you a diplomat.

When confronted with challenging situations, your immediate response may well be less assertive and positive than that of many Sun sign Sagittarians. However, once you have drawn your conclusions, your Sagittarian Sun sign usually points you in the right direction.

There is an easygoing side to your nature, and you could give the impression that you cannot be rushed.

You may need to persuade yourself to be a little more self-disciplined and better organized if you are to make the best of your potential.

Romance

You are probably rather more romantic than many Sagittarians, and enjoy setting a glamorous scene in which to make love. Once committed, you make a wonderful partner. You will always be fair and listen to your lover's ideas.

Your well-being

The Libran organ is the kidneys and, if you are at all prone to headaches, there could be a minor problem with them. Very often those with a Libran influence get totally bored with exercise and just give up. Aim to avoid this, because Sagittarians have a lot of physical energy to burn, and lethargy does not suit them. Your Libran Moon may encourage you to

The Moon in Libra

eat too much sweet food, and you could well suffer from excessive weight gain as a result. Even the balance by becoming a member of a good health club with a variety of exercise programs.

Planning ahead

You are very generous and may not be terribly sensible with money. Both your Sagittarian gambling streak and your Libran Moon's sympathy for a hard-luck story may be a source of money problems. Do not overinvest in one area, do not lend money, and do not gamble more than you can afford to lose. Always aim to get professional advice in this area.

Parenthood

While you are a very enthusiastic and kind parent, you are capable of spoiling your children. Remember that indecisiveness on your part makes it difficult for them to know where they stand. If you keep up with their ideas, you will have few difficulties with the generation gap.

THE MOON IN
SCORPIO

YOUR SAGITTARIAN BREADTH OF VISION IS ENHANCED BY A NATURAL ABILITY TO DELVE DEEPLY INTO PROBLEMS. THIS DERIVES FROM YOUR MOON SIGN. YOU HAVE AN INTENSE, FIERY PASSION, BUT YOU SHOULD CURB ANY TENDENCY TO JEALOUSY.

Sagittarius and Scorpio are both charged with a great deal of physical and emotional energy. Sagittarians express this in a lively, positive way, while Scorpios tend to be deeply penetrating, incisive, and generally very intuitive.

Self-expression
You obviously have extremely powerful resources on which to draw, and striking potential. You have breadth of vision and the ability to deal with any aspect of a challenge or problematic situation. Your powers of endurance, under both difficult physical conditions and intellectually demanding ones, are second to none. With all of this in mind, it is obvious that you need to be totally committed to your objectives in life, and that your reach must always exceed your grasp. If you are unfulfilled and life seems empty, few Sagittarians will suffer more than you.

Romance
Your passion for a full life is second only to your expression of love and sex. In this area you are very enthusiastic and, while you contribute a great deal to the success of a permanent emotional relationship, you are also very demanding, and need an extremely energetic and passionate partner.

The worst Scorpio fault is jealousy – something that your Sagittarian Sun sign will deplore. You may find yourself reacting negatively to a partner's mildly flirtatious behavior, while you yourself enjoy an element of freedom within a relationship.

Your well-being
The Scorpio body area covers the genitals; anyone, whatever their Sun sign, should get regular checkups in that area. But it is your emotional and physical energy that has the strongest influence on your general health and

The Moon in Scorpio

well-being. Aim to get regular exercise; all kinds of water sports should suit you.

Planning ahead

You could be very clever with money, provided that you allow your instinctive business sense and intuition to express themselves. Financial risk-taking could attract you, and you may end up taking an unwise plunge. At such times, the Scorpion is wiser than the Centaur.

Parenthood

While you are always enthusiastic and encouraging, you could be a somewhat demanding parent. Children like a well-structured life, which gives them a sense of security. Be careful not to overdo this, however, or to allow tradition and discipline to interfere with the sheer enjoyment of your children's company. Encourage their interests and ideas, and keep abreast of them in order to avoid the generation gap.

THE MOON IN
SAGITTARIUS

BECAUSE BOTH THE SUN AND THE MOON WERE IN SAGITTARIUS
AT THE TIME OF YOUR BIRTH, YOU WERE BORN UNDER A
NEW MOON. SAGITTARIUS IS A FIRE SIGN, SO THIS ELEMENT
INFLUENCES YOUR PERSONALITY AND REACTIONS.

Should you study a list of your Sun sign characteristics, you will probably recognize that a great many of them apply to you. Out of a list of perhaps 20 traits of a Sun sign listed in books or magazines, most people will strongly identify with 11 or 12. For you, however, the average increases considerably because the Sun and Moon were both in Sagittarius when you were born.

Self-expression

Not only do you have the attributes of your Sun sign, but you also respond to situations in the same manner. When someone suggests an idea to you, your natural enthusiasm ignites, and you are eager to get involved.

You probably do not worry too much about possible pitfalls or problems, regarding them as something to be dealt with when you come to them. But it is important that you keep your initial enthusiasm on the boil, because if you do not, you could easily succumb to the most serious Sagittarian fault: restlessness. You are capable of enormous versatility, but must learn to be selective and to develop a degree of consistency. You have a high level of intellectual and physical energy, and neither must be allowed to stagnate.

Romance

You are passionate and will enjoy love and sex with a youthful exuberance. You must have a full love and sex life, and need a partner who is intellectually very stimulating.

Fidelity may not come naturally to you, and your partners must learn that you need a good measure of freedom in this sphere of your life.

Your well-being

If you turn to pages 422 to 423, you will read about Sagittarian health and well-being. As you are a "double

The Moon in Sagittarius

Sagittarian," those comments will most definitely apply to you. Be careful not to overindulge in heavy food. You are prone to weight gain, and unwanted flesh is likely to gather around your hips and thighs – especially if you are a woman. Good workouts and some of the more daring sports are excellent for you.

Planning ahead

Your Sagittarian gambling instinct could get the better of you from time to time, and you may be strongly attracted to get-rich-quick schemes. You must be careful to curb these enthusiasms and to always get professional financial advice when you have some money to invest, no matter how convincing a deal may seem at the time.

Parenthood

You are among the most enthusiastic of parents and will always encourage your children to make the most of their potential. You probably try to see to it that they fill their days as completely as you do. You do not find it difficult to keep up with their ideas and should not incur problems with the generation gap.

THE MOON IN
CAPRICORN

YOU HAVE A GREAT DEAL OF POTENTIAL AND ARE ALWAYS VERY
EAGER TO GET INVOLVED IN AMBITIOUS SCHEMES. YOUR
EARTHY CAPRICORNIAN MOON ADDS PRACTICALITY TO YOUR
CHARACTER — AND PERHAPS A TENDENCY TO GRUMBLE.

There are some striking contrasts between Sagittarius and Capricorn and, as a result, you possess a multifaceted personality, with a great deal of potential that can be expressed in a variety of ways.

Self-expression
Your Sagittarian Sun sign gives you fiery enthusiasm and a positive outlook on life. On the other hand, the earth element of your Moon sign makes you instinctively cautious and far less likely to take risks than are many Sagittarians.

You are very ambitious and, when presented with a challenging situation, will at once be able to foresee the end result. You will then begin to plan your moves constructively toward that goal.

Sagittarians are, on the whole, good communicators, and you will certainly let it be known if you are being impeded by some form of inefficiency. Should you be accused of grumbling too much, which is usually very uncharacteristic of Sagittarians, you must take note.

Romance
You are less gushing in expressing your emotions than many people of your Sun sign, and could tend to hold back a little in the initial stages of a relationship. This does not mean that you cannot enjoy a truly rewarding and fulfilling love and sex life.

You could be more faithful, and have less of a roving eye, than other Sagittarians, and may take a while to commit yourself to a relationship.

Your well-being
The Capricornian body area covers the knees and shins. Yours will be vulnerable, especially if you engage in a lot of sporting activities. Treatment can save a great deal of pain and prevent serious problems.

The Moon in Capricorn

The teeth, skin, and bones are also in Capricorn's domain, so beware of stiffness in the joints, and keep moving. Do not neglect regular dental checkups, and wear a protective cream when the sun is strong.

You may have a rapid metabolism; if so, weight gain is unlikely to be a problem for you.

Planning ahead
Anyone with a Capricornian influence is usually careful, and often good with money. You like to see it grow, so your Sagittarian gambling streak is probably kept under control. You only take financial risks if you are sure you can afford to lose the money involved.

Parenthood
Your sense of humor is a great asset to you as a parent, but you could, surprisingly for a Sagittarian, react a little coolly to some of your children's suggestions and ideas. If you enjoy the challenge of keeping up with them, you will manage to leap across the generation gap.

THE MOON IN
AQUARIUS

SAGITTARIUS AND AQUARIUS ARE BOTH SIGNS THAT REQUIRE INDEPENDENCE. TRY NOT TO ALLOW A TENDENCY TO RESPOND COOLLY AND DISTANTLY TO OTHER PEOPLE SPOIL YOUR WONDERFUL SAGITTARIAN APPROACH TO LOVE.

The fire element of Sagittarius and the air element of Aquarius blend well, not only making you the individualist of your Sun sign peers, but also putting you among those who greatly need independence and freedom of expression.

Self-expression
You may well have built a lifestyle that has certain individual features. You are a warm-hearted and very friendly person, but definitely need both physical and psychological space. Pettiness, unnecessary detail, and people who nag are not for you.

Romance
The Moon in Aquarius adds a certain glitz and glamour to your personality, but you may also respond coolly and distantly when first approached by prospective partners. You need a good period of friendship and intellectual rapport before the lively passion of

your Sagittarian Sun can be fully expressed. Your love and sex life is probably rewarding, but you must cater to your need for independence. You may postpone a full commitment until you find a partner who sees this and is willing to allow you space.

Your well-being
The Aquarian body area covers the ankles, and yours are vulnerable. The circulation is also ruled by Aquarius and, if you like crisp, cold weather, you must try to keep warm.

You may enjoy skiing, skating, or dancing. In any case, you should get involved in some form of exercise. You thrive on a light diet, even if you like the heavier foods often favored by your Sun sign.

Planning ahead
You may find it quite difficult to save money regularly. You are probably attracted to fashionable clothes and

The Moon in Aquarius

fine and unusual things for the home. You could go all out for some apparently excellent savings plan and invest heavily in it, only to find that it runs into difficulty.

It may be well worth your while to seek professional financial advice when you have some money to invest. Best of all, you should seriously consider taking part in some option where a certain proportion of your regular paycheck is invested at the source before you can squander it.

Remember, your Sagittarian gambling spirit is very much attracted to exciting but risky schemes.

Parenthood

You are an extremely lively parent and do not find it difficult to know what your children are thinking. If you keep up with their ideas, you should have few problems with the generation gap. Aim to display warm affection toward your children, and avoid unpredictable responses.

THE MOON IN
PISCES

SAGITTARIUS AND PISCES ARE DUAL SIGNS OF THE ZODIAC, AND YOU
ARE THEREFORE VERY VERSATILE. HOWEVER, YOU DO NEED
TO DEVELOP CONSISTENCY OF EFFORT, AND MUST BE DISCIPLINED
IF YOU ARE TO DEVELOP TO YOUR FULL POTENTIAL.

Sagittarius and Pisces are both mutable signs, and their combination makes you very flexible and easygoing. In addition, both are dual signs. Pisces is represented by two fishes swimming in opposite directions, Sagittarius by a creature who is both man and horse. These symbols represent a high degree of versatility, with enviable potential, but suggest a similarly high degree of restlessness.

Self-expression
While it is very important for you to have a variety of very different interests, you should also develop staying power and complete any project that you start, if it is to give you inner satisfaction.

Your response to challenges is complex. At first, you probably feel somewhat hesitant and lacking in confidence, but then you may decide on a line of action. Finally you will,

for no apparent reason, do precisely the opposite, which may turn out to be a mistake. Your Sun sign gives you an excellent, sharp intellect and a rich imagination, possibly adding creative potential. Be firm with yourself, and exploit these qualities.

Romance
You are caring, loving, and passionate, but need a strong partner who will bring out the best in you and ignite your Sagittarian enthusiasm. You are capable of giving much to a lover, and should enjoy a rich and rewarding love and sex life.

The worst Piscean fault is deceitfulness; do not lie to yourself, especially when considering your lovers' attitudes to you.

Your well-being
The Piscean body area is the feet, and you may find it difficult to obtain comfortable shoes. You could easily

The Moon in Pisces

fall back on eating too heavily, and may be prone to putting on weight unless you are actively involved in some form of sports, for example, dancing or skating.

Planning ahead
You are sometimes left wondering where your money has gone. The answer is that you have spent it on frivolous things. You may need help from a stronger, more down-to-earth partner or a friendly bank officer in working out a sensible budget. If you have some spare money, make sure that you get financial advice before investing it. You should neither lend money, nor give so readily to charity that you get yourself into trouble.

Parenthood
You are probably a very warm and caring parent, who may well spoil your children. Take disciplinary measures when you must, even if you do not enjoy being strict, since this will help give your children a more secure background. You will always listen to your children's problems, so they will know where they stand with you. There should be no problems with the generation gap.

SUN & MOON SIGNS

CAPRICORN

DECEMBER 22 – JANUARY 20

INTRODUCING
CAPRICORN

CAPRICORN, WHO IS TRADITIONALLY REPRESENTED AS THE
HALF-GOAT, HALF-FISH FIGURE, IS THE TENTH SIGN OF
THE ZODIAC. SUN SIGN CAPRICORNIANS GENERALLY HAVE
RATHER COMPLEX CHARACTERS.

There are two distinct types of Capricornian. One type will be ambitious and enterprising, while the other will never find the motivation to move forward in life and will spend a great deal of time complaining about the real or imagined obstacles that hold them back. Even the most famous and successful Capricornian may have a tendency to grumble, and all people of this sign can feel that they are forced to carry undeserved burdens. A fondness for solitude is another Capricornian characteristic.

Traditional groupings

As you read through this book you will come across references to the elements and the qualities, and to positive and negative, or masculine and feminine signs.

The first of these groupings, that of the elements, comprises fire, earth, air, and water signs. The second, that of the qualities, divides the Zodiac into cardinal, fixed, and mutable signs. The final grouping is made up of positive and negative, or masculine and feminine signs. Each Zodiac sign is associated with a combination of components from these groupings, all of which contribute different characteristics to it.

Capricornian characteristics

Capricorn belongs to the earth element, and its subjects often have a great deal of practical common sense. It is of the cardinal quality, which may make you outgoing. However, as a negative, feminine sign Capricorn also inclines its subjects to introversion. All of these characteristics find expression in the Capricorn personality. Saturn, your ruling planet, also guides your destiny, and "saturnine" is an adjective that often applies to you. Capricornians generally prefer subdued colors such as gray or dark green.

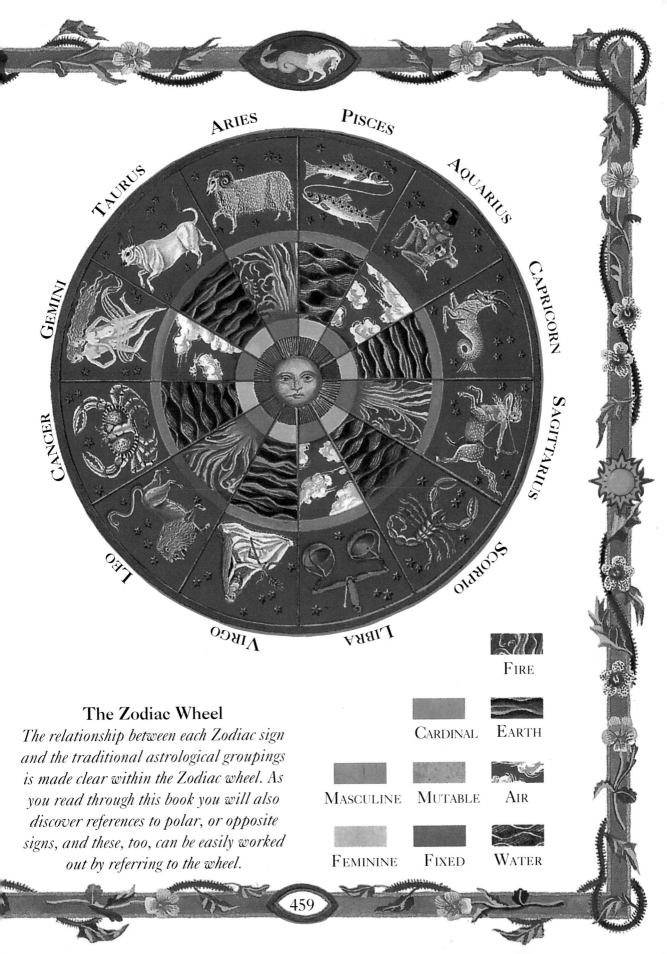

The Zodiac Wheel

The relationship between each Zodiac sign and the traditional astrological groupings is made clear within the Zodiac wheel. As you read through this book you will also discover references to polar, or opposite signs, and these, too, can be easily worked out by referring to the wheel.

ARIES

PISCES

TAURUS

AQUARIUS

GEMINI

CAPRICORN

CANCER

SAGITTARIUS

LEO

SCORPIO

VIRGO

LIBRA

FIRE

CARDINAL

EARTH

MASCULINE

MUTABLE

AIR

FEMININE

FIXED

WATER

MYTHS & LEGENDS

THE ZODIAC, WHICH IS BELIEVED TO HAVE ORIGINATED IN
BABYLON AS LONG AS 2,500 YEARS AGO, IS A
CIRCLE OF CONSTELLATIONS THROUGH WHICH THE SUN
MOVES DURING THE COURSE OF A YEAR.

Many Zodiacal figures were first carved on Babylonian boundary stones. This is where Capricorn makes his first appearance, as the Goat-Fish. He is shown as Ea, a man walking in a great fish-shaped cloak, with the fish head over his head and the cloak trailing into a tail. One of his Babylonian titles was "antelope of the subterranean ocean." He was said to rise from the waters during the day in order to tutor man in the arts of civilization and to return to the depths at night.

Ea's name means "House of the Water," and perhaps this indicates the significance that was placed upon him in a country where water was such a precious commodity. He had the role of god of knowledge and presided over the work done by men. Because of this, he was devoutly worshiped by many different types of craftsmen.

Pan pipes
This bronze statuette of Pan and the syrinx dates from 430 B.C.

Later myths

The later mythological associations of Capricorn are obscure and difficult to follow. There is a distant association with Pan, no doubt because although he had a human torso and arms, other parts of his body consisted of the legs, ears, and horns of a goat. He was the son of Hermes, the messenger of the gods, but his mother's name is uncertain. According to some sources it was Callisto, but others sometimes mention Penelope.

Pan and Syrinx

Pan is perhaps best remembered as the being who was responsible for inventing the panpipes; he called them syrinx in honor of a nymph who was turned into a reed to escape his amorous attentions.

Pan loved mountains, caves, and lonely places, and it was while frisking with nymphs in one such desolate place that he gave chase to Syrinx. Just as he was about to capture her, she called out for help to her father, Ladon the river god. At her request, Ladon turned her into a reed and Pan was foiled. To console himself, Pan cut down a clump of reeds and made some pipes. The music that Pan was able to produce on his syrinx was apparently so sweet that on one occasion he challenged Apollo, the god of music and the personification of beauty, to a musical competition.

Panic fear

The feeling of loneliness that can afflict people traveling on their own through wild or inhospitable terrain was sometimes attributed to the presence of Pan. Any fear that seemed unattributable to an obvious cause has come to be known as "panic fear" – or panic for short.

The music of Pan
The image on this dish, which dates from 1515, shows Pan playing his syrinx to a couple of shepherds.

Although it does at first seem to be an extremely slender association, astrologers throughout the ages have attempted to play up with the Capricornian qualities that can be related to the goat.

The domestic animal is, for instance, often tethered in one small space, while for the wild mountain goat the mountains and hills seem to be as accessible as they once were to the god Pan himself.

Many Sun sign Capricornians have a fondness and perhaps even a real need for solitude.

CAPRICORN
SYMBOLISM

CERTAIN HERBS, SPICES, FLOWERS, TREES, GEMS, METALS, AND
ANIMALS HAVE LONG BEEN ASSOCIATED WITH PARTICULAR
ZODIAC SIGNS. SOME ASSOCIATIONS ARE SIMPLY AMUSING, WHILE
OTHERS CAN BE GENUINELY USEFUL.

Pansies and ivy
*Pansies and ivy are two of the
decorative plants said to be
ruled by Capricorn.*

PANSIES

IVY

Spices

No spice is traditionally associated with Capricorn, but angostura bitters and cloves are sometimes attributed to this sign.

CLOVES

Trees

Capricornian trees include the somewhat austere pine and yew, as well as the graceful willow, aspen, elm, and poplar.

BELLADONNA

Herbs

The poisonous belladonna is ruled by Capricorn. Knapweed, which is good for healing sores, and plantain, which is used almost indiscriminately to treat a wide variety of illnesses, are also traditional Capricornian herbs.

KNAPWEED

CAPRICORN
SYMBOLISM

Metal

The traditional metal of the sign is lead, no doubt because of its gray color. When Capricornians choose jewelry, however, they often show a preference for silver items.

LEAD ORE

LEAD
PENCILS

TURQUOISE CHIPS
AND BOX

AMETHYST
FRAGMENT
AND NECKLACE

Gems
*The Capricornian gem is traditionally
said to be the amethyst, although
some astrologers make a connection
with turquoise.*

BRONZE
GOAT

Animals
*Goats are, of course,
Capricornian animals, but so
too are all animals with horns
and cloven hooves, and those
that live on mountain slopes.*

CAPRICORN
PROFILE

YOUR OVERALL LOOK WILL BE CONVENTIONAL WITHIN YOUR OWN PEER GROUP. CAPRICORNIANS USUALLY WALK QUICKLY, TAKING LONG STRIDES. THEY HOLD THEIR HEADS EITHER UP OR DOWN, ACCORDING TO THEIR PREVAILING MOOD.

Many Capricornians are tall, and they may have a tendency to stoop, sometimes with their knees bent. However, when they are feeling positive they will stand erect and tall, and may occasionally appear to look down on the rest of the world.

The body

As Capricorn rules the bones, the skeletal frame is likely to be strong, with rather obvious bony wrists, elbows, and knees. A large number of Capricornians are tall and thin, with a fairly gaunt appearance. Another type of Capricornian will have a slim build, but will often be on the short side. Members of this second group can tend to have rather bony knees.

The Capricornian face
A high forehead and a direct gaze characterize the Capricorn face.

Capricornian legs are likely to be long and slim and, in the case of many women, extremely beautiful. They will quite rightly be shown to their best advantage, for example, swathed in black hosiery.

The face

Capricornians often have rather heavy hair, which tends to be sleekly styled and cut. The forehead can be high, and the eyes show directness; they are steady, although perhaps downcast. The nose is often emphasized by lines joining its sides to the corners of the mouth, which are usually turned down when the individual smiles. The chin can sometimes be fairly sharp. The shape of the entire face – the temples,

The Capricornian stance

Capricornians are often tall, perhaps with a tendency to stoop. When feeling positive they will, however, stand tall and proud.

nose, cheekbones, jaw, and chin – may reflect the rather prominent Capricornian bone structure.

Style

The Capricornian image is conventional: both men and women look marvelous in well-cut, chic suits and dark colors. A "little black dress," perhaps adorned by dramatic jewelry, is a particular favorite with women. Stylishness is the rule, even with casual clothes. Quality is important, too, and you are likely to favor designer labels. Exaggerated fashion will not appeal to you; classic clothes will.

In general

Capricornians do not like to stand out in a crowd. A reserved, quiet image is far more acceptable. Because you like to impress, but will be reluctant to make too strong a statement, you will often choose to wear high-quality, formal clothes. With experience, you will discover ways in which a dramatic but restrained look can be achieved by the addition of subtle and interesting jewelry or accessories. Capricornians tend to be attracted to high-quality belts, handbags, and briefcases. You may also have a preference for traditional fragrances, as opposed to more overpowering modern scents.

Clothes made from natural fibers such as cotton and wool, perhaps in shades of pale gray and dark green, are likely to flatter you.

CAPRICORN PERSONALITY

CAPRICORNIANS SHOULD SET THEIR SIGHTS HIGH AND ASPIRE TO
GREAT THINGS. MANY ARE TRUE ACHIEVERS, BUT
OTHERS TEND TO GRUMBLE OVER THE OBSTACLES THAT
PREVENT THEM FROM BEING SUCCESSFUL.

Many fine and noble qualities, for example prudence, caution, circumspection, and practical common sense, are shared by members of this Sun sign group. However, unlike the other Zodiac signs, this one produces two very contrasting types.

The symbol of the sign is a goat with a fish's tail, and this fact is significant. The fish's tail represents a powerful psychological factor in the Capricornian makeup that can curb ambition, produce a negative response to other people's suggestions, and generally spoil things not only for the Capricornian, but for others as well.

At work
You may sometimes take on a gloomy attitude because you feel that much of your success at work depends on your being thoroughly reliable in what you do, so that you must stick to a regular routine. This could make you feel perennially depressed.

You will no doubt place great value upon retaining a sense of security, and are unlikely to take extravagant risks.

Your attitudes
Your depressing inner voice will all too often make itself felt when you try to be at all daring, or want to do something just for the fun of it. Try not to let it hold you back.

There is, however, another, fun-loving side to the Capricornian goat. Many people of this sign seem to manage metaphorically to slough off the fish's tail and become all goat – in fact, a giddy goat who simply will not have anything to do with the wet-blanket, depressive attitude expressed by some Capricornians. They will have fun, love life, and thoroughly enjoy the process of achieving the ambitious objectives that they decide to set themselves. These latter Capricornians are able to take care of themselves very well.

Saturn rules Capricorn

Saturn, originally an agricultural god, represents the Capricornian ruling planet. It can make its subjects practical and cautious, but also selfish and narrow-minded.

They are highly motivated people who will attempt to reach for the sky, and may well go so far as to touch it.

The overall picture

You should try to recognize which type of Capricorn you resemble most closely. Remember, however, that yours is one sign, not two; you may seem to be a placid valley goat, happily tethered to a restricting pole, but you can escape and play the giddy goat. You might lack confidence, but this should not be allowed to hold you back. Even the most successful person is, of course, entitled to grumble from time to time, but you should be aware of how this tendency affects you and those around you, and try not to succumb to it too often.

CAPRICORN
ASPIRATIONS

YOUR NEED FOR SECURITY CAN CONFLICT WITH AMBITION, AND YOU MAY NOT LIKE TAKING CHANCES. A FONDNESS FOR ROUTINE MAKES YOU A VALUABLE EMPLOYEE, AND YOU MAY HAVE WHAT IT TAKES TO COPE WITH A TOP JOB.

The building trade
In the same way that Capricornians are excellent at "building" their lives, you may find inner satisfaction from working in the building trades.

TROWEL
AND
CEMENT

MINIATURE
GLOBE

Property management
Managing the land is an attractive profession for Capricornians. You will enjoy working on site as much as in an office.

Teaching
The dry Capricornian sense of humor will be an asset to you if you decide to become a teacher. You may specialize in geography.

DOCUMENTS AND WAX SEAL

Civil service
A need for security and the chance to make gradual progress, plus the possibility of involvement with those in power, attracts Capricornians to civil service.

APPLICATOR FOR DENTAL CEMENT

PLANS AND SPIRIT LEVEL

Dentistry
The powerful astrological tradition linking Capricorn with the skeletal system could draw you to the dental profession.

CAPRICORN
HEALTH

CAPRICORNIANS ARE OFTEN TOO CONCERNED WITH WORLDLY
MATTERS AND CARRY HEAVY BURDENS OF RESPONSIBILITY;
YOU MAY TEND TO NEGLECT YOUR PHYSICAL WELL-BEING AND
COULD AGE MORE QUICKLY THAN YOU SHOULD.

The Capricornian body area covers the knees and shins, but the skin, bones, and teeth are also ruled by this sign. It is important for all Sun sign Capricornians, both young and old, to keep moving. An excessively static life may result in stiffness of the joints, and rheumatism and even arthritis could eventually set in.

Your diet
Most Capricornians have a rather fast metabolism, so weight gain is less likely to be a problem for you than other Zodiac types. You might benefit from adding the cell salt calcium phosphate (calc. phos.) to your diet. As the principal salt contained in the bone structure, it may be of particular importance to you.

Taking care
Many Capricornians are interested in sports, and some may be great athletes. You could find that knee injuries will affect you more frequently than they do people of other signs. Make sure that you get medical attention for even the slightest trouble; more severe problems may develop if you are at all negligent in this area.

Even if regular dental checkups appear to be little more than an unnecessary expense, they are especially desirable for Capricornians. You might feel justifiably proud when the dentist congratulates you on your high level of oral hygiene, but you should not take this as an excuse to stop making regular visits.

As a Capricornian you may well possess unusually beautiful, fine skin, and that too could need some extra-special care. It may be ultrasensitive, in which case it would be advisable for you to use a high-factor protective cream in very strong sun to prevent redness, blotchiness, or something more serious from developing.

Astrology and the body

For many centuries it was not possible to practice medicine without a knowledge of astrology. In European universities, medical training included information on how planetary positions would affect the administration of medicines, the bleeding of patients, and the right time to pick herbs and make potions. Each Zodiac sign rules a particular part of the body – from Aries (the head) to Pisces (the feet) – and textbooks always included a drawing of a "Zodiac man" (or woman) that illustrated the point.

CAPRICORN AT
LEISURE

EACH OF THE SUN SIGNS TRADITIONALLY SUGGESTS SPARE-TIME
ACTIVITIES, HOBBIES, AND VACATION SPOTS.
ALTHOUGH THESE ARE ONLY SUGGESTIONS, THEY OFTEN WORK
OUT WELL FOR CAPRICORNIANS.

Going to the races
*A day at the races involves
dressing up and mixing with the
"right" people, and therefore
gives satisfaction to
ambitious Capricornians.*

BINOCULARS

MODEL SPINNING
WHEEL

Weaving
*The creation of fabrics
from natural materials may
prove attractive to creative
Capricornians.*

Golf

Many Capricornians like to get out in the fresh air, and golf also provides a good opportunity to meet other active, upwardly mobile people.

GEOLOGIST'S
HAMMERS

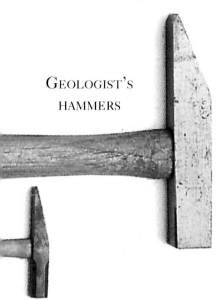

SET OF GOLF
TEES

Pottery

Working with clay gives creative Capricornians a great sense of inner fulfillment and pleasure because it puts them in touch with their earth element.

Geology

Capricornians are often interested in the distant past, and may develop a fascination with the formation of the Earth's surface.

POSTAGE STAMPS

Travel

You will enjoy planning your trip almost as much as taking it. Destinations might include the Orkney or Shetland Isles in Great Britain, or Mexico or India.

TOOLS USED FOR POTTERY

CAPRICORN IN
LOVE

CAPRICORNIANS USUALLY KEEP THEIR EMOTIONS UNDER CONTROL
AND CAN BE PEOPLE OF FEW WORDS. WHAT THEY DO SAY,
HOWEVER, THEY USUALLY MEAN. TO ACHIEVE FULFILLING LOVE
LIVES, THEY SOMETIMES NEED TO LEARN HOW TO RELAX.

Very possibly, it may take some time for you to realize you are in love. Once you fall for someone, however, your commitment will be deep. Your natural caution encourages you to make quite sure of your ground before committing yourself, or even before declaring your love. You may fear the thought of rejection, and it is likely to hurt you much more than it would most other Zodiac types.

As a lover

You can be very reserved indeed in the way that you express your feelings towards others, and may even take this to the point where you give the distinct impression of being rather cold and distant. This characteristic is most likely to emerge if you had a repressive or overly disciplined childhood. But with the right partner, all Capricornians will blossom and show their fun-loving characteristics. Your tendency always to do the right and proper thing will help to ensure your fidelity once you are committed to a permanent relationship. When this occurs, a strong urge to protect and look after your partner and, in due course, your children, will probably develop in you. If, however, you are ambitious, a tendency to concentrate on material progress may impinge on your family life, leaving insufficient time for all of you to be together. You may not be averse to a little genteel social climbing and will be delighted and proud to date your boss's son or daughter – or even the boss.

Types of Capricornian lover

Capricornians express their love in one of five different ways: you may, for instance, be a highly sexed and very demanding partner. Jealousy can sometimes emerge, and must be controlled. On the other hand, you may have a more free, passionate approach to love. Other Sun sign Capricornians will be pure in spirit, and will agree with most of the general comments that have been expressed here. They will aim to be constant and faithful, but must try to overcome feelings of reticence in their relationships with their partners. Members of a fourth group have a charismatic effect on their partners, but tend to act rather coolly until a lover has broken the ice. Finally, there are those Capricornians who tend to throw caution to the winds when they are in love.

CAPRICORN AT HOME

DEPENDING ON WHAT TYPE OF CAPRICORNIAN YOU ARE, YOUR HOME WILL EITHER BE FURNISHED AND DESIGNED CHIEFLY TO IMPRESS OR EXTREMELY SPARTAN. YOU WILL PROCLAIM YOUR TRUE PERSONALITY THROUGH THE STYLE YOU CHOOSE.

Many Capricornians move from one residence to the next with unusual frequency. This is generally due to the fact that as they gradually make their way up the social ladder they want their homes to match their newfound status accordingly.

China coffee set
Articles made from china or fine porcelain are likely to be proudly displayed.

Furniture
Financially conscious Capricornians are highly unlikely to throw money away on trendy or impractical flippancies. This holds particularly true when it comes to their choice of furniture.

Your taste is possibly rather conventional, so you will choose traditional styles and, if you can afford them, antiques that are made in a traditional fashion. To obtain them you will often search at auction houses rather than large department stores. You are probably attracted to beautiful, good-quality, wood, either polished or left in its natural state. One thing that might well be worth bearing in mind is the Capricornian tendency to want to impress other people. This could end up governing your choice and, as a result, comfort may be sacrificed in a search for the correct type of appearance.

Soft furnishings
You will usually keep soft furnishings to a minimum. Curtains and drapes will be well shaped and cut, and perhaps made of natural materials such as linen. Pure silk may be another favorite with you. Your

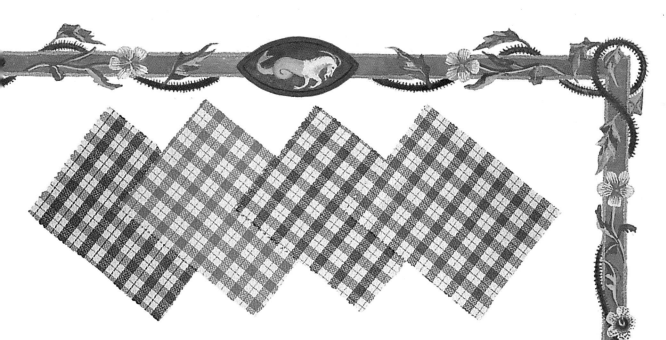

preference for natural materials is due to the influence of the earth element of your sign. The overall effect of the Capricornian home is elegant, tasteful, and without doubt expensive-looking, even if the individual is poor. A certain severity can, however, also be present.

Decorative objects

Any inherited articles will be proudly displayed, especially if they are silver, and family portraits will be placed in prominent positions.

A tendency to show off objects on stands is common. Capricornians are often attracted to unusual rocks or shells. You may have a piece of amethyst, the Capricornian stone, glinting away on a windowsill. A restrained flower arrangement containing a few carefully placed blooms may also have a place in your home. China or pieces of porcelain will often be carefully displayed.

Gingham cloth
Materials with a subdued pattern often characterize the Capricornian home.

Elegant armchair
Settees and easy chairs may be covered in natural materials, such as wool, and are likely to be rather hard.

THE
MOON
AND
YOU

THE SUN DECREES YOUR OUTWARD
EXPRESSION, YOUR IMAGE, AND MANY
IMPORTANT PERSONALITY TRAITS. THE
MOON, ALTHOUGH MERELY THE EARTH'S
SATELLITE, IS ASTRONOMICALLY THE
SECOND MOST IMPORTANT BODY IN THE
SOLAR SYSTEM. FROM THE SIGN THAT IT
WAS IN AT YOUR BIRTH, IT INFLUENCES HOW
YOU REACT TO SITUATIONS, YOUR
EMOTIONAL LEVEL, AND, TO A CERTAIN
EXTENT, WHAT YOU HAVE INHERITED FROM
YOUR PARENTS AND ANCESTORS. AFTER
FINDING YOUR MOON SIGN IN THE SIMPLE
TABLES ON PAGES 606 TO 609, TURN TO THE
RELEVANT PAGES AND TAKE A STEP
FORWARD IN YOUR OWN SELF-KNOWLEDGE.

THE MOON IN
ARIES

YOUR ASSERTIVE ARIEN MOON PROVIDES YOU WITH A POSITIVE AND
ENTHUSIASTIC RESPONSE TO AMBITIOUS CAPRICORNIAN
OBJECTIVES AND SCHEMES. IT HELPS QUELL ANY TENDENCY
TO TAKE YOURSELF AND LIFE TOO SERIOUSLY.

You respond to most situations with a positive, lively enthusiasm that adds a sparkle to your practical, earthy Capricornian qualities. Your powerful motivation to be aspiring and ambitious is supported by an instinctive urge to win.

Self-expression
You have the potential to be a truly high achiever. Very few situations frighten you, and you are in an excellent position to overcome any inhibiting feelings. The emotional energy of your Arien Moon is very potent. Express it by getting involved in work that you find really rewarding.

Romance
You are among the most passionate of Capricornians, and may fall in love more quickly, and express yourself less cautiously, than many people of your Sun sign. Your partners will appreciate your positive approach to

this sphere of your life. Allow your passion plenty of free expression, and do not hesitate to sweep your lovers off their feet. The worst Arien fault is selfishness, and you should be aware that it may lead to problems.

Your well-being
The Arien body area is the head, and you may consequently be rather prone to headaches. These are probably stress-related, so perhaps you would benefit from a relaxation technique such as yoga. Otherwise, there is a relationship between headaches and the kidneys, and it is possible that yours could be slightly out of balance.

Ariens are hasty and prone to minor accidents. As a Sun sign Capricornian you have enough caution and patience to overcome this tendency, but you could sometimes become uncharacteristically careless. You usually cope very well with quite vigorous sports and exercise.

The Moon in Aries

Planning ahead

In true Capricornian style, you are probably careful with money and smart with investments. Your Arien Moon gives you an enterprising spirit that encourages you to start money-making schemes.

People with an Arien emphasis commonly have two sources of income; you may well fall successfully into this category. You are probably more generous than many Sun sign Capricornians, and your immediate response to any form of need is to take direct action, often by donating some money.

Parenthood

All Capricornians like to have some time to themselves, perhaps for reading or listening to music. Make sure that you have enough of this spare time. You should not find it difficult to keep up with your children's ideas, so the generation gap will pose few problems for you.

THE MOON IN
TAURUS

YOUR SUN AND MOON ARE BOTH IN EARTH SIGNS. YOUR TAUREAN MOON COMPLEMENTS YOUR CAPRICORNIAN SUN, AND ADDS A WARM AND AFFECTIONATE RESPONSE TO THE HIGHLY PRACTICAL, MORE CAUTIOUS ASPECTS OF YOUR CHARACTER.

You are among the most practical and cautious of all Sun and Moon sign combinations. Your gift is for the steady, sound development of your talents and abilities, and for solid material growth.

Self-expression

It is worth remembering that there is a lively, almost flighty side to Capricorn. If, however, you are too concerned with your career and family, and with finding a way to ensure that your children have everything they need, your livelier qualities could be somewhat subdued.

The Moon is traditionally "well placed" in Taurus. This means that its influence on you is rather stronger than on many people. Among other traits, it emphasizes an attraction to the good life and pleasure-seeking. You should allow yourself to respond positively to this, since it will let you enjoy the fruits of your labors.

Romance

Your Taurean Moon encourages your instinctive need for emotional and material security. You need a stable, permanent relationship and a reliable partner with whom you can stride forward through life.

You are a warm and sensual lover, and should enjoy a rich and rewarding love and sex life. Do, however, remember that possessiveness is the worst Taurean fault, and that you could well be too overbearing toward a lover, perhaps creating a rather claustrophobic atmosphere.

Your well-being

The Taurean body area covers the neck and throat, and you should therefore take care of it.

Those with a Taurean emphasis are often somewhat lazy when it comes to exercise and can have a rather slow metabolism. This is not usually the case with Capricornians. If you are

The Moon in Taurus

prone to weight gain, you may need to make exercise a regular part of your no doubt well-planned life. You may also have quite a sweet tooth and a preference for rich foods. The calories, and the pounds, could have an effect on your figure.

Planning ahead
You have the capacity to be very good with money. You may even have chosen a career in banking or insurance. In any case, you will certainly make your money work for you. You will not want to take financial risks of any kind and will devote a great deal of care and thought to avoiding them.

Parenthood
While you are ambitious for your children and respond warmly to them, you may be very conventional and rather strict. Try hard to make a conscious effort to remain aware of their changing problems and concerns. Otherwise the generation gap is likely to yawn wide.

THE MOON IN
GEMINI

YOUR ASPIRING, AMBITIOUS QUALITIES ARE LIGHTENED BY YOUR
GEMINIAN MOON, WHICH MAKES YOU VERSATILE AND
SOMETIMES GIVES YOU A TENDENCY TO DITHER IN DAUNTING
SITUATIONS. YOU HAVE A GREAT SENSE OF HUMOR.

The earth element of your Capricornian Sun sign, and the air element of your Geminian Moon sign, suggest that you have many interesting facets to your personality.

Self-expression
You have a lighthearted, but intellectual, response to challenges, being both inquisitive and skeptical. You are extremely lively in debate and are happy to play devil's advocate just to get your point made.

You are less single-minded than most Capricornians, and a natural versatility, a disposition to do more than one thing at a time, makes you interesting company. You probably know a little about a great many things and may be the typical collector of useless trifles.

Being a good communicator, working in some branch of the media would probably be most fulfilling for you. If you manage to guard against

superficiality, you can certainly put the excellent qualities of your Geminian Moon to good use.

Romance
You may take your love life rather less seriously than many Capricornians, and can, at times, be quite flighty and flirtatious. You particularly enjoy the friendship stage of a new relationship, and friendship and intellectual rapport are essential in the long term. Your sex life may be both lively and experimental, and you should take this into account when forming a relationship. Bear in mind the Geminian tendency to duality; it can cause complications.

Your well-being
The Geminian body area covers the arms and hands, and these are therefore likely to be vulnerable. Make sure you find a hobby that encourages you to use your fingers

The Moon in Gemini

energetically; this should help avoid developing any Capricornian stiffness of the joints.

You will probably enjoy fast-moving and intellectually demanding exercise. Your low boredom threshold may, however, prove a problem when it comes to this area of your life, so endeavor to persevere.

Planning ahead

You could be less successful in organizing your financial affairs than many of your Capricornian brothers and sisters. Indeed, you may be among the few Capricornian Sun and Moon combinations who should seek financial advice when they have money to invest.

Parenthood

You keep up with your children's ideas and may sometimes even be ahead of them. Beware that you do not respond to your children too critically. Logic is admirable, but a hug and some real enthusiasm are also reassuring and encouraging.

THE MOON IN
CANCER

CAPRICORN AND CANCER ARE OPPOSITE OR POLAR ZODIAC SIGNS,
WHICH MEANS THAT YOU WERE BORN UNDER A FULL MOON.
YOU MAY BE RATHER PRONE TO RESTLESSNESS, BUT HAVE A WARM,
EMOTIONAL RESPONSE TO OTHER PEOPLE.

Each of us is, in one way or another, likely to express the attitudes of our polar, or opposite, Zodiac sign. Every sign has its partner across the horoscope; for you this is Cancer and, since the Moon was in that sign when you were born, the polarity is strongly emphasized. As the Moon also rules Cancer, its influence on you is extremely potent.

Self-expression
The influence of your Moon sign encourages you to respond warmly and sensitively to other people, but it may also mean that you have a defensive system that springs into action whenever you are challenged. It is possible that you are not particularly self-confident.

Romance
You are far more emotional than many Sun sign Capricornians and are prepared to give a great deal of yourself in a relationship. Being a very responsive lover, you will instinctively know how to please your partner sexually. You should be aware, however, that your desire to create a warm and secure environment could make it somewhat claustrophobic.

You are a natural worrier and this, plus a very powerful imagination, means that you can work yourself up into a positive frenzy if, for instance, your partner is simply late arriving home. You would be best advised to direct your imagination creatively.

Your well-being
The Cancerian body area covers the chest and breasts. There is no connection between the name of this sign and that of the disease but, as always, it is desirable for women to examine their breasts regularly.

The tendency to worry can affect your digestion, and your food could upset you when you are worried.

The Moon in Cancer

Restlessness could also affect your health. A relaxation technique like yoga may offset the tendency.

Planning ahead

As well as being a practical Capricornian, you have an instinctive shrewdness that comes from your Cancerian Moon. You are good at making your money work for you and should follow your instincts, especially when you are planning to make an investment.

You may sometimes feel that you are less well off than is the case. You will do well to review your financial situation from time to time, just to reassure yourself that you can, in fact, allow yourself to enjoy the fruits of your labors more wholeheartedly than you at first thought.

Parenthood

You make a wonderfully caring parent. You may, however, tend to resent it when your children decide to leave home; you should take up some new and demanding interest that will fill the gap. Make a conscious effort to keep up with your children's opinions and concerns, in order to avoid difficulties with the generation gap.

THE MOON IN
LEO

ALLOW THE WARMTH OF YOUR FIERY LEO MOON TO COLOR YOUR
PERSONALITY AND REACTIONS, AND TO INCREASE YOUR
ORGANIZATIONAL ABILITY. BE VERY CAREFUL, HOWEVER, THAT
YOU DO NOT LAPSE INTO POMPOSITY AND BOSSINESS.

The fire of your Moon sign adds warmth and an optimistic enthusiasm to your response to challenges. Your instinctive organizational ability readily springs into action and, in most situations, you probably end up well in control.

Self-expression
When taking matters into your own hands, as you almost invariably do, remember to smile and charm people, so that you can achieve your objectives without being accused of undue autocracy.

Most people with a Leo emphasis have creative potential. Music, acting, wood carving, or painting could all appeal to you.

Romance
Leo and Capricorn have a fine sense of style and are not averse to showing off. This quality will certainly be in the forefront when you fall in love.

Avoid bossiness at all times and, if you are accused of it, take the allegation seriously. It could detract from a relationship that would otherwise be good fun.

Your well-being
The Leo body area covers the spine and back, and you should exercise regularly to keep your spine supple. If you spend a great deal of time behind a desk, get a back-support chair.

The Leo organ is the heart, and it must be kept well exercised if it is to serve you long and well. You probably enjoy the usual Capricornian outdoor sports, like hiking and jogging, but may also be attracted to something that is a little more aesthetic, such as dancing or skating.

Planning ahead
Although in many ways Capricorn and Leo are very unlike each other, they have at least one thing in common:

The Moon in Leo

they both love and really appreciate true quality, and have somewhat expensive tastes.

There is a difference between them even here, however. Leos usually spend on quality simply because they get such a kick out of doing so, while Capricornians often spend money on impressing other people, particularly those who may be useful to them. One way or the other, you will undoubtedly end up spending a great deal of money. If your Sun sign makes you feel somewhat guilty about this, bear in mind that you generally invest wisely and are sensible about saving. You will probably not need to get professional financial advice when you have money to invest.

Parenthood

You have what it takes to be a marvelous parent, as long as you do not allow a distance to yawn between you and your children. Follow your instinct and express warm enthusiasm; encourage your children when they show you the results of their latest efforts. If you keep up with their opinions and concerns, you will avoid the generation gap.

THE MOON IN
VIRGO

ALWAYS ALLOW THE AMBITIOUS, ASPIRING CAPRICORNIAN ELEMENTS OF YOUR PERSONALITY FREE EXPRESSION, AND TRY NOT TO BE HELD BACK BY INTUITIVE FEELINGS OF INFERIORITY. YOU MAY BE A WORRIER, BUT YOU WILL ALSO BE A GOOD COMMUNICATOR.

Both Capricorn and Virgo are earth signs and, as a result, you are extremely practical, with an above-average amount of straightforward, basic common sense.

Self-expression
You approach problems in a rational, logical way, although you may become rather nervous and lack self-confidence when challenged or confronted with tricky situations. If this happens, try to develop a little more Capricornian coolness.

You have a sharp and analytical mind, and are marvelous at assessing problems in detail. In doing so, do not ignore the overall pattern. Develop breadth of vision; it will be of great advantage to you.

You may be rather shy, and to cover this tend to assume a chilly, aloof air. If you were strictly brought up, it may be that you were put down by your parents once or twice too often, and

that this has inhibited you a little more than it might have with other people. No doubt you have what it takes to rationalize such a background, and to deal with any problem that may have arisen as a result of it.

Romance
While you are a naturally adept communicator, you may not find it very easy to talk about your emotions. Do not be too modest. Try to relax and let your relationship develop.

Virgoans can be very critical, and you should beware of nagging your partners too much.

Your well-being
The Virgoan body area is the stomach. You really need a high-fiber diet, and could be attracted to vegetarianism. You are probably exceptionally susceptible to worry, and this will definitely affect your stomach.

The Moon in Virgo

Because you have a great deal of nervous energy, you may be prone to stress and tension, and could find it difficult to sit still, let alone really relax. A study of yoga or some other relaxation technique will go a long way toward conquering the problem.

Planning ahead
You are usually careful and very practical with money. You may, in fact, be somewhat too cautious and go for such safe investments that your money might not be working as hard for you as it could. Study various investment programs; your critical nature will ensure that you will benefit a great deal by doing so.

Parenthood
While you are fair in dealing with your children, you could respond to them more critically than you realize, which could damage their self-confidence. Encourage them; they may be just as ambitious as you are.

THE MOON IN
LIBRA

YOUR LIBRAN MOON MAKES YOU VERY DIPLOMATIC, AND YOU
HAVE THE ABILITY TO CHARM OTHERS. YOU RESPOND
WELL TO AN ENJOYABLE SOCIAL LIFE, BUT MAY SOMETIMES
SUCCUMB TO SNOBBISH SOCIAL CLIMBING.

Your Sun sign and your Moon sign are both cardinal signs, and as a result you are outgoing. You can develop excellent sympathy, even empathy, with other people.

Self-expression
When you are confronted by tricky situations, your initial response may be rather hesitant. Your Capricornian determination then takes over, letting you know where you stand and what you should do.

You live a full and busy life but, because you always find time for other people, especially if they are in trouble, you can give the impression that you are at best laid-back and, at worst, lazy. The latter is certainly not true, and neither, really, is the former.

Romance
You will probably not feel psychologically whole until you have contrived a satisfying and permanent partnership for yourself. You really do need that all-important rapport with another person who is close to you. But you also need space and time to yourself. When choosing a partner, it is important to keep this in mind.

You are among the more romantic of Sun sign Capricornians and will enjoy the most memorable, and often expensive and luxurious, occasions with your lovers.

Your well-being
The Libran body area is the kidneys, and if you suffer from constant headaches, it might be worth getting a checkup in case you have a slight kidney disorder. The lumbar region of the back is also Libra-ruled. If you suffer from pain in this region, get a back-support chair or follow a series of back-oriented exercises.

You could be less enthusiastic about exercise than most Sun sign Capricornians. Since you may also

The Moon in Libra

enjoy rich, sweet food, you could be vulnerable to weight gain. You need to exercise in a place where there is a pleasant social life – for example, in a friendly health club or gym.

Planning ahead

You are probably among the least careful of Capricornians where money is concerned. You may not waste it, but will like to own beautiful things.

Capricorn will rule at times when you have money to invest. If, however, you know that you tend not to save too determinedly, you would probably be wise to seek independent professional financial advice.

Parenthood

You will be a kind parent, as responsive to your children's needs as to everyone else's. Do not, however, let Libran indecision come between you and your children. Help them to aspire; your encouragement will pay off in the long run. Because you are always fair and attentive, you should leap across the generation gap.

THE MOON IN
SCORPIO

YOU POSSESS A POWERFUL SOURCE OF EMOTIONAL ENERGY THAT INCREASES YOUR CAPRICORNIAN DETERMINATION TO SUCCEED IN ALL OF YOUR OBJECTIVES. BEWARE, HOWEVER, OF DEVELOPING OBSESSIVE TENDENCIES.

The earth element of your Capricornian Sun and the water element of your Scorpio Moon blend well. You should be able to get the best out of both of these influences.

Self-expression

You have intense emotional and physical energy that springs into action the moment you are challenged. Combined with Capricornian determination and ambition, this gives you the potential to be extremely successful.

It is important for you to be emotionally involved in your work. If you are merely working at some boring job in order to make money, your motivation and energies will stagnate. Try some self-analysis if you feel any danger signals, and make changes if necessary.

Be careful not to be too ruthless with your colleagues. You would be wise to remember the old saying: do not tread on people on the way up, since you may well encounter them again on the way down.

Romance

Your powerful emotions make you a passionate lover who needs a rich and fulfilling love and sex life. You will be a demanding partner and will need an enthusiastic lover.

The worst Scorpio fault is jealousy, and it might be that you occasionally succumb to this useless, negative emotion. Listen to rational explanations from your partner.

Your well-being

The Scorpio body area covers the genitals. Men with this Sun and Moon combination should regularly examine their testicles for irregularities, and women should have cervical smears.

Scorpios usually enjoy living it up, which means eating rich food and drinking fine wine. As a result, you

The Moon in Scorpio

may have a tendency to put on excess weight. If you have to diet, you will probably not find it easy; on reaching your ideal weight, you may rush off for a celebratory banquet. You may enjoy the discipline and steady routine of a regular sports interest.

Planning ahead

You should cope well with money and may have a considerable flair for making it. Your Sun and Moon sign combination suggests that you are good in business, and that you could build a successful business of your own. You should have no problems when you have money to invest.

Parenthood

You have the capacity to enjoy parenthood, but could be so involved with your career that you may have less time for your children than is wise. Listen to your children, and always encourage them in their ambitions and interests.

THE MOON IN
SAGITTARIUS

SAGITTARIAN BREADTH OF VISION AND ABILITY TO ACCEPT
CHALLENGE WORKS WELL WITH YOUR STRONG CAPRICORNIAN
AMBITION. YOUR CAPRICORNIAN SENSE OF
HUMOR IS FUELED BY YOUR SAGITTARIAN MOON.

The influence of your Sagittarian Moon adds some remarkably varied qualities to your personality. By expressing them you should be able to achieve a great deal.

Self-expression

Your Moon sign gives you a natural optimism, but there could be conflict here, for Sun sign Capricornians can sometimes be pessimistic and gloomy. If you tend to swing between one mood and another, try to allow Capricornian common sense and ambition to override gloom and doom.

You have a good mind and a good intellect. Do not let them stagnate; it is important for you to have an intellectual challenge of some kind, perhaps a language.

Romance

Sagittarius is a warm, loving, and emotional sign. You will not find it difficult to express these qualities.

You are passionate and will want to enjoy a rich and rewarding love and sex life. Perhaps you do not take this sphere of your life as seriously as do others of your Sun sign, but the chances are that you get a lot more fun out of it. You need a measure of freedom within a relationship and should bear this in mind when considering a permanent liaison.

The worst Sagittarian fault is restlessness. Try not to take this out on your partner, or to allow that ever-so-slightly roving eye to cause too many problems.

Your well-being

The Sagittarian body area covers the hips and thighs, and women with this sign emphasized are prone to putting on weight around this area. Special exercises will help and should encourage good muscle tone. A diet of lighter food than you may like is also advisable.

The Moon in Sagittarius

The Sagittarian organ is the liver and, because it is common for people of that sign to enjoy rich, meaty foods, heavy desserts, wine, and beer, it might be wise to keep some hangover cures handy. Keep generally active with energy-consuming interests and you will thrive.

Planning ahead

Although you are practical to a fault and sensible with money, you may have a deeply ingrained gambling instinct. You are likely to enjoy the occasional financial risk, and this may take the form of a bet on a big race or some marginally unsavory stock purchase. For the most part, you can easily control this tendency. When making important financial decisions, seek the advice of an expert.

Parenthood

You will be a lively and enthusiastic parent, eager to stimulate your children's minds and to encourage their efforts. Be ambitious for them without being too heavy-handed. You should have few problems with the generation gap and will find coping with older children somewhat easier than understanding toddlers.

THE MOON IN
CAPRICORN

BECAUSE BOTH THE SUN AND THE MOON WERE IN CAPRICORN AT
THE TIME OF YOUR BIRTH, YOU WERE BORN UNDER A
NEW MOON. THEREFORE THE EARTH ELEMENT POWERFULLY
EMPHASIZES YOUR PERSONALITY AND REACTIONS.

When you read a list of the characteristics of your practical, aspiring Sun sign, you will probably recognize that a great many of them apply to you. On average, out of a list of perhaps 20 personality traits of a Sun sign, most people will identify with 11 or 12. For you, the average increases considerably, as both the Sun and the Moon were in Capricorn when you were born.

Self-expression
The influence of your Moon sign encourages you to appreciate ambitious schemes and daunting projects, which you will usually want to accept as soon as they are put to you. You may, however, tend to swing between positive, ambitious thinking and a negative, self-doubting attitude.

No doubt you have the marvelous, offbeat sense of humor that is so characteristic of Capricorn, and it will surface very spontaneously. But you are not beyond slumping into a grumbling mood and complaining that nothing is right with your world. Try to allow the positive side of your personality to dominate.

Romance
You may not express your emotions very freely. This is probably due to your natural Capricornian caution and your self-protective instinct.

Once committed, you are very faithful and will enjoy a rich, rewarding love and sex life. You will be ambitious for your partner's progress in life, but it is possible that you may have slightly old-fashioned or conventional ideas as to how your relationship should develop.

Your well-being
The pages dedicated to health and well-being (*pages 472 to 473*) are especially relevant to you, as your vulnerabilities are extremely

The Moon in Capricorn

Capricornian. You could be even more prone to rheumatic pain and arthritis than most Sun sign Capricornians.

Planning ahead
You will not be averse to making an effort to impress important people. On the whole, however, you will use your money well, although you may sometimes think you are less well off than you actually are. Make an effort to follow your naturally cautious instinct when investing, and you will not go far wrong.

Parenthood
You will want to do a lot for your children and will work hard to this end. However, because you are always busy, you may not spend as much time with them as you should, and they may feel that you are a rather distant parent.

You will be conventional in your attitude and could be rather strict. This is all right, provided that you make an effort to understand your children's concerns and problems, and thus avoid the generation gap.

THE MOON IN
AQUARIUS

YOU MAY NEED TO BE INDEPENDENT, BUT TRY TO AVOID GAINING A REPUTATION FOR BEING COOL AND DISTANT. WHILE YOU ARE ATTRACTED TO THE UNCONVENTIONAL, YOU WILL ALWAYS WANT TO DO WHAT IS CONSIDERED ACCEPTABLE.

Aquarius and Capricorn are neighboring Zodiac signs and, until the discovery of Uranus in the eighteenth century, the planet Saturn ruled them both. They therefore have a certain amount in common, but in some respects they could not be more different. Your Capricornian Sun, for instance, inclines you toward conventionality in outlook and manner, while your Aquarian Moon sometimes makes you respond to situations in an unconventional way.

Self-expression

Both Capricorn and Aquarius share the tendency not to show emotion very freely. While you have a dynamic, magnetic personality that is very attractive to the opposite sex, you may instinctively send out vibes telling admirers that, while they may certainly admire you, they should also keep their distance. In spite of this, you have a romantic streak that is

quite wonderful once ignited. Another aspect of your attitude to romance is that you may put off deepening an emotional relationship, or certainly committing yourself to marriage, for longer than most people. This is probably because you enjoy your independence so much.

Your well-being

The Aquarian body area covers the ankles, which are vulnerable. You may well enjoy wearing fashion shoes and could easily twist your ankle. The circulation is also Aquarius-ruled, and yours may not be too brisk, so make sure you wear several layers of light clothes in cold weather.

You will like various forms of exercise, particularly if they are an outlet for your creative flair; all kinds of dance, or perhaps skating, will probably suit you. Exercise will aid your circulation and is excellent for preventing Capricornian stiffness and

The Moon in Aquarius

rheumatic pain. Aim to keep your diet on the light side. Many Capricornians favor the great classical dishes of the world; you probably do best on poultry, fish, and a salads.

Planning ahead

You will spend money more freely than most Capricornians and may well be attracted to exciting, but perhaps not very sound, investment schemes. You must aim to be careful and should not gamble any more than you can afford to lose. In all situations, allow your Capricornian common sense to rule the day.

Parenthood

You will make a lively and well-informed parent. You should not find the generation gap to be a problem, provided that the strict, conventional Capricornian side of your personality balances your unconventional Moon sign. Bear in mind that children like to know where they stand.

THE MOON IN
PISCES

YOUR PISCEAN MOON HEIGHTENS YOUR EMOTIONAL LEVEL, AND
WARMS AND SENSITIZES YOUR REACTIONS. YOU
MAY, HOWEVER, NEED TO CONSCIOUSLY BUILD SELF-CONFIDENCE.
DO NOT SMOTHER YOUR CAPRICORNIAN AMBITION.

Your earth sign Sun and water sign Moon combine well. As a Capricornian, you are practical and cautious, but you will respond sensitively to situations and should not find it difficult to show tender emotion. You may not, however, be very self-confident and could have to make a conscious effort to allow your positive, aspiring, and ambitious Capricornian qualities full expression.

Self-expression
Because you are sensitive, there is a chance that you may have suffered more deeply than most people from parental put-downs. This could have made you fearful of taking firm steps onward and upward. Make an effort to develop your ambitions and to summon up the inner strength to achieve them.

You are a warm, kind person, who could do especially well in a career in the caring professions.

Romance
You respond warmly and lovingly to partners and are capable of a truly rewarding love and sex life. The worst Piscean fault is deceptiveness. As a Capricornian you will loathe this characteristic and should therefore be able to combat it successfully.

When you fall in love, you may have a tendency to see your partner through rose-colored glasses. Consciously allow your Capricornian qualities full expression, especially when considering a long-term commitment. Never slip into the bad habit of telling white lies in order not to hurt your partner since, in the long run, the implications could be ghastly.

Your well-being
The Piscean body area covers the feet, and yours are vulnerable. You may well enjoy going barefoot, but be careful: you are more vulnerable than most people to foot infections.

The Moon in Pisces

Pisceans tend to put on weight rather easily, usually because of a reliance on junk food. Capricornians are often lean, or perhaps even gaunt. If you do have a slow metabolism, you will need to keep a careful check on your diet. Exercise such as dancing, swimming, and downhill or cross-country skiing will help a lot.

Planning ahead

Pisceans are generally not too good at handling money, and your immediate reaction to financial problems may well be one of utter confusion. Do not make sudden decisions if you have money to invest, and be careful not to fall for get-rich-quick schemes. Let your Capricornian gift for finance overrule any Piscean impracticality.

Parenthood

You will be a good parent, who will sensitively and intuitively understand your children's needs. If you follow your Piscean instincts when dealing with your children, they will always work well, and you will have very few problems with the generation gap. Always remember to express warmth and tenderness to children, as well as Capricornian forthrightness.

AQUARIUS

JANUARY 21 – FEBRUARY 18

INTRODUCING
AQUARIUS

AQUARIUS, THE SIGN OF THE WATER BEARER, IS THE ELEVENTH
SIGN OF THE ZODIAC. AQUARIANS ARE THE MOST
ENIGMATIC OF ALL ZODIAC TYPES, AND ALSO THE MOST
INDIVIDUAL AND INDEPENDENT.

People of this Sun sign have a powerful desire for a lifestyle that is in some way unique. They are often so devoted to it, and so intent on achieving independence, that it is somewhat difficult for them to commit themselves to permanent relationships. At the very least, such a relationship can come rather late in an Aquarian's life.

Traditional groupings

As you read through this book you will come across references to the elements and the qualities, and to positive and negative, or masculine and feminine signs.

The first of these groupings, that of the elements, comprises fire, earth, air, and water signs. The second, that of the qualities, divides the Zodiac into cardinal, fixed, and mutable signs. The final grouping is made up of positive and negative, or masculine and feminine signs. Each Zodiac sign is associated with a combination of components from these groupings, all of which contribute different characteristics to it.

Aquarian characteristics

People of this sign tend to be intellectual and, since the sign is of the fixed quality, you may also be surprisingly stubborn.

Uranus is your ruling planet, and many Aquarians are trendsetters, the leaders of their generation. Perhaps because of the fixed quality of your Sun sign, you can sometimes become a little too set in the opinions that you may have formed when you were young and may consequently lag behind current thought.

Since it is a positive, masculine sign, Aquarius inclines its subjects toward extroversion.

The Aquarian colors are traditionally considered to be electric blue and turquoise.

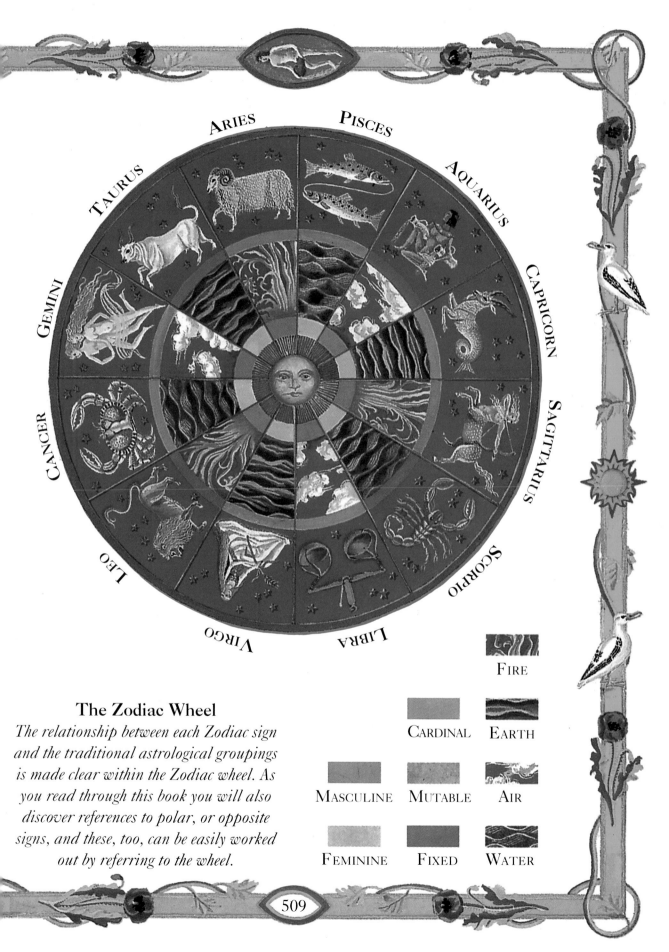

ARIES

PISCES

TAURUS

AQUARIUS

GEMINI

CAPRICORN

CANCER

SAGITTARIUS

LEO

SCORPIO

VIRGO

LIBRA

FIRE

CARDINAL   EARTH

MASCULINE   MUTABLE   AIR

FEMININE   FIXED   WATER

The Zodiac Wheel

The relationship between each Zodiac sign and the traditional astrological groupings is made clear within the Zodiac wheel. As you read through this book you will also discover references to polar, or opposite signs, and these, too, can be easily worked out by referring to the wheel.

MYTHS & LEGENDS

THE ZODIAC, WHICH IS RECOGNIZED TO HAVE ORIGINATED IN
BABYLON POSSIBLY AS MANY AS 2,500 YEARS AGO, IS
A CIRCLE OF CONSTELLATIONS THROUGH WHICH THE SUN
MOVES DURING THE COURSE OF A YEAR.

Was Aquarius originally male or female? The Babylonian name for Aquarius, gu. la, has been translated as meaning both a goddess of childbirth and healing, and "constellation of the great man." The latter is thought to refer to the giant Enkidu, described in the ancient epic of Gilgamesh as a man who grew up in the desert among the wild beasts, who became his friends. He devoted his time to protecting the animals and is often shown watering an ox.

The god of fresh water

In ancient Babylon there was also a god of fresh water called Ea, known as "the god with streams," or "house of the water," who was said to dwell in the city of Eridu on the Persian Gulf. He was normally depicted with water streaming from his arms and hands, but is sometimes shown holding a pot. This seems to be a more likely Aquarian figure.

Later, the ancient Egyptians pictorially associated the constellation of Aquarius with the god Hapi, who watered the ground from two jars held in his arms and was a symbol of the River Nile.

Zeus and Ganymede

Manilius, the Roman writer who, in the first century B.C. set down several astrological myths, firmly suggests that the original Aquarian was Ganymede, the son of Tros, king of Troy. He refers to the earliest Greek myths, in which Ganymede appears to be recognized as the deity responsible for showering the earth with the heavens' rain.

The popular myth of Ganymede describes him as the most beautiful boy alive and goes on to relate how Zeus, king of the gods, fell in love with him. Turning himself into an eagle, Zeus carried the boy off to be his cup-bearer, who would pour wine,

Worshipping Ea

The Babylonian water god, Ea, whose name means "house of the water," seems a likely candidate for one of the earliest characters to prefigure Aquarius.

not water, for the gods from a golden bowl. When King Tros quite understandably protested, Zeus sent him two fine horses as compensation, and explained that his son would now be an immortal, exempt from the pains of old age.

The symbol of Ganymede

Although in the Middle Ages Ganymede became renowned as the symbol of homosexual love, during the Renaissance his flight to heaven came to symbolize the soul's ascent to the absolute.

The Age of Aquarius

One modern myth might be said to be the Age of Aquarius, which was made notorious through the radical 1960s musical *Hair*.

Every 2,500 years the Earth passes through a sign of the Zodiac, and these periods are known as ages. The Age of Aquarius may have started a century ago, or it may not begin for another century – opinions differ. One thing that can, however, be said with certainty is that few signs so frequently confer such romantic good looks on their subjects.

AQUARIUS
SYMBOLISM

CERTAIN HERBS, SPICES, FLOWERS, TREES, GEMS, METALS, AND
ANIMALS HAVE LONG BEEN ASSOCIATED WITH PARTICULAR
ZODIAC SIGNS. SOME ASSOCIATIONS ARE SIMPLY AMUSING, WHILE
OTHERS CAN BE GENUINELY USEFUL.

Flowers

*Aquarian flowers include those
ruled by Taurus and Capricorn,
but particularly the orchid and
goldenrod. The latter is often used
as a herbalist's cure for "inward
hurts and bruises."*

ORCHID

GOLDENROD

Trees

Most fruit trees, such as the pear and the peach, are said to be ruled by Aquarius.

PEAR TREE

ELDER

Spices

No spice is particularly associated with Aquarius, but cinnamon, which is used to flavor apples and other fruit, and pepper are sometimes mentioned.

Herbs

Taurean herbs are, for the most part, also ruled by Aquarius. This is particularly true of common sorrel, which helps counter inflammations, and elder.

PEPPER

CINNAMON

AQUARIUS
SYMBOLISM

AQUAMARINE

AMETHYST
FRAGMENT
AND
NECKLACE

Gem
The Aquarian gem is the amethyst, but many astrologers also suggest the aquamarine, a bluish green beryl whose color particularly seems to appeal to Aquarians.

AMETHYST
CHIPS

ALUMINUM
FOIL

Metal
Aluminum is the Aquarian metal, perhaps because of its malleability.

Animals
Large, far-flying birds,
especially those that migrate
over great distances, are
ruled by Aquarius.

EAGLE
FEATHERS

GOOSE
FEATHERS

LEAD
ALBATROSS

AQUARIUS PROFILE

DUE TO THE FACT THAT AQUARIANS ARE SO INDIVIDUALISTIC, IT IS VERY DIFFICULT TO GENERALIZE ABOUT THEM. THEY ARE USUALLY FAIRLY LANKY AND, ON THE WHOLE, TEND TO HOLD THEMSELVES WELL WHEN STANDING OR WALKING.

The Aquarian stance is usually very correct. You may use your hands to gesture in an elegant, somewhat superior way, and you hold your head high, in order to make the most of your height.

The body
Perhaps because Aquarius is an air sign, the Aquarian body gives an overall impression of lightness, even if you are overweight. Many Aquarians are rather lanky, although their bones are usually fairly well covered by flesh. You no doubt have an upright, erect carriage, with a long back and narrow waist.

Aquarian shoulders tend to be square and broad, and the body joints are prominent. Your ankles will be trim and elegant, with a high calf, and

The Aquarian face
Fine, neatly styled hair and pale eyes characterize the Aquarian face.

your arms and hands are perhaps longer than most people's. There is probably a certain fineness to your bone structure; your features are likely to have a chiseled appearance, as opposed to the more rounded features of, for instance, Librans and Taureans, both of which are ruled by Venus. In fact, curves are very unlikely to play a large part in the make-up of an Aquarian body. It will instead be based upon lines and geometric masses.

The face
Your hair is probably fine, well cared for, and carefully styled, and your forehead is likely to be broad and open. Aquarian eyes are typically pale

The Aquarian stance

A very correct and upright stance is characteristic of many Aquarians. They may appear to possess a certain dignity.

and may have slightly drooping lids. There is a chance that your nose may be a little on the large side, perhaps even a shade imperious; a well-shaped mouth, ready to offer a friendly smile, is also a typical Aquarian characteristic. Your chin may add dignity to your whole face.

Style

Aquarian style is very up to the minute, although some of you may cling to a look that you decided suited you years ago. This is because Aquarians become less adaptable as they age and feel most at home in the initial style that they feel defines them. You may go all out to shock, or use your originality to make a very interesting statement. Pale turquoise or "Aquarian blue" is really your color, and smooth fabrics with satin or silky textures, as opposed to rough ones, will probably suit you best.

In general

Because its subjects are so individualistic, it is very difficult to generalize about this sign. Aquarians usually carry themselves well, giving the impression that they are somewhat superior or even noble.

There is a certain wildness about some Aquarians. This can manifest itself in the the way they dress – they may, for instance, find some small way in which to bend the rules of a particular dress code. Other Aquarians are, however, impeccably neat and rather conventional.

AQUARIUS
PERSONALITY

AQUARIANS ARE THE INDIVIDUALISTS OF THE ZODIAC. YOU CAN BE
INVENTIVE AND UNIQUE, BUT ALSO STUBBORN AND,
AT TIMES, UNPREDICTABLE; YOU ARE FRIENDLY, KIND, AND
HUMANITARIAN, BUT ALSO VERY PRIVATE.

The only thing two Aquarians will agree upon when reading a list of characteristics of their Sun sign is that they share none of them. This is chiefly because Aquarians are the individualists of the Zodiac and, either consciously or unconsciously, they like to make this known. Because of a perverse streak, they will enjoy being as different from their Sun sign brothers and sisters as they are from other people. Nevertheless, they do share certain characteristics.

At work

Your ideal career will include a good deal of human contact. Because of your happy, kind, and caring attitude, you might make an excellent social worker. Furthermore, you will not find it hard to distance yourself from suffering and will be of real assistance in difficult situations. A large number of Aquarians seem to veer toward careers that are based in the sciences.

You may be involved in the development of communication techniques, or in some other field where a degree of inventiveness and originality is needed.

From time to time, real brilliance can emerge from members of this sign, and anyone close to such individuals should be careful not to write them off as harmless eccentrics.

Your attitudes

It is very difficult to talk of "knowing" an Aquarian; while people of this sign make very good, kind, and helpful friends, it usually becomes clear that because they are so private no one really knows very much about them. If they are questioned (which will seem like prying to many Aquarians) they will very kindly but firmly ease their way out of providing an answer, and put the inquisitors firmly in their place without them even noticing it.

Uranus rules Aquarius

Uranus, a rather unattractive mythical figure, represents the Aquarian ruling planet. It can make its subjects original, versatile, and independent, but also perverse and rebellious.

You will occupy your spare time in a variety of ways, perhaps by going to lectures, rehearsing with a local drama group, or even working on a local charity committee.

The overall picture

There is a tendency among Sun sign Aquarians to be forward-looking when they are young, but to become rather set in their opinions as they get older. It can be very difficult to encourage them to reassess their outlook.

Aquarians are inventive and should develop their potential originality, since they can be very creative. The need to have a distinctly individual lifestyle, as well as overall independence, is likely to provide a great motivation in your life.

AQUARIUS
ASPIRATIONS

YOU LOVE WORKING WITH OTHER PEOPLE, SO THE SOCIAL SERVICES
MAY APPEAL TO YOU. HOWEVER, YOU ALSO NEED SPACE TO
DO THINGS YOUR WAY. AS LONG AS YOUR COLLEAGUES DO NOT
CROWD YOU, YOU WORK WELL WITH THEM.

Science

*The branches of science that allow
experimentation, the expression of
originality, and creative flair, are those that
Aquarians find most rewarding.*

ARTIST'S
MATERIALS

SCIENTIFIC IMPLEMENTS

The fine arts

*An Aquarian who is
attracted to the fine arts will
produce original and very
imaginative work. It may be
spiced with eccentricity.*

HAIRDRESSER'S TOOLS

The beauty industries
The Aquarian attraction to glamour could make you a marvelous makeup artist, beautician, or inventive hairdresser.

EASTERN THEATER PUPPET

The theater
Many Aquarians have dramatic flair and will be stagestruck from an early age, perhaps thinking that the acting profession is more glamorous than it is.

Teaching older students
Many Aquarians enjoy teaching older students, and become very popular because they express themselves in a friendly, if somewhat eccentric, way.

CHALK

AQUARIUS
HEALTH

AQUARIANS TEND TO SUFFER FROM STIFFNESS OF THE JOINTS,
WHICH CAN LEAD TO ARTHRITIS. IT IS THEREFORE
ESSENTIAL THAT YOU SHOULD KEEP MOVING AND GET
IMMEDIATE TREATMENT FOR ANY SPORTS INJURIES.

While the ankles are the traditional Aquarian body area, and they are certainly vulnerable, another tradition suggests that joint pains can be a problem. Most Aquarians like keeping active, and it is important that they do so.

Your diet
Natrum muriaticum in its crude form is simple salt, and you may benefit from including it in your diet.

Remember, however, that a balanced diet should give you all the salt you need. Do not oversalt your food.

Taking care
The circulation is Aquarian-ruled, and you may enjoy cold, crisp weather, but make sure that you keep warm.

Because Aquarians need a lifestyle that is unique to their own rather special needs, they tend to become ill if something conflicts with this urge. Should you find yourself falling ill without quite understanding why, or if you seem to be catching every minor infection that is going around, you should take a close look at your lifestyle – unease about this could be lowering your resistance.

Apples
Foods that preserve well, such as apples and citrus fruits, are traditionally ruled by Aquarius.

Astrology and the body

For many centuries it was not possible to practice medicine without a knowledge of astrology. In European universities, medical training included information on how planetary positions would affect the administration of medicines, the bleeding of patients, and the right time to pick herbs and make potions. Each Zodiac sign rules a particular part of the body – from Aries (the head) to Pisces (the feet) – and textbooks always included a drawing of a "Zodiac man" (or woman) that illustrated the point.

AQUARIUS AT LEISURE

EACH OF THE SUN SIGNS TRADITIONALLY SUGGESTS SPARE-TIME ACTIVITIES, HOBBIES, AND VACATION SPOTS. ALTHOUGH THESE ARE ONLY SUGGESTIONS, THEY OFTEN WORK OUT WELL FOR AQUARIANS.

ANCIENT COLUMBIAN ARTEFACTS

Archaeology
An attraction to the deep past often encourages Aquarians to become archaeologists. This profession enables them to combine inspiration with practical research.

Ballooning
Aquarius is an air sign, and its subjects love unpolluted fresh air. The idea of taking off in a balloon or glider could therefore be extremely attractive to them.

CIGARETTE CARDS SHOWING BALLOONING

MODEL OF 1930s BENTLEY

Collecting old cars
Many Aquarians are attracted to unusual hobbies, and some of them enjoy the challenge of restoring and driving old cars.

FACE MASKS

Drama
Like those of their polar sign, Leo, most Aquarians enjoy taking center stage. Amateur theatricals are therefore a popular leisure activity.

Travel
You will relish the thought of boarding a plane bound for Iran, Israel, Syria, Russia or Sweden, and will love flying. You will be eager to savor new experiences, and may prefer to avoid package tours.

POSTAGE STAMPS

Astronomy
Many Aquarians make excellent astronomers. The combination of science and the wonder of the universe is a great source of inspiration.

CALCULATING TOOLS

AQUARIUS IN
LOVE

AQUARIANS ARE KNOWN TO BE ROMANTIC BUT CAUTIOUS. THEY
CAN BE COOL, GLAMOROUS, AND ATTRACTIVE, WITH
MAGNETIC PERSONALITIES. THE ACT OF FALLING IN LOVE IS AN
ESPECIALLY MEANINGFUL EXPERIENCE FOR AN AQUARIAN.

When Aquarians fall in love they are, perhaps more than any other Zodiac type, confronted with some very specific problems.

Unless you are very young you will be intent on building a lifestyle that is in some way unique, which you will be reluctant to disturb. This relates to your need for privacy, and to the fiery independent streak that persuades you to live your life in your own particular way.

Partnership clearly signifies that a great deal of change will occur in one's life; in your case, this might mean a measure of sacrifice. This can sometimes be a rather heavy burden for Aquarians, and it is the reason why many of them frequently put off marriage or forming a permanent relationship until quite late in their lives. Very often this is not a bad thing, since it can prevent a series of relationship breakdowns and a lot of unenviable heartache.

As a lover

Enjoyment of love and sex is extremely unlikely to be a problem for you. Even so, you will always be inclined to put a distance between yourself and your partners. You will, of course, want to see relationships develop, and to enjoy increasing intellectual and physical rapport with your partners, but you will also want to maintain a great element of freedom, even while enjoying the most passionate of affairs.

Types of Aquarian lover

You may express love and sex with warm enthusiasm, and might be very flirtatious, with a roving eye. On the other hand, you could take this sphere of your life extremely seriously. In this case, you will be faithful and will express your emotions sparingly. A third group of Aquarians will identify with all of the general comments that have been made so far. They will not want to be pressured by a lover into making a commitment before being entirely ready for it. The fourth Aquarian group is sensitive, emotional, caring, and frequently starry-eyed. If you belong to this group you will need to be very cautious in this sphere of your life, since any mistakes could cause a great deal of damage both to you and to others. People in this group take great pleasure from love and sex, but also value their independence within a relationship.

AQUARIUS AT
HOME

AQUARIAN INDIVIDUALITY WILL PROCLAIM ITSELF IN YOUR HOME.
DO NOT, HOWEVER, FURNISH IT SO TRENDILY THAT IT WILL
LOOK DATED IN A FEW YEARS. YOU MAY POSSESS A TALENT FOR
CREATING ORIGINAL LIGHTING EFFECTS.

Most Aquarians are quite capable of organizing their lives to meet with the requirements of any particular environment. They are therefore equally at home living in either the country or a big city. Even if their dwelling place is quite small, they will make it feel spacious.

Furniture
Aquarians need a feeling of space, so there will probably be as little furniture as possible in your home.

The pieces that you choose are often somewhat clinical in design and usually very modern. If they are not modern items, they will probably have originated in the 1920s or 1930s, when slickness of line and a minimum of decoration were preferred.

Since Aquarius is an air sign, heaviness and too much solidity in furniture is not usually favored. Therefore glass dining tables or

Unique ornaments
Any ornaments in an Aquarian home are likely to be unusual, perhaps because of the owner's interest in the past.

occasional tables are likely to be in evidence. It is, however, surprising how comfortable an insubstantial, angular Aquarian chair can be.

Soft furnishings

While soft furnishings do not usually abound in the Aquarian home, they most certainly add a considerable, possibly Hollywood-style, glamour to it. Aquarians love shiny fabrics, so taffetas and silks are popular among them. Transparent net curtains, or attractive blinds, pulled over only when the sunlight becomes uncomfortable, may also be apparent.

White is a very popular choice for plain walls, and it is sometimes the color used for leather furniture. It is often combined with shiny chrome, which forms the basic structure of tables and chairs. Generally, Aquarians prefer plain or striped fabrics to elaborate patterns.

Decorative objects

All kinds of glass will probably have honored places in your home. You will favor tinted vases, pieces of crystal, and Lalique or other sophisticated glass ornaments. The paintings that you are likely to prefer will be abstract and intellectually demanding, and therefore unlikely to bore you, even after many years.

Since Aquarians are often attracted to the deep past and the distant future, fossils or antiquities may have a place in a well-displayed collection. Nearly all Aquarians love mirrors; they have an unfortunate reputation for being a little vain.

Display of frosted glass fruit
Trendy and glamorous are two words frequently used to describe the Aquarian home. Glass of all kinds is very popular.

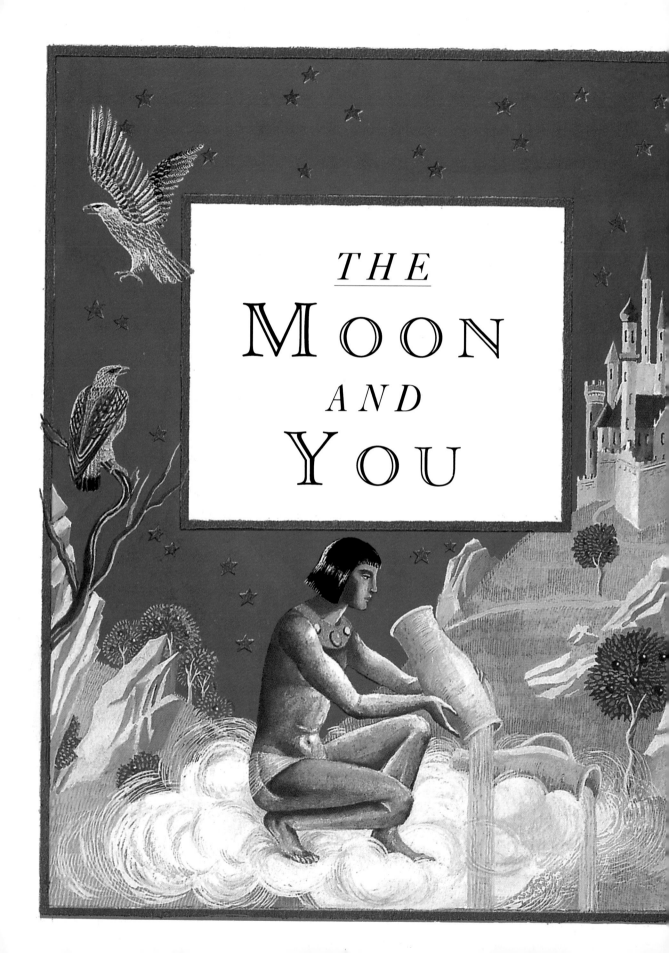

THE
MOON
AND
YOU

THE SUN DECREES YOUR OUTWARD EXPRESSION, YOUR IMAGE, AND MANY IMPORTANT PERSONALITY TRAITS. THE MOON, ALTHOUGH MERELY THE EARTH'S SATELLITE, IS ASTRONOMICALLY THE SECOND MOST IMPORTANT BODY IN THE SOLAR SYSTEM. FROM THE SIGN THAT IT WAS IN AT YOUR BIRTH, IT INFLUENCES HOW YOU REACT TO SITUATIONS, YOUR EMOTIONAL LEVEL, AND, TO A CERTAIN EXTENT, WHAT YOU HAVE INHERITED FROM YOUR PARENTS AND ANCESTORS. AFTER FINDING YOUR MOON SIGN IN THE SIMPLE TABLES ON PAGES 606 TO 609, TURN TO THE RELEVANT PAGES AND TAKE A STEP FORWARD IN YOUR OWN SELF-KNOWLEDGE.

THE MOON IN
ARIES

YOUR AQUARIAN NEED FOR INDEPENDENCE IS HEIGHTENED BY YOUR
ARIEN MOON. YOU ARE ALSO LIKELY TO BE A VERY WARM,
PASSIONATE PERSON, WHO WILL EXPRESS EMOTION MORE FREELY
THAN MANY OTHER SUN SIGN AQUARIANS.

The elements of Aquarius and Aries, air and fire, blend well and, as a result, you respond to most situations with warm enthusiasm. You thrive on challenge, and always want to be well ahead of your rivals.

Self-expression
Your Aquarian Sun gives you originality, which is complemented by a straightforward, uncomplicated approach to life. You are not inhibited by side issues or petty details.

In spite of your natural Aquarian friendliness, you should be aware that your rapid responses may upset other people. It could be that you organize them too sharply, hinting at incompetence on their part. Try to be considerate as well as competent.

Romance
You are among the warmest, and most passionate and highly sexed, of Sun sign Aquarians. Your Moon sign contributes a wealth of emotion to your personality and also gives you the ability to express it positively.

Aquarius and Aries are both very high on the list of Zodiac people who need independence and freedom of expression, and your partners must recognize this. When contemplating a permanent relationship, make sure you discuss this part of your character thoroughly with your partner.

Your well-being
The Arien body area is the head, and when you are subjected to tension or stress, you may incur headaches. If there is no apparent reason for these, it could be that they stem from a slight kidney imbalance, so get a medical checkup.

An Arien Moon always tends to make one impulsive and hasty. As a result, you could be slightly accident-prone. Make an effort to develop a more cautious approach.

The Moon in Aries

You enjoy sports and most forms of exercise, and should have a fast metabolism. You will therefore probably burn up calories quickly.

Planning ahead

Your originality and flair may well be expressed through enterprise; you may have two sources of income. You could invest impulsively and be attracted to unsound schemes. Keep your Aquarian cool when investing, and seek professional advice.

Parenthood

You are probably a lively parent and much of your instinctive, warm enthusiasm is likely to surface quite naturally in your children's company.

Because you are rather modern in outlook and enjoy keeping in touch with current trends, it is very unlikely that you will end up falling victim to the generation gap. In fact, the situation could even arise where your children may find it difficult to keep up with you.

THE MOON IN
TAURUS

YOUR TAUREAN MOON MAKES YOU WARM AND AFFECTIONATE IN
YOUR RESPONSES TO OTHERS AND GIVES YOU AN INSTINCTIVE
BUSINESS SENSE. HOWEVER, SINCE BOTH AQUARIUS AND TAURUS
ARE FIXED SIGNS, BEWARE OF BEING TOO STUBBORN.

The characteristics of these two signs are very different, and your immediate responses to situations could consequently be somewhat out of step with your general attitude toward life.

Self-expression

Your Moon gives you considerable stability, and a great need for emotional and financial security. Furthermore, while Aquarius is known for its unconventionality, Taurus has a liking for tradition and a mistrust of change.

Your Moon will encourage and help you to express your originality. It is very likely that you have creative flair of some kind, perhaps for music or singing, and you may want to develop this along traditional, conventional lines. Your Taurean creativity should help you to express your natural Aquarian flair and originality in a very satisfying way.

Romance

The contrast between a need for emotional security and an equal need for freedom of expression will be most marked in the area of your personal relationships. You will place some contrasting demands on your partners. Almost inevitably, you will have to make some sacrifices and compromises, and your lovers must be aware of your different needs.

Your well-being

The Taurean body area is the throat, and it is likely that when you get a cold it will start with a sore throat and end in a cough that is hard to lose.

Most people with a Taurean emphasis enjoy rich, sweet food, and you may therefore be prone to weight gain. Much depends on your metabolism. If it is slow, make sure that you exercise regularly. Also bear in mind that there is a relationship between your Taurean Moon and the

The Moon in Taurus

thyroid gland. If you eat very lightly but still find that you put on weight, get a medical checkup.

Planning ahead

There is a chance that you could be very adept at handling money. You may spend freely on your possessions, and therefore need to earn a good, regular salary.

You have a naturally good business sense and, with Aquarian flair, could do extremely well running a business of your own.

Parenthood

You probably express warm affection toward your children, but may have a tendency to be strict one moment and favor a freer style of parenthood the next. Bear in mind that your children should always know where they stand with you.

Aquarius will help you keep up to date with your children's ideas. However, your Taurean instinct for not breaking the rules may not endear you to them. Make sure that you always aim for compromise.

THE MOON IN
GEMINI

YOUR AQUARIAN ORIGINALITY AND QUICK MIND BLEND VERY WELL WITH YOUR SPEEDY GEMINIAN RESPONSES AND COMMUNICATIVE ABILITY. YOU MUST BEWARE OF BEING TOO TRENDY IN YOUR IMAGE AND OUTLOOK, AND SHOULD NOT SUPPRESS YOUR EMOTIONS.

Both Aquarius and Gemini are air signs, and this element emphasizes an intellectual approach to life. You are therefore more than likely to be in possession of distinctive ideas, logic, and originality.

Self-expression
You should be able to muster your various qualities without much difficulty, although actually realizing your plans may not always be easy; you may enjoy theorizing more than taking practical action.

You probably have a very low boredom threshold, and your inherent versatility will encourage you to learn a little about a great many things. You would do better to study a few well-chosen subjects in depth.

Romance
Neither Aquarius nor Gemini is noted for being able to express their emotions very freely, and this may

inhibit you. You always need a high level of friendship and intellectual rapport with a lover.

Your well-being
The Geminian body area covers the arms and hands, and they are therefore vulnerable. In addition, Aquarians are somewhat prone to arthritis, so it is a good idea for you to have at least one hobby that will keep your hands and fingers very active.

The Geminian organ is the lungs, and bronchitis could trouble you. Seek medical advice if a cough hangs on for more than a few days.

The worst Geminian fault is restlessness, which can impair achievement and sometimes lead to a buildup of tension. A calming discipline such as meditation or yoga will be most helpful.

You probably have a fast metabolism. If you do not, you may need to take regular exercise to fight

The Moon in Gemini

the flab. Fast games such as basketball, badminton, squash, and tennis are excellent for you, and you should also aim to keep your diet as light and as healthy as possible.

Planning ahead
You probably have the ability to sell ice in Alaska and will certainly strike a good deal when, for instance, you want to sell your car. But be careful: you may not be as clever as you think when you have money to invest. Seek professional financial advice and take it. If possible, favor a savings scheme to which contributions are extracted from your paycheck at the source.

Parenthood
You make a tremendously lively parent, challenging your children's opinions and keeping up with them. The generation gap will therefore never be a problem for you. You could sometimes appear a little distant to your children. Bear in mind that logic is a good thing, but a warmhearted hug is also very necessary at times.

THE MOON IN
CANCER

YOUR AQUARIAN ORIGINALITY SHOULD WORK WELL, AND PERHAPS
CREATIVELY, WITH CANCERIAN IMAGINATION AND INTUITION.
IT WOULD BE A GOOD IDEA FOR YOU TO ENDEAVOR TO CURB ANY
UNPREDICTABILITY AND SUDDEN CHANGES OF MOOD.

Your Aquarian Sun and Cancerian Moon bestow some very contrasting characteristics. They can make you a unique, interesting, extremely individualistic, and rather complex character.

Self-expression
You are probably among the most individual of Aquarians. No doubt you respond to most situations in a sensitive and emotional manner, and it is in this respect that Cancer and Aquarius meet most happily.

Aquarians give help generously where it is needed, and do so simply because the need is apparent. They are cool, logical, and rational, rather than emotional. Your Cancerian Moon allows you to be emotionally moved by the plight of others.

At a first meeting, you may give the impression of friendliness tempered by a certain degree of coolness. As acquaintance ripens into friendship, others will recognize that in some ways you can be quite a softy. But you never lose the ability to snap back when a sharp answer is required.

Romance
In emotional relationships, you may have experienced conflict. On the one hand you have a very deep-rooted longing for a home and family, while on the other there is an Aquarian insistence on retaining your own individual lifestyle.

You respond marvelously to partners and are capable of a really rich and rewarding sex life. Take care, however, that you do not create a claustrophobic atmosphere.

Your well-being
The Cancerian body area covers the chest and breasts. Although there is absolutely no connection between this sign and the disease that bears the same name, it is perhaps

The Moon in Cancer

particularly important for women with the Moon in Cancer to check their breasts regularly just in case there are any problems.

Cancerians are very prone to worry, and Aquarians are detrimentally affected by stress and tension. You may therefore suffer from headaches or even migraines. Learn to relax – yoga and other techniques might well help you to do this.

Planning ahead

You are among those Aquarians who cope very well with money, provided that you allow a naturally shrewd and clever business instinct free expression. Aim to invest in well-established companies and schemes.

Parenthood

As a protective, caring parent, you may sometimes worry unduly about your offspring. At the same time, your modern Aquarian spirit encourages them to be as independent as you are. Be understanding when they decide that it is time to leave home. As long as you curb a tendency to go on about how things were when you were young, the generation gap should not prove to be a problem.

THE MOON IN
LEO

AQUARIUS AND LEO ARE POLAR OR OPPOSITE SIGNS, WHICH MEANS
THAT YOU WERE BORN UNDER A FULL MOON. RESTLESSNESS
MAY BE A PROBLEM, AND YOU MUST AVOID BEING STUBBORN. LET
LEO CREATIVITY BLEND WITH AQUARIAN ORIGINALITY.

We all express some of the characteristics of our polar sign (the sign opposite ours across the Zodiac circle). For Aquarians, this is Leo and, because the Moon was in that sign when you were born, this polarity is strikingly emphasized.

Self-expression

You are a good organizer who is able to take over any situation at a moment's notice. However, you should be careful not to appear bossy. At times, you may seem a little distant and unapproachable.

You may have creative potential, which could be expressed through painting, acting, or maybe fashion designing. Your inventiveness could lean toward a scientific expression.

Romance

You will express your feelings with passion and with all the fire of your Leo Moon. Both in and out of bed,

you will make a rewarding partner. As with all Aquarians, you need a good measure of independence, but you will also want to look up to your partners and be a power behind the throne, as well as sharing it.

Beware of a tendency to dominate your lover; anyone with a Leo emphasis can fall into this trap. Keeping a balance is essential.

Your well-being

The Aquarius and Leo polarity is at its strongest in health matters. Aquarius rules the circulation, which is, of course, driven by the heart – the Leo organ. The two influences combine most potently and call for your special attention. Exercising your heart will assist your circulation, and you must keep moving to avoid any buildup of arthritic conditions in your joints. The spine and back are Leo body areas, and they also need exercise. If you have to spend long

The Moon in Leo

hours sitting at a desk, you may benefit greatly from using an ergonomic chair.

You may like rich food but provided that you keep moving, you will burn up any unwanted calories.

Planning ahead

Aquarians are glamorous, and Leos like the best and the most expensive things. To meet these needs, you will need to earn a relatively high salary. Your Leo Moon may well also give you quite a clever flair for investment, perhaps in well-established companies making quality goods. If you ever need financial advice, you will seek it from the most knowledgeable expert you can find.

Parenthood

Leo is a sign traditionally related to parenthood, and you should get great pleasure from your children, always encouraging them to greater achievements. Always express loving, warm enthusiasm, especially when they show you their efforts. Be rational and forward-looking, and discipline your children positively. You should have no problems with the generation gap.

THE MOON IN
VIRGO

YOUR VIRGOAN MOON GIVES YOU EXCELLENT DOWN-TO-EARTH
QUALITIES. DO NOT LET ANY INHIBITING OR REPRESSIVE
FEELINGS SUPPRESS THE DEVELOPMENT OF ORIGINAL IDEAS
AND UNCONVENTIONAL SELF-EXPRESSION.

Your cool and rational Aquarian Sun combines with the natural common sense and logic of your Virgoan Moon. You are therefore able to look at every aspect of a problem in a critical, analytical way.

Self-expression
You are both original and practical, and should express those qualities fully. They are a source of excellent potential, perhaps for some unique form of craftwork.

You sometimes have a tendency to nitpick, and this can cause you to lose sight of the overall pattern of a situation. Only when your Aquarian Sun takes over are you be able to see the problem in a broader way.

Romance
Your modesty may sometimes cramp your style where love and sex are concerned. However, if you manage to relax into your relationships, you will manage to achieve a really rewarding and ultimately fulfilling love and sex life.

Your well-being
The Virgoan body area is traditionally said to cover the stomach, and you may benefit from a high-fiber diet. Like many people with a Virgoan influence, you could also respond well to vegetarianism. You may sometimes be rather prone to worry, and this could end up affecting your health, via your stomach.

Stress, tension, and a degree of restlessness can lead to migraine if you do not learn to relax. A discipline such as yoga could be of help.

Planning ahead
You will no doubt be as profoundly attracted to glamour as all Aquarians are. However, if you indulge in an excessive amount of glamorous purchases, you could end up feeling

The Moon in Virgo

very guilty. This is far less likely to be the case if the things that you buy actually have a practical purpose of some sort and, even better, if they are made of natural materials.

You may sometimes be inclined to think that you are rather less well-off financially than is in fact the case. While you are generally quite good at managing your financial affairs, you would probably be wise to seek independent professional advice when you want to start saving, or if you find yourself in possession of a substantial amount of money that you wish to invest.

Parenthood

You could be far more critical of your children than you realize. Be careful, since this could sap their confidence.

Your Aquarian Sun will no doubt enable you to keep abreast of your children's ideas. Make sure that you also provide them with adequate warmth and affection.

THE MOON IN
LIBRA

YOUR LIBRAN MOON HELPS YOU TO EXPRESS YOUR THOUGHTS
FREELY AND WITH ORIGINALITY. YOU ARE SOCIABLE,
BUT YOU MAY NEED TO DEVELOP A MORE SERIOUS, PRACTICAL
APPROACH TO SOME SPHERES OF YOUR LIFE.

Both Aquarius and Libra are air signs, so they blend very well. As a result, you are among the friendliest, most sympathetic, understanding, and diplomatic of all Aquarian Sun and Moon sign combinations.

Self-expression
Your Libran Moon gives you the instinctive ability to see all sides of a problem and to follow another person's argument sympathetically. Understandably, this characteristic can sometimes make you indecisive, and others may occasionally find it annoying because they do not know exactly where they stand with you. It may be worth trying to develop a more down-to-earth attitude.

Romance
Your Libran Moon brings out the real romance that is always lurking somewhere in the Aquarian spirit. You enjoy setting a scene for love. You

will, however, react to your partners in one of two distinct ways. On the one hand, you may feel that you are incomplete as a person when you are not sharing an emotional relationship, and may rush into partnerships. On the other hand, because of your Aquarian independent streak, it is possible that you keep your distance even when a good opportunity arises. You are, of course, capable of building a rewarding and loving relationship with someone who understands you.

Your well-being
The lumbar region of the back is ruled by Libra. If you have a job that involves spending long hours at a desk, you should consider getting a back-support chair.

The Libran organ is the kidneys, and you may suffer from headaches as a result of either a buildup of stress or a slight kidney disorder. If your metabolic rate is unusually slow, you

The Moon in Libra

are quite likely to end up putting on excess weight, so it may prove wise for you to indulge in some regular exercise. You might, for example, consider skiing or working out at a friendly health club.

Planning ahead

You probably love luxury and may well have expensive tastes. Never be tempted to lend money, since you are likely to be a soft touch for unscrupulous people, and take professional advice before buying stock or starting a savings scheme. Enjoy your money, but keep a firm check on how you spend it.

Parenthood

You may have a tendency to bribe your children for a bit of peace and quiet. This is a bad idea in the long run. Be decisive, and try to be firm, so that your children know exactly where they stand with you. You will be able to keep up with their concerns and should have few problems with the generation gap.

THE MOON IN
SCORPIO

YOU HAVE A POWERFUL EMOTIONAL FORCE WITH WHICH YOU MAY HAVE FOUND IT HARD TO COME TO TERMS. STUBBORNNESS COULD SOMETIMES CAUSE PROBLEMS FOR YOU. ALWAYS AIM TO BE OBJECTIVE AND TO KEEP AN OPEN MIND.

Both Aquarius and Scorpio are fixed signs, which may make you somewhat stubborn and increase your determination in life. This will help you in difficult or stressful times.

Self-expression
You are a typically free, independent Aquarian spirit, but also have all the depth and intensity of a Scorpion Moon and the need to live a really fulfilling life.

You will only be really happy in a career that gives you psychological satisfaction and burns up your great resources of emotional and physical energy. If you do not have such a career, you could stagnate.

Romance
Your powerful source of emotional energy is quite different from your Aquarian qualities. More than any other Aquarian Sun and Moon combination, you need a rich and

rewarding love and sex life. You are passionate and sexually demanding, and therefore require an exuberant and responsive partner. Bearing in mind your Aquarian Sun, you also need to feel free and independent.

The worst Scorpio fault is jealousy – your Aquarian self will hate it if you allow this negative emotion to surface.

Your well-being
The Scorpio body area covers the genitals. Male Scorpios should therefore regularly examine their testicles for irregularities, while women should have cervical smears.

Scorpios enjoy living it up. They are, in many ways, the party people of the Zodiac. Too much rich food and quality wine can therefore result in excessive weight gain among people of this sign. If this is the case with you, make a disciplined and gradual change in your eating habits, however boring you may find this. In theory,

The Moon in Scorpio

you should enjoy sports and exercise. However, unless you are an enthusiast for one particular kind of exercise or team game, you may need variety – water sports, speed skating, and karate should suit you.

Planning ahead
You have a shrewd business sense, and possess what it takes to make a lot of money. This will be useful, since you could well spend money liberally. When investing you may

benefit from professional advice, but tell your adviser what your instincts suggest – they could be right.

Parenthood
You could sometimes appear quirky to your children. You may be conventional one moment, and all for a modern outlook the next. Try to let your children know where they stand with you. If you fully express your Aquarian traits, you will have no problems with the generation gap.

THE MOON IN
SAGITTARIUS

AQUARIUS AND SAGITTARIUS ARE BOTH SIGNS THAT NEED SPACE
AND INDEPENDENCE. ALLOW THE WARMTH OF YOUR
MOON SIGN ADEQUATE FREEDOM OF EXPRESSION. THIS WILL
MELT THE COOL DETACHMENT OF AQUARIUS.

The air element of your Aquarian Sun and the fire element of your Sagittarian Moon blend well, making you a very enthusiastic, optimistic person. You no doubt respond with a sense of immediacy and intensity when challenged or faced with a demanding situation.

Self-expression
You are likely to have a positive outlook on life, and will be a free spirit with a wide-ranging mind and breadth of vision. You may, however, cope badly with detail, which might be best left to others.

There is an element of the eternal student about you. You are likely to need an element of intellectual challenge in order to thrive, and should always have some interest that encourages the positive expression of this quality. Although you are a versatile person, you should make sure that you do not spread your interests too thin, since this could easily encourage you toward inconsistency of effort.

Romance
You have a marvelous source of very positive emotion and probably do not find it difficult to express your feelings. You make a very lively partner, and love and sex are a joy to you. You need a partner who is capable of recognizing your powerful need for freedom and independence, since anything smacking of claustrophobia in a relationship will be fatal to its happiness.

Your well-being
The Sagittarian body area covers the hips and thighs. Sagittarian women in particular often put on weight in this area. To make matters worse, you may have a liking for heavy foods. You should try to lean toward the more typical Aquarian diet of salads,

The Moon in Sagittarius

fish, and poultry. You clearly need a good deal of exercise and will probably enjoy one or more sports.

The Sagittarian organ is the liver, which may well be disturbed by the heavy food mentioned already. You may like taking risks, but should make sure that every one of them is carefully calculated.

Planning ahead
You have something of a gambling spirit and could be excited by moneymaking schemes that sound rewarding but may not be secure. If therefore you cannot resist a gamble, make quite sure that you do not invest more money than you can afford to lose. Take professional advice before investing; you may make mistakes here from too much optimism.

Parenthood
You are probably progressive and modern in outlook; rational and logical but, at the same time, able to show warmth and tenderness toward your children, especially when they are upset. You will encourage all their efforts and will contribute much to their education. The generation gap will not be a problem for you.

THE MOON IN
CAPRICORN

YOU NO DOUBT HAVE WHAT IT TAKES IN ORDER TO REACH THE TOP, BUT YOUR AMBITIOUS CAPRICORNIAN MOON MAY TEND TO MAKE YOU A LONER. YOU COULD EXPERIENCE CONFLICT BETWEEN CONVENTIONAL AND ECCENTRIC BEHAVIOR.

Before the planet Uranus was discovered in the eighteenth century, Saturn ruled both Aquarius and Capricorn. There are therefore some interesting links between these signs, but also some vivid contrasts.

Self-expression
You will initially respond to situations in a very matter-of-fact, practical way, and will be very cautious. Subsequently, however, your more extrovert Aquarian personality is likely to come into its own. In this way, you will possess a secure basis from which to express yourself.

Capricorn is known for being very conventional, whereas Aquarius is renowned for being unconventional, and likes to surprise and sometimes shock people. You must find a compromise if you are to achieve a balance, and get the best out of both instincts without causing problems to other people. If you are particularly ambitious, you are likely to lead a very rewarding life and achieve the successful career that you desire.

Romance
Neither Aquarius nor Capricorn is a very emotional sign. You may consciously need to relax into a relationship in order to enjoy a really rich and rewarding love and sex life.

Your Aquarian Sun makes you glamorous and attractive to the opposite sex, but your Capricornian Sun may be an inhibiting factor. Even before a romance begins, you may tell yourself that it is doubtful whether you have found a suitable partner.

Your well-being
The Capricornian body area covers the knees and shins, which are therefore vulnerable. It is important for you to keep moving, and to keep exercising, since anyone with a Capricorn emphasis is particularly

The Moon in Capricorn

susceptible to rheumatic pain and stiffness of the joints. The skin and teeth, as well as the bones, are also Capricorn-ruled.

Perhaps you are fairly lean, with a fast metabolism, and therefore have no weight problem. If this is not the case, you may need to take some regular exercise.

Planning ahead

Your instinctive caution will stand you in good stead, preventing you from frittering money away. You will want the feeling of security that regular savings bring. Although you probably do not need to take financial advice, you should seek it, if only to confirm how good your own ideas are.

Parenthood

You may appear rather cool and distant to your children. While you are kind and friendly, you should make a conscious effort to reassure them in a warm and loving way when they are upset. Be progressive, and you will avoid the generation gap.

THE MOON IN
AQUARIUS

BOTH THE SUN AND THE MOON WERE IN AQUARIUS AT THE TIME OF YOUR BIRTH, SO YOU WERE BORN UNDER A NEW MOON. BECAUSE AQUARIUS IS AN AIR SIGN, THIS ELEMENT POWERFULLY INFLUENCES YOUR PERSONALITY AND REACTIONS.

Should you study a list of your Sun sign characteristics, you will probably recognize that a great many of them apply to you. On average, out of a list of perhaps 20 traits of a Sun sign listed in books or magazines, most people will strongly identify with 11 or 12. In your case, however, the average increases considerably because the Sun and Moon were both in Aquarius when you were born.

Self-expression
You are perhaps among the most independent and self-contained of all Zodiac Sun and Moon sign combinations. Kind and friendly almost to a fault, you have a unique and individual lifestyle that you have developed over the years and may still be refining. You need psychological space but, since you are a very private person, you also need privacy. Even friends who truly love you may not really know you. You are not

concerned with other people's private lives, and expect them not to be concerned with yours.

Romance
Your expression of love no doubt fits the general descriptions on pages 526 to 527. You should study the comments on the different ways in which your Sun sign expresses love and affection, since these variations will add a considerable dimension to your attitudes to love and sex. You have an almost magnetic appeal, but your instinctive reaction to lovers is to let them admire you, but to make them keep their distance.

Your well-being
Because the Sun and the Moon were both in Aquarius at the time you were born, your ankles (the Aquarian body area) are particularly vulnerable. There is also a chance that your circulation may not be very good. In

The Moon in Aquarius

cold weather you should keep warm by wearing several layers of light clothing rather than one heavy sweater. In addition, you should take special care of your spine and back. If you stick to a light diet, you should not incur excessive weight gain.

Planning ahead
In coping with finance you will express originality and flair. This may not be such a good thing, because neither of these traits is necessarily effective when it comes to increasing your bank balance. Always seek professional financial advice.

Parenthood
While you should experience few problems with the generation gap, you may not be sufficiently reassuring, warm, and loving toward your children. This can leave them feeling a little insecure. Remember that they may need stricter discipline than you think is necessary.

THE MOON IN
PISCES

IN DIFFERENT WAYS, BOTH AQUARIUS AND PISCES ENCOURAGE HUMANITARIAN, CHARITABLE WORK. YOUR INSTINCT TO HELP OTHERS IS VERY POWERFUL, BUT DO NOT LET IT GOVERN YOUR AQUARIAN DETACHMENT AND OBJECTIVITY.

The qualities attributed to these signs are very different, making you a multifaceted person. Contrary to your Sun sign character, the influence of your Piscean Moon gives you powerful emotion that readily surfaces, and which you can express in a variety of ways.

Self-expression
You are extremely kind, friendly, and helpful – your Aquarian Sun sees to that. However, since Aquarius is humanitarian and Pisces is charitable, you can sometimes be swept up into making considerable sacrifices in order to help others in need.

You have a great deal of creative potential and must express it in a fulfilling manner.

Romance
You are more sensual and expressive in love and sex than many Aquarians. No doubt you fall in and out of love very easily, since it is not hard for you to identify with that romantic streak that so often lies deeply buried in the Aquarian personality. However, you still need Aquarian space, and an element of independence within your relationships. Equally, you need a strong partner who will encourage you in all your efforts and help to develop your self-confidence.

Deceptiveness is by far the worst Piscean fault. Do not resort to it, especially if you think it will provide an easy way out of a tricky situation. Furthermore, do not be self-deceptive when you fall in love.

Your well-being
The Piscean body area covers the feet, and yours will therefore be vulnerable to all kinds of injury. You will find exercise sandals attractive and comfortable. Pisceans tend to put on weight rather more easily than Aquarians, and you could rely too

The Moon in Pisces

heavily on junk food, or simply may not bother to eat sensibly. This can be disastrous both for your well-being and for your figure.

You will enjoy rather unusual forms of exercise and sport. Modern free-form dance, roller or ice skating, and sequence swimming are all likely to appeal to you.

Planning ahead
Money probably slips through your fingers. You may give away much more than you can afford, which is wonderfully noble, but can cause problems when you are unable to pay the rent. If you have a regular job, try to find a savings plan to which contributions are paid out of your income. Otherwise, you should always seek sound professional advice.

Parenthood
You will be a rational, sensitive, and caring parent, but must try to curb Aquarian unpredictability, since sudden changes of mind and mood do not go over well with children. You will always be prepared to give your children a hug when things go wrong and should have no problems with the generation gap.

SUN & MOON SIGNS

PISCES

FEBRUARY 19 – MARCH 20

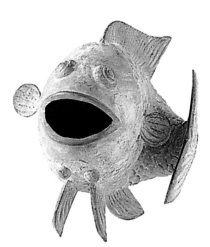

INTRODUCING
PISCES

PISCES, THE SIGN OF THE TWO FISHES, IS THE TWELFTH SIGN OF THE ZODIAC. THE PISCEAN CHARACTER IS MARKED BY A NATURAL QUIRKINESS, AND THIS IS SYMBOLIZED BY THE FISH SWIMMING IN OPPOSITE DIRECTIONS.

The two fishes that symbolize this sign are connected by a cord held in their mouths and are always portrayed swimming in opposite directions. They suggest a strong characteristic of the Piscean personality: Pisceans often decide on one line of action, and then take precisely the opposite course. Not surprisingly, this may impede your progress through life.

Traditional groupings

As you read through this book you will come across references to the elements and the qualities, and to positive and negative, or masculine and feminine signs.

The first of these groupings, that of the elements, comprises fire, earth, air, and water signs. The second, that of the qualities, divides the Zodiac into cardinal, fixed, and mutable signs. The final grouping is made up of positive and negative, or masculine and feminine signs. Each Zodiac sign is associated with a combination of components from these groupings, all of which contribute different characteristics to it.

Piscean characteristics

The water element is a powerful source of emotion and, because Pisces is of the mutable quality, you are likely to be flexible in your views. You are full of marvelous creative potential, but may sometimes doubt yourself. If you lack self-confidence, you will need continual support and encouragement in order to develop and fulfill your promise.

Neptune, the god of the sea, is the Piscean ruling planet. Although you are probably very kind, Neptune's influence can persuade you to seek easy ways out of difficult situations. All too often this involves deceit. The sign is negative and feminine, so Pisceans tend to be introverts.

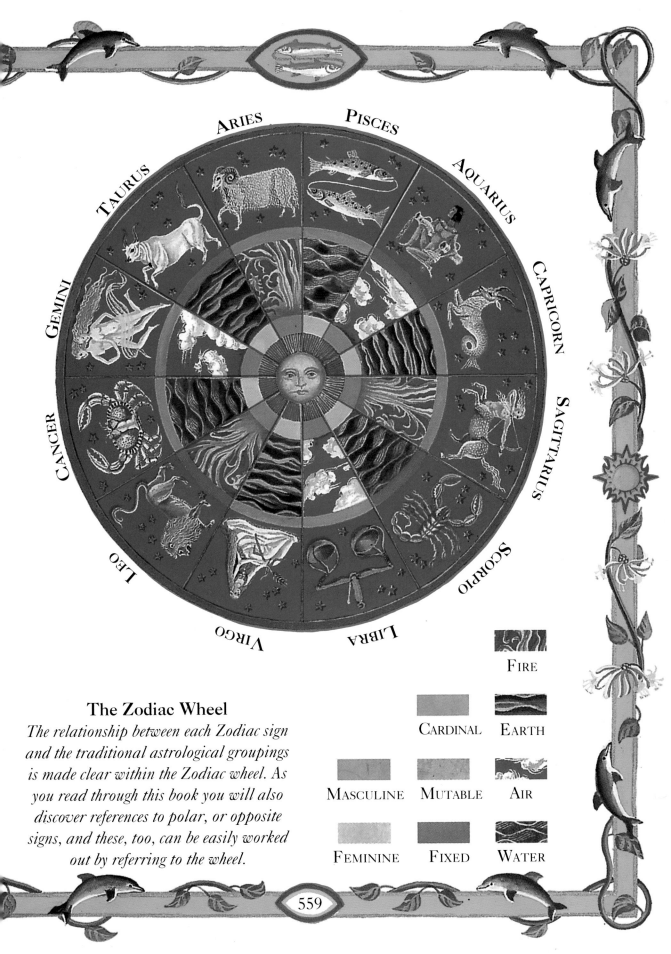

ARIES

PISCES

TAURUS

AQUARIUS

GEMINI

CAPRICORN

CANCER

SAGITTARIUS

LEO

SCORPIO

VIRGO

LIBRA

The Zodiac Wheel

The relationship between each Zodiac sign and the traditional astrological groupings is made clear within the Zodiac wheel. As you read through this book you will also discover references to polar, or opposite signs, and these, too, can be easily worked out by referring to the wheel.

FIRE

CARDINAL   EARTH

MASCULINE   MUTABLE   AIR

FEMININE   FIXED   WATER

559

PISCES
MYTHS & LEGENDS

THE ZODIAC, WHICH IS BELIEVED TO HAVE ORIGINATED IN
ANCIENT BABYLON AS LONG AS 2,500 YEARS AGO, IS
A CIRCLE OF CONSTELLATIONS THROUGH WHICH THE
SUN MOVES DURING THE COURSE OF A YEAR.

The ancient Babylonian name for this constellation was *kun*, meaning "the tails." This title referred to the tails of the two fishes that were associated with the goddesses Anunitum and Simmah, who once represented the rivers Tigris and Euphrates. The great Roman writer Manilius, who set down a number of astrological myths, gives us a stronger link with the sign of Pisces. It actually derives from the earlier literature of the Greek writer Hyginus, who wrote one of the first works on mythology.

Typhon
Made in the sixth century B.C., this terracotta figure shows the monster Typhon.

Venus and Cupid

Hyginus's story involved Venus and Cupid, who were the Roman versions of the Greek Aphrodite and Eros.

The former was the goddess of love, who was said to preside over a love that bonded all living creatures, and to inspire all of Nature's creations. The latter was her son by her husband, the graceless and ugly god Vulcan. Cupid was originally conceived as the god who was responsible for harnessing the different elements of the universe, allowing life to develop. Clearly there is a link between the role of Cupid and that of his mother. From these abstract origins, he came to be seen as an immortal child with the ambition to infect both mortals and the gods with the virus of love. Cupid is often shown firing arrows from a bow.

Venus and her son Cupid

This representation of Venus, the goddess of love, and her son Cupid was created in the 1500s by Agnolo Bronzini.

These arrows were invested with the power to stir great passion in the hearts of all those that they struck.

Typhon the monster

Far removed from the notions of love and beauty associated with Cupid and his mother was Typhon, the youngest child of Mother Earth and the largest monster ever born.

From the thighs downward he was nothing but coiled serpents, and his arms, which were said to span a hundred leagues in any direction, ended in countless serpents' heads. As his name suggests (it is the root of the word *typhoon*), Typhon was said to be responsible for any unusually strong winds.

Venus and Cupid are transformed

According to the myth, Venus and Cupid were strolling along the banks of the Euphrates one day when they were confronted by an enraged Typhon. In order to evade him they immediately turned themselves into fish, and swam off rapidly in opposite directions. To commemorate the event, Zeus, king of the gods, placed the constellation now known as Pisces in the heavens.

The two fishes

Even today, the fishes used to represent the sign face in different directions, although they are connected by a single golden cord. This perfectly indicates the perversity that is such a powerful characteristic of Sun sign Pisceans. They will almost inevitably argue strongly for one course of action only to eventually decide to take precisely the opposite course.

PISCES
SYMBOLISM

CERTAIN HERBS, SPICES, FLOWERS, TREES, GEMS, METALS, AND
ANIMALS HAVE LONG BEEN ASSOCIATED WITH PARTICULAR
ZODIAC SIGNS. SOME ASSOCIATIONS ARE SIMPLY AMUSING, WHILE
OTHERS CAN BE GENUINELY USEFUL.

PINKS

Plants
*Dandelions, lime-flowers, mosses, lichens,
waterlilies, and pinks – in fact most
plants that grow in Piscean colors – are
all associated with this Sun sign.*

Moss

Trees

The lime, birch, mulberry, chestnut, ash, oak, birch, and all trees that grow near water are ruled by Pisces.

BIRCH

SAGE

CHESTNUT

Herbs

Herbs ruled by Cancer and Sagittarius come under the influence of Pisces. They include sage and saxifrage.

Spices

No spice is particularly associated with Pisces, but coriander and cinnamon are sometimes mentioned.

CORIANDER

CINNAMON

PISCES
SYMBOLISM

FISH MOULD

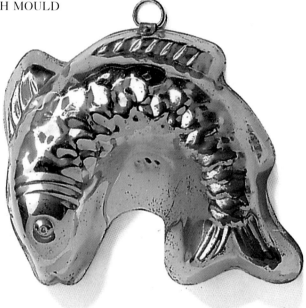

Gem
The Piscean gem is traditionally said to be the colorless moonstone. Magical properties are often attributed to it.

MOONSTONE

PLATINUM
NUGGET

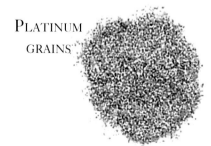

Metal
The Piscean metal is platinum, but traditional astrology also mentions tin and titanium, which emit the entire color range of the spectrum and are therefore well suited to Piscean taste.

PLATINUM
GRAINS

FISH PRINTER'S BLOCK

DOLPHIN EARRINGS

Animals

All fishes are, of course, Piscean animals, and so are all mammals – for instance, dolphins, whales, and porpoises – that live near or in the water.

WOODEN FISH ORNAMENT

PISCES
PROFILE

PISCEANS OFTEN SEEM TO WALK AROUND IN A DREAM, FAR AWAY FROM THE BUSTLE OF EVERYDAY LIFE. BECAUSE THEY CAN BE FORGETFUL AND MAY HAVE THEIR MINDS ON HIGHER THINGS, THEY HAVE A TENDENCY TO DRESS CARELESSLY.

Many Pisceans stand with their feet crossed, like a fish's tail. This distinctive stance is often noticeable at social gatherings or at cocktail parties.

The body

It is not difficult to recognize Pisceans who have an undisciplined and unhealthy approach to life. They will tend to look overweight, and have flabby, shapeless bodies and rather dull eyes. However, Pisceans who decide to dedicate themselves to some grueling physical activity like skating or dancing will appear to be fitness itself, even if they possess typically pale Piscean complexions. Piscean creative potential and inspiration will be likely to keep them practicing at the barre long after many other people would have decided to give up.

The Piscean face
Pisceans often have gentle eyes and unstyled, natural-looking hair.

The face

Pisceans will either style their hair heavily, or lean in quite the opposite direction and leave it in its natural state. You will tend to frown if you are worried or confused. The eyes are a dominant feature in many Pisceans and will probably appear to be gentle, perhaps showing a capacity to be very emotional. A dominant feature is very often a drooping line at the corner of the eye. Your nose is likely to be well shaped and from small to medium in size; some Pisceans tend to have noticeably high bridges to their noses.

The Piscean stance
Pisceans frequently stand with both feet crossed, forming the distinctive shape of a fish's tail.

Style
The Piscean image is romantic. Many Piscean men love to own velvet jackets, while Piscean women can look stunning whether they are dressed in a Paris creation or simply have a length of fabric pinned around them. Unless career commitments force you to dress conventionally, you will probably have an extremely original image and may like wearing unusual antique clothes. You are unlikely to become too great a slave of fashion, unless some aspect of your life demands it.

You will look your best wearing soft fabrics such as wool, and you may veer toward an ethnic look.

Your feet are very likely to betray the fact that you are a Piscean. Perhaps without even realizing it, you could have a tendency to wear rather broken down, well-worn shoes.

In general
A softness and gentleness, an eagerness to sympathize, is very apparent on first meeting a typical Piscean. There is nothing pushy

about these people. They will always listen to others with interest, and their eyes reflect the emotions of the people they are conversing with. As has been said, the eyes are nearly always a very dominant Piscean feature. Piscean women will probably not take long to discover that they can use their eyes to their advantage. Many will develop a range of subtle expressions and inflections.

PISCES
PERSONALITY

PISCEANS ARE SAID TO BE THE POETS OF THE ZODIAC. WHILE
NOT ALL OF THEM WILL SPEND HOURS PENNING
VERSES TO THEIR LOVERS, MANY DO SEEM TO SHARE
THE INSPIRATION ASSOCIATED WITH THIS ART.

Words such as unworldliness, dreaminess, and inspiration are all frequently used to describe head-in-the-clouds Pisceans; but so are charity, kindness, and helpfulness. You probably have a great willingness to ease other people's burdens.

Many Pisceans find it difficult to face up to reality. While you may have an ability to identify with suffering and often actually the means to do something about it, you may also have a tendency to retreat into your own little world. You could be a recluse.

At work
It should come as no surprise to find that the characteristics mentioned above may influence your choice of career. You would do best to find work that offers plenty of variety, and that does not force you to labor through the same hours every day. A predictable job might provide you with a sense of security, but it could

prove to be stifling. Well-defined regulations or guidelines may provide you with a useful sense of direction, and you should have no problems in following them. Try to study and learn from the way that your superiors handle authority and manage to cope with decision making.

Your attitudes
Many Pisceans need peace and quiet. This can mean the quiet of the cloister or, ironically, it can cause you to disconnect yourself from the everyday world by blasting loud music into your ears through a personal stereo. Either way, you will probably find the experience restorative.

The overall picture
The symbolism of the sign is opposite and represents a true Piscean problem. Just as the two fishes of Pisces swim in opposite directions, Pisceans will often fail to

Neptune rules Pisces

Neptune, the Roman god of the sea, represents the Piscean ruling planet. It can make its subjects idealistic, imaginative, and sensitive, but also careless, indecisive, and deceitful.

act in their own best interests. It may be that a certain lack of self-confidence often prompts you to decide on one line of action – and to then do just the opposite. Unfortunately, you may find this happening just when you are attempting to act particularly positively and assertively. You must be careful not to rely on excuses in order to avoid starting new projects. If, for example, you say that you have no time to start something new, you are probably actually falling victim to a lack of self-confidence – whether or not there is an element of truth in your excuse. You must make an effort to harness your complete potential.

PISCES
ASPIRATIONS

It is possible that you do better working behind the scenes than occupying a high-profile position. If you learn to interpret your imagination practically, it will be a valuable asset to you.

Painting

Many Pisceans are very creative, and the work they can produce as painters may be both beautiful and imaginative. They should not underestimate their potential.

WATERCOLOR
PAINTS AND BRUSHES

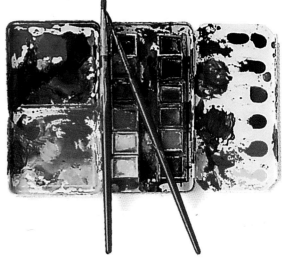

PRISON
OFFICER'S KEYS

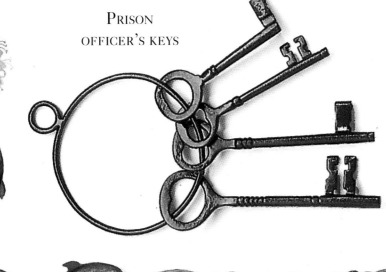

Prison work

If you work in the prison service you will be very sympathetic to your charges. The ability to listen to problems is a great asset in this profession.

CLOWN'S MASK

Medical research
The motivation to help others and reduce suffering can attract Pisceans to medical research.

The theater
Pisceans are natural mimics and have an attractive sense of humor. This may lead to a career as a comedian or a mime.

MICROSCOPE

The shoe trade
Pisces rules the feet, and some creative people of this sign become successful shoe designers, while others find the fitting and selling of shoes rewarding.

SHOE TREES

PISCES
HEALTH

PISCEANS TEND TO BE UNDISCIPLINED, AND YOU MAY SOMETIMES NEGLECT YOUR HEALTH AND GENERAL WELL-BEING. YOU WOULD THEREFORE BE WISE TO NOTE THE FOLLOWING SUGGESTIONS AND WARNINGS.

The feet are ruled by Pisces, so people of this sign often have problems with this area of their bodies. Exercise sandals are the ideal footwear for them. More serious than problem feet may be your inclination to fall back on forms of escapist behavior, such as drug-taking and excessive drinking. This is because you often have difficulties facing up to reality, as well as a self-deceptive attitude that encourages you to take any easy way out of a problem situation. Sun sign Pisceans should recognize their vulnerability and call upon other, stronger areas of their personality to counter it. The Piscean system often tends to be sensitive, so other people's reactions or bad attitudes can have an adverse physical effect on you.

Your diet
You may benefit from supplementing your diet with Ferrum phosphate (ferr. phos.), which is a combination of iron and oxygen that enriches the blood and soothes inflammation.

Taking care
Interestingly, many Sun sign Pisceans do not respond well to medically prescribed drugs – an allergy to antibiotics is common. Alternative medicine could be the solution to this problem in some cases.

Cucumber
Cucumbers and melons are among the foods traditionally linked with Pisces.

Astrology and the body

For many centuries it was not possible to practice medicine without a knowledge of astrology. In European universities, medical training included information on how planetary positions would affect the administration of medicines, the bleeding of patients, and the right time to pick herbs and make potions. Each Zodiac sign rules a particular part of the body – from Aries (the head) to Pisces (the feet) – and textbooks always included a drawing of a "Zodiac man" (or woman) that illustrated the point.

PISCES AT LEISURE

EACH OF THE SUN SIGNS TRADITIONALLY SUGGESTS SPARE-TIME ACTIVITIES, HOBBIES, AND EVEN VACATION SPOTS. ALTHOUGH THESE ARE ONLY SUGGESTIONS, THEY OFTEN WORK OUT WELL FOR PISCEANS.

POSTAGE STAMPS

Travel

You will enjoy wandering aimlessly on one of the small Mediterranean islands or in the Sahara. Portugal and Scandinavia may also be favorite destinations. You will be eager to try local food, but should watch your digestion.

Flying

The idea of "getting away from it all" is restorative to Pisceans. They will become excited at the thought of taking off in an airplane to enjoy vacations.

1916 AVIATOR'S MAPS

Dance

Lyrical dance movement can provide a non-competitive, steady, rhythmical, and therefore rewarding form of self-expression for Pisceans.

Flower arranging

Sensitivity, artistic flair, and a love of nature are Piscean traits that often make people of this sign talented flower arrangers.

CHICKEN WIRE
AND FLOWERS

Fishing

The peace and quiet of a solitary afternoon's fishing allows a Piscean to calm down and escape from the rat race.

FLY-FISHING HOOKS

BALLET SHOES

PISCES IN
LOVE

PISCEANS GIVE A GREAT DEAL OF THEMSELVES TO THEIR LOVERS.
THIS CAN EITHER BE MARVELOUS FOR BOTH PEOPLE
INVOLVED, OR IT CAN MEAN THAT THE PISCEAN WILL SACRIFICE
TOO MUCH AND BECOME A DOORMAT

Many Sun sign Pisceans have a tendency to view the world through rose-colored glasses when they are in love. They often delude themselves. You may have to develop a much thicker skin than you naturally possess, and make sure that you are not taken in by a combination of flattery and good looks. Your tendency to idealize your prospective partner may sometimes cause you to either ignore or conveniently overlook the true picture.

Deceptiveness, the main Piscean fault, can surface in another way: because Pisceans hate to hurt others, they may sometimes tell white lies in order to take the easy way out of a difficult situation.

As a lover

Pisceans give a great deal of themselves to their lovers. This can either be marvelous for both people involved, or it can mean that the Piscean will sacrifice too much and become a doormat. They also often instinctively know what their partners are feeling and thinking. This is a useful, if sometimes embarrassing, asset. You are capable of sharing and maintaining an extremely rewarding, long-lasting sex life, which will be a great source of pleasure and fun. If you have partners who are able to recognize and encourage the full development of your potential, and above all else help you to become more self-confident, every aspect of your life will be rewarding.

Types of Piscean lover

One group of Pisceans is not quite as gushing or gullible as has been suggested. People belonging to a second group have a rather special glamour. They need to retain their independence and might tend to be a little cool and distant toward their partners. While enjoying love and sex, they may delay making a total commitment. A third type of Piscean is a true Piscean, who will easily recognize all of the general comments made so far. Yet another group is made up of enthusiastic, passionate Pisceans, who do not find this area of their lives to be particularly complicated. They contribute a great deal to a partnership once they settle down. People in the final group are very sensual, passionate, and affectionate. They usually need to have a great deal of emotional and financial security within their relationship.

PISCES AT HOME

YOU LIKE YOUR HOME TO BE A HAVEN OF PEACE AND TRANQUILLITY. PALE BLUE OR GREEN SOFT FURNISHINGS WILL REFLECT YOUR QUIET GOOD TASTE, AND A TROPICAL FISH AQUARIUM MAY ADD TO THE OVERALL RELAXED ATMOSPHERE.

The majority of Pisceans like to live near a source of water, ideally in a coastal area. If this is not possible they may design their own small haven of peace and tranquillity in even the most run-down or unappealing type of area. While doing so they may become heavily involved with the local community, and perhaps lend their enthusiastic support to various charitable groups or conservationist organizations.

Bronze vase
A vase or jug in the shape of a fish is not uncommon.

A Piscean home is always guaranteed to be a most interesting place to visit.

Furniture
Comfortable furniture is essential, but because Pisceans tend to be artistic and creative, the appearance of pieces is also important. If you are short of money, the look of your secondhand furniture may be enhanced by imaginative repairs and repainting. Settees and beds are generally jumbo-sized and very soft. You use them to retreat into your own blissfully private, imaginative world. Scrubbed pine is popular for kitchen and dining tables, and you may own a large china

Subtly patterned cushions
Pretty designs and soft colors will feature heavily in any Piscean decorative scheme.

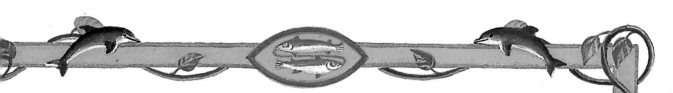

cabinet or cupboard which will be full to the brim not only with cups and plates, but all types of clutter.

Soft furnishings

Piscean invention and imaginative creativity are expressed in the creation of unusual cushions and small items of furniture that enhance more important pieces. Patchwork, screen printing, and sculpting all find their place in the Piscean home.

The curtains and drapes will be either chintzy and floral, or rather shimmery, giving a waterlike appearance. Moiré silk in pale pastel shades of green, blue, or sometimes silvery gray, often features in the Piscean decorative scheme. Floor coverings are generally heavily textured or thick-piled, with Greek flokati rugs being special favorites.

Decorative items

Any paintings that you choose probably have a romantic air, and those that are psychologically restorative and calming are usually preferred. Lighting comes from shaded lamps placed in discreet

corners. There may be an aquarium in your home; this will serve as both a container for extoic tropical fish and a purely decorative feature. Pisceans are often good at flower arranging, and dried flowers and bowls of potpourri may be prominently displayed around your home.

Lamp and books

Generous lampshades and piles of books typify the Piscean home.

THE
MOON
AND
YOU

THE SUN DECREES YOUR OUTWARD EXPRESSION, YOUR IMAGE, AND MANY IMPORTANT PERSONALITY TRAITS. THE MOON, ALTHOUGH MERELY THE EARTH'S SATELLITE, IS ASTRONOMICALLY THE SECOND MOST IMPORTANT BODY IN THE SOLAR SYSTEM. FROM THE SIGN THAT IT WAS IN AT YOUR BIRTH, IT INFLUENCES HOW YOU REACT TO SITUATIONS, YOUR EMOTIONAL LEVEL, AND, TO A CERTAIN EXTENT, WHAT YOU HAVE INHERITED FROM YOUR PARENTS AND ANCESTORS. AFTER FINDING YOUR MOON SIGN IN THE SIMPLE TABLES ON PAGES 606 TO 609, TURN TO THE RELEVANT PAGES AND TAKE A STEP FORWARD IN YOUR OWN SELF-KNOWLEDGE.

THE MOON IN
ARIES

YOUR FIERY, EMOTIONAL, AND LIVELY MOON LENDS A STRONG
POSITIVE FORCE TO YOUR PISCEAN PERSONALITY. DO
NOT BE AFRAID TO EXPRESS THIS FREELY. IT ADDS STRENGTH
AND ASSERTIVENESS TO YOUR RESPONSES.

While Aries is strong, positive, and assertive, Pisces is gentle, tender, and not at all pushy. The influence of your fiery Moon gives you a powerful source of physical and emotional energy.

Self-expression

You initially respond boldly to challenges, but could later have second thoughts that eat away at your self-confidence and cause you to backtrack. Aim to move forward steadily, and to allow the gentler, more conscientious elements of your Piscean Sun to be stimulated by the strong forces of your Arien Moon.

Romance

You possess both the fiery, expressive emotion of Aries and the deep, intense emotion that derives from Pisces. In addition to these qualities you are passionate and are likely to fall in and out of love very quickly.

Your Arien Moon probably makes you more resistant to being upset than most Pisceans, and you have the ability to detach yourself once you realize that an affair is over. You have what it takes to enjoy a rewarding, fulfilling relationship, although the worst Arien fault, selfishness, could surface at times.

Your well-being

The Arien body area is the head, and you could suffer from more than an average number of headaches. These are probably the result of worry and tension. There can be a link between headaches and slight kidney disorders, so it is worth getting a medical checkup if they persist.

Like many people with an Arien emphasis, you are usually in a hurry. Because of this, you could be somewhat accident-prone; consciously take care, particularly when working with sharp tools or hot dishes.

The Moon in Aries

Although you probably enjoy sports and exercise, you do need to watch your diet. You may not worry much about it, and Piscean haste could encourage you to consume an excessive amount of junk food.

Planning ahead

You may well have an enterprising spirit that could supply you with a useful second income. However, seek financial advice when you have money to invest. Otherwise you may make serious mistakes. These will be the result of combining soft-hearted Piscean traits with those of an over-enthusiastic Arien.

Parenthood

You will be a sympathetic parent and will be anxious to see your children make progress. You will not find it difficult to keep up with their ideas. Try not to continually change your mind, or your children will not know where they stand with you.

THE MOON IN
TAURUS

YOUR PISCEAN KINDNESS AND SYMPATHY DO NOT ALWAYS WORK TO YOUR COMPLETE ADVANTAGE. LISTEN TO YOUR SENSIBLE AND PRACTICAL TAUREAN MOON, AND MAKE AN EFFORT TO CURB POSSESSIVE REACTIONS.

The water element of your Piscean Sun and the earth element of your Taurean Moon blend well. You are far more reliable and stable than many Sun sign Pisceans.

Self-expression

The Moon is traditionally well placed in Taurus, which means that its influence on you is particularly strong. It gives you backbone and acts as a marvelous anchor to your personality, calming what can sometimes be a turbulent spirit.

When challenged, you face up to reality with great practicality. You can be very firm and decisive, and should always follow your most deep-rooted instincts and intuition.

Both Pisces and Taurus have considerable creative potential, and Taurus is particularly appreciative of beauty. If you enjoy embroidery, pottery, craftwork, and music, you should develop these interests.

Romance

It is very important for you to have a secure background. Material security does not always interest Pisceans, but your Taurean Moon puts an emphasis on both it and emotional security.

You will relax into and enjoy a relationship with a partner who you feel you can trust. You are a powerful source of affection and sexuality, being sensual and passionate. When you feel secure, these qualities do much to enhance your relationship.

The worst Taurean fault is possessiveness, and you will sometimes try to own your partners. Be aware that they may need some independence within a relationship.

Your well-being

The Taurean body area is traditionally said to cover the throat and neck. Your colds are likely to begin with a very sore throat and end with a cough. Make sure that you

The Moon in Taurus

keep the appropriate medicines on hand so that you can relieve any discomfort as soon as possible.

Taurus loves rich and often sweet food, so you may have a tendency to gain weight, especially since Pisceans can suffer from a similar difficulty. Discipline yourself into a reasonable diet and a regular exercise routine.

Planning ahead

You have an above-average capacity to cope with finance; it is far better than that of most Pisceans. If you do seek financial advice, you will be surprised at how close your own ideas are to those of your adviser. You will probably want to own your own home as early in life as possible.

Parenthood

You will be stricter with your children than most Pisceans and will discipline them sensibly. They will know where they stand with you, but you may have to make a conscious effort to understand their problems if you are to avoid the generation gap.

THE MOON IN
GEMINI

YOUR MOON HELPS YOU TO RATIONALIZE YOUR POWERFUL PISCEAN
EMOTIONS. PISCES AND GEMINI ARE BOTH DUAL SIGNS,
WHICH MEANS THAT YOU ARE NATURALLY VERSATILE. YOU MUST
CURB SUPERFICIALITY AND BE CONSISTENT.

The chances are that you will be a free-thinker with a flexible, open mind. This is largely because Pisces and Gemini are both mutable signs. You are also extremely versatile, enjoying a great variety of interests, and finding it easy to converse with many different kinds of people on a wide range of subjects.

Self-expression
You are a marvelous communicator and are able to get your ideas across very easily. It is, however, entirely possible that you may alter your opinions at a moment's notice.

You respond to proposals with a flurry of words, showing great enthusiasm if you like what is put to you and producing a variety of hastily invented excuses if you do not. Because of your Piscean Sun, you may lack self-confidence and could try to cover the fact by being nervously talkative. Try to take your time, and

remember that a few well-chosen sentences can make a far better impression than a tumble of words.

Romance
You are probably unlikely to be completely overwhelmed by your emotions. You may rationalize your feelings, especially when you first fall in love. Try not to restrain your emotions. A certain measure of skepticism from your Geminian Moon is valuable, but do not let it smother the heart's affections. Bear in mind, too, that friendship and a good measure of intellectual rapport are as essential for you in a long-term relationship as a good sex life.

Your well-being
The Geminian body area covers the arms and hands. Yours are therefore vulnerable, perhaps to minor accidents. The Geminian organ is the lungs. Do not allow a cough to hang

The Moon in Gemini

on for more than a few days before resorting to prescribed antibiotics. Anyone with a Geminian emphasis should not smoke.

Restlessness can affect your health, but a relaxation discipline could help counter this. If your metabolism is fast, you will be less likely than most Pisceans to suffer from weight gain.

Planning ahead

Pisceans are often not particularly adept at finance, and money tends to burn holes in Geminian pockets. Resist sob-stories from those who wish to borrow your money, and get financial advice, especially before leaping into get-rich-quick schemes.

Parenthood

You will be both a loving and a very lively parent: youthful and alert, and with few generation gap problems. You may need to be a little more strict than you are if your children are to know precisely where they stand with you. Remember that they need a sense of security.

THE MOON IN
CANCER

BOTH PISCES AND CANCER ARE SIGNS OF THE WATER ELEMENT, SO YOUR EMOTIONS, INTUITION, AND IMAGINATION ARE HIGHLY REFINED. YOU MUST TRY TO CHANNEL THEM IN A CONSTRUCTIVE AND POSITIVE WAY.

With Pisces and Cancer both being water signs, you have some very powerful, emotionally oriented forces within your personality. The Moon rules Cancer and is at its strongest and most influential from that sign. It will have a deep effect on your personality.

Self-expression

You have considerable strength and determination; when you are challenged in any way, an immediate and powerful self-defensive system springs into action. You respond strongly, either kindly and sympathetically or sharply, according to your opinions and the way you feel.

Both Pisces and Cancer enhance your powers of imagination, and you should always try to express your creativity, perhaps inventively. If you do not, your imagination may work overtime in a negative way. Your instincts and emotions are very

powerful. If you feel that you should take a particular line of action, you will probably be right to do so. But always calm yourself down before doing anything important.

Romance

You will be a very passionate, sensual lover and will make a wonderful partner in a long-term relationship or marriage. You know how to please your lover both in and out of bed, and will not find it difficult to achieve sexual fulfillment. Make sure that you do not nag your partner, and remember that in expressing your love, it can be all too easy for you to create a claustrophobic atmosphere.

Your well-being

The Cancerian body area covers the breasts and chest. It is therefore advisable for Cancerian women to be particularly diligent in examining their breasts regularly, although there

The Moon in Cancer

is, of course, no connection between the Zodiac sign Cancer and the disease with the same name.

You enjoy good food and may well be prone to weight gain. Try to discipline yourself into getting regular exercise, perhaps swimming.

Planning ahead

Those with a Cancerian emphasis have a very shrewd business sense and are talented at making the most of what money they have. You will have some good ideas about what to do with your money, but your Piscean Sun may detract from them, and you could be overly generous to charity. Seek professional advice when you have money to invest.

Parenthood

You will be among the most sensitive and caring of all Piscean Sun and Moon sign parents, and will stimulate your children's imagination and encourage their efforts. You will be strict enough to discipline your children as and when necessary, but warm and comforting when they are distressed. Make sure that you do not get too sentimental; this could lead to problems with the generation gap.

THE MOON IN
LEO

YOU HAVE MARVELOUS POTENTIAL, CAN RESPOND POSITIVELY TO
MOST SITUATIONS, AND ARE PROBABLY BETTER ORGANIZED
THAN MOST PISCEANS. AT TIMES, YOU MAY BE PRETTY BOSSY —
BUT THAT CAN BE USEFUL TO A SENSITIVE PISCEAN.

There are some very vivid contrasts between the qualities of Pisces and Leo, but this is still a stunning combination. It makes you a fascinating individual with exciting, dynamic potential.

Self-expression
Your fiery Moon contributes a wonderfully positive enthusiasm when you are challenged. No doubt you are far more self-assured than many people of your Sun sign, and certainly much better organized. You could also be more self-confident and, at times, perhaps rather bossy.

Pisces and Leo are probably the two Zodiac signs with the most creative potential. Pisceans often do not have the confidence to develop this quality, but your Leo Moon will help you to overcome your inhibitions. Always aim to achieve the highest standard and to make a dramatic impact, whatever you do.

Romance
Like Pisces, Leo is a very emotional sign. You express your passion with great feeling and are a very ardent lover. You make a caring partner, but probably fall in love often and suffer heartbreak just as much as, if not more than, other Pisceans.

You are very sensitive and, when hurt, will instinctively creep into your lair and lick your wounds in private. It is probable that you will want to look up to and admire your partner. You will always be a splendid power behind a throne, but you also need to share it. Avoid any inclination to dominate your partner.

Your well-being
The Leo body area covers the back and spine, and yours may be vulnerable. If you work at a desk you might benefit from an ergonomic chair. Exercise will also keep the back and spine in good order.

The Moon in Leo

The Leo organ is the heart, and it also needs exercise. Work out at a health club, or find some form of exercise that expresses your sense of drama and creative talent.

Planning ahead
Unlike most Pisceans, you enjoy doing things in style and spend freely on luxuries. Since you are also generous by nature, you will need to earn a relatively high salary.

You will probably be inclined to invest in fairly safe, well-established companies making quality products. Make sure that you get your decisions confirmed by a professional financial adviser before you invest large sums of money.

Parenthood
Leo is a sign that is traditionally related to parenthood. You will make an enthusiastic parent, always ready to praise and encourage your children.

While you should not suffer from too many generation gap problems, you should try to allow your children to develop their own interests, and refrain from forcing your ideas upon them. Do not expect them to achieve goals that have always eluded you.

THE MOON IN
VIRGO

PISCES AND VIRGO ARE POLAR OR OPPOSITE ZODIAC SIGNS, WHICH
MEANS THAT YOU WERE BORN UNDER A FULL MOON.
INNER DISCONTENT AND RESTLESSNESS MAY BOTHER YOU, BUT DO
NOT BE WEIGHED DOWN BY BAD FEELINGS.

We all have a tendency to express the attitudes of our polar, or opposite, Zodiac sign. Every sign has its partner across the horoscope; for you this is Virgo, and since the Moon was in this sign when you were born, the polarity is expressed in a very interesting way.

Self-expression
Virgo is an earth sign, and this element blends well with the water element of Pisces, making you practical and rational. You are an excellent communicator, and enjoy a good, lively discussion or argument.

It is possible that you may not be very self-confident, and a certain shyness can inhibit you. You are very good at covering this up, perhaps by being overly talkative, but your lack of self-confidence is very deeply rooted. When asked to organize something, or when an opportunity for promotion occurs, you may well not be willing to accept it. It is entirely possible that you are seriously underestimating your abilities.

Romance
Lack of confidence could also emerge when someone makes a romantic approach to you. You have a delightful natural modesty, but do not let it inhibit you to the extent where you lose the opportunity for what might be a rewarding relationship.

Also bear in mind that the worst Virgoan fault is to be overcritical. Beware of a tendency to nag your partner; it could be devastating.

Your well-being
The Virgoan body area covers the stomach, and since those with a Virgoan influence are very prone to worry, the physical effects usually center around an upset stomach, pains, and cramps. You need a high-fiber diet, and may be sympathetic to

The Moon in Virgo

vegetarianism. Perhaps you are less prone to weight gain than many Pisceans. This could be because you have a high metabolism and therefore a lot of nervous energy to burn. Exercising will alleviate restlessness and encourage sleep. You will favor outdoor sporting activities.

Planning ahead

You are careful with money, and may be too worried about losing it to take any undue risks. You would be wise to go for safe investments with steady growth and to obtain financial advice when you have money to invest.

Parenthood

You will be sensitive and caring with your children, but may tend to be hypercritical. Help them to develop their imaginations and creative abilities by expressing your own. It should not be hard for you to keep up with your children's ideas and thus avoid the generation gap.

THE MOON IN
LIBRA

PISCES AND LIBRA ARE GENTLE SIGNS. YOU COULD FEIGN A VERY
CALM ATTITUDE WHEN MAKING DECISIONS. TRY TO
MAKE AN EFFORT TO DEVELOP A MORE PRACTICAL APPROACH
TO LIFE, OR YOU MAY NOT FEEL FULFILLED.

The effect of both Pisces and Libra can be to make their subjects charming, friendly, kind, and very sympathetic. You show gentle understanding when challenged or confronted, but may not be eager to make essential snap decisions.

Self-expression
You should consciously try to be more forthright and assertive, and perhaps also more rational and constructively self-critical.

You are diplomatic and always have time for other people, especially if they are upset or in trouble. You have the knack of relaxing them and making them feel much better.

Your Sun and Moon sign combination does not give you a great deal of inner strength, although it is perfectly possible that the influence of other planets within the Solar System have strengthened your psychological muscle.

Romance
You are probably extremely romantic and have a tendency to fall in love with love itself. You may well not feel psychologically whole until you are sharing an emotional relationship.

You are very attractive to the opposite sex, and capable of enjoying a highly rewarding love and sex life.

Your well-being
The lumbar region of the back is ruled by Libra, and you may therefore benefit from an ergonomic chair. The Libran organ is the kidneys, and it is possible that you suffer from an above-average number of headaches. Pressure from other people may provoke these but, if this is not the case, it will be well worth getting a checkup, just in case you have a slight problem with your kidneys.

You probably loathe exercise, but may put on weight if you avoid it completely. Try to be disciplined

The Moon in Libra

about this and about what you eat. Do remember that too much smoking, drinking, or any kind of negative escapism is not good for you. Also note that you can react very badly to many drugs.

Planning ahead

You enjoy your creature comforts, so much of the money that you make probably slips too easily through your fingers. It would be wise for you to follow a savings plan in which a regular payment is deducted from your salary. You are also so generous that some people may seek to take advantage of you. Seek professional advice in all money matters.

Parenthood

You will be a very easygoing parent, and your children will discover that they can manipulate you. They will appreciate your tremendous kindness and sympathy, but remember that children also benefit from a certain amount of discipline. The generation gap should not prove to be a problem.

THE MOON IN
SCORPIO

BOTH PISCES AND SCORPIO ARE SIGNS OF THE WATER ELEMENT, WHICH WILL HEIGHTEN YOUR ALREADY ABUNDANT PISCEAN EMOTIONS. LET DETERMINATION OVERCOME INHIBITION AND ANY LACK OF SELF-CONFIDENCE. SUPPRESS JEALOUSY.

Scorpio is, in many respects, the strongest of the 12 Zodiac signs. Since it is of the water element, its influence blends well with that of your Sun sign.

Self-expression
In addition to your Piscean qualities, you have further inner strength, and considerable resilience and determination when faced with a challenge or a demanding situation. These qualities encourage you to overcome any Piscean reticence, shyness, or lack of self-confidence.

You need to be emotionally involved with your work. While you enjoy making money, it is still more important for you to obtain inner satisfaction from your job.

Romance
You are highly sexed and very passionate. You need an energetic partner who can match your passion,

who will challenge you and keep you stimulated. The worst Scorpio fault is jealousy, and you may sometimes succumb to it. Bear in mind that you could create a somewhat claustrophobic atmosphere within your relationship.

Your well-being
The Scorpio body area covers the genitals. Male Scorpios should therefore regularly examine their testicles for malformations, and women should have cervical smears.

Those with a Scorpio emphasis love good food and wine, and are therefore likely to gain weight. Moderation is the best solution to this problem.

Planning ahead
You will probably cope well with money; much better, in fact, than many Sun sign Pisceans. You may have a certain financial flair, but could tend to put too many eggs in a single

The Moon in Scorpio

basket. If you feel that this tendency is likely to affect you, you should go for safe savings plans and, if you are feeling adventurous, seek professional financial advice.

Although many Scorpio types manage to do well in their own businesses, they sometimes get rather bored, make an attempt to organize a change, and finally end up going too far. In the end they are faced with no real choice but to start again at the very bottom.

Parenthood

While Pisces is likely to make you a kind and easygoing parent, your Scorpio Moon encourages you to be much stricter. This is fine, since it enables you to give your children a good, secure background. You will, however, probably have to make a conscious effort to learn about your children's concerns and problems if you are to avoid running into the many problems associated with the generation gap.

THE MOON IN
SAGITTARIUS

BEFORE NEPTUNE WAS DISCOVERED, THE PLANET JUPITER RULED BOTH SAGITTARIUS AND PISCES. THERE IS THEREFORE A NATURAL SYMPATHY BETWEEN THEM, WHICH IS HEIGHTENED BY THE FACT THAT THEY ARE DUAL AND MUTABLE SIGNS.

Many Sagittarians respond to challenges in a lively, optimistic, and enthusiastic way. In fact they thrive on them and derive a great deal of excitement from them.

Self-expression
Although you are very good at grasping the overall view of any situation, you could find the details terribly boring. You have a tremendous zest for life and enjoy action more than many Pisceans. Your outlook is philosophical, and you have an admirable mind that should always be engaged in study of some kind, perhaps of a foreign language.

Romance
You have the positive, fiery emotion of Sagittarius, as well as the more sensitive emotion of Pisces. They combine well when it comes to love and sex. You could well have something of a roving eye, and will

certainly get a lot of fun out of this sphere of your life. You tend to fall in and out of love rather often, but will take a broken heart in your stride and readily accept the challenge of finding someone new.

Once you have settled down, other factors come into play, and you will get great satisfaction from a rewarding love and sex life with a partner who is also a good friend.

Your well-being
The Sagittarian body area covers the hips and thighs, and women with this sign emphasized are more than likely to put on weight in those areas. The Sagittarian organ is the liver, and hangovers are often common, so keep a remedy on hand.

A preference for rather heavy dishes and good wine and beer can mean a buildup of weight, so follow your Sagittarian Moon and keep up with sports. Riding is traditionally a

The Moon in Sagittarius

Sagittarian form of exercise. Restlessness is the worst Sagittarian fault. You should try to curb it, or it will lead to stress and tension because of feelings of unfulfillment. Alternating from physical to mental interests and vice versa provides an excellent antidote.

Planning ahead

It is important for you to seek financial advice when you want to start an investment or savings plan. Being a Piscean soft touch is one thing, but having a Sagittarian inclination to take a gamble is quite another. You could fall very easily for get-rich-quick schemes. If you must place a bet, never stake more money than you can easily afford to lose.

Parenthood

You will be an enthusiastic parent and will be extremely eager to encourage your children to stimulate their minds. In addition to this, you will have a great deal of fun with them, and should have almost no difficulty in keeping up with their ideas. The specter of the generation gap should therefore hold no real terrors for you.

THE MOON IN
CAPRICORN

YOU HAVE HIGH ASPIRATIONS, BUT YOUR SENSITIVE PISCEAN SUN SIGN COULD INHIBIT PROGRESS. BE SELF-CONFIDENT AND AMBITIOUS, AND FOLLOW YOUR INSTINCTS. THEY MAY WELL BE MORE PRACTICALLY FOUNDED THAN YOU REALIZE.

The elements of water, for Pisces, and earth, for Capricorn, blend well and give you some very positive common sense.

Self-expression
When challenged, you could be somewhat overcautious. This is fine for a Sun sign Piscean, provided that your natural caution does not sap your self-confidence. To avoid this, set yourself ambitious but attainable objectives, and make sure that you continually aspire to meet every one of them.

There is another side to the Capricornian influence, which could cause you to grumble or to take a negative view of life. Try not to let this tendency get the better of you.

Romance
Your Capricornian Moon prevents you from being gullible in your love life, and you are less likely than many

Pisceans to don rose-colored spectacles when falling in love. Capricorn is not a sign that bestows a high emotional level; Pisces, on the other hand, gives you a capacity to express emotion forcefully towards a partner. You are probably very faithful and eager to see your partner progress in life. Possibly more than most people, you need security within your relationship. You will work really hard for this and do everything in your power to make it work. Do not allow feelings of inferiority to creep into your attitude.

Your well-being
The Capricornian body area covers the knees and shins, as well as the bones, teeth, and skin. It is important for you to get exercise to keep you moving. Jogging, aerobics, or even walking will ensure that you keep rheumatic pains and stiffness of the joints, especially in the knees, at bay.

The Moon in Capricorn

Your skin could be rather sensitive, whatever your race, and it is best to protect it from the sun. You should also have regular dental checkups.

Most people with a Capricornian influence are not heavy eaters. Provided that your Piscean influence does not make you lazy, you should have no problems with your weight.

Planning ahead

You probably cope fairly well with money, although you may have a tendency to think that you are less well-off than you really are. You must get value for your money, so seek financial advice when investing.

Parenthood

You will be a kind, understanding parent and will discipline your children fairly whenever it is necessary. Be careful to avoid undue criticism or put-downs, and allow your tender Sun sign qualities plenty of expression. If you listen to your children, you will leap across the generation gap.

THE MOON IN
AQUARIUS

YOU ARE ALL EMOTION, BUT THE COOL DETACHMENT OF AQUARIUS
WHICH COLORS YOUR REACTIONS MAY MAKE YOU APPEAR A
LITTLE BRITTLE. YOUR SENSITIVE, CHARITABLE PISCEAN WARMTH
USUALLY EMERGES WHEN PEOPLE GET TO KNOW YOU.

The tender warmth of Pisces is contrasted in a very vivid and exciting way against the cool glamour and originality of Aquarius. When challenged, you find it easy to distance yourself from a problem and to respond logically.

Self-expression
You may sometimes give the impression of being cool and distant. However, once people get to know you, they discover a very different person. Aquarius is known for general friendliness and kind, humanitarian qualities, and Pisces for charity. You will therefore give a great deal of yourself to people in need.

Romance
You are a very caring, loving, and tender partner with a high emotional level. While you are extremely attractive to the opposite sex, you may distance yourself when you feel that a prospective lover is pressing you too fast. You have a very independent streak that may well influence your whole lifestyle. Perhaps you have built a life that is in some way unique. If this is the case, do not allow yourself to be pressured into changing it. Aim to achieve a rewarding love and sex life with partners who recognize your strong need for independence.

Your well-being
The Aquarian body area covers the ankles. Because Pisces rules the feet, and since your ankles are vulnerable due to your Moon sign's influence, you need to make sure that you always buy comfortable footwear.

The circulation is also ruled by Aquarius but, while you may feel the cold fairly easily, you also enjoy cold, clear winter weather. Make sure that you keep warm by wearing several layers of light clothing.

The Moon in Aquarius

It is advisable for you to try to get aesthetic satisfaction from exercise, so that your mind, body, and spirit will be at one. You also need to keep moving because of possible circulation problems. You could well be a natural iceskater, skier, or synchronized swimmer.

Planning ahead

Coping with money may not be very easy for you – unless other planets within the Solar System contribute a positive influence to this sphere. You may spend heavily on glamorous items. Always seek professional advice before investing.

Parenthood

Your attitude toward your children may be unconventional. You have plenty of ideas about bringing them up; make sure they always know where they stand. You look to the future, so the generation gap should not trouble you.

THE MOON IN
PISCES

BECAUSE THE SUN AND THE MOON WERE BOTH IN PISCES AT THE MOMENT OF YOUR BIRTH, YOU WERE BORN UNDER A FULL MOON. SINCE PISCES IS A WATER SIGN, THIS ELEMENT POWERFULLY INFLUENCES YOUR PERSONALITY AND REACTIONS.

When you read a list of the characteristics of your sensitive and emotional Sun sign, you will probably recognize that many of them apply to you. On average, out of a list of perhaps 20 personality traits attached to a Sun sign, most people identify with 11 or 12. For you the average increases greatly, since the Sun and the Moon were both in Pisces when you were born.

Self-expression

Your Sun sign makes you highly imaginative and gives you some very powerful emotions; because the Moon was also in Pisces when you were born, you will sometimes react very emotionally to situations.

Far more than most Sun sign Pisceans, you will be inclined to decide on one line of action, and then do the opposite. As a result of this, you may cause yourself a considerable amount of worry and confusion.

Romance

You will give a great deal of yourself to your lovers and readily make sacrifices for them. Think about this, and make sure that you do not compromise too often.

You want a good, stable relationship and a partner who will encourage and support you, spurring you on to express your potential. You are a very sensual lover, and will enjoy a rich and rewarding sex life with your partner. It is possible that you fall in love too easily, and you could well deceive yourself about your lovers' qualities, ignoring their faults and foibles. Be cautious in this sphere.

Your well-being

The comments made on pages 572 to 573 about Piscean health and well-being really do apply to you. You can hardly escape having problem feet and must recognize their great vulnerability. Only go barefoot in the

The Moon in Pisces

house; otherwise you will pick up foot infections very easily. Also watch your eating habits. Many Pisceans are prone to weight gain, and this tendency will probably affect you more than most. Although you may not be enthusiastic about the idea, you should discipline yourself in the way that you eat, and make sure that you take regular exercise.

Planning ahead

In regard to money, the less you have to do with balancing your books the better. This may be something that a partner should take care of. If you have money to invest, then get professional advice. If you have a regular income, embark on a savings plan in which contributions can be deducted at the source.

Parenthood

You may find disciplining your children rather difficult, and you could spoil them. For their sakes, and your own peace of mind, work on disciplining them when they start to grow up. Because you have an instinctive understanding of human nature, you should have no problems with the generation gap.

MOON CHARTS

THE FOLLOWING TABLES WILL ENABLE YOU TO DISCOVER YOUR MOON SIGN. THEN, BY REFERRING TO THE PRECEDING PAGES, YOU WILL BE ABLE TO INVESTIGATE ITS QUALITIES, AND SEE HOW THEY WORK WITH YOUR SUN SIGN.

By referring to the charts on pages 607, 608, and 609 locate the Zodiacal glyph for the month of the year in which you were born. Using the Moon table on this page, find the number opposite the day you were born that month. Then, starting from the glyph you found first, count off that number using the list of Zodiacal glyphs (below, right). You may have to count to Pisces and continue with Aries. For example, if you were born on May 21, 1991, first you need to find the Moon sign on the chart on page 609. Look down the chart to May; the glyph is Sagittarius (♐). Then consult the Moon table for the 21st. It tells you to add nine glyphs. Starting from Sagittarius, count down nine, and you find your Moon sign is Virgo (♍).

MOON TABLE

DAYS OF THE MONTH AND NUMBER OF SIGNS THAT SHOULD BE ADDED

DAY	ADD	DAY	ADD	DAY	ADD	DAY	ADD
1	0	9	4	17	7	25	11
2	1	10	4	18	8	26	11
3	1	11	5	19	8	27	12
4	1	12	5	20	9	28	12
5	2	13	5	21	9	29	1
6	2	14	6	22	10	30	1
7	3	15	6	23	10	31	2
8	3	16	7	24	10		

ZODIACAL GLYPHS

♈	Aries
♉	Taurus
♊	Gemini
♋	Cancer
♌	Leo
♍	Virgo
♎	Libra
♏	Scorpio
♐	Sagittarius
♑	Capricorn
♒	Aquarius
♓	Pisces

	1923	1924	1925	1926	1927	1928	1929	1930	1931	1932	1933	1934	1935
JAN	♊	♏	♈	♌	♐	♈	♍	♑	♉	♎	♓	♋	♏
FEB	♌	♐	♉	♍	♑	♊	♏	♓	♋	♐	♈	♌	♑
MAR	♌	♑	♉	♍	♒	♋	♏	♓	♋	♐	♉	♍	♑
APR	♎	♓	♋	♏	♈	♍	♑	♉	♍	♒	♊	♎	♓
MAY	♏	♈	♌	♐	♉	♎	♒	♊	♎	♓	♋	♐	♈
JUN	♑	♉	♍	♒	♋	♏	♓	♌	♐	♉	♍	♑	♊
JUL	♒	♋	♏	♓	♌	♐	♈	♍	♑	♊	♎	♓	♋
AUG	♈	♌	♐	♉	♍	♒	♊	♏	♓	♋	♐	♈	♌
SEP	♉	♎	♒	♋	♏	♓	♌	♐	♈	♍	♑	♊	♎
OCT	♊	♏	♓	♌	♐	♉	♍	♑	♉	♎	♓	♋	♏
NOV	♌	♑	♉	♍	♑	♊	♏	♓	♋	♐	♈	♌	♑
DEC	♍	♒	♊	♎	♓	♌	♐	♈	♌	♑	♉	♍	♒

	1936	1937	1938	1939	1940	1941	1942	1943	1944	1945	1946	1947	1948
JAN	♈	♌	♑	♉	♍	♒	♊	♎	♓	♌	♐	♈	♍
FEB	♉	♎	♒	♊	♏	♈	♌	♐	♉	♍	♑	♊	♎
MAR	♊	♎	♒	♋	♐	♈	♌	♐	♉	♎	♒	♊	♏
APR	♌	♐	♈	♌	♑	♉	♎	♒	♋	♏	♓	♌	♑
MAY	♍	♑	♉	♎	♒	♊	♏	♓	♌	♐	♉	♍	♒
JUN	♎	♒	♋	♏	♈	♌	♑	♉	♎	♒	♊	♏	♓
JUL	♏	♈	♌	♑	♉	♍	♒	♊	♏	♓	♌	♐	♈
AUG	♑	♉	♎	♒	♋	♏	♈	♌	♐	♉	♍	♑	♊
SEP	♓	♋	♏	♈	♌	♑	♉	♍	♒	♋	♏	♓	♌
OCT	♈	♌	♑	♉	♎	♒	♊	♎	♓	♌	♐	♈	♍
NOV	♊	♎	♒	♊	♏	♈	♌	♐	♉	♍	♑	♊	♏
DEC	♋	♏	♓	♌	♑	♉	♍	♑	♊	♎	♒	♋	♐

	1949	1950	1951	1952	1953	1954	1955	1956	1957	1958	1959	1960	1961
JAN	♑	♊	♎	♓	♋	♏	♈	♌	♑	♉	♍	♒	♋
FEB	♓	♋	♐	♈	♍	♑	♉	♎	♒	♊	♏	♈	♌
MAR	♓	♋	♐	♉	♍	♑	♊	♏	♓	♋	♏	♈	♌
APR	♉	♍	♒	♊	♎	♓	♋	♐	♈	♌	♑	♊	♎
MAY	♊	♎	♓	♋	♐	♈	♍	♑	♉	♎	♒	♋	♏
JUN	♌	♐	♈	♍	♑	♊	♎	♓	♋	♐	♈	♌	♑
JUL	♍	♑	♊	♎	♓	♋	♏	♈	♌	♑	♉	♍	♒
AUG	♏	♓	♋	♐	♈	♍	♑	♉	♎	♒	♊	♏	♈
SEP	♐	♈	♍	♑	♊	♎	♒	♋	♐	♈	♌	♑	♊
OCT	♑	♊	♎	♓	♋	♏	♓	♌	♑	♉	♍	♒	♋
NOV	♓	♋	♏	♈	♍	♑	♉	♎	♒	♊	♏	♈	♌
DEC	♈	♌	♑	♊	♎	♒	♊	♏	♓	♌	♐	♉	♍

	1962	1963	1964	1965	1966	1967	1968	1969	1970	1971	1972	1973	1974
JAN	♏	♓	♌	♐	♈	♍	♑	♊	♎	♒	♋	♐	♈
FEB	♐	♉	♍	♒	♊	♏	♓	♋	♏	♈	♍	♑	♉
MAR	♐	♉	♎	♒	♊	♏	♈	♌	♐	♉	♍	♑	♊
APR	♒	♋	♏	♈	♌	♑	♉	♍	♒	♊	♏	♓	♋
MAY	♓	♌	♐	♉	♍	♒	♊	♎	♓	♋	♐	♈	♍
JUN	♉	♎	♒	♊	♏	♓	♌	♐	♉	♍	♑	♊	♎
JUL	♊	♏	♓	♌	♐	♈	♍	♑	♊	♎	♓	♋	♐
AUG	♌	♐	♉	♎	♒	♊	♏	♓	♋	♏	♈	♍	♑
SEP	♍	♒	♋	♏	♓	♋	♐	♉	♍	♑	♊	♎	♓
OCT	♏	♓	♌	♐	♈	♍	♒	♊	♎	♒	♋	♐	♈
NOV	♐	♉	♎	♒	♊	♎	♓	♋	♐	♈	♍	♑	♉
DEC	♑	♊	♏	♓	♋	♐	♈	♌	♑	♉	♎	♒	♊

	1975	1976	1977	1978	1979	1980	1981	1982	1983	1984	1985	1986	1987
JAN	♌	♑	♉	♍	♒	♊	♏	♓	♌	♐	♉	♍	♑
FEB	♎	♒	♋	♏	♈	♌	♐	♉	♍	♒	♊	♎	♓
MAR	♎	♓	♋	♏	♈	♍	♑	♉	♎	♒	♊	♏	♓
APR	♐	♈	♍	♑	♊	♎	♒	♋	♏	♈	♌	♑	♉
MAY	♑	♉	♎	♒	♋	♏	♓	♌	♐	♉	♍	♒	♊
JUN	♓	♋	♐	♈	♌	♑	♉	♎	♒	♊	♏	♓	♌
JUL	♈	♌	♑	♉	♍	♒	♋	♏	♓	♌	♐	♉	♍
AUG	♉	♎	♓	♋	♏	♈	♌	♐	♈	♎	♒	♊	♎
SEP	♋	♐	♈	♌	♐	♊	♎	♒	♊	♏	♓	♌	♐
OCT	♌	♑	♉	♍	♒	♋	♏	♓	♋	♐	♉	♍	♑
NOV	♎	♓	♋	♏	♓	♌	♐	♉	♍	♒	♊	♎	♓
DEC	♏	♈	♌	♐	♉	♍	♑	♊	♎	♓	♋	♐	♈

	1988	1989	1990	1991	1992	1993	1994	1995	1996	1997	1998	1999	2000
JAN	♊	♎	♒	♋	♏	♈	♌	♑	♉	♎	♒	♊	♏
FEB	♋	♐	♈	♍	♑	♉	♎	♒	♋	♏	♈	♌	♐
MAR	♌	♐	♉	♍	♒	♊	♎	♓	♋	♏	♈	♌	♑
APR	♍	♒	♊	♏	♓	♋	♐	♈	♍	♑	♊	♎	♓
MAY	♏	♓	♌	♐	♈	♍	♑	♉	♎	♒	♋	♏	♈
JUN	♐	♉	♍	♑	♊	♎	♓	♋	♐	♈	♌	♑	♉
JUL	♑	♊	♎	♒	♋	♐	♈	♌	♑	♉	♎	♒	♋
AUG	♓	♌	♐	♈	♍	♑	♉	♎	♓	♋	♏	♓	♌
SEP	♉	♍	♑	♊	♏	♓	♋	♏	♈	♌	♑	♉	♎
OCT	♊	♎	♒	♋	♐	♈	♌	♑	♉	♎	♒	♊	♏
NOV	♌	♐	♈	♍	♑	♉	♎	♒	♋	♏	♈	♌	♑
DEC	♍	♑	♉	♎	♒	♋	♏	♈	♌	♐	♉	♍	♒

THE
SOLAR SYSTEM

THE STARS, OTHER THAN THE SUN, PLAY NO PART IN THE SCIENCE OF ASTROLOGY. ASTROLOGERS USE ONLY THE BODIES IN THE SOLAR SYSTEM, EXCLUDING THE EARTH, TO CALCULATE HOW OUR LIVES AND PERSONALITIES CHANGE.

Pluto

Pluto takes 246 years to travel around the Sun. It affects our unconscious instincts and urges, gives us strength in difficulty, and may emphasize any inherent cruel streak.

Neptune

Neptune stays in each sign for 14 years. At best it makes us sensitive and imaginative; at worst it encourages deceit and carelessness, making us worry.

Uranus

The influence of Uranus can make us friendly, kind, eccentric, inventive, and unpredictable.

Saturn

In ancient times, Saturn was the most distant known planet. Its influence can limit our ambition and make us either overly cautious (but practical), or reliable and self-disciplined.

SATURN

PLUTO

NEPTUNE

URANUS

Jupiter

Jupiter encourages expansion, optimism, generosity, and breadth of vision. It can, however, also make us wasteful, extravagant, and conceited.

Mars

Much associated with energy, anger, violence, selfishness, and a strong sex drive, Mars also encourages decisiveness and leadership.

JUPITER

The Moon

Although it is a satellite of the Earth, the Moon is known in astrology as a planet. It lies about 240,000 miles from the Earth and, astrologically, is second in importance only to the Sun.

MERCURY

THE MOON

VENUS

MARS

EARTH

The Sun

The Sun, the only star used by astrologers, influences the way we present ourselves to the world – our image or personality; the face we show to other people.

Venus

The planet of love and partnership, Venus can emphasize all our best personal qualities. It may also encourage us to be lazy, impractical, and too dependent on other people.

Earth

Every planet contributes to the environment of the Solar System, and a person born on Venus would no doubt be influenced by our own planet in some way.

Mercury

The planet closest to the Sun affects our intellect. It can make us inquisitive, versatile, argumentative, perceptive, and clever, but perhaps inconsistent, cynical, and sarcastic.

Index

ACKNOWLEDGMENTS

ARIES
Photography p 10 British Museum, London/Bridgeman Art Library, London;
p 11 Bradford Art Galleries and Museums/Bridgeman Art Library, London;
p 16 Tim Ridley. Stylist pp 28-29 Lucy Elworthy.

TAURUS
Photography p 61 by courtesy of the Board of Trustees of the Victoria
and Albert Museum/Bridgeman Art Library, London; p 66 Tim Ridley.
Stylist pp 78-79 Lucy Elworthy.

GEMINI
Photography p 110 Museum of Antiquities, Newcastle Upon Tyne/Bridgeman
Art Library, London; p 111 Ronald Sheridan/Ancient Art and Architecture
Collection; p 116 Tim Ridley. Stylist pp 128-129 Lucy Elworthy.

CANCER
Photography p 160 Ronald Sheridan/Ancient Art and Architecture Library;
p 161 ©Michael Holford/British Museum; p 166 Tim Ridley.
Stylist pp 178-179 Lucy Elworthy.

LEO
Photography p 211 © Michael Holford/British Museum; p 216 Tim Ridley.
Stylist pp 228-229 Lucy Elworthy.

VIRGO
Photography p 260 ET Archive/British Museum; p 261 CM Dixon;
p 266 Tim Ridley. Stylist pp 278-279 Lucy Elworthy.

LIBRA
Photography p 311 © Michael Holford/British Museum; p 316 Tim Ridley.
Stylist pp 328-329 Lucy Elworthy.

SCORPIO

Photography p 360 CM Dixon/British Museum; p 361 CM Dixon/British Museum; p 366 Tim Ridley. Stylist pp 378-379 Lucy Elworthy.

SAGITTARIUS

Photography p 411 Ronald Sheridan/Ancient Art and Architecture Library; p 416 Tim Ridley. Stylist pp 428-429 Lucy Elworthy.

CAPRICORN

Photography p 460 © Michael Holford/British Museum; p 461 CM Dixon/British Museum; p 466 Tim Ridley. Stylist pp 478-479 Lucy Elworthy.

AQUARIUS

Photography p 511 British Museum, London/Bridgeman Art Library, London; p 516 Tim Ridley. Stylist pp 528-529 Lucy Elworthy.

PISCES

Photography p 560 CM Dixon/British Museum; p 561 National Gallery, London/Bridgeman Art Gallery, London; p 566 Tim Ridley. Stylist pp 578-579 Lucy Elworthy. Illustration pp 610-611 Kuo Kang Chen.

Computer page make-up Patrizio Semproni. **Jacket illustrations** Peter Lawman. With thanks to Hilary Bird, Louise Candlish, John Filbey, Caroline Hunt, Carolyn Lancaster, Tracy Hambleton-Miles, Sean Moore, Des Reid, and David Williams.

Notes

Notes

Notes

Notes